Ace the Programming Interview

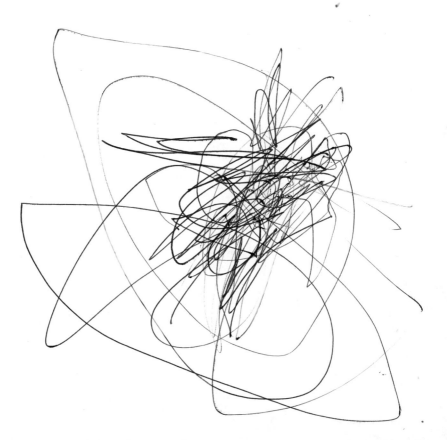

Ace the Programming Interview

160 Questions and Answers for Success

Edward Guiness

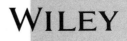

Ace the Programming Interview: 160 Questions and Answers for Success

Published by
John Wiley & Sons, Inc.
10475 Crosspoint Boulevard
Indianapolis, IN 46256
www.wiley.com

Copyright © 2013 by John Wiley & Sons, Inc., Indianapolis, Indiana

Published simultaneously in Canada

ISBN: 978-1-118-51856-4
ISBN: 978-1-118-51862-5 (ebk)
ISBN: 978-1-118-75796-3 (ebk)

Manufactured in the United States of America

10 9 8 7 6 5 4 3 2 1

For Lisa

About the Author

Edward Guiness is a software developer who has been programming since before the birth of Windows 1.0. A great love of programming has led Edward through a career involving mainframes, mini-computers, PCs, and many different programming languages. As a software development hiring manager since 2004, Edward has interviewed and worked alongside hundreds of programmers in New Zealand, Australia, the United Kingdom, and India.

In 2012 Edward founded SocialCoder, a volunteering organization for programmers, designers, and other technical people.

Edward lives in the town of Flitwick, England, with his wife and two daughters.

Credits

Executive Editor
Carol Long

Project Editor
Maureen Spears

Technical Editor
Todd Meister

Production Editor
Christine Mugnolo

Copy Editor
Paula Lowell

Editorial Manager
Mary Beth Wakefield

Freelancer Editorial Manager
Rosemarie Graham

Associate Director of Marketing
David Mayhew

Marketing Manager
Ashley Zurcher

Business Manager
Amy Knies

Production Manager
Tim Tate

Vice President and Executive Group Publisher
Richard Swadley

Vice President and Executive Publisher
Neil Edde

Associate Publisher
Jim Minatel

Project Coordinator, Cover
Katie Crocker

Proofreader
James Saturnio,
Word One New York

Indexer
Robert Swanson

Cover Designer
Ryan Sneed

Acknowledgments

Writing this book has been an incredible experience for me, and it has only been possible because of the following people.

First of all, a huge thank you to my wife, Lisa, for her constant support, for her angelic patience, and for her unwavering belief that I would, eventually, send the final chapter to the publisher.

To my beautiful daughters, Danielle and Laura, thank you for giving up some of our play time so I could write about programming and pirates. (The pirates are in Chapter 11.)

I have been fortunate to have had comments and suggestions from two excellent technical editors, Elizabeth Naramore and Todd Meister. Thank you both. Thanks also to Matthew-Baxter Reynolds for providing valuable comments in the early stages.

Many thanks to the superb team at John Wiley & Sons; acquisitions editor Carol Long, project editor Maureen Spears, copy editor Paula Lowell, and production editor Christine Mugnolo.

To Keith Purdie and Jacob Fardell at the Bedford i-Kan Business Centre; thank you for providing the best flexible working space in Bedfordshire, for your patient good humor, and for putting up with my mood swings, from jelly baby dispensing mania to sullen, hunched-over silence at the keyboard.

Finally, to the programmers I've interviewed and worked alongside over the years, thank you for giving me the best education a hiring manager can have. Most of the truly important things I learned about interviewing I learned from you.

Contents at a Glance

Introduction   xxiii

Chapter 1   Hiring Programmers: The Inside Story   1

Chapter 2   Handling the Phone Interview with Confidence   29

Chapter 3   In-Person Interviews   39

Chapter 4   Negotiating a Job Offer   53

Chapter 5   Programming Fundamentals   63

Chapter 6   Code Quality   109

Chapter 7   The Usual Suspects   157

Chapter 8   Quirks and Idioms   193

Chapter 9   Testing — Not Just for Testers   245

Chapter 10   The Right Tools   265

Chapter 11   Notorious Interview Questions   303

Chapter 12   Programming Wisdom   351

Appendix   Preparing Your Cheat Sheets   389

Index   401

Contents

Introduction		xxiii
Chapter 1	**Hiring Programmers: The Inside Story**	1
	Reasons They Recruit	2
	Planned expansion	3
	The interviewer's motivation and approach	3
	Your approach	3
	Specific projects	5
	The interviewer's motivation and approach	5
	Your approach	5
	Replacing someone	6
	The interviewer's motivation and approach	6
	Your approach	6
	Talking to Managers	7
	Tech talk—don't hold back	7
	Using metaphors	8
	Preparing Your CV	8
	Include relevant keywords but keep them in context	9
	Write as well as you can	9
	Justify your claims of experience	9
	Ignore anyone who tells you "strictly one or two pages"	10
	Emphasize skills that match the job advertisement	10
	Don't leave unexplained gaps between jobs	10
	"Reading, music, and cinema"	11
	Use a logical layout	11
	Graduate CVs	11
	CVs containing more experience	12
	CVs of those returning to work	12
	Avoiding common CV blunders	13

Poor spelling or grammar 13
Vague or nonspecific accomplishments 13
Unclear or cluttered layout 13
Unprofessional e-mail address 14
Using Job Sites 14
Comparison of major job boards 15
Recruitment Agencies 15
Working effectively with a recruiter 17
Searching for Jobs Yourself 17
Networking for introverts 18
Finding potential employers 20
Approaching potential employers 20
Being persistent 21
Timing 22
Emerging Alternatives 22
Using Twitter 22
Using Facebook 23
Using LinkedIn 24
Writing a Blog 25
Careers at Stack Overflow 26
Skills matter: "Find Your Ninja" 27

Chapter 2   **Handling the Phone Interview with Confidence**   **29**
Knowing What to Expect 30
Preparing your cheat sheets 32
Relating your experience 32
Answering hard questions 33
Asking good questions 34
Having a phone interview checklist 35
Using a phone interview cheat sheet template 35

Chapter 3   **In-Person Interviews**   **39**
Preparing for the Interview 39
Knowing what to expect 40
Doing your homework 41
Dressing appropriately 42
Handling different types of interview questions 42
Fielding social and behavioral questions 43
Handling design problems 43
Tackling technical pop-quiz questions 43
Fielding the general intelligence test 44
Dealing with the stress test question 44
The Most Important Thing 45
Establishing rapport 46
It takes work 47
Be a good listener 47
Ask good questions 47

	Mirror your interviewer	47
	Look for ways to interact	47
	The Second Most Important Thing	48
	Speaking up	48
	Being aware of how much time you have	48
	Stories are good, evidence is better	49
	Communicating Effectively	49
	Using your passion to combat nerves	49
	Using your hands	49
	Speaking slower than usual	50
	Starting and finishing clearly	50
	Repeating your main point	50
	Spontaneity improves with practice	51
Chapter 4	Negotiating a Job Offer	53
	Understanding the Market	54
	Doing the Numbers	54
	Considering the whole package	55
	Must have, should have, could have	56
	Must have	56
	Should have	56
	Could have	57
	Won't have	57
	The Role of the Recruiting Agent	57
	Start as You Mean to Go On	57
	Avoid overcommitting	58
	Realism and idealism	58
	Evaluating a Contract	59
	Intellectual Property (IP)	59
	Non-compete clauses	60
	Non-solicitation clauses	60
	What to Do If Things Go Wrong	60
	"It's a standard contract"	60
	The silent treatment	61
	Escalation and ultimatums	61
	Summary of Negotiating Tips	61
Chapter 5	Programming Fundamentals	63
	Understanding Binary, Octal, Hexadecimal	64
	Converting hexadecimal to binary	66
	Using unicode	67
	Understanding Data Structures	68
	Using arrays	68
	Using hash tables	69
	Using queues and stacks	70
	Using trees	70
	Using graphs	72
	Understanding graph traversal	72

Sorting   73
Working with Recursion   75
Modeling with Object-Oriented Programming   76
    Understanding classes and objects   76
    Untangling inheritance and composition   78
    Exploring polymorphism   78
    Data-hiding with encapsulation   80
Thinking Like a Functional Programmer   81
Understanding SQL   81
    What is ACID?   81
    Set-based thinking   82
Full-Stack Web Development   82
Decipering Regular Expressions   83
    Finding content with anchors and word boundaries   85
    Matching character classes   86
    Constraining matches with quantifiers   88
    Working with groups and captures   89
    Avoiding gotchas   90
    More reading   92
Recognizing Hard Problems   92
Questions   93
Answers   95

Chapter 6   Code Quality   109
Writing Clear Code   110
Writing Expressive Code   112
Measuring Efficiency and Performance   112
    Big-O notation   113
        Constant, O(1)   113
        Logarithmic, O(log n)   114
        Linear, O(n)   114
        Quadratic, O(n²)   116
        Using big-O   116
    Measure performance   117
    Consider context   118
    Have a goal   118
    Measure more than once, take an average   118
    Divide and conquer   118
    Try the easy things first   119
    Use a profiler   119
Understanding What "Modular" Means   119
Understanding the SOLID principles   121
    Single Responsibility Principle   121
    Open/Closed Principle   123
    Liskov Substitution Principle   123
    Interface Segregation Principle   124
    Dependency Inversion Principle   125

	Avoiding Code Duplication	126
	Questions	128
	Answers	134
Chapter 7	**The Usual Suspects**	**157**
	Concurrent Programming	158
	Race conditions	160
	Locks	160
	Deadlocks	165
	Livelocks	166
	Relational Databases	167
	Database design	167
	Normalization	168
	First normal form: "No repeated values"	168
	Second normal form: "No partial dependencies"	169
	Third normal form: "No transitive dependencies"	169
	Boyce-Codd normal form	169
	Beyond BCNF	170
	Denormalization	170
	Populating a normalized database	170
	Pointers	171
	Functions in C receive arguments by value	173
	Arrays in C are handled like pointers	174
	Passing values and references	175
	Design Issues	177
	YAGNI is not an excuse to take shortcuts	177
	Design for performance	178
	Do not trade common sense for a methodology	178
	Bad Habits	179
	Mishandling exceptions	179
	Not being paranoid enough	180
	Being superstitious	181
	Working against the team	182
	Copying and pasting too much	182
	Eager loading	183
	Questions	184
	Answers	186
Chapter 8	**Quirks and Idioms**	**193**
	Binary Fractions and Floating Point Numbers	194
	Questions	195
	JavaScript	195
	Questions	195
	C#	198
	Questions	198
	Java	200
	Questions	200

Perl   201
Questions   202
Ruby   205
Questions   205
Transact-SQL   206
Questions   206
Answers   208

Chapter 9   **Testing — Not Just for Testers**   **245**
Unit Tests   246
Test-Driven Development   246
    Behavior-driven development   247
    Red, green, refactor   247
Writing Good Unit Tests   247
    Run quickly   247
    Be simple   248
    Be self-evident   248
    Be helpful when failing   248
    Be self-contained   248
Testing Slow Things   249
Unit Testing Frameworks   249
Mock Objects   251
Questions   253
Answers   256

Chapter 10   **The Right Tools**   **265**
Exploring Visual Studio   266
Questions   266
Exploiting Command-Line Tools   268
Questions   269
Understanding PowerShell   271
Questions   271
Troubleshooting with Utilities from Sysinternals   272
Questions   272
Managing Source Code   272
    Source control with Team Foundation Server   273
Questions   273
    Source control with Subversion   273
Questions   274
    Source control with git   274
Questions   275
Answers   275

Chapter 11   **Notorious Interview Questions**   **303**
Estimating on the Spot   303
Questions   304
Solving Puzzles and Brain-Teasers   304
Questions   304

	Solving Probability Problems	306
	Questions	306
	Coping with Concurrency	307
	Questions	307
	Doing Tricks with Bits	308
	Questions	309
	Devising Recursive Algorithms	309
	Questions	309
	Understanding Logic Gates	311
	Questions	313
	Writing Code to…Prove You Can Code	315
	Questions	315
	Answers	316
Chapter 12	**Programming Wisdom**	**351**
	Questions	352
	Answers	357
Appendix	**Preparing Your Cheat Sheets**	**395**
	General and Behavioral	396
	Programming, General	397
	Programming Concepts	397
	Work History	398
	Questions to Ask, If Given the Opportunity	399
Index		**401**

Introduction

I found my first proper computing job in the classified section of our local newspaper. At the time I was living with my mother in the small New Zealand town of Featherston, and the year was 1987. Just like many kids my age, I had been bitten by the computing bug and would have swept floors at night to work with—or even just to be near—computers.

At the interview, my great enthusiasm for computing was enough to impress Neville, the operations manager. My dream came true and soon I was working the evening shift, changing tapes, loading the printer, and yes, I swept the floor at night. Later I learned that, among other things, Neville had been impressed that I had turned up wearing a smart new jumper (sweater).

How times have changed.

Interviewees today, even those with smart jumpers, might face a whole series of tough technical interviews spread over several days. They might be quizzed on their knowledge of language quirks. They could be asked to write a complete and syntactically correct implementation of a linked list while standing at a whiteboard. Their knowledge of mathematics might be probed. And then, after running this gauntlet, they might be rejected because one interviewer out of ten gave the thumbs down.

I have great sympathy for the programmer who is looking for work today. I also have a confession to make. For some years I was the stereotypical geek promoted to hiring manager; single-handedly dreaming up increasingly difficult hurdles for interviewees to jump over. I used a white board for interview exercises (though I didn't quite go so far as to insist that hand-written code should be syntactically perfect) and I made lists of technical trivia questions. Although I was never seriously tempted to pose the brain teasers made notorious by Microsoft (such as how one might move Mt. Fuji), I'm sure that in the early days of being the interviewer, I was guilty of asking a few dubious questions of my own. It is said that we learn by making mistakes, and I've certainly learned a lot over the years.

With that confession out of the way—and the disclaimer that, to this day, I'm still learning new things—let's move on to the much more positive subject of how you, the programmer preparing for an interview, can use the content of this book to ace those tough interviews.

Code for this Book

You can find code for this book at www.wiley.com/go/acetheprogramming interview, or you can visit: https://github.com/EdGuiness/Ace.

How This Book is Organized

This book is notionally divided into two parts. The first four chapters cover what I refer to as the soft stuff—the intangible things that you need to know and understand about how programmers are hired. Then, from Chapter 5 on, we dive deep into the actual questions you will face as an interview candidate.

Chapter 1 covers the entire process of finding a programming job, from writing your CV through to the interview. This first chapter will put the process into perspective and give you an idea of what can happen along the way. If you've ever applied for a programming job, much of this will be familiar. What might be less familiar to you, in chapter one, is the insight into how the hiring manager experiences the process and the pressures that drive companies to recruit programmers.

Chapter 2 is about phone interviews. In a number of important ways a phone interview can be more harrowing than an in-person interview. As a candidate, you will have fewer environmental clues about the company you're talking to. You can't see the décor, how people are dressed, the atmosphere, etc. The first phone-based interview is like a cold sales call—and programmers are typically not too keen on receiving let alone making these kinds of calls. The key to a confident and effective phone interview lies in preparation and being somewhat organized. It's common and natural to be apprehensive about the phone interview, but being overly nervous can get in the way of communicating effectively. We will look at strategies to calm excessive nerves, including a look at what to expect on the call. Cheat-sheets are invaluable when answering tough questions on the phone, and this chapter discusses how to prepare these cheat-sheets.

Chapter 3 covers in-person interviews. As with phone interviews the key to a successful face-to-face interview is preparation. The in-person interview is usually longer than the phone interview and will cover more aspects of your application in greater depth. We will look at how to prepare for the interview, how to ensure you communicate effectively, and we will look at what makes a good answer to a tough interview question.

Handling the job offer and negotiating a great deal is covered in Chapter 4. Despite its importance, this final stage is often overlooked by applicants and employers alike. A poorly-negotiated deal can set an undesirable tone to the employer/employee relationship and the benefit of taking time to consider the agreement before signing up cannot be over emphasized. It should not, and does not need to be difficult or drawn-out, but it does need some careful handling.

Then we will dive deep into a long list of many questions you might face at an interview. Starting from chapter five, each chapter contains a categorized set of questions you might face at the interview.

Chapter 5 covers programming fundamentals. Regardless of whether you are a recent graduate or a software development veteran, if you cannot demonstrate mastery of programming fundamentals you will struggle in most technical interviews. If you are confident and experienced then you may wish to skim-read this chapter; otherwise, you should start here to ensure you can nail the basics.

Chapter 6 covers a subject of increasing importance as employers get wise to what really matters. Here we look at the vital topic of writing good-quality code. This is a slightly elusive subject because programmers are not unanimously agreed about every aspect of what makes code good. On the other hand there are many widely accepted practices that will be in the "top-ten essential" lists of experienced programmers. In this chapter, along with a good list of questions and answers, you will find a condensed version of good practices that enjoy near-universal acceptance. Whatever your personal view on these so-called "best practices" happens to be, you ignore them at your peril. Interviewers want to know that you are at least aware of if not fully conversant with them.

In Chapter 7 I've collected a group of tough interview problems that some hiring managers will hold dear to their hearts. These are the problems that, in all likelihood, they have gathered from their own efforts as programmers, based on the hardest or most thorny problems they have faced. Multi-threading, race conditions, locks, and deadlocks—here lie some of the more challenging areas for most programmers, and the questions in this chapter might challenge even the most experienced programmers. There are almost endless pitfalls and gotchas, and here we will look at some of the most common. Experienced developers must be able to demonstrate familiarity with these problems along with their solutions, and if you are less experienced you should at least be aware of them.

The subject of Chapter 8, language quirks and idioms, is somewhat controversial. It contains a list of what might be considered "pop-quiz" questions, the kind that are trivially answered by searching the web. The point of these questions is that most experienced programmers have explored these dark corners of their programming languages, and can therefore reasonably be expected to know of edge cases that can bite the less experienced.

Testing, the kind that programmers do, is covered in Chapter 9. Unit testing and test-driven development (TDD) is big these days, and for good reason. All programmers should be confident writing good tests. They should be able to describe what makes a good test, what kinds of things to avoid, and have some familiarity with the more common test frameworks. This chapter tests and perhaps improves your knowledge in this area.

Chapter 10 covers software development tools. It was once the case that a programmer was fully equipped if they had a text-editor and a compiler. In the modern world almost no programmer goes without an integrated development environment (IDE). This is especially true in the Microsoft stack of technologies, where Visual Studio has a near-monopoly over all kinds of development. There is so much packed into the modern IDE that even experienced developers might learn a new trick or two—I certainly did when researching material for this chapter. Command-line tools are particularly worthy of some study. If you can belt out a command-line to filter and sort a collection of text files while other, less-knowledgeable programmers labor to write a helper utility in some high-level language, you will only go up in an interviewer's estimation.

Many interviewers still want to explore the implementation details of a linked list during their interviews, so Chapter 11 covers what you need to know. I also drop in to sort out the hapless dining philosophers (a problem of concurrency), and frown over a chess board at the eight queens problem (a problem with a surprising number of interesting solutions, including one based on regular expressions).

Finally, in Chapter 12 you have a collection of questions where the answers of experienced and skillful developers will truly shine. This is where the difference between knowledge and wisdom becomes apparent. It is the hallmark of a veteran programmer that they possess sophisticated views on some or all of the issues presented in this chapter, views that are nuanced and smoothed by years spent toiling at the keyboard. There is no substitute for experience, but less experienced developers reading and reflecting on the issues in this chapter will be taken a bit further down the path toward mastery of programming—if indeed such mastery is possible.

It is my sincere wish that you find this book useful in some way. I welcome any and all comments; you can send them to me at `edward@socialcoder` `.org` or talk to me directly on Twitter at `@KiwiCoder`.

Good luck, and may you truly ace the programming interview.

# CHAPTER 1

Hiring Programmers: The Inside Story

When I was a young boy, making new friends seemed easy. I had grown up with the surreal humor of Monty Python and my usual approach to a potential new friend would be something like *"I am a knight who says Ekki-Ekki-Ekki-PTANG!"* I thought it was hilarious. I made a few great friends (one is still a friend 30 years later), but I also had a lot of misses. Actually, mostly I had misses, nearly all the time. Sometimes my approach would generate open hostility. I couldn't understand it.

What my young self didn't realize was that enthusiasm for the absurd was not a universal constant. Not all kids my age had seen Monty Python, and even if they had, not everyone loved and appreciated it like I did. I was seeing the world through my own Python-shaped glasses, and I did not appreciate the diversity of other childhood experiences. Not everyone was on the same wavelength.

As naïve as this might seem, many hiring managers make the same basic mistake when interviewing. Perhaps they suppose that because they have a lot of hard-won experience in a certain area then *of course* everyone with experience in that area will see things the same way. Further, they might assume that their thought process will be similar. At the interview the hiring manager might abruptly open the conversation with the equivalent of my Python-inspired icebreaker:

> *"Nice to meet you; now, could you please describe a situation where it would be inappropriate to normalize a set of database tables into Boyce-Codd normal form."*

It might be that you love Monty Python and, for you, meeting an interviewer who quotes from Python might seem like a dream come true. If that is the case, then I wish you all the best; just be careful how you respond when the interviewer asks you to *"Please, walk this way."*

For the rest of us, establishing a level of communication that is easy and familiar will take some preparation and effort.

It might have occurred to you that I'm hinting at the concept of rapport. *Rapport* is an excellent word; it describes feelings of harmony, of sympathy, and of being on the same wavelength. I hesitate to use this word only because it has been somewhat hijacked in recent times and now comes loaded with connotations of insincerity, like the fake grin of a novice salesman.

But for an interview to be really effective, to have the ideal degree of communication, and to put yourself on common ground with the interviewer, you really do need to work on establishing a rapport.

One of the simplest and most effective ways to start building rapport is to try to see things from the interviewer's perspective. If you understand the motivations of the interviewer, establishing a common ground and adapting your responses appropriately becomes much easier. You can quickly home in on what the interviewer is looking for, in both a positive and negative sense.

In this chapter, I will take a thorough look at the process of finding a programming job including:

- What motivates a hiring manager, and how to tailor your approach appropriately
- How to prepare a CV that will get you to an interview
- How to use job sites
- Understanding recruitment agencies; how they work and how to work effectively with them
- How to find jobs without a recruitment agency (it can be done!)

Let's start by taking a look at some of the most common reasons why a company might want to hire a programmer.

Reasons They Recruit

Without exception, a company hiring a programmer will have a reason for hiring. If you know what that reason is and understand the motivation for it, then you can optimize your approach accordingly.

Planned expansion

A common scenario—one that will become increasingly common as the major world economies resume growing—is for companies to make medium- to long-term plans for expansion that require them to take on more programmers in accordance with their plans for business growth.

The interviewer's motivation and approach

Because the role is part of longer term plans, the interviewer is unlikely to feel a great sense of urgency. Well-prepared interviewers will have a job profile, perhaps also a person profile, and be comparing candidates to these. With time on their side, they are less likely to compromise their pre-determined requirements, and although they might not realistically expect to perfectly match every aspect, they will probably be less open to considering candidates who deviate by any significant degree.

Your approach

Your approach should be to highlight areas where your skill and experience matches well with the advertised job profile. That is the easy part.

What about skills that aren't a good fit? For example, suppose you apply for the role of a .NET programmer and during the interview it becomes apparent that the interviewer has an expectation that the ideal candidate will have experience of a certain component library, which happens to be one you've not used. In areas where your background is not such a good fit, you have three basic options.

Play it down

Your first option is to downplay the perceived gap in skills—including the option of substituting other experience as being of equivalent value. If you decide to play it down, you might say:

"It's been my experience that it never takes long to learn the basics of a new component library, since, as programmers, we face an endless supply of new components and frameworks both open source and from the major vendors."

You might also comment that learning is part of the job:

"One thing I really like about programming is the experience of learning new technologies and platforms. It's part of the ongoing attraction of the job."

The biggest risk in taking this approach is that you might appear evasive, so be wary of overdoing it. After all, it is unlikely the interviewer chose the requirement at random, and if you push too hard at downplaying the requirement you might inadvertently maneuver yourself into an argument. Be sure to avoid that.

Take it on the chin

Your second option is to take it on the chin, so to speak. Take ownership of the "development opportunity" and perhaps talk briefly about how you have acquired other, similar skills or experiences.

If you decide to take it on the chin, simply agree with the interviewer's observation and at the same time show your enthusiasm for learning something new:

"I don't have experience of that particular technology but I would really enjoy learning it."

If the interviewer persists, you might feel it appropriate to ask how other developers in the team might learn new skills:

"Could you describe how the developers in your team generally learn new skills?"

Each example of learning given by the interviewer is an opportunity to show how, as a part of the team, you would benefit from the same approach and so acquire the necessary skill.

Understand the requirement

Your third option is to explore the interviewer's motivation, to gently probe the motives underpinning the requirement.

Exploring the underpinning motivation of the requirement gives you the best chance of looking good, but to take this approach you must have established a reasonable rapport; otherwise, you risk appearing argumentative. The basic idea is that you explore the requirement looking to show that you understand and can meaningfully address the underlying requirement despite lacking a specific skill or certain experience.

For instance, you might lack experience of a particular IoC container, let's say Microsoft Unity. You might ask the reason for using that particular implementation of IoC:

"I know there are a few good reasons for using an inversion of control pattern; could you describe how the Microsoft Unity framework helps with the kind of work you do here?"

If the answer is to encourage loose-coupling of components, then this gives you an opening to talk about your understanding of dependency injection principles. If the answer is to encourage the writing of code that is structured in a way that better supports unit testing, then you can talk about your experience

"Can I ask whether there have been issues about how the team has been working together that make this ability particularly important?"

Talking to Managers

It is a story often told. A capable and bright programmer impresses everyone and is promoted to team leader or manager. The newly promoted manager takes on the responsibility of hiring new programmers and uses his awesome interpersonal skills to hire more bright programmers.

The problem is that this is almost never how it happens. Many otherwise excellent programmers simply don't have awesome interpersonal skills, and sometimes these are the people who will be running the interview and interviewing you.

Is that a good thing, or is it bad? It depends. It could mean you suffer a terrible interview experience—in which case, count yourself lucky you won't be working for a poor communicator—or it could be a huge advantage. Think of it like this: In every human relationship, having things in common helps, and the more you have in common the easier breaking the ice and enjoying a conversation will be.

Now, as one programmer talking to another programmer (even if the manager isn't currently working as a programmer) what might you have in common? The answer is "lots." Have you ever spent hours or days tracking down a difficult bug? Sure you have—and almost certainly the manager has, too. What do you like about a particular programming language? The manager might feel the same. Do you regularly visit a website for programmers? The manager might, too. Do you have a favorite XKCD cartoon? Do you visit `http://thedailywtf.com`? What is your favorite programming book? Have you ever used the word "nullable" in conversation with a non-techie? What annoys you about the IDE you use? There are lots of topics you can discuss together.

Tech talk—don't hold back

It might become apparent during the interview that the interviewer is not as technical as you might have assumed. He might have a background in project management or product marketing, for example. How should you react? Don't make the mistake of thinking you need to "dumb it down" for the interview. The problem with "dumbing it down" is that you put yourself at a disadvantage when the interviewer compares your responses to another candidate. He might not understand everything you say, but his impression of your response will be colored by the language you use, and if you talk purely in metaphors (for example) then you risk giving the impression that you don't actually know the subject as well as the other candidate who talks about specific language or framework features using their proper names.

If a non-technical interviewer asks you a technical question then he expects a technical answer. The case might be that he has a "cheat sheet" of his own, a list of questions and answers, for example.

Don't hold back—answer the question fully and as you would if talking to a technical interviewer. If the non-technical interviewer wants you to explain something in non-technical terms, then you could use a metaphor (see the next section "Using metaphors"). As a rule, keep your answers grounded in reality using real names and proper terms for things.

Using metaphors

Sometimes a non-technical interviewer wants to assess how well you can explain a technical subject to someone who is non-technical. In this case, a metaphor is your best bet.

For example, suppose you are asked to explain the concept of an IP address in non-technical terms. Here is the definition from Wikipedia:

> **An Internet Protocol address (IP address) is a numerical label assigned to each device (e.g., computer, printer) participating in a computer network that uses the Internet Protocol for communication.**

The first metaphor that might occur to you is that an IP address is much like a mailing address. A mailing address is used to deliver mail, and an IP address is used to deliver packets of information, so the metaphor seems to work. On the other hand, mailing addresses vary widely in format and local conventions, whereas an IP address conforms to a strict set of rules that are consistently and globally applied. Perhaps a better metaphor would be latitude and longitude?

While metaphors might conveniently help a non-technical person relate to an aspect of a technical subject, they are almost by definition an imperfect representation. They have limits, and you should never cling to an imperfect metaphor after reaching those limits. For example, if you use latitude and longitude as a metaphor for an IP address, presumably you don't mean to imply that IP addresses are assigned purely due to the physical location of the computer or device.

Preparing Your CV

A good CV (also known as a resumé) gets you past the filters of recruitment agencies and human resource (HR) departments. A good CV will mean your application is not rejected out of hand, and it could give you an opportunity to talk to someone about the job role. A CV by itself is never going to win you the job. In other words, no hiring manager ever decides to hire someone purely on the strength of her CV alone.

Include relevant keywords but keep them in context

Knowing that, in most cases, non-technical agents will filter your CV has one very important implication—you need to be sure to include keywords that are relevant to the job and in particular to the job advertisement. The technical hiring manager might well understand that working on the ECMAScript specification means you have excellent knowledge of JavaScript, but the typical recruiter will not see the connection unless you spell it out and include the keyword "JavaScript" in your CV. Of course, you also want to avoid the appearance of insincerely stuffing your CV full of keywords, so ensure that any list of keywords is presented in proper context.

Write as well as you can

Poor writing puts you at a severe disadvantage. What you write must be clear and concise. You must proofread (or have a friend proofread) and ruthlessly rewrite or delete anything that isn't clear or relevant.

When I am unsure how to write something, I find that pretending to tell it to a friend is helpful. If you have no friends, tell it to your hand, and then write down the words you used. It doesn't matter what they are at first because the next step is to revise those words into shape. Showing a bit of personality is good, but don't ramble. Also keep in mind that what might seem funny to you while writing your CV might not necessarily look so clever to everyone who reads it. A much better strategy is to let your personality show at the interview after you've established a rapport. If in doubt, always err on the side of plain and simple writing.

Some managers don't care so much about spelling and grammar, but others (like me) care a great deal. I think my distaste stems from years of reviewing poor code that is often full of spelling errors. Using the spelling checker in your word processor or browser doesn't take a lot of extra effort. Don't ignore the red squiggly lines!

Most people find that writing well takes a bit of effort and discipline, so be realistic and allow yourself plenty of time to write and revise.

Justify your claims of experience

If you claim to have experience in an area, or if you claim knowledge of a particular technology, the hiring manager needs to understand how you acquired it. If your CV doesn't show how you got "five years of experience of ASP.NET" then you risk appearing insincere. If you claim to have the experience then the hiring manager will to want to see where you got it. If I don't see it, I won't necessarily assume you're lying, but you will be at a disadvantage when I have another CV that clearly shows where the experience was obtained.

If you claim to be good at anything, it should be reflected in the details of your employment or education history. You need to be explicit. Also be aware that job titles today are almost meaningless. Being an "analyst" could mean just about anything and doesn't necessarily imply analysis skill of any kind. A "web developer" could mean someone with programming skills or someone with Photoshop skills. A "programmer" should mean someone who produces code, but I've seen it used for jobs where the work amounted to configuring systems via drop-down lists. You need to describe the technology, and how you used it.

Ignore anyone who tells you "strictly one or two pages"

Ignore all the advice about keeping a CV short. That's for people with short attention spans and for recruiters who in many cases don't care for details. If you have lots of experience it should be reflected in your CV. As a hiring manager I want to see it, and more importantly you should be proud of it, not ashamed.

This is not an excuse to ramble—the advice about being clear and concise still applies, and you still need to make effective use of keywords and summaries.

Emphasize skills that match the job advertisement

There's nothing wrong with emphasizing certain skills to match a job advertisement. As a candidate, it took me a long time to appreciate that emphasizing different skills depending on the job in question is perfectly fine. I used to think it was deceptive, but I don't think that any more. See it from the hiring manager's point of view—if a CV clearly calls out skills that match the job description then that CV will appeal more than some other CV that contains the same skills but buries them among other, less-relevant skills.

In other words, highlighting relevant skills helps everyone.

If you have experience in a variety of areas, consider writing more than one CV, each one emphasizing different areas. You might write one that targets database-centric roles, and another that emphasizes your business analysis skills. Having these prepared and ready to send means you can respond quickly to job advertisements without the need to revise your CV before applying.

Don't leave unexplained gaps between jobs

Don't leave gaps in your CV, especially big ones. It risks making you appear shifty or evasive. If you were volunteering in Africa, that's great. If you took time off to retrain, or to pursue a start-up idea, or to raise a child, that's all good. The only thing you have to prove is that you can do the job. Yes, in some cases, a gap in your experience might mean you have to accept a lesser salary, but a savvy employer will see that as an opportunity rather than a problem, and savvy employers also know that life experience counts for something.

"Reading, music, and cinema"

My estimate, based on reading many hundreds of CVs, is that 80 percent of CVs contain a "personal interests" section, and that 80 percent of these sections contain the exact same list of things; reading, music, and cinema.

You really don't need this section in a CV, especially if it contains the same interests listed by everyone else. If you do happen to be a Tiddlywinks world champion, maybe that is something to show off, but in general, rather than trying to show how well-rounded and interesting you are in this odd little corner of your CV, try to let that show through in the rest of your CV, through your experience, and at the in-person interview.

On the other hand, if you have (for instance) used your programming skills to support a non-profit organization, perhaps a charity, then you should mention it. I know a person who worked with inner-city kids at one point, and as a hiring manager I would definitely be interested to read that. Anything you've done that demonstrates enthusiasm, altruism, or any other noble quality is worth including. Just avoid being boring because you felt compelled to include this section—better to leave it out.

Use a logical layout

In general, the layout of your CV should be easy to scan and arranged logically. A key goal of any CV is to make it easy for someone to check boxes off when comparing your experience and skills against a job specification. I recommend starting your CV with a well-written summary that includes an overview of your key skills and significant experiences. The next section should be your job history shown in reverse chronological order, followed by a section for projects including any voluntary or unpaid work experience, and the final section should be education and training.

Every page of your CV should contain your contact information—your name, e-mail, and phone number, for example, within the header and footer areas. Contact information does not need to be a dominant feature but you do need to ensure that employers or recruiters have no trouble finding your contact details when they want to contact you.

Graduate CVs

With a relatively small amount of work experience, you will need to show off your abilities by listing projects, at or out of school, and the role you played in each. If you led a project, played a key role, solved a difficult problem, or designed a complicated component, then be sure to highlight that as an accomplishment. Testimony from someone who assessed your work or benefited from it in some way adds authenticity.

CVs containing more experience

Experience is wonderful, and there is no substitute. However, a lot of experience can be interpreted in a number of ways and not all the ways are flattering. Twenty years with a single employer might give the impression, right or wrong, that you have never been challenged professionally. No doubt within those twenty years you overcame many tough challenges, so you should ensure that these are made visible in your experience. You should include subheadings for:

- Major projects where you had significant responsibility
- Different roles or major responsibilities
- Organizational changes that required you to adapt

CVs of those returning to work

If you've taken time off to raise children, travel, or study, then you've absolutely nothing to hide or to cover up. Be honest in your CV about why you have not been working. A single sentence is probably enough. Also, be honest with yourself about areas in which you might be somewhat out of date.

If you've been out of work due to redundancy—perhaps a down-sizing due to poor economic conditions—or if you were outright fired then, please, be honest in your CV. You don't need to use the word "fired" (if you were), but you don't want to hide your circumstances or pretend it was according to some plan. Hiring managers are hyper-vigilant for this kind of deception, and (trust me on this point) if a manager feels you are being deceptive in any way, you will have zero chance of landing the job.

Redundancies happen, and now and then people are fired. A simple and honest summary of the situation is by far the best strategy.

If you were fired, you may find some doors are closed. I can't pretend otherwise. The most practical advice I can give is to omit your "firing" from your CV, and be prepared with a good answer when asked why you left that job. A good answer is something like:

"I was fired following a disagreement with my team leader. We fell out after I took an initiative she disagreed with. It was difficult, but I feel I learned a lot from the experience."

You may have strong feelings about a firing and that is, of course, quite natural. What you mustn't do, even if the interviewer encourages it, is to complain about your past employer. Let the facts speak for themselves, and allow the interviewer to come to their own conclusion.

Think of it this way: If you are composed, dignified, and reasonable at an interview, the interviewer will be more inclined to believe your side of the story. If you are emotional and allow yourself to vent, the interviewer may be more inclined to sympathize with your past employer.

It is difficult, but be sure to consider how you will answer this question, before the time comes (as it surely will).

Avoiding common CV blunders

It is a sad truth that many hours of good work can be undone by a moment of carelessness. The first impression a hiring manager will have of you is based on your CV. Not only that, but your CV will sit alongside a stack of other CVs. Most hiring managers sift this stack into a smaller "short list" stack, and to do, that they must somehow discriminate. All other things being equal, the small mistakes in your CV could result in rejection. Let's go over some of these "small" things so you are sure to avoid them.

Poor spelling or grammar

Poor spelling or grammar can ruin an otherwise good CV. It happens so often that it is almost a cliché. Be sure to proofread your CV, or better, have an eagle-eyed friend check it for you. If English isn't your first language then you really should have a native English speaker review your CV, even if it means paying for it.

Vague or nonspecific accomplishments

When describing accomplishments, you need to keep two things in mind: Be specific, and describe the accomplishment in terms that most people can understand. For example, if you discovered and fixed a performance issue in a framework component, someone unfamiliar with that component (but otherwise technically informed) will find it more impressive if you describe the impact of your performance tweak rather than the mechanics of the tweak itself. Describing a "200 percent performance improvement" is much better than describing how you implemented a custom sort method. You will have plenty of opportunity to show off your technical skills in more detail at the interview.

Unclear or cluttered Layout

Of all the mistakes, fixing a cluttered layout is the easiest to detect and to fix. Simply hold up the page—without trying to read it—and let your eyes focus on whatever leaps out of the page. If nothing leaps out, it's too cluttered—or too empty! If the wrong things leap out then the CV isn't arranged well enough.

Don't be afraid to add whitespace around things you want to highlight, and whatever you do, don't use a tiny font hoping to cram in more information.

Unprofessional e-mail address

No matter how hilarious your friends think it is, "jojo_2hot4u@hotmail.com" is never going to be appropriate on a CV. Think how this address looks to someone who's never met you and is trying to form an opinion based purely on the presentation in your CV.

Domains are cheap to register and easy to maintain, and unless you have a very common name then *yourfirstname@yourlastname.com* or a variation like *@yourname.info* will probably be available.

If you don't want to spend any money then at least consider signing up for a more "professional" e-mail from one of the many free providers such as Google or Yahoo!.

Using Job Sites

All online job sites function similarly. You can upload your CV and thereby make it searchable by employers (or more likely, by recruiters), browse and search for jobs, subscribe to receive e-mailed notifications of new jobs, and apply for jobs.

For the job seeker, these sites are always 100 percent free to use. They all have a huge following of recruiters and employers. From a purely statistical point of view, you have a better chance of making contact with a potential employer than if you go it alone.

Some of the search tools on these sites make them truly useful. For example, you can limit your search to a very specific location, salary, or job title.

The sheer volume of users on job sites means that your CV is less likely to be noticed. You join a very large crowd of job seekers, and it is harder to differentiate your CV from the many thousands of others. It can be disheartening to send your CV and hear nothing back.

Unfortunately, it doesn't take much time reading through job advertisements to realize that almost all the jobs posted on these sites are posted by recruiting agencies. This means you're almost never going to be dealing directly with an employer. This can sometimes (though rarely) work in your favor should the agency take a special interest in your application, but, for the most part, these agencies represent another layer of obstacles between you and the interviewer.

Also, it doesn't take too much imagination to see how these job boards might potentially be abused by unscrupulous agencies who post fake job adverts in order to gather CVs from applicants, CVs which are then redacted and forwarded to prospective clients as the agents tout for business. This may not be common but it would be naïve to think it never happens.

Be on your guard, and don't invest too much mental or emotional energy in the "perfect" job after submitting your application. If you don't hear back soon after submitting an application for which you are obviously suited, the job may never have existed in the first place.

Comparison of major job boards

All job sites operate similarly and have the same pros and cons, so how you choose which site to use is a question of personal preference. It might be helpful to see which sites post the most jobs for programmers, in which case refer to the numbers in Tables 1-1 and 1-2. The search query used to obtain these numbers was "programmer OR software developer" and the search was limited to "posted within the past seven days." The query was run in June 2012.

Table 1-1: Job Listings on Major U.S. Sites

SITE	NUMBER OF JOBS LISTED
CareerBuilder.com	1,950
Monster.com	1,000+
Jobserve.com	718
ComputerJobs.com	685
Dice.com	152

Table 1-2: Job Listings on Major UK Sites

SITE	NUMBER OF JOBS LISTED
CWJobs.co.uk	3,018
Reed.co.uk	2,439
Jobserve.co.uk	930
Monster.co.uk	531

Recruitment Agencies

All recruitment agencies work on behalf of employers to find and match job seekers to vacancies. While all agents will initially appear very interested in your career prospects, the extent to which they are committed to finding you a job is limited by how likely they think it is that they can "sell" you to an employer. If they don't have a live vacancy that matches your profile, you might never hear from them after the initial contact.

Almost all agencies work on a contingency basis, which means they charge their clients (the employers) a percentage of the salary they will pay to the person they hire following an introduction. If the agency doesn't place someone with that employer then it gets nothing. The fees of recruiting agencies vary a lot, but are usually somewhere between 10 and 30 percent of the new hire's first-year salary. This might seem like a lot of money for very little work, but the uncertain nature of this work—and the fact that many employers are willing to pay these fees—appears sufficient justification for the recruiters to continue charging what they charge.

Job seekers are not normally asked to pay any fees to recruitment agencies so you should treat any such request with great suspicion.

In exchange for the promise of this contingent fee, the agency might advertise the job vacancy on a number of online job sites and will probably also search its database of candidates looking for a match between candidate skills and the skills listed in the job description provided by the employer. Most recruiters will also put the word out via their network of contacts, hoping to attract suitable candidates they can then introduce to their client.

Interestingly, almost all recruiting agents involved with sourcing and placing software developers have no significant first-hand (and sometimes not even second-hand) experience with software development. When working with employers and programmers, their role is purely sales and (social) networking. Inevitably some of the more experienced agents will pick up a basic vocabulary of technical and programming terms that enable them to communicate a bit less awkwardly, but as a programmer you might occasionally find yourself explaining the most elementary programming terms to a recruitment agent. What you need to remember is that although agents might lack technical comprehension, whatever you say to them will (hopefully) be replayed to a potential employer. To minimize the chance of Chinese whispers, avoiding the temptation to relate your experience in great detail is usually the best strategy. Save that information for when you talk directly with the employer. Good agents will ensure that the most relevant aspects of your experience are relayed to the potential employer. They will also be aware of their own limited technical knowledge when communicating with employers, and, for the most part, they will (and should) refer technical questions to you. If you ever find that an agent has "made stuff up" about your experience (and incredibly some do) then you should distance yourself from that agent as soon as possible. He or she won't be helping you find the right employer and might even damage your reputation.

Some agencies want to interview you prior to making an introduction to any employer. This is an interesting and sometimes amusing affair, where the agent, who knows next to nothing about the technologies in your CV, asks you questions about your experience with those technologies. Pragmatic agents will recognize their own limitations and restrict themselves to asking generic interview questions such as those related to your motivation, your aspirations, your attendance, and sickness-absence record, and so on. One important thing to remember is that apart from a routine confirmation of your background and experience, the agent also wants to gain a clear impression of your "personality," which he or she can then relate to the potential employer. This is one way agencies and agents "add value," though the actual value added from this subjective assessment is perhaps questionable.

Working effectively with a recruiter

Remember that recruiters are paid by employers, and so their motivation to help you can vary depending on the prospects currently on their books. Investing too much emotional energy with any individual agent or agency, regardless of how exciting the job on offer might be, is generally not advisable. Certainly never be tempted to rely exclusively on a single recruiting agency, regardless of how effective it might appear.

Also remember that agents act as middlemen, and that whatever you say might be replayed to a potential employer. Although you need to convince the agent that your credentials and experience are genuine and relevant, being somewhat guarded in disclosing anything that isn't clearly advantageous to your application also makes sense. You can't avoid obvious questions, such as gaps in employment, but avoid volunteering unflattering or "complicated" information that might be misrepresented to the employer.

When waiting for news from an agent, don't waste your time and energy fretting if she doesn't return your calls. Be assured that an agent will waste no time in contacting you when she has news—she doesn't get paid unless she places you. Remember, too, the agent is at the mercy of the employer and is therefore just as likely as you to be anxious when waiting for news. Keeping in touch with the agency doesn't hurt—perhaps do a weekly "check in" call to ensure the agency has you in mind and is aware of your continued enthusiasm—but avoid pestering agents. It doesn't help.

Searching for Jobs Yourself

An alternative to relying on recruitment agencies is to find and contact employers yourself. This task isn't as hard as you might think. After all, most employers want to spread the news of a job vacancy as widely as they can, and many have an area on their website dedicated to advertising current vacancies. Very large employers might have an arrangement with a number of preferred supplier agencies or have a dedicated team in their Human Resources department that handles all incoming employment queries, but—and I cannot stress this enough—most hiring managers still welcome direct approaches from suitable candidates, provided, of course, that the contact is respectful and personalized.

If you make contact with a hiring manager who then refers you to the HR department, don't be disheartened. The manager is very probably obliged due to corporate rules of "efficiency and uniformity" to send you through to HR. Unless you feel that the contact was unwelcome then nothing prevents you from remaining in touch with the hiring manager as your application progresses through the necessary HR channels. Remember that the corporate "rules" don't apply to you unless and until you're an employee. Always remain respectful and forthright in all your communication, and don't be put off by the bureaucracy.

A word of caution—don't be tempted to send a generic letter or e-mail. To the potential employer this approach puts you in the same category as the bothersome agencies that send out unsolicited and unwelcome junk mail about "exciting opportunities" or "hot candidates." Always personalize your message as much as you can, including addressing the letter or e-mail to the hiring manager rather than "To whom it may concern," and mention specific and genuine reasons why you are interested in joining the company. If you are stuck for ideas then ask yourself these questions: Does the company produce a product you've used? Is it working in an area with potential that excites you? Have you heard something interesting about the company from friends or in the news?

One of the best ways to find a potential employer is through your own personal network of friends and contacts. Perhaps you're lucky and have naturally built up a large social network over the years, or perhaps (more likely) as a programmer you don't have a particularly large social network. Many of us know intellectually that having a large network can be a tremendous asset, especially when looking for a new job, but how many of us (and I sheepishly include myself in this number) have failed to invest time and energy into establishing and maintaining this kind of network?

If you don't have a significant network of contacts because you are—and let's call a spade a spade—an introvert, then don't despair. This next section is especially for you. I only wish I had followed this advice myself from an earlier age.

Networking for introverts

The problem with most of the advice you may have read about networking is that it was written *by extroverts for extroverts*. If, like many programmers, you are not particularly extroverted by nature, most of this advice is wasted on you. What's even worse is you might feel guilty or stressed about not being able to follow what is presented as "simple and easy" advice for networking.

Don't feel guilty. Instead, play to your strengths as an introvert.

Introverts are often quite thoughtful, preferring to spend time thinking about a topic rather than talking about it. This trait can be a major advantage when "preparing to network." If you want to make contact with someone, set yourself a goal of making a list of thoughtful questions to ask that person when the opportunity arises. Most people love talking about themselves and sharing their opinions. This is not a cynical view; it's just basic human psychology— the sharing of personal experience is fundamental to any human relationship. Thoughtful, open-ended questions asked at the right time break the ice and set the relationship off to an excellent start.

Introverts are often more comfortable talking to individuals rather than to groups of people. It also happens that communicating one-on-one is much more effective in terms of exchanging ideas and building relationships. Look for situations where you can engage a new contact one-on-one, even if that interaction happens in a public place. Perhaps ironically, the open and public space of Twitter is a good environment for an introvert to make contact. The 140-character limit works well for those who prefer thoughtful and concise exchanges over wordy and extended conversations, and after you're followed by a Twitter user you can send him direct (and private) messages. You'll learn more about using Twitter and other social networking tools later in this chapter.

Many introverts find the job of building a network somewhat daunting. It needn't be. The trick is to think of it as a game with a well-defined goal—to make new contacts and build meaningful relationships with them. The hardest part for introverts is that the "rules of engagement" are vague. *"Exactly how,"* an introvert might wonder, *"do I go about building a network?"* If you're introverted, these vagaries are annoying and off-putting—*"What on earth should I do next?"* If you're extroverted these vagaries are exciting—*"I can do whatever I wish!"* (Though if you're extroverted you've probably skipped this section or are reading it out of curiosity.) For introverts, here's a cheat sheet for how to build a network:

- Make a list of potential contacts.
- Sort the list into order, from "most desirable and probable" to "least desirable and improbable."
- Starting at the top, think about what kind of questions the contact might find interesting, and write down a short list of questions.
- In a suitable environment, ask those questions of up to five potential contacts (more than five might be difficult to do, depending on your personal capacity and energy).
- Engage with those who respond.
- Keep adding to your list so you always have five potential new contacts.
- Repeat!

Finally, if you find that networking drains your energy, be sure to protect your energy reserves by pacing yourself. Take time out to reflect and process information gathered from social exchanges, and in this way prepare yourself for the next opportunity to build and maintain your network. It's a marathon, not a sprint.

Finding potential employers

Potential employers are out there. Unfortunately, many of them are unthinkingly patronizing recruitment agencies, or perhaps (more fairly) they exclusively use agencies because they don't know of any better way.

Consider the problem of finding candidates from the hiring manager's perspective—wouldn't it be nice if a suitable candidate contacted the company directly? Wouldn't it save the company a lot of money and time? Too right, it would! With that in mind, here are some of the channels you can use to unearth these potential employers:

- Your personal network of contacts, including Twitter, Facebook, and LinkedIn
- Regional business directories
- Chambers of commerce job fairs
- Job sites, limiting your search to jobs that have been "posted by employer"
- Web search for "careers" + "*employer name*"
- Professional journals

Searching for a job is no time to be bashful. Add a note to your online profiles that you're available; you never know who might see it.

Approaching potential employers

Approaching a potential employer "cold" is probably the hardest aspect for many job seekers, and I won't pretend otherwise. If you can, having someone (other than a fee-seeking agency) introduce you is much better. If you use LinkedIn, check to see whether anyone in your network can help, and of course, ask around and make use of your other social networks. You've probably heard of the idea that everyone is on average six steps away, by way of introduction, from any other person.

If you don't have a connection then you'll need to contact the hiring manager without an introduction. Don't panic; this isn't necessarily a problem. The first thing to do is to find out as much as you can about the company, the department, and the people who influence and make hiring decisions. I say "as much as you can," but I don't mean you should spend an unlimited amount of time researching a company. Set yourself a reasonable limit, perhaps a few hours at most, by which time you will have all the useful information you need plus some insight into how the company is structured and who makes the decisions.

Obviously, you need to look at the company website where, quite often, you will find most of the information you need. At the very least you will find a contact telephone number. Call it. Don't pretend to be anything other than a job seeker, and ask the person who answers the phone whether he or she can help you. You only need a few bits of information, and if you are up-front and honest most people are happy to help. It doesn't hurt that many receptionists have been in your position (job seeking) and therefore have some sympathy for job seekers. Be warned, though: The first hint of deception or evasiveness will cut your conversation short. Having had the benefit of sitting near receptionists, I've heard this happen over and over. Companies receive endless cold calls from sales people and recruiting agencies, and most receptionists have developed finely tuned senses to detect these types of calls. A naïve sales person will call asking to speak to the software development manager about "a business opportunity" and, inevitably, he achieves nothing but having his details taken on a Post-It note that is soon discarded. Don't let that happen to you!

I do not recommend that your very first contact should be via e-mail. Think of what happens to the unsolicited e-mails that land in your own inbox. You need to call up and talk to someone. The aim of the first call is very simple: You want to get the name and contact details of the person who makes hiring decisions in whichever department hires programmers. Ideally you will also find out a bit about the structure of the company and whether or not it is hiring, but at minimum you must obtain the name and e-mail address of the hiring manager. If the first-contact conversation goes well, you might ask the person you talk to if he or she will pass on a message to the hiring manager that you're a software developer, you're available, and that you're hoping to have a chat. Don't fret about the possibility of the message being lost or ignored. That might happen, but more than likely this message will serve as a kind of introduction in lieu of one from a common connection in your social network.

Being persistent

One thing that is drilled into trainee sales people is that persistence can pay off. This is a double-edged sword, for although it is true that persistence can pay off it can also taint your reputation and result in you being labeled as a pest. A fine line exists between persistence and pestering but, at its most basic, persistence is the idea that you should not give up at the first hurdle.

This can mean that you need to make more than one phone call to get the information you desire. It can mean that you need to send follow-up e-mails rather than assuming the worst. It might mean that your e-mail was accidentally filtered into a "junk mail" folder and you need to send a personally addressed letter, which is something I recommend in any case. Ultimately, you must be the judge of when your efforts have crossed the line, but remember that if you have consistently been polite, respectful, and direct in all your communication then there is no good reason why anyone would consider you a pest.

Timing

Many large companies are constantly in the news for various reasons. If you have an ambition to join one of these companies, you should keep a lookout for any news that suggests expansion plans are afoot. For instance, many publicly traded service companies announce whenever they win major new contracts or business. Submitting (or resubmitting) your application after learning of news like this might provoke a favorable response, when otherwise the answer would have been "no current vacancies."

Also, most companies make plans for expansion that coincide with their financial year. If you find out when this financial year starts—and this information is readily available for all publicly listed companies—then you might stand an improved chance if you submit an application just as the hiring process kicks off.

Emerging Alternatives

If you've spent much time online then almost certainly you have heard of or are active on one or more social networking sites. Here's a quick overview of some of the more popular sites, and how suited they are (or can be) to finding your next job as a programmer.

Using Twitter

Twitter is a social networking service where users can post and exchange messages. These messages are known as "tweets" and they are limited to 140 characters. Twitter claims to have more than 140 million active users who collectively post 340 million tweets daily.

When you're looking around for potential employers, don't forget that the reason most people join and use Twitter is to exchange funny tweets, interesting thoughts, and useful information. A steady stream of similar-sounding tweets won't gain you many followers, and neither will tweets that are impersonal and stuffy. To be interesting, you also need to be a little bit vulnerable, sharing your ideas even if they won't necessarily be universally popular. This is not to suggest you should continually air your unpopular opinions (should you have any), but rather that you should not be afraid to—always respectfully—say what you think. A monotonous repetition of dull links to your website won't gain you many followers.

If you are new to Twitter, spend the first few days reading the tweets of others, noting what kind of tweets are popular and retweeted, and also noting what kind of tweets are less popular or ignored.

You can pay to gain followers, but I don't advise you do this. The followers you gain won't be at all interested in you, and they won't be interesting to follow. You can also pay for software that automates the "following" and "unfollowing" process in order to gain a large number of followers. You might find this helpful, perhaps as a minor ego boost, but again I don't recommend you do this. You can distinguish these robotic accounts from real users because they will inexplicably follow you one day, and if you don't reciprocate they will unfollow you in short order. Real relationships in Twitter, just like in life, are not something you want a robot attending to, at least not if you want real, potentially helpful connections with real, potentially helpful people.

In summary,

Do:

- Engage with others, including retweeting tweets you find interesting or relevant.

- Update your profile to include mention of your availability.

- Include a link in your profile to your CV (or better, your website where your CV can be found along with other interesting material you've written or compiled).

Don't:

- Post unprofessional or offensive tweets (this includes not retweeting the potentially offensive tweets of others).

- Limit your tweets to just advertising yourself and your job search. Tweet about what you find interesting or amusing.

- Follow obvious spammers or "follow back" robots. Yes, this increases your number of followers but at the same time it taints your account by association.

Using Facebook

Facebook is probably the best known and most widely used of all social networks. You might have seen the film *The Social Network*, and the chances are you have a Facebook account no matter where in the world you happen to live.

The popularity and the ubiquity of Facebook is a double-edged sword; a potential employer might have a presence on Facebook, which can give you some insight into their company and culture. On the other hand, consider the sobering thought that every potentially embarrassing thing you've ever posted on Facebook is at risk of being discovered by that employer. You should also be aware that the U.S. Federal Trade Commission recently came to an agreement with Facebook over their accusation that Facebook "deceived consumers by telling them they could keep their information on Facebook private, and then repeatedly allowed it to be shared and made public." You could assume that this agreement between Facebook and the FTC will lead to better privacy controls at Facebook, or you could take a more cynical view that Facebook is unlikely to care for your privacy unless it is forced to by external regulation.

There is another privacy aspect to Facebook, although perhaps it has been exaggerated in the popular media. It has been reported that employers and academic institutions have begun asking for access to the accounts of Facebook users, or to become Facebook "friends" with potential employees or students. Whether this is right or wrong or even legal is largely irrelevant; the implications for many job seekers faced with this kind of request is unpleasant. At the very least, this gives many people a reason to hesitate before freely posting social updates.

Ultimately, Facebook is great for purely social networking, but not so great for the job seeker.

Using LinkedIn

If you had to choose exactly one networking site for the purpose of finding a programming job, you are well-advised to choose LinkedIn. More than any other networking site, LinkedIn clearly targets professionals; that is, those in paid employment and employers. LinkedIn's mission statement makes it clear beyond any doubt that this is the site for connecting with other professionals.

The mission of LinkedIn is to connect the world's professionals to enable them to be more productive and successful.

Using LinkedIn is mostly self-evident. You connect with people you know, join groups that interest you, keep your employment history up to date, and post occasional updates. You can also interact with other LinkedIn users by sending "InMail," which is handy if you don't have any other contact details for that person.

LinkedIn also provides a convenient way to showcase recommendations from your colleagues and business associates. You can display (or hide) these recommendations in your profile.

For a monthly fee LinkedIn also offers a number of extra features for job seekers, including:

- Five "InMails," which allow you to contact anyone on LinkedIn (normally you are limited to contacting just your immediate network).

- Information about who has viewed your profile (normally you can see just limited information).

- Your profile displays a "job seeker" badge, though this is optional.

- When you apply for a job via LinkedIn, your profile appears as a "featured applicant" at the top of the list as viewed by the job poster.

- Recruiters (in fact, anyone on LinkedIn) can send you messages via "OpenLink," which appears as an icon displayed in your profile. This is an optional feature.

Writing a blog

Writing a blog is incredibly effective as a way to connect you with potential employers. If you write well, and have interesting or amusing things to say, you can reach a very large audience who will return to your blog or sign up for your RSS feed. Over time, you can develop a group of loyal readers, and the value of that loyalty for the job seeker is huge.

That's the good news.

The reality is that many blogs are started with the best of intentions, and then fall silent after an initial burst of enthusiasm. Why is this so? It's because writing takes time, accumulating readers takes time, and building up a significant following can take months or even years.

If you regularly post on Twitter or any social network then blogging might be the option for you, in the sense that every interesting thing you might post to a social network can instead be posted to your blog. If not, then you have to ask yourself whether you have the capacity to sustain a blog. The content has to come from somewhere, and if your heart isn't in it, then it will probably show in your writing—and consequently you won't gain many readers.

Getting started blogging is easy, and many free services are available to get started with. I don't recommend these. Hosting your blog on your own domain and with a paid hosting provider lends credibility to your blog but perhaps more important, gives you ultimate control over your blog and your content. In contrast, anything you post on a "free" site is subject to terms that detract from a professional image. For example, some free sites adorn your blog with unrelated advertising. Similarly, if you post your content on one of the well-known social networks, you probably don't have much control over that content, and depending on the terms and conditions you agreed to when signing up (you do remember those, right?) then the possibility exists that you might not even own the content you've created.

If you decide to set up a blog, here's what I recommend:

- Choose a topic for your blog that is relevant to your career interest. Programmers are lucky—we have an enormous number of very interesting topics to talk and write about. Resist the temptation to blog about random unrelated things—a focused blog is more likely to attract loyal readers.

- Pay for hosting and buy a suitable domain name.

- Set yourself a reasonable schedule for writing, one that is regular and to which you can realistically commit over the long term.

- Try to build up a buffer of blog posts for those inevitable times when for whatever reason (for example, holiday or sickness), you can't write new material.

- Use blogging software. If you don't know which blogging software to use then I recommend WordPress as a good starting point.

- Enable comments on your blog posts. Yes, this attracts spammers, but the benefit of engaging with your readers far outweighs the hassle of filtering spam comments. People love being heard, so don't ignore them when they leave comments.

Careers at Stack Overflow

At some point, most programmers find themselves searching the Web for answers to a difficult or obscure problem. Many of these programmers find the answer on Stack Overflow, a relatively new site that has become a mecca for programmers and a truly valuable resource. Most programmers reading this will know of Stack Overflow and will have visited it many times.

What isn't quite as well-known is that the good people at Stack Overflow have branched out from their initial programming Q&A site and now also run a site for employers and job seekers at `http://careers.stackoverflow.com/`.

The operation of this site is similar to most job sites: You can submit your details to allow employers and recruiters to find your profile, and employers and recruiters can search for profiles using keyword and location. The unique aspect of `http://careers.stackoverflow.com` lies in its connection with Stack Overflow. If you have contributed answers to Stack Overflow then your "top answers" display in your profile along with how you rate in various subjects. Your Stack Overflow reputation will also be on display.

Whether your involvement with Stack Overflow is seen as a significantly positive aspect of your application depends on the attitude of the potential employer. Tech-savvy employers might be impressed, and some might even browse your contributions (including your questions!) to gain insight into your style of communication and to see how well you can express yourself. On the other hand, the possibility exists that some employers won't see your involvement with Stack Overflow in quite the same light. For example, they might understandably have concerns about the time you might spend on this site versus actually working for them. If you have a particularly high reputation, this might be an issue you must prepare to address during a phone or in-person interview. If your involvement with Stack Overflow was during a period of unemployment, the time you've spent on Stack Overflow probably won't be an issue, but otherwise you should consider how you can credibly respond to the question when it is asked.

Skills matter: "Find Your Ninja"

An interesting alternative to the usual approach to matching employers with programmers is the Find Your Ninja project run by the training company Skills Matter, London.

The basic idea is that employers who want to hire a programmer pay a fee to attend, and pitch their company and project to an audience of programmers. Programmers attend the event for free.

This event sounds similar to a traditional job fair, but an important difference exists. Because the audience consists mostly of experienced programmers who have heard about the event while attending training at Skills Matter, the presentations (that is, the "pitches") are more technical than usual. Rather than emphasizing general benefits, employers focus more on the technology and programming environment in addition to the usual information about the company. Employer presentations are usually given by technical leads within the company rather than by recruiting representatives.

Fundamentally, the Find Your Ninja project and other similar events are based on the assumption that the audience is filled with highly motivated and competent programmers. If you see yourself in that category and you live in or live close to London, then perhaps this kind of event is for you.

If you don't live near London then contact technical/programmer training companies near where you live, or near where you want to work, to see if they run similar events.

# CHAPTER 2

Handling the Phone Interview with Confidence

I once nearly shot an interviewer in the head with a rubber band. I was nervously fiddling and it slipped and went sailing just over his head. Somehow he didn't notice, but it settled my nerves because it was kind of funny.

This technique was effective for me, but I don't suggest you try it. Your aim might not be as good as mine.

If you pick up a generic book on interviewing and flip to the chapter on handling nerves, you can find a lot of helpful-sounding advice, like remembering to breathe, imagining interviewers in their underwear, and role playing the interview with a friend.

If that kind of advice works for you then go for it. But if you've tried those kinds of things and they haven't worked, here is some advice specifically for programmers.

What you need to realize is that programmers are special. If you take away the project manager, the tester, the document writer, the business analyst, the systems analyst—even if you take away the UX expert and the architect—a programmer can still write code. Maybe it won't be as good as if all those experts had pitched in, but the point is the programmer on the team is the one who writes the code. The others help.

Now imagine that team of people without a programmer. See? That coder-less team might produce an impressive set of PowerPoint slides, or a shiny mock-up of what the product might have looked like, but it takes a programmer to write code that compiles and does something useful.

Don't forget that.

Here is another thing to remember: Good programmers are scarce. At times, it might seem like you are competing with hundreds of other programmers and you might be, but you have a big advantage—you are a good programmer or you want to be, and that will make you stand out.

I might not hire a programmer for many reasons, but first and foremost among the reasons to hire is the ability of the programmer to be capable of writing code. Of course, exceptions exist, such as when a non-technical manager is the only interviewer, or when the job turns out to be something other than actually writing code, such as working with spreadsheets or spelunking around with MS Access.

After all these interviews, just one thing still surprises me, and that is when I ask a candidate programmer to write some code and he can't, or when he writes code without any apparent knowledge of looping constructs, arrays, or basic Boolean logic. I'm not making this up.

Does that make you feel more confident? It should, because you know the basics of programming like the back of your hand, and on top of that you know much, much more. If you need to brush up on some things, no problem—that's why you're reading this book.

Knowing What to Expect

As an interviewer, here's how I run a standard phone interview.

Prior to the interview, I have read the curriculum vitae (CV) and perhaps highlighted a few things. The kinds of things I might highlight vary from CV to CV, but the most basic thing I look for (and highlight) is relevant experience. If you have no commercial experience, I look for relevant school projects. On top of that, I look for anything "extra" (that is, not strictly necessary for the job in question) that might be worth discussing during a phone interview. I can't give you a rote list of things to include in your CV, but here are some things I might highlight in order to ask you about them:

- Non-work-related software projects
- Any kind of special achievement, in any field
- Experience building a framework of any kind
- Experience in less-common programming languages or technologies
- Your personal website

I will have previously arranged a time to call you, and when you answer I will introduce myself and confirm you were expecting my call, and that you do indeed have the time to talk. Of course, if the interview has been pre-arranged I won't be expecting you to say, "Well, actually now is an awkward time"—but it has happened, more than once!

Then I will make some small talk. I might ask how your day has been. I'm not going to pretend to be your friend the instant we start talking, but I will be trying to build a basic level of rapport in the hope that you feel more comfortable talking to me about yourself. Not all interviewers do this, and if you get a call that launches straight into difficult questions you just have to go with it. The interviewer necessarily won't learn a lot about you, and that will be her loss.

Then it will be my turn to talk, and I'll describe the opportunity on offer and talk a bit about the company (more so for smaller companies).

Next, I ask all candidates to "describe what you've been doing recently." It's an open question, and you can answer it any way you like, but I would normally expect you to talk about your most recent job, perhaps an interesting project you worked on, or something you've been doing that is relevant to your application.

I will usually always ask you some specifics about your most recent experience. Here are some of the questions I might ask:

- Were you working by yourself or in a team?

- If on a team, who else was in the team with you, and how well did the team work together?

- What did you like about your last job?

- What things could have been done better?

- What would your boss say about you if I called to ask?

- What specific technologies did you use? What did you think about those technologies?

I won't ask all these questions every time, but you get the idea.

Next, unless something you've said is a deal-breaker (such as not having essential prerequisites, should there be any) I will go through a list of short technical questions. All I'm trying to find out by asking these questions is whether you can communicate at a basic level. I do expect you to know the answers, but what I'm really testing is your ability to communicate.

Technical questions I might ask during a phone interview include:

- In object-oriented terms, what is the difference between a class and an object?

- What does it mean to pass a variable "by reference"?

- What is a partial class, and what is a key benefit of a partial class?

- What are some differences between an interface and an abstract class?

I won't give you any feedback about your answers unless, as before, something you've said is a deal-breaker. I will have made notes about your answers so that I can digest and reflect on them after the phone interview. The reason I avoid giving feedback at this stage is not to torture you—it's to give me a little time to think about our conversation and to fairly assess your answers, and perhaps compare them to answers from other candidates.

Finally, you get to ask me whatever you like. This is when you ask me the questions you've listed on your cheat sheet.

Preparing your cheat sheets

Now that you know what to expect in a standard interview, it's time to prepare your cheat sheets. These little bits of paper are invaluable references during the phone interview, especially if you expect to be nervous at all.

How many times have you faced an awkward question, stumbled through an answer, and then afterwards had a brilliant flash of genius about what you could have said? Preparing cheat sheets gives you an opportunity to have that flash of genius *before* the phone interview. You can lay the questions out in front of you while you talk.

The idea of a cheat sheet is simply to help you think about and formulate answers to difficult questions. If you think about these difficult questions before the interview, you are less likely to be put on the spot during the interview. Cheat sheets also serve as reminders of things you specifically want to mention if and when the opportunity arises during the interview.

The key is to think of awkward questions you might be asked. For example, if you've been unemployed for a time you will probably be asked about it. Ditto if you were fired, or if anything is unusual about your work history.

Let's be real—if you don't think about how you'll respond to awkward questions before the interview then you will have to think of something to say on the fly, when giving a good answer will be much harder.

As well as posing and answering the hardest questions about your work history and your experience, you need to think about how to answer common interview questions as well. You'll find a long list of questions to assist with your preparations in Appendix A.

Relating your experience

Every question the interviewer asks gives you an opportunity to illustrate the relevance of your experience. When posing a problem, quite often interviewers will ask you for an example of when you faced a similar problem. Even if they don't, you can still answer in those terms when you do have relevant experience.

So, for example, suppose you were asked how you might go about resolving a bug that was difficult to reproduce in testing. You would talk about the time you visited a customer site to observe a customer reproducing a bug that no one could reproduce on the development servers. Or if asked what you think makes a good software development framework, you might talk about your experience with in-house and third-party frameworks that you've used.

The idea is that you take every reasonable opportunity to demonstrate how your experience can be brought to bear in the situations raised by the interviewer. Relating your experience helps the interviewer to more easily imagine you filling the role, which gives you an advantage over those who speak more generally or in more theoretical terms.

Answering hard questions

The hardest questions are unlikely to be the technical ones. Those will be hard, no doubt, but you should have an opportunity to work through them with the interviewer.

The hardest questions you will face during an interview are the ones where you are asked for your opinion when the question has no clear "correct" answer. One dangerous aspect of questions like this is that you might be tempted to respond in black-and-white terms when the reality—and usually more satisfactory answer—is less clear. Let me give you an example:

"Which is more important, software quality or customer satisfaction?"

Ouch! There seems to be no clear best answer to this question. Without customer satisfaction the business is unlikely to sustain development, but a low-quality product is unlikely to satisfy many customers.

Wait—did I just fall for the trap? (Yes, I did.) Software quality and customer satisfaction are certainly not mutually exclusive; there's no good reason you can't have both, so an answer that chooses one of them and argues how the other is "less important" is probably not the best possible answer. In slightly more formal terms, questions like this present a *false dilemma*, where there appear to be just two choices (or two extremes) when, in fact, more choices are available than presented or a balanced position exists between the two extremes.

Whatever you do, avoid a situation where you give a dubious answer and then feel obliged to defend that point of view at all costs. If you realize your answer is perhaps not the best, admit it and explain your thinking. Being confident and giving confident answers is good, but clinging to a sinking ship is foolish and counterproductive, especially if it means defending a losing argument.

Another trap for the unprepared interviewee is to answer with a long, rambling discussion of (for example) the various considerations of software quality and customer satisfaction. If you've ever answered a hard question in this fashion you've probably done it hoping that sooner (or later) you would stumble upon a good answer. Try to avoid a rambling answer. Nothing is wrong with taking time to think about the question—just be sure to let the interviewer know you are thinking, or else she might think you've been stunned into silence:

"That's an interesting question; let me think about it for a moment."

Also, don't forget that you can ask the interviewer for clarification. When the interviewer poses a difficult question, and you can't immediately think how to answer it, you could ask for an example of how that situation might arise. This might give you a clue about the interviewer's motive for asking. Perhaps the company has had a recent spate of quality issues, and wants to hire someone with a sound view on what software quality means. Perhaps it has had some poor customer feedback, and wants to emphasize customer satisfaction. Either way, listen carefully for clues when the interviewer clarifies the question.

Being really stumped isn't necessarily the end of the world. Resist the temptation to start rambling and confess that you are at a loss for an answer. If the interviewer has asked this question a number of times at previous interviews, then you probably won't be the first person to come up blank. He might even expect candidates to be stumped, looking to see whether you are inclined to waffle or whether you are more honest and open in your response.

Asking good questions

The phone interview is unlikely to give you much of an opportunity to ask questions of the potential employer, but you should prepare some in any case. If you don't have an opportunity during the phone interview then save them for the in-person interview.

You should consider asking two broad categories of question. The first are questions where you are, in effect, demonstrating interest and enthusiasm to the potential employer. Questions in this category include:

- *"Could you describe a typical week in this position?"* (Shows you have an interest in the realities of the job)

- *"If I were made an offer, what kind of objectives would I be given in the first few months?"* (Shows you are already thinking how you might meet goals and objectives)

- *"What things do you think are the most important for this company to focus on over the next few months or year?"* (Shows you are interested in the bigger picture)

The second broad category includes questions that might affect your decision if you are made an offer such as:

- *"What things do you (the interviewer) like about working here, and what don't you like as much?"* (Might reveal some less-appealing aspects of working with this employer)

- *"How many of this company's senior managers were promoted to their position from within the company?"* (Can indicate prospects for advancement within the company).

Depending on your personal circumstances, asking about the company policy toward overtime might be important for you, such as whether it is expected or assumed, and whether you are expected to travel and stay away from home. Be sure to have a list of important questions prepared before the interview, but choose your moment—the phone interview is almost certainly not the best time to ask the interviewer challenging questions.

Try to avoid asking trivia questions just for the sake of appearing interested. A trivia question is any question that you could easily find the answer to with a web search or by reading the company website.

Always make a point of asking about the expected time frame for the interview to get back to candidates with interview results. You don't want to be left wondering when you will next hear something.

Having a phone interview checklist

Here is a short checklist of things you must prepare before a phone interview:

- A hands-free phone or a headset so you can use your hands while you talk. Not only does this make referring to your cheat sheets (or laptop) easier, but also being able to make gestures with your hands while talking can help you feel more comfortable, and therefore more relaxed.
- A quiet place where you can concentrate and talk undisturbed.
- If using a mobile device, good phone reception (check the reception before the interview!)
- Your printed CV and your cheat sheets, or a laptop (plugged in) with these documents loaded.
- A short list of questions to ask the employer, if given the chance.
- Confidence that comes from knowing how to write code.

Using a phone interview cheat sheet template

Use the following table to consider how you would answer each question if you are asked. Don't write a "script" for answers; otherwise, you will tend to read them out when on the phone and sound unnatural. Instead, after considering how you want to reply, make short notes to jog your memory when on the phone.

Some of these questions won't necessarily apply to you or your situation so just ignore those.

If I'm honest, some of these questions make me cringe. I include them only because many interviewers still like to ask them, and answering them can be difficult if you aren't prepared.

Table 2-1: Phone Interview Preparation

QUESTION	HINT
Describe your experience with...	Go through the job description or advertisement and list the technologies relevant to the job; for example, scalable websites, big data, and information security. Consider your own experience with each of these. You want to identify areas where your experience is lacking, and what you will say when asked them.
Tell me about a project you're proud of.	Consider what made you proud—was it your work or someone else's? What part did you play in the project?
Explain a gap between jobs and anything else unusual about your work history.	Having taken time off work for personal reasons is fine, and you needn't feel pressured to explain personal matters on the phone. Be prepared for a follow-up question about the recency of your experience; that is, "So after that time off, does that mean you are out of practice with...?"
How do you rate yourself in each of the major technologies mentioned in the job description or advertisement?	Be honest; this question often precedes a technical "pop-quiz."
What would your previous manager say was your biggest weakness?	Again, be honest; the potential employer might well contact your previous or current employer when seeking references.
Why are you looking to leave your current employer?	Good reasons include: ■ Self-improvement, career advancement ■ Broadening your experience ■ Relocating Poor reasons include: ■ "I was fired for incompetence" ■ "I felt like a change" (sounds suspicious)
You haven't been with your current employer for very long—why are you looking to move so soon?	Perhaps you were mis-sold a job, and it turned out to be something other than what you expected. That reason is valid, but you need to be careful, whatever your reason, that you avoid the appearance of having acted capriciously.

QUESTION	HINT
You have been with your current employer for a long time—why are you looking to move after so long?	The concern of a potential employer might be that you were settled (in a rut?) and were forced out only by changing circumstances.
What are you least skilled at (either technical or non-technical)?	This is a variation of the old question, "What is your biggest weakness?" You should either pick something that is less relevant to the job, or pick something that, depending on the context, could be considered a strength, such as assertiveness or impatience.
Describe a bug or a problem that you couldn't resolve.	Don't be afraid to 'fess up here. Every mortal programmer will face a bug like this sooner or later. These are opportunities for learning, remember? Describe what you learned.
Which is more important: code quality or code efficiency?	This is another false dilemma—why not have both?
Which is more important: getting things done or doing things properly?	This is also a false dilemma. A balance is called for.
What is the most important part of the software development life cycle (SDLC)? Explain your choice.	The only wrong answer is "all of them," which avoids the question. Think of this as an opportunity to demonstrate your understanding of the SDLC and how, depending on context, analysis, testing, or even documentation might be key to the success of a project.
Should testers (or project managers and so on) know how to write code?	If you don't already know the culture of the team, this would be a good time to ask. As to whether you think testers should know how to write code, go with your judgment, but be prepared to explain your reasoning—and be sure to avoid diminishing the role of testers.
Describe the worst team you've been part of, and what you did to try to improve that team.	The interviewer is asking whether you are aware of "team dynamics" and how they might be improved.
What makes you stand out from all the programmers we could interview?	This is no time to be modest. It's also not a good time to waffle. Get to the point, list your best qualities, and briefly describe how these qualities match those required for the job.

Continued

Table 2-1 *(continued)*

QUESTION	HINT
Describe how you handled a situation where you disagreed with a decision for technical reasons, but were overruled for business reasons.	This question is to find out two things: how passionate you are about your opinions, and how pragmatic you are about decision-making. You should aim for a balance.
What is the most difficult question you've ever been asked at an interview?	As a programmer familiar with recursion you might be tempted to answer, "What is the most difficult question you've ever been asked at an interview?" But the interviewer has probably heard that one before. My advice is to answer this question with an example of a difficult (or impossible) technical question; something the interviewer will probably agree is hard.
What is the one question an interviewer should ask during an interview?	This is another "clever" question. The interviewer is asking what you think is important. Be prepared to answer whatever question you suggest.

In-Person Interviews

Human beings and interviews, as a rule, are wonderfully unpredictable. You never really know what you're going to get. This might lead you to think that preparing for an interview is pointless, but that is about as wrong as it is possible to be. Preparation is your secret weapon. The interview might go any which way, but that won't matter if you are prepared.

> "It usually takes me two or three days to prepare an impromptu speech."
>
> —*Mark Twain*

Preparing for the Interview

The well-prepared programmer brings a lot more than just technical readiness to an interview. No doubt there will be questions on data structures and algorithms, perhaps a few brain-teasers, and probably a coding exercise. But technical questions are just part of the interview. There will usually also be questions about teamwork, getting things done, and questions designed to see if you are a good match for the culture of the company. The interviewer might want to see how you handle stress, how well you communicate, and how you react to criticism.

If the interview was just about how well you code, you could do it online. Face-to-face interviews are much more than just a technical assessment. Although some companies like to give the impression that the "best programmer" will get the job, I can tell you first hand that being technically best will not always win you the job. This might seem unfair, but that, as they say, is life.

Knowing what to expect

Every workplace is different. Companies might have similar décor and facilities, but no two companies are exactly alike when it comes to philosophy and culture. What determines the culture of a company? It's the people, and more specifically it is the people at the top that set the tone for everyone else. If the people at the top are relaxed and friendly, that attitude will tend to dominate. If the people at the top are formal and serious, that is what you will tend to find in the offices and in the break rooms. Smaller companies tend to be less formal than bigger companies, but the size of a company alone won't tell you much.

You probably already have a good grasp of the cultures at Microsoft, Google, and Amazon (and if not, there are plenty of public web sites that talk about nothing but the culture of these companies) but other, lesser-known companies will require you to do a bit of research.

By far the best way to research the culture of a company is to talk to someone who works there. If you are lucky enough to know someone on the inside, then I suggest you buy them lunch and hit them with 100 questions. The rest of us will need to find other ways.

A web search should be the first thing you do. (Incidentally, the hiring manager will probably search for information about you, too.) You will find the carefully constructed marketing image of the company, but without too much digging you should be able to find some clues about the company culture. If you are lucky, you might find a statement of company values, or, even better, a company blog. If you can find the names of the people at the top you can search for news items where things they've said may have been quoted. These quotes can be revealing.

If you happen to be working with a recruiting agent, ask them about the culture of the company. A good agent will have first-hand experience of working with the company, albeit as a supplier, and should be able to give you some useful insight.

If all else fails, call the company and ask directly. This need not be awkward; it is a perfectly reasonable question.

> *"Hello, I'm calling because I have an interview with your company next week and I was wondering if you could tell me a bit about what it is like to work there?"*

The worst that can happen is that you talk to someone unwilling to help, but no one is going to hold this approach against you. If the person you call is unhelpful, ask to be put through to the HR department, or even better, to the department that is looking to hire you. It almost goes without saying that you should be polite and respectful of the time people give to you, but, in general, people love sharing opinions, especially about their employer, and who better to share those opinions with than a potential workmate? You might find that some companies have a communications policy that forbids employees talking about their employer, but that in itself is useful information.

After researching the culture of the company you should turn your attention to the hiring manager. Again, talk to people who know, do a web search, and ask the recruiting agency. I would be a little wary of calling to ask about the hiring manager directly, but if you call to ask about working at the company then you could also ask about how interviews for this role are typically organized.

At the very least you should be sure to find out about the structure of the interview:

- How long will the interview last?
- Are there multiple in-person interviews or just one?
- Will there be a technical test? If so, how will it be administered?
- Will you write code during the interview?
- How many interviewers will be present, and who are they?
- Is there anything specific the company advises you to prepare for?

Doing your homework

Once you have done your research, it is time to start practicing, with particular focus on the things you've learned about the company and the hiring manager.

If the interview is with a high-tech company (like Google, or perhaps some start-up companies) then you will benefit from focusing on data structures, algorithms, and how software can be designed to scale up. Very small tech companies are likely to expect their programmers to be knowledgeable in a wide variety of areas so you should brush up on server administration, network troubleshooting, database configuration, and so on. You are unlikely to need this kind of knowledge at larger companies because they have dedicated teams (if not entire departments) to look after servers and infrastructure.

Something you really need to do at this point, if you haven't already, is to ask yourself the questions that you dread being asked.

Be honest—what question would make you drop dead at the interview? Perhaps you have a morbid fear of sorting algorithms. Perhaps you don't quite understand the difference between BFS and DFS. Maybe you quit your last job after a big blow-out with your team lead. Maybe you have a controversial opinion; maybe you think code comments are a pernicious form of code duplication?

If you don't face your fear before the interview, you will have to face it during the interview. It's a no-brainer, as they say. Face it before the interview.

Dressing appropriately

Once you have come face-to-face with and conquered your worst interview fears, you will need to choose a nice outfit to wear.

Ok, I will be honest here. I'm a little dismissive of all the advice so freely given about how to dress for the interview. What I will concede is that how you dress does have some impact on how you are perceived. Exactly how much difference your shirt or blouse will make is a point of debate, but I accept that it can make some difference. Unless you've been living the life of a hermit, wearing sack cloth and ashes, you will have a variety of clothes in your wardrobe to choose from. Here's how to choose what to wear.

First, try to find out about the prevailing dress code at the company. If you live close, you could visit during the lunch hour and observe what people are wearing as they come and go. If not, you will need to ask someone. As before, your options are to ask someone who works there, ask the recruiting agent, or ask directly by calling up.

"Hello, I have an interview next week and just wanted to check the dress code in your office."

If you really have no idea what to wear then you should default to smart office attire, which for men means a nice dress shirt with a collar, and no jeans or sports gear. Motorbike leathers are not ideal, and gang insignia is right out. Don't ever be tempted to dress in a provocative fashion. The same rules apply if you are female; a nice blouse and skirt (not a mini) or trousers. Dressing like a gigolo might score you short-term points with a certain class of interviewer, but think ahead to how you will be perceived once you land the job. Do you really want to be known for the length of your skirt or the tight fit of your shirt?

Men, wear a tie if you are comfortable wearing one, but be aware that some companies, particularly companies with a strong geek culture (which should be obvious) will not have much time for someone who turns up in a suit. If you really aren't sure then take a tie to the interview in your bag and put it on if it seems appropriate. (Put it on before going in to the interview; don't start dressing yourself after the interview starts.)

Finally, whatever you wear, make sure you are comfortable. You will face enough challenges at the interview without struggling with your outfit. If you are hot and sweaty because of your jacket, politely excuse yourself while you take it off. Don't sit and suffer; you really don't need the distraction.

Handling different types of interview questions

Broadly speaking, interview questions fall into the following categories. How you answer a question depends on the category.

Fielding social and behavioral questions

Social and behavioral questions are often asked so that, in theory, the interviewer can assess your style or approach in different situations.

> *"How would you settle a team debate about whether source code should be format-ted with spaces or tabs?"*

Your answers should be direct and backed up with examples. This kind of question tends to encourage rambling answers, and rambling answers should always be avoided at the programming interview.

> *"I usually take the approach that it doesn't matter provided the source code is for-matted consistently. When I worked at Acme we used the SpaceMeister utility to ensure consistency, so that would probably be the approach I'd take with the team."*

Handling design problems

To answer *design problems* need you to go into analysis mode. The interviewer doesn't necessarily want you to come up with a single "correct" answer, which in any case may not exist, but rather wants you to demonstrate how you think about and work toward a feasible design. You will recognize a design problem in one of two ways; either the interviewer will pointedly use the word "design," or the problem will initially appear to be impossible, difficult, or vague.

> *"Design an algorithm to calculate how an international aid fund should be divided up between beneficiaries."*

The only way to answer questions like this is to ask questions of your own. You need to demonstrate an analytical yet goal-focused approach. If you ask the right questions the answer will eventually become obvious (or it might become obvious that there is no good answer) and you can proceed with the design (or identify the reasons why no good design is possible).

> *"Do we want to optimize for a fair distribution?"*
> *"How is a 'fair' distribution to be defined?"*
> *"Do we need to account for factors other than what is 'fair'?"*
> *"What are the inputs to this algorithm?"*
> *"What are the expected outputs?"*
> *"Is there any useful precedent we can build on?"*

Tackling technical pop-quiz questions

Some interviewers still like to ask *technical pop-quiz questions*. You can easily recognize these because they will be obscure or excessively specific.

> *"How many overloads are there for the Tuple.Create method in .NET version 4.5?"*

There is little you can do to prepare for this kind of questioning. Unless you have a good memory for programming then you will just have to answer as best you can:

"Oh, I'm not sure; I would guess 8 or 9 based on the idea that the Tuple data structure is for holding a set of values. I would need to look that up to be sure. Also, in general, I've found that if a method has many overloads then it can be difficult to choose the right one, especially if each method has different behavior, so I would think there shouldn't be too many."

You might try to relate the question to things you do know well, but if the interviewer is fixed on their favorite trivia questions then you can only take comfort that they will probably end up hiring the programmer they deserve. Unfortunately, your wise words might be wasted on a pop-quiz interviewer who will hear nothing but your "8 or 9" answer.

Fielding the general intelligence test

Another type of question that is rightly falling out of favor is the *general intelligence test*. These questions are dubious even in an appropriate context (mental health assessment) and are even more dubious in a programming interview. Nonetheless, some interviewers want "only the smartest" and see no problem undertaking an IQ test where even a trained psychologist would hesitate. If you have ever taken an IQ test (and again, many programmers have) then you will recognize these questions immediately.

"Find the next value in the sequence …"
"Pear is to apple as potato is to …?"
"If two typists can type two pages in two minutes, how many fingers am I holding up behind my back?"

(I made up that last question; I hope you are never asked that at a programming interview.)

IQ questions tend to be similar in style and, with practice, it is possible to get better at answering them. If you have an idea that your interviewer might favor this style of questioning then you should seek out and practice IQ tests in preparation for the interview. IQ tests are widely available, and they can be fun in a nerdy kind of way. If you search for IQ tests on the web, make sure you try a test from at least two different sites so that you aren't inadvertently misled by one site that might have a unique (non-standard) approach to IQ testing.

Dealing with the stress test question

One kind of question that you can and should practice is the *stress test*. For this you will need to enlist the help of a friend, preferably an aggressive and loud programmer. Ask your shouty friend to find (or write) a list of really hard questions. Set aside an hour or more, and grind through these questions, acting out the roles of candidate and hard-nosed interviewer. The role your friend needs to play is "merciless interrogator with an inexplicable grudge." The idea with this kind of practice is not so much to come up with the right answers (although you should try) but rather to build up *stamina* for the real interview. One hour can be a grueling marathon, but some interviews run for much longer. Train like an athlete for these interviews.

The Most Important Thing

Kirk, McCoy, and Spock are around a camp fire, Kirk andMcCoy are singing "Row Row Row your Boat."

Kirk: Come on. Spock... Why didn't you jump in?

Spock: I was trying to comprehend the meaning of the words.

McCoy: It's a song, you green-blooded... Vulcan. You sing it. The words aren't important. What's important is that you have a good time singing it.

Spock: Oh, I am sorry Doctor. Were we having a good time?

—*From Star Trek V: The Final Frontier (1989)*

I briefly touched on the importance of *rapport* in Chapter 1, and now I'm going to look at in more detail.

Despite the importance of rapport, I will confess some mixed feelings on the subject. No one likes a fake smile, and no one likes insincerity. There is an uncomfortable association between rapport and cheesy sales tactics.

As a teenager I had an extremely strong aversion to insincerity in any form. I felt particularly aggrieved by advertising campaigns that I perceived were trying to induce an emotional reaction in me for the purpose of selling me something. I walked around with a deliberately neutral expression so that no one could accuse me of insincerity. In conversation, I was blunt and candid to the point of rudeness. Frankly, I was a right sourpuss.

Then, in my twenties, I had a revelation.

Of course, this revelation involved a young woman. This young woman taught me that people who smile and who are generally agreeable can be just as sincere, perhaps even more so, than a person made prickly by a stoic aspiration to be sincere. What people want, for the most part, is to get through their day without antagonism and conflict. Politeness is simply a lubricant for the wheels of human interaction. Strangers waiting for a train might smile and nod in mutual acknowledgement, and neither one will have an agenda beyond passing time comfortably while they wait for the train. You can usually spot the exceptions; people with an agenda often have a conspicuous name tag and a clipboard.

These days, a reliable source informs me, I am still a sourpuss. I flatter myself that I am a sourpuss with an insight that helps me get along with people. Is this insincere? I hope not, and I don't believe it is.

If you are interested in this topic and think you can stomach the full-strength dose of how to get along with people, then I (sincerely) recommend the classic book by Dale Carnegie; *How to Win Friends and Influence People* (1936). It isn't necessarily a book for everyone, and in some places it shows its age, but I still recommend it for its brilliant insight into the mechanics of human interaction. Spock could have used it.

Establishing rapport

What is an interview candidate to do if they want to establish a rapport? Let's start from the basics; rapport is much more likely to exist when two people share a common goal. On the face of it, the interviewer wants to find the best person for the job, and the candidate wants to convince the interviewer that they are that person. That isn't an ideal starting point, because it puts the candidate firmly into the role of *selling* something to the interviewer (themselves). It would be much better if the interviewer and the candidate had something in common.

As it turns out, they do. They both want to find out if this job is going to be suitable for the candidate. Both want to see how well the candidate matches up to the job specification. Both want to get a realistic view of what it would be like if the candidate took the job.

Don't misunderstand me—I am not suggesting that the balance of power (something I will discuss later) is equal in an interview. What I do firmly believe is that the interviewer and the candidate have a very strong starting point for establishing a good rapport. In a very real sense they both want the same thing. It is a subtle but important shift in perspective. Instead of *claiming* to be a perfect match, the candidate will be working *with* the interviewer to see if that is true, or to what extent it is true. This is the fundamental starting point of an effective interview.

With an attitude that you are working *with* the interviewer, you will see things a little differently. Instead of waiting passively for challenging questions you will be genuinely interested in details about that job so that you can see for yourself how you experience matches up. Instead of worrying about theoretical questions about how you would handle *this* situation or *that* kind of problem, you will be trying to relate how your experience has prepared you for the concrete circumstances of the job. You will be taking notes of things you might need to brush up on, and you are more likely to acknowledge those things you may need to learn on the job.

This attitude, more than anything else, will put your interviewer at ease. You are in effect making their job easier, relieving them of their burden of playing the role of interrogator. Some interviewers don't seem to mind playing that role, but for most interviewers this is the quickest way to establish an effective rapport.

It takes work

It would be nice if a change in attitude was enough to make everything go swimmingly at the interview, but there is still a lot more you can do. You might be a gifted conversationalist, but everyone will benefit from reviewing the following basic guidelines.

Be a good listener

Don't ever interrupt rudely, and if you feel compelled to jump in then at least apologize for doing so:

> *"Sorry to interrupt you, I just need to mention that you appear to have the wrong CV."*

Listening effectively is more than just sitting quietly. A skilled listener will replay what they hear using their own words. This reassures the interviewer that you are actually listening and that you understand. This is such an important technique that is has a special name: *active listening.*

Ask good questions

Also remember that an interview is supposed to be a mutual exchange of information. You need to ask questions as well as answer them. Similar to the technique of active listening, asking good questions will reassure the interviewer that you have heard them, and also that you are interested in finding out more.

Mirror your interviewer

Sometimes it can be effective if you consciously imitate some of the postures and behavior of the interviewer. So if they sit up, you sit up. If they relax and sit back, so do you. I'm not suggesting you perform an impromptu silent comedy of mime, as amusing as that might be, but rather that reflecting the attitude of your interviewer does wonders for establishing rapport. This is a proven technique that can help put the interviewer at ease. The name for this technique is *mirroring.* You can look it up when you look up *active listening.*

Look for ways to interact

If you are naturally introverted, it isn't a problem; so are many software developers. Your interviewer might even be an introvert by nature. Remember that introversion doesn't necessarily mean that you are compelled to be shy. Look for common ground. Look for opportunities to talk about things that are relevant and that interest you. If you are naturally shy, do try to make eye contact at least once or twice, and remember that the clear words in your head need to be equally clear when you speak them. Slow down your rate of speech, and pause for confirmation now and then. In many ways, introverts have an advantage in one-on-one conversation, since they tend to be much better at reflecting on what they hear.

The Second Most Important Thing

Even the very best rapport will be wasted if the interviewer is not left with a strong impression of your competency as a programmer. The second most important thing to remember is that you need to *show your stuff* in the time available to you.

Speaking up

Interviewers are supposed to let you do most of the talking. Unfortunately, my observation from sitting on both sides of the interview desk is that many interviewers like to talk at least as much as they like to listen. If you encounter an excessive talker then you have little option but to politely interrupt when you have something to say. You will be listening for opportunities to relate your experience to the job. If the interviewer is really hammering away then you will be wise to choose your moments rather than constantly interrupt. If you have the misfortune to be interviewed by a pathological chatterbox then you may need to wait until they pause for breath. Use the time to prepare, try to keep your concentration up, and jump into the conversation when the interviewer pauses to inhale.

Being aware of how much time you have

You will usually know in advance how long the interview is scheduled to run. If the interview is short then you will need to focus on the most important aspects of your experience as it relates to the job. You might be very proud of the open-source data-grid control you wrote, but if time is limited you will need to ensure that you clearly and specifically target the key criteria of the job specification. If they aren't clear to you before the job interview (they should be) then you will need to ask the interviewer:

"What would you say are the most important skills needed for this job?"

Stories are good, evidence is better

If possible, you should try to relate the answer to this question to your concrete experience and to your achievements. Tell a story to illustrate your experience if you can, but avoid veering off track into the realm of making stuff up. It might be entertaining to make up a hypothetical situation to illustrate a point, but the problem is that the interviewer will remember you for the stuff you didn't actually do. You want them to look at your CV afterward and think *"oh yes, that is the programmer who sorted out that big performance problem"* rather than *"oh yes, this is the programmer who, uh…what did he actually do again?"*

Communicating Effectively

When it comes to getting your point across at the interview, there are some simple but powerful techniques you should know about. These tricks, though I hesitate to call them that, can transform the effectiveness of your communication.

Using your passion to combat nerves

Almost everyone experiences nerves. It is a basic physiological response we all experience in challenging situations. It used to be caused by Velociraptors but now it is the fear of speaking or being in the spotlight that gives us an adrenaline rush and sets us trembling.

What you need to do is distract yourself. If you have children you will have noticed how the worst catastrophe in the world can often be fixed by the possibility of an ice cream. Use the same trick on yourself. If you find yourself fixated on something that is causing your anxiety then change the channel in your mind. Think of something fascinating or intriguing to push away the trembles. You are a good programmer, what is it you like about programming? What are your pet annoyances with code written by others? Should code be formatted with tabs or spaces? Which is the better editor, Vim or Emacs? Channel your nerd rage, and, while you do, notice how your nerves fade away.

Using your hands

When politicians go to politician finishing school, one thing drummed into them is the power of using their hands while they talk. Watch any political speech and you will see a dramatic performance involving hands. This is less true in England than the rest of the world, but at the highest levels of politics anywhere in the world you will always see pointing and chopping gestures, open palms and pinching motions.

The reason for all this hand waving is simple. Reliable studies have shown that body language counts for at least as much as the words coming out of our mouths. It stands to reason and intuition as well; enthusing about anything is difficult when you are slumped lifeless in your chair like a koala bear. Sit on the edge of your chair and use your hands to emphasize important points. If you aren't used to this it will take some practice, and you might feel a bit theatric at first, but take your lead from the best speakers and get those hands up.

Speaking slower than usual

When you speak rapidly, it makes you sound nervous. When you slow it down, you sound calm and in control. If you are prone to blurting out then you will really need to practice slowing it down. Record yourself speaking to see what I mean. Ask your close friends for their opinion. Listen to professional speakers, especially leading politicians, and you will notice how they almost never blurt out anything. They breathe, they pause, they hold up their hands up as if carrying a large vase, and they speak slowly and clearly.

Starting and finishing clearly

Nothing ruins the delivery of a good sound bite more than rushing the beginning or the end:

"I once saved a whale by coding up a ...mumble."

If you say something and then realize you rushed it, then repeat yourself. You need to make sure you are heard and understood. If you don't take care with your enunciation then a lot of your important points will be lost on an impatient interviewer.

Repeating your main point

When public figures wants to make sure that their key messages are heard, they repeat themselves. Not like a parrot does, of course, key messages are emphasized by focusing on the same point from different perspectives. They might relate different anecdotes to underline a recurring theme. The message is repeated in different ways and at different times. If you have something that you really want to ensure an interviewer remembers then you should do the same. Look for opportunities to repeat your key message as it relates to things the interviewer says.

Spontaneity improves with practice

At the interview more than at any other time, you need to be able to draw on your experience to deliver spontaneous answers to important questions. The best advice I can give you for improving your ability to spontaneously give good answers is to know your source material inside out, and back to front. This means you have to know and recall the details of what you've written in your CV. It means you really do have to know your technologies as well as you claim. It means you have prepared a list of relevant stories to tell, a list of problems you have solved, and a list of challenges you have overcome. When the opportunity arises, as it always does, you draw on that material to talk "spontaneously." If you aren't used to speaking spontaneously, you need to practice it before the interview. Use your friends to practice with. Take it seriously and get them to ask you random questions about your CV or the technologies in your CV so that you can rehearse relating your experience to those questions. If, during practice, you draw a blank, great! You've just found a hole in your preparation that you can plug before the interview. Offer a prize to the friend who stumps you the most.

Practice, practice, practice.

# CHAPTER 4

Negotiating a Job Offer

Negotiating is something a programmer might associate with high-pressure sales techniques, or with the ravenous profiteering of the Ferengi. Most programmers would rather write code than spend time negotiating.

Negotiating a job offer *can* be like that, but it doesn't need to be. With preparation and with the right attitude, you can establish a satisfying agreement with your potential employer. If you or your potential employer has an adversarial attitude, or if you don't prepare properly, then you risk coming out of the negotiation feeling aggrieved or hard done-by. If you are unhappy with the deal, you probably won't stay for long. If your employer enters into an agreement that he resents, again, you probably won't stay for long.

Before you enter into any negotiation you must consider what your reaction will be if things don't work out as you hope. You should hope for the best, but be prepared for the worst. What will you do if negotiation completely breaks down? Will you be prepared to walk away? You need to understand which things are important to you, and on which things you are prepared to compromise.

Walking away from a job offer is not the worst outcome. The worst outcome is being stuck with a job you hate, with terms and conditions that make leaving or doing anything else difficult.

Understanding the Market

The reason you need to understand the market is very simple. If programmer unemployment in the region is high, you have less negotiating power. If programmers are scarce in the region, you have more negotiating power. If your skills are in demand but relatively scarce, then you have more power. If your skills are common then you have less power, and so on.

Career programmers will do well to keep an eye on their local IT job boards, regardless of whether they are looking for work. Being familiar with the rate of job postings and salaries being offered gives you a feel for what is going on in the market.

For a more serious analysis you can turn to official figures of employment.

In the UK, the Office of National Statistics (`http://www.ons.gov.uk`) compiles and publishes detailed information about employment (and unemployment) in different professions, with specific categories for Information Technology and Telecommunications Professionals including:

- IT specialist managers
- IT project and programme managers
- IT business analysts, architects, and system designers
- Programmers and software development professionals
- Web design and development professionals

In the U.S., the Bureau of Labor Statistics (`http://www.bls.gov`) publishes a number of helpful indicators such as the projected change in the number of computer programmers employed between 2010 and 2020. You can also find occupational employment statistics at both the national and state level, and further broken down into metropolitan and non-metropolitan areas (`http://www.bls.gov/oes`).

Doing the Numbers

If you are offered a deal that involves options other than a straight salary or wage then you must crunch some numbers to work out what value these options actually represent.

If you are offered a bonus or incentive scheme, look very closely at whether the conditions attached to that bonus or incentive are within your control. Having bonuses be contingent on overall business performance is perfectly reasonable, but you should downplay the value of a bonus that is based on the subjective assessment of your line manager or some committee. This is not suggesting you take a deliberately negative attitude toward bonuses and incentive schemes, but you should realistically assess the value of the offer.

Share options are often a good value at larger or established companies, but they can be essentially worthless at smaller companies. The value of a share or stock option depends entirely on the success of the business, which is something that might not be in your direct control. How you view these options depends on your personal preference for risk versus reward. Young programmers and those without a family will probably be more open to the idea of exchanging a portion of their salary for a potentially greater reward.

Considering the whole package

Salary is very likely to be the biggest part of a package, and this is why almost everyone focuses on it when negotiating. Realizing that other parts of a package can not only be significant in their own right, but can also be much easier to negotiate is important. You can score big wins by focusing on these instead of the base salary. Consider how much an extra week of paid leave is worth, for instance. Would you value being able to work from home once a week? Is there a significant commuting cost the company could help with? Here is a list of items you should consider in addition to base salary:

■ Commuting cost and time

■ Paid vacation days

■ Training

■ Paid study time

■ Medical insurance and health plans

■ Share options

■ Childcare schemes

■ Perks such as on-site meals and stocked fridges

■ Gym membership

Some companies also offer "discount" schemes through certain retailers. These *can* be worthwhile although, as always, you need to shop around and compare prices before assuming they are a good deal.

Other, less tangible factors can be even more important depending on your circumstances. Don't forget to consider:

■ Is the work going to be interesting?

■ Who do you get to work with?

■ Does the potential exist for career advancement?

- Is the company culture one you will enjoy?
- How will this job look on your curriculum vitae (CV)?
- How does this job fit into your overall career plan?

Technical and product management considerations are also important for most programmers. A company that doesn't use source control, or that refuses to fix bugs in favor of releasing new features is unlikely to be a satisfying place to write code. Think about things like the following:

- Will you have a technically literate boss?
- Will projects be run with an agile approach?
- Which tools are used for source-code control and bug tracking?
- Will you have a high-spec workstation and multiple monitors?
- Will you be using the latest frameworks?

Must have, should have, could have

Must Should Could Won't (MoSCoW) is a technique you can use to help you clarify priorities before entering into negotiation. MoSCoW is originally a technique for prioritizing the requirements of a software project, but is easily adapted for prioritizing aspects of your employment offer.

Must have

"Must haves" are the things that are non-negotiable. In this category you might have (for example) a minimum base salary, and perhaps a minimum amount of paid leave.

These are the things that are deal breakers: You either get them or you will refuse the offer. Some programmers will want to include specific technologies or projects in this category.

Should have

The "should haves" are the things that are perhaps as important as those in the "must" category, but where an alternative might be acceptable. In this category (for example) you might have formal training, where you would consider "in-house training" as an alternative.

Try to list as many of these as you can, and for each of them consider what alternatives would be acceptable to you.

Could have

"Could haves" are the things that are desirable, but not deal breakers. If you don't get them you will probably still accept the offer. Things in this category might include free meals, a gym membership, and so on.

Won't have

In the original MoSCoW classification the *W* stands for *won't* as in, "won't be included in this release, but maybe in a future release."

You can use this category in two ways: to list the things that you won't tolerate, or to list the things that won't make any difference to your acceptance of the offer. Either way, this category is optional when prioritizing aspects of the offer.

The Role of the Recruiting Agent

You might have the impression that the agency that introduced you to the potential employer will have your financial interests at heart. After all, you might reason, its fee is proportional to the size of your remuneration package. That might be true to some extent, but think about the numbers. If you manage to negotiate an extra 10 percent then the agent gets another 10 percent as well. On the other hand, if the deal falls through she might get nothing. From the agent's perspective, the potential increase in her fee is very unlikely to be worth the increase in the risk of losing her fee altogether. Closing the deal is a much higher priority for the agent than negotiating a better deal for you.

An agency might negotiate on your behalf if you have a strong bargaining position, but most of the time it is more likely to quietly line up alternative candidates for the employer. Never make the mistake that an IT recruitment agency works primarily for your interests. If a more agreeable candidate turns up, someone who appears less likely to agitate for a better deal, then most agencies will prefer to work with that candidate instead of you.

Start as You Mean to Go On

When negotiating, don't forget that you will be giving your future employer its first insight into how you operate and the things you value. Passively taking whatever is on offer colors the employer's impression of you in the future. Similarly, making an aggressive and argumentative impression will also stick.

Think about how you want your employer to perceive you, and then proceed with negotiation on that basis. "Firm but fair" is the approach I recommend.

Avoid overcommitting

A big trap for inexperienced negotiators is when an employer makes a small concession and then asks you for a big concession in exchange. Perhaps you have asked for an extra five percent salary, and in exchange for agreeing to this the employer asks you to be on call at weekends and holidays, which, he or she might reassure you, "won't be a lot of work."

When considering this kind of deal, look at what it could mean in the worst case. It could mean that in exchange for a small increase in your base salary you have given up all your free time. Even if you don't actually end up doing a lot of extra work in your free time it could mean that your ability to make plans, socialize, pursue hobbies, and so on is limited simply because you need to stay available in case you are called in. That isn't a good deal. If you are offered a deal like this, be sure to work out the details up front, before the signing the contract. If you make a large commitment then ensure that it is accompanied by reasonable limits; in other words, that it is not open ended. Verbal assurances are usually not adequate protection. If a situation on the job goes badly and it ends up in a dispute, you don't want it to boil down to "your word against theirs." Having details written down and agreed to (signed) by both parties always pays off. Every business knows this; it is both good practice and common sense.

Realism and idealism

Every programmer who has read *Peopleware* by Tom DeMarco and Timothy Lister will be aware that working in a quiet office is one of the major factors affecting programmer productivity. Yet, although the need for a quiet office is almost universally acknowledged, most programmers work in noisy offices located somewhere between the chirpy marketing team and the chatty customer support team. There is a stark contrast between the ideal conditions a programmer wants and the reality he or she will face in almost all workplaces.

This is not to suggest that you should compromise at every turn, but rather that you should have a realistic sense of what to expect. Many top companies will not tick all your boxes, and you won't be able to change that overnight. Think about what is important to you, use the MoSCoW technique for prioritizing, and be prepared to compromise in some areas if it means you get the things you really want.

Evaluating a Contract

Some types of clauses in contracts of employment deserve special attention. The following section lists some of them.

NOTE   If you find anything that you don't understand, or that causes you concern, you should consult with a lawyer. Paying for expert advice is always worthwhile when you consider the potential cost of entering into a contract with unfavorable terms and conditions.

Intellectual property (IP)

Some employment contracts are very one-sided about intellectual property, saying in effect that anything you create, even those things you create in your own time, will belong to the company. In most cases this clause simply ratifies the reasonable expectation that the company owns the work you do for it, but this type of clause might also affect you in some surprising ways. For example, you might no longer be able to work on open source projects because that work would be in conflict with your new contract. If you have any thoughts of potentially working on your own stuff, you must look closely at any clauses in the contract relating to IP.

Note that sometimes the question of who owns the intellectual property of your side projects is settled in law, which makes anything written in an employment agreement redundant. A good example is the California Labor Code, section 2870, which reads as follows:

(a) Any provision in an employment agreement which provides that an employee shall assign, or offer to assign, any of his or her rights in an invention to his or her employer shall not apply to an invention that the employee developed entirely on his or her own time without using the employer's equipment, supplies, facilities, or trade secret information except for those inventions that either:

(1) Relate at the time of conception or reduction to practice of the invention to the employer's business, or actual or demonstrably anticipated research or development of the employer; or

(2) Result from any work performed by the employee for the employer.

(b) To the extent a provision in an employment agreement purports to require an employee to assign an invention otherwise excluded from being required to be assigned under subdivision (a), the provision is against the public policy of this state and is unenforceable.

Retrieved November 2012 from http://www.leginfo.ca.gov/cgi-bin/displaycode?section= lab&group=02001-03000&file=2870-2872

Non-compete clauses

A *non-compete clause*. Asking their employees to not work for competitors makes sense for employers, but sometimes these clauses can be much further reaching than necessary. If you have one of them in your contract, be sure you understand the implications. You don't want to find your options unreasonably restricted if things do not work out.

Non-solicitation clauses

Similar to a non-compete clause, is a *non-solicitation clause*. This kind of clause is fairly common, but, just as with the non-compete clause, it can sometimes be too far reaching in scope.

If you have any thoughts of potentially striking out on your own at some point in the future, carefully consider the implications of such a clause.

What to Do If Things Go Wrong

Whenever you enter a negotiation, at the outset you must consider what your reaction will be if things go wrong. You might find that the employer is open to negotiation and things go well, but in some cases you might get a negative reaction or even a refusal to enter into any discussion regarding the terms of your employment.

"It's a standard contract"

A common reaction to the suggestion of negotiating aspects of a contract is that "it (the contract) is a standard template and can't be changed." That is nonsense. What it means is that it would be *awkward* for the hiring manager to have it changed without recourse to a legal team or (more often) to an unyielding human resources department. You should politely but firmly say that it will be worthwhile making the effort because of the importance you place on it. Being specific about the changes you want to make, including the actual wording of the changes, can also help. You should try to make it as easy as possible for the hiring manager (and whoever else might be involved) to agree to your changes. Always get legal advice if the changes are anything but simple and straightforward.

The silent treatment

One of the hardest things to handle as a candidate is the silent treatment. You might have made a counteroffer or asked to change a clause in the employment contract, and then you find that it goes quiet and you hear nothing for days or even weeks.

Hiring managers are typically very busy, but failing to respond is not a good sign in any circumstance. Even if legitimate reasons exist for the hiring manager not getting back to you, writing an e-mail saying something like "Sorry, we are very busy, and will respond by the end of the week," only takes a few minutes.

If you get the silent treatment, you should be realistic. Wait for a reasonable amount of time, perhaps a day or two, and then carry on with your job search. It is unlikely you will be happy working for a company that does not prioritize this kind of communication. Don't waste your emotional energy chasing a company that behaves this way.

Escalation and ultimatums

Making a reasonable request that is met with a disproportionate response, perhaps even a threat of withdrawing the offer, is another situation in which you need to be realistic. Do you want to work for an employer that reacts this way? How will it be if you agree to a contract and then later want to negotiate a raise or a change to the conditions of your employment? The answer is that it won't be good. If an employer escalates a point of negotiation into an argument, your being happy working for the company is unlikely. Be glad you dodged this bullet and move on.

Summary of Negotiating Tips

Negotiating can be a difficult and stressful experience. Here is a list of key points to help keep down the stress and to help you stay focused on what truly matters:

- Work with your prospective employer, not against them
- Avoid an adversarial approach
- Wait for an offer before attempting to negotiate
- Understand the balance of power
- Do the numbers

- Think of the longer-term working relationship you want to have
- Consider aspects of the package other than the base salary
- Be clear about what is important to you
- Be prepared to compromise on less important parts of the package
- Be prepared to walk away if necessary
- Watch out for overly restrictive clauses in your contract
- Don't expect a recruiting agent to negotiate for you

Programming Fundamentals

Many interviewers (including me) like to "warm up" an interview by starting with an easy question that looks at some fundamental aspect of programming. If a candidate falls at this first hurdle, I might even terminate the interview. Knowledge of fundamentals really is that important.

A thorough knowledge of the elements takes us more than half the road to mastership.

—Aron Nimzowitsch

Many programmers are also disadvantaged by the lack of a formal education in computer science. It might have seemed like a load of stuffy irrelevance when you were learning it (though I hope not), but many situations exist in which this knowledge can mean the difference between doing a quality job and a late night wearing your fingers to nubs while you reinvent the wheel.

Programmers love solving problems, which is just as well because programmers face so many of them. What isn't quite so serendipitous is that many otherwise pragmatic and sensible programmers seem to enjoy solving problems that were comprehensively solved decades earlier. It is true that some of these problems are trivial and have obvious solutions, in which case not much harm is done (and the programmer enjoys the thrill of the learning experience), but other commonly encountered problems such as the manipulation of dates and the choosing of a random number are deceptively difficult. Reinventing solutions to these harder problems inevitably leads to buggy software. I know this from first-hand experience.

This chapter covers many common "algorithm and data structure" interview questions, but please don't think that everything you need to know is contained here: There is no substitute for a good reference book on algorithms and data structures. I recommend *Algorithms* by Robert Sedgewick and Kevin Wayne.

Before diving into the glamorous world of trees and graphs, let's start with a quick look at the most fundamental of topics: numbers.

Understanding Binary, Octal, Hexadecimal

> **There are only 10 types of people in the world: those who understand binary and those who don't.**

You might find it hard to believe, but once upon a time a computer programmer had to be conversant with binary, octal, and hexadecimal. In those days it was fairly common that a programmer could convert between these three bases without the aid of a calculator.

Today it is true you don't need quite the same level of familiarity with binary, octal, and hexadecimal, but in case you think an understanding of them is redundant, let me offer some modern examples.

Hexadecimal is used to represent colors in a web page:

```
<body bgcolor="#007F7F">
```

Octal is used in UNIX/Linux-based operating systems when setting permissions of a file.

```
chmod 0664 myfile
```

Binary is necessary to understand subnet masks in an IP network.

```
192.168.0.24/30
```

Still not convinced? Perhaps the fact that some interviewers like to start their tech-quiz at this most basic level will convince you to double-check your understanding of these items.

Counting in base 10 seems the most natural thing in the world. Most of us have 10 fingers and 10 toes, and we learn to count our digits from an early age. Can you imagine a world where everyone had 11 digits?

From our sophisticated vantage point of being supremely familiar with base 10, base 2 (binary) might seem primitive. Yet this is what we have, and it underpins the entire digital age, so there's little point complaining about it. Indeed, far from being primitive, the accomplishment of building a modern computer from the building blocks of 1 and 0 seems nearly magical when you think about it.

The quickest way to understand a number system other than decimal (base 10) is to first understand what base 10 actually means.

It means that for a number such as 7,337 you have:

$$7 \times 1000+$$
$$3 \times 100+$$
$$3 \times 10+$$
$$7 \times 1$$

Or you could have written:

$$7 \times 10^3+$$
$$3 \times 10^2+$$
$$3 \times 10^1+$$
$$7 \times 10^0$$

Now, if you take a leap and interpret "7337" as a hexadecimal (base 16) number you would have:

$$7 \times 16^3+$$
$$3 \times 16^2+$$
$$3 \times 16^1+$$
$$7 \times 16^0$$

Hexadecimal is as simple as that. Octal (base 8) is equally straightforward:

$$7 \times 8^3+$$
$$3 \times 8^2+$$
$$3 \times 8^1+$$
$$7 \times 8^0$$

All this is very simple, but it isn't quite the end of the story. Decimal numbers have the digits 0, 1, 2, 3, 4, 5, 6, 7, 8, and 9. But how do you write numbers in base 16?

The answer is that you borrow letters from the alphabet after you get past 9. For hexadecimal you therefore have

0, 1, 2, 3, 4, 5, 6, 7, 8, 9, A, B, C, D, E, and F.

For octal, you simply drop the digits 8 and 9, and for binary there's nothing beyond 0 and 1. You can't take the "7,337" number and treat it as binary because those digits don't exist in binary. Take another random number, "1001," and give it the same treatment:

$$1 \times 2^3+$$
$$0 \times 2^2+$$
$$0 \times 2^1+$$
$$1 \times 2^0$$

Converting hexadecimal to binary

It might sound like an interview nightmare that an interviewer asks you to convert a hexadecimal number to binary without the help of a calculator or a computer, but doing the calculation is actually quite easy. With a bit of practice you should be able to do it in your head. Here's how:

Converting hexadecimal to binary is like eating an elephant. You just need to take one nibble at a time.

Remember that a *nibble* is half a byte, or four bits. Each digit of a hexadecimal number converts neatly into a nibble. Table 5-1 shows the complete list of hexadecimal digits and their binary equivalents.

Table 5-1: Converting Hexadecimal to Binary

HEXADECIMAL	BINARY
0	0000
1	0001
2	0010
3	0011
4	0100
5	0101
6	0110
7	0111
8	1000
9	1001
A	1010
B	1011
C	1100
D	1101
E	1110
F	1111

With this table in mind you can now convert any hexadecimal number to binary without using any kind of arithmetic. You simply look up the binary equivalent of each hexadecimal digit and concatenate them to get the answer.

Here is the hexadecimal number BEEF converted to binary:

```
B is 1011
E is 1110
E is 1110
F is 1111
```

Put it all together and you have:

$$B\ E\ E\ F\ (hex) = 1011\ 1110\ 1110\ 1111\ (bin)$$

Converting a binary number to hexadecimal is equally simple if you take it a nibble at a time:

$$1111\ 1110\ 1110\ 1101\ (bin) = F\ E\ E\ D\ (hex)$$

Using unicode

One can easily forget that all the text processed by a computer is ultimately stored as binary and that what you see on the screen is an interpretation of those binary numbers according to some kind of *encoding* scheme. Many programmers are so accustomed to working with ASCII that they come to think of ASCII as being "plain text" and everything else as being an annoying inconvenience. Those same programmers are quite surprised when they open up a "plain text" file in their favorite editor and find that it looks like Figure 5-1.

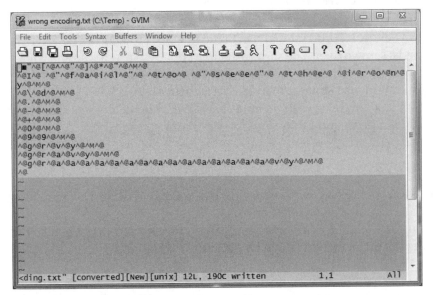

Figure 5-1: Wrong encoding

This situation happens when a program chooses (or is forced to use) the wrong encoding. It shows you a misinterpretation of the raw numbers, Unicode or otherwise. Just for the record, Vim is a fine editor and handles Unicode perfectly well. I forced it to use the wrong encoding, as shown in Figure 5-1.

Unicode was designed to provide a single, unambiguous, and unifying representation of character in all written languages, a much bigger set of characters than those used in the English language. Prior to Unicode programmers used 7-bit ASCII and what came to be known as *code pages*. Code pages evolved as an attempt to standardize the interpretation of numbers greater than 127 (the upper limit of a 7-bit number) for different languages and cultures. Unicode was intended to take away the need for code pages, but it hasn't quite achieved that goal. Code pages are still needed for backward compatibility, and (ironically) they are also used to indicate which character set encoding applies to a Unicode file.

A very common misconception is that Unicode means each that character takes up 2 bytes instead of 1. That isn't quite right. Unicode characters can and often do take up 2 bytes in memory, but they can take 1 byte (UTF-8 usually takes 1 byte per character) or more than 2 bytes (UTF-16 takes either 2 or 4 bytes per character). Version 6.2 of the Unicode standard supports more than $110,000$ characters. This is far more than the limit of 65,536 that would be imposed if Unicode were actually restricted to just 2 bytes.

Understanding Data Structures

You wouldn't expect a professional mechanic to work on your car with only a hammer and a screwdriver. The same principle applies to programmers whose toolboxes contain only primitive data structures. At risk of overloading my metaphors I might also suggest that data structures are like LEGO pieces; you can make almost anything with the most basic LEGO brick, but using specialized bricks for wheels and motors is a lot easier and quicker.

Using arrays

An array is a sequence of *elements* where each element is identified by a number. This number is known as an *index* or a *key*.

Accessing an element in an array is always a quick operation because the address of each element is obtained by a simple calculation:

$$offset = index \times size\ of\ (element)$$

In other words, the offset of an element at a given index can be calculated by multiplying the index number by the size of the element.

The size of an array is normally declared before the array is used, which can be awkward when you don't know how many elements the array will be required to hold. All modern frameworks have data structures that serve better than an array; for instance, .NET has the generic List<T>, so the constraints of traditional arrays are no longer the problem they once were. Nevertheless, remaining aware of underpinning structures, such as arrays still pays off.

Using hash tables

Also known as an *associative array*, a *hash map*, and sometimes simply a *hash*, a hash table is one of the most useful and widely used data structures.

A hash table is similar to an array in that it allows you to store a collection of values, but instead of accessing elements via sequential integers, the elements of an associative array are accessed using arbitrary data types such as strings, dates, or even classes you've created yourself.

The following Hashtable shows strings used as keys (and coincidentally also as values):

```
Hashtable h = new Hashtable();

h.Add("JAN", "January");
h.Add("FEB", "February");
h.Add("MAR", "March");
h.Add("APR", "April");
h.Add("MAY", "May");
h.Add("JUN", "June");
h.Add("JUL", "July");
h.Add("AUG", "August");
h.Add("SEP", "September");
h.Add("OCT", "October");
h.Add("NOV", "November");
h.Add("DEC", "December");

Console.WriteLine(h["SEP"]);  // Prints "September"
```

Hash tables are always implemented with the help of a *hash function* that converts each key (that is, "SEP" in the preceding example) into an index of the element where the corresponding value is stored. Hash functions typically produce a number that is the result of a fixed set of calculations based on the input key. You can think of this number as roughly equivalent to an array index, except that you are not exposed to these numbers as you are to array indexes. They are calculated and handled behind the scenes by the framework.

Keys in a hash table must be unique; you cannot store more than one of each key. Values can be duplicated as many times as you like.

While keys may be arbitrarily large, the resulting index value will always be a relatively small size (otherwise it wouldn't be suitable for use as an index).

Every now and then a hash function might calculate the same index for two different keys. This event is known as a *hash collision*. When this happens, the hash function resolves the collision by either recalculating the hash with a different set of calculations (*rehashing*) or by storing the element in a secondary data structure using a method known as *chaining*. Again, this detail is not normally exposed to the programmer using the hash table.

Hash functions run in constant time, which means that hash tables are quick to store and retrieve elements.

Modern languages such as C# and Java provide a number of concrete data types on top of the basic building block of the hash table. In C# using the strongly typed `Dictionary` data type is very common. Here is an example with keys of arbitrary type `Foo` and values of another arbitrary type `Bar`:

```
var myDictionary = new Dictionary<Foo,Bar>();
```

Storing more than one value against a key is nearly as straightforward, because storing lists as values is perfectly acceptable:

```
var myDictionary = new Dictionary<Foo,List<Bar>>();
```

Using queues and stacks

Queues and stacks are both lists of values. A queue and a stack both store values in the order in which they were added. The difference between a queue and a stack is simply that items are retrieved from a *queue* in the order in which they were added (FIFO—first in, first out), whereas items are retrieved from a *stack* in reverse order (LIFO—last in, first out). The queue data structure can be understood intuitively—everyone has queued for something—and a stack is not much more difficult to visualize—just think of a stack of plates. You put plates on the top, and you take plates off the top rather than from the bottom. That's LIFO.

Using trees

A tree is a structure in which values are stored in *nodes*, and each node is the parent of zero or more *child nodes*. A node without a parent is the *root node*. A tree in which all nodes have at most two nodes is a *binary tree*. A binary tree in which there are no duplicate nodes and in which all nodes are arranged in a sorted order is a *binary search tree*. A *B-tree* is a sorted tree that allows more than two children per node, which makes it more suitable for reading and writing large sets of data because the height of a B-tree will be smaller than that of an equivalent binary tree.

Despite the fact that most trees in nature grow upward and extend their branches toward the sky, a tree data structure is conventionally drawn with branches and child nodes descending down the page from a root node.

Figure 5-2 shows a simple binary tree. This tree has a height of 3 and a size of 7. This tree is unbalanced and unsorted.

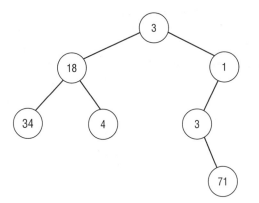

Figure 5-2: Binary tree

Figure 5-3 shows a binary search tree (BST). The left subtree of any node in a BST contains only nodes with keys less than the node's key. Subtrees on the right contain only nodes with keys greater than the node's key. Notice also that the node with key 9 has just one child—it is not required that all nodes have two children.

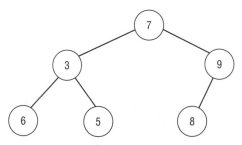

Figure 5-3: Binary search tree

Figure 5-4 shows a B-tree illustrating that each node may have more than two children.

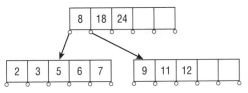

Figure 5-4: B-tree

Using graphs

A graph is like a tree but it can sprawl in all directions at once. The nodes in a graph are not necessarily connected, and nodes can be connected to themselves as well as to other nodes. Two nodes may have more than one connection between them. In terms of structure, it's almost a free-for-all.

As if node connections weren't already complicated, the connections between nodes (called *edges*) can be directed, meaning they can be traversed in only one direction. After you've gone over a directed edge, you can't go back to the node you just left unless you go back by another route.

Figure 5-5 shows a graph with a number of interesting features: Node 2 is connected to itself, and two edges exist between nodes 8 and 9. The graph is disconnected because, for instance, no path connects node 1 to node 5.

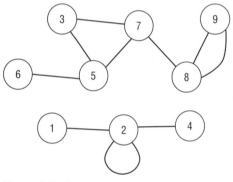

Figure 5-5: Graph

Understanding graph traversal

Interviewers often want to check that you have at least a basic understanding of tree and graph traversal. You might recall the two basic approaches: *depth first*, which means following a path all the way down to a leaf node before you follow adjacent nodes, and *breadth first*, where you visit the children of a node before visiting any further-removed descendants of that node.

Algorithms that perform breadth-first traversal normally use a queue (FIFO) to keep track of nodes, whereas algorithms that perform depth-first traversal normally use a stack (LIFO).

When visiting nodes in a depth-first algorithm the three distinct orders of traversal are *preorder*, *inorder*, and *postorder*. See question 8 in this chapter if you need to brush up on the difference.

Sorting

Sorting data is such a common operation that the collection classes in most programming frameworks expose a `sort` method or powerful native sorting capabilities such as those found in Perl and Ruby.

In C# you can sort a list of integers in a number of ways; here are a few examples:

```
var list = new List<int>
            { 1, 4, 1, 5, 9, 2, 6, 5, 3, 5, 8, 9, 7};

// Method 1 - the simplest way to sort a list of integers
list.Sort();  // list now contains
            { 1, 1, 2, 3, 4, 5, 5, 5, 6, 7, 8, 9, 9 }
```

For sorting objects you can use the `OrderBy` extension method:

```
var listOfPeople = new List<Person>
{
    new Person {Name = "Fred", Age = 29},
    new Person {Name = "Barney", Age = 27},
    new Person {Name = "Wilma", Age = 22},
    new Person {Name = "Betty", Age = 23}
};

// Method 2 - sorting with an extension method and a Lambda expression
var sortedListOfPeople = listOfPeople.OrderBy(item => item.Name);
```

You can also use LINQ to Objects:

```
// Method 3 - uses LINQ to Objects
var anotherSortedList = from p in listOfPeople orderby p.Age select p;
```

Behind the scenes of the `Sort` method in .NET is an implementation of the quick sort algorithm. You should be familiar with how this algorithm works because some interviewers (thankfully a decreasing number) still want candidates to code up a quick sort implementation from scratch while standing at a whiteboard. Merge sort is another common sorting algorithm that competes with quick sort for title of "most popular sorting algorithm." Both of these sorting algorithms run quickly with average time of O $(n \log n)$, but quick sort can run in O (n^2) time in the worst case.

If you are wondering which sorting algorithm is the best, there is no clear answer. Each algorithm has advantages in certain contexts. Even the lowly bubble sort can be optimal in some cases; for example, a nearly sorted list will be sorted quickly by a bubble sort with minimal memory overhead.

Table 5-2 provides a cheat sheet for some of the more common sorting algorithms.

Table 5-2: Sorting Algorithms

ALGORITHM	WORST-CASE RUNNING TIME	AVERAGE RUNNING TIME	OBSERVATIONS
Bubble sort	$O(n^2)$	$O(n^2)$	Adjacent pairs are compared and swapped if they are in the wrong order. Can be efficient for very small and nearly sorted lists. Easy to implement. Almost never used.
Merge sort	$O(n \log n)$	$O(n \log n)$	Repeatedly divides the list into sub-lists until each list contains just one item, then repeatedly merges the lists to produce a single (sorted) list. Fast. Very commonly used.
Quick sort	$O(n^2)$	$O(n \log n)$	Repeatedly divides the list into two sub-lists based on a pivot value until all lists contain a single value (or no values). Sorted sub-lists are concatenated around their pivot values to eventually form the complete, sorted list. Fast. Very commonly used.
Heap sort	$O(n \log n)$	$O(n \log n)$	Creates a heap data structure from the list, then repeatedly extracts the largest value into an array until all values are removed from the heap. The heap speeds searches while constructing the sorted array.
Insertion sort	$O(n^2)$	$O(n^2)$	Iterates over a list, removing elements and inserting them into their sorted location in another list. Faster than quick sort for very small arrays.

Working with Recursion

Recursion happens when a method calls itself. If you've never encountered recursive code you might think a method that calls itself is asking for trouble in the form of a stack overflow, and you would be right—except that all correctly written recursive methods test for a condition that terminates the recursion when the method reaches the *base case*, as in the following example:

```
int factorial(int n)
{
    if (n <= 1) // the base case, terminates recursion
        return 1;
    else
        return n * factorial(n-1); // the recursive call
}
```

Recursion is more than an academic exercise. It is an essential tool for implementing algorithms that take advantage of the technique known as *divide and conquer*, where a complex problem is repeatedly divided into similar (but smaller) problems until a simple case (the base case) is reached. The biggest practical problem with recursive calls (and with the general approach of divide and conquer) is that running out of memory or exceeding the number of calls allowed by a framework is very easy to do.

The Fibonacci sequence of numbers is generated by adding the numbers 0 and 1 (equals 1), then adding 1 to 1 (equals 2), then adding 1 to 2 (equals 3) and so on as per the following sequence:

0, 1, 1, 2, 3, 5, 8, 13, 21, 34, 55, 89, 144, …

An iterative algorithm for generating the first *n* numbers in this sequence might be something like:

```
int FibonacciIterative(int n)
{
    if (n <= 1)
        return n;

    int firstNumber = 0;
    int secondNumber = 1;
    int result = 0;

    for (int i = 2; i <= n; i++)
    {
```

```
        result = secondNumber + firstNumber;
        firstNumber = secondNumber;
        secondNumber = result;
    }
    return result;
}
```

In contrast, a recursive algorithm requires much less code and is easier to read:

```
int FibonacciRecursive(int n)
{

    if (n <= 1)
        return n;

    return FibonacciRecursive (n - 1) + FibonacciRecursive (n - 2);
}
```

If these classic textbook examples aren't sufficiently inspiring you could look to the spectacular 1997 chess match where a computer named Deep Blue convincingly beat the world champion Garry Kasparov. This was the first time ever that a computer beat a world champion in match play. It is also a fine example of recursion because at the heart of all chess-playing programs is the *minimax* algorithm, a recursive algorithm that searches the move space of a chess game looking for optimal moves. Without this algorithm it is doubtful that computer chess would have been as advanced as it was in 1997.

Modeling with Object-Oriented Programming

At the heart of object-oriented programming is an emphasis on modeling the entities of a domain as a collection of objects. These objects combine data with behavior and perform operations on data when prompted by a message, a method call, or an event that triggers an action.

Object-oriented programming is one of the most fundamental areas of programming knowledge to have when you are developing line-of-business applications. If you don't know the difference between a *class* and an *object* then you will be in trouble at most interviews.

Understanding classes and objects

Let's get the most obvious question out of the way. What exactly is the difference between a class and an object?

Very informally, a class is like a blueprint, and an object is the thing you get by following the blueprint.

Slightly more formally, an object is an instance of a class. You can't create an object without a class. When a program runs, objects spring into existence and are eventually destroyed, whereas classes normally exist throughout the entire run-time of an application.

```
// Here is the definition of a class called MyClass
public class MyClass {

    // This class contains a method that does something
    public void DoSomething()
    {
        Console.WriteLine("Don't panic");
    }

}

// And here is another class that creates an instance
// of MyClass so it can do something...
public class MyOtherClass {

    // Here we create an object
    var foo = new MyClass();

    // And now we can do something with the newly created object
    foo.DoSomething();
}
```

In practice, the difference between a class and an object can be somewhat academic, because declaring classes in such a way that they can be used as if they were objects is perfectly possible (and reasonably common).

```
public class MyClass {
    public static void DoSomething()
    {
        Console.WriteLine("Don't panic");
    }
}

// And here is another class that uses MyClass
// directly, no object is explicitly created.
public class MyOtherClass {

    // We don't need an object to use the static method
    MyClass.DoSomething();
}
```

Notice that the method DoSomething has been declared as static, which allows it to be used without first creating an object. In this example I can still create an instance of the class even though I don't need to. If I were writing a utility class then I would normally also declare the class as static because it tells the compiler that this class may not be inherited and that all the methods in this class will also be static.

Untangling inheritance and composition

Inheritance is simultaneously one of the greatest strengths and one of the greatest weaknesses of object-oriented programming. It provides for very strong modeling of a domain, and it also provides for effective code reuse where a derived class can take advantage of inherited methods and properties. It isn't all roses, however, because in practice it turns out that naïve enthusiasm for inheritance leads to complex class hierarchies where the behavior of a program becomes difficult to predict, where debugging is far from easy, and where the correctness of a program is impossible to prove. To be fair, the same might be said of any sufficiently complex program, but complex hierarchies of inheritance have contributed to some of the worst headaches in my programming career to date. Untangling and making sense of a complex hierarchy of inheritance can take days, and for that reason I advise programmers to consider *composition* before inheritance. Here is an example of the difference:

```
// Foo inherits from Bar
// Foo *is a* Bar
public class Foo : Bar
{
    . . .
}
// Foo is composed of a Bar
// Foo *has a* Bar
public class Foo
{
    Bar bar = new Bar();
    . . .
}
```

How does composition help? For one thing, the maintenance programmer no longer needs to worry about whether changes in a base class will break the functionality of derived classes somewhere along the chain of inheritance. You can switch out the use of Bar in the Foo class for something else and be confident that changes are localized to the Foo class, with no unpleasant ripples downstream in descendants of the class.

Exploring polymorphism

A typical textbook example of polymorphism describes how a cat and a dog are both animals and yet the dog barks while the cat meows. You usually see examples like this:

```
public class Animal
{
    public string MakeNoise()
    {
        return string.Empty;
    }
}
public class Cat : Animal
{
    public new string MakeNoise() {
        return "Meow!";
    }
}
public class Dog : Animal
{
    public new string MakeNoise()
    {
        return "Woof!";
    }
}
class Program {
    static void Main()
    {
        var cat = new Cat();
        var dog = new Dog();

        Console.WriteLine("Cat goes " + cat.MakeNoise());
        Console.WriteLine("Dog goes " + dog.MakeNoise());
    }
}
```

And when you run this (silly) program you get

```
Cat goes Meow!
Dog goes Woof!
```

Examples like this might lead you to two conclusions: that polymorphism is somehow connected with animals and that polymorphism implies overriding, as shown here with the MakeNoise method. The connection with animals is common in textbooks but merely coincidental. The connection with overriding is also common but is not essential for polymorphism. You can also have polymorphism when classes implement an interface or inherit an abstract class. In both of those cases the subclasses are not overriding the method of a base class but still provide different implementations of a method and are therefore polymorphic. Here is an example of polymorphism without overriding:

```
interface IAnimal
{
    string MakeNoise();
}
public class Cat : IAnimal
{
    public string MakeNoise()
    {
        return "Meow!";
    }
}
public class Dog : IAnimal
{
    public string MakeNoise()
    {
        return "Woof!";
    }
}
class Program
{
    static void Main()
    {
        var cat = new Cat();
        var dog = new Dog();

        Console.WriteLine("Cat goes " + cat.MakeNoise());
        Console.WriteLine("Dog goes " + dog.MakeNoise());
    }
}
```

Data-hiding with encapsulation

The word most commonly associated with encapsulation is *hiding*. Things that are hidden include the implementation details of a class and the data that belongs to a class. If a class exposes data members, encapsulation means that these members are accessed via *getters* and *setters* (called *accessors*) rather than directly as public *fields*.

Encapsulation encourages programmers to think of objects as black boxes. Data goes in, data comes out, and the processing performed by an object is hidden from the programmer. This approach can be very effective in simplifying the model of a system, because the programmer does not need to hold so many implementation details in her head, but when things go wrong—a bug in the black box perhaps—then this approach can make debugging harder. For this reason the "1.0" release (the first version) of a framework is often treated with suspicion by many experienced programmers.

Thinking Like a Functional Programmer

Functional programmers think about problems and model their solutions differently from object-oriented programmers. Some key differences include:

- You use functions instead of mutable objects.
- Results are obtained by evaluating expressions rather than performing actions on data.
- Functions are always stateless and have no side effects.
- Recursion is the norm rather than the exception.

It is said that functional programs scale up better than object-oriented programs. One reason for this scalability is that functional programs completely avoid the complications associated with concurrent operations on data such as race conditions and thread safety.

Understanding SQL

You can't go very far into a software development career without dealing with a requirement for data storage and retrieval, and you can't go very far into the requirement for data storage and retrieval without encountering some form of database. One of the earliest and certainly one of the most widespread forms of database is the *relational database management system* or RDBMS. SQL is the language a programmer uses to manage data stored in a RDBMS. If you are new to SQL I have some good news and some bad news: The good news is that there are just four statements to learn that will allow you to add, retrieve, update, and delete data. The bad news is that every major RDBMS vendor (including Oracle and Microsoft) has a very different implementation of SQL, so a lot of what you might learn about one RDBMS will not be transferable to another.

What is ACID?

A cornerstone of RDBMS is adherence to ACID, a set of properties that are intended to guarantee operations on a database are processed reliably:

- **A** is for *atomicity*, which requires that you apply an update in its entirety or not at all. If one part of an update operation fails, then all parts should fail.
- **C** is for *consistency*, which requires that you only make an update if it results in data that is valid according to all defined rules.

- **I** is for *isolation*, which requires that concurrent execution of updates has the same result as if the updates had been run one after the other.

- **D** is for *durability*, which requires that after an update is committed to a database, the resulting data persists even if the database crashes, the power is shut off, or the server room is overrun by pigeons.

Set-based thinking

By far the biggest adjustment a programmer must make when learning SQL is to think about processing data in sets rather than iteratively. This does not necessarily mean writing monstrous, impenetrable 100-line SQL statements, but it does mean thinking in terms of partitioning, selecting, and processing sets of data in preference to selecting and processing individual rows one at a time. Apart from anything else, RDBMSs are excellent at optimizing set-based SQL statements. If you process one row at a time the RDBMS can do little to optimize your code.

Full-Stack Web Development

Developing software for the World Wide Web requires that a programmer (or a team of programmers) possess a diverse set of skills. So many technologies are involved that a new term has been invented to describe a programmer who has competency in all of them: *a full stack web developer.*

A full stack web developer is a programmer who might one day code up a responsive web page with HTML and CSS, and the next day write JavaScript code with jQuery and Ajax, and the next day write a stored procedure to optimize a data retrieval routine. I've barely scratched the surface; full stack web development can also require knowledge of:

- Graphic design
- Principles of usability, also known as "UX"
- Flash or Silverlight
- Content Management Systems (CMS)
- XML and JSON
- A programming language such as Java, Ruby, or .NET and supporting frameworks
- MVC frameworks
- SQL (or, increasingly, NoSQL)
- ORM frameworks
- Data modeling

- Database administration

- Server and network administration

- Browser quirks (and there are many)

- Website configuration

- Website performance testing and optimization

The technology that underpins the Web, by which I mean primarily the Hypertext Transfer Protocol (HTTP), was not designed to be stateful. It was designed for the transmission of independent requests and responses, and in itself it has no mechanism for retaining information about a session. This is what people mean when they say "The Web is stateless."

Fortunately, or unfortunately, depending how you look at it, every modern programming framework provides a range of ways in which a façade of session state can be maintained. Cookies, hidden form values, and many forms of server-side session management all contribute to the façade of a stateful user session.

All mechanisms for maintaining session state struggle with the same fundamental problem; they all struggle with user behavior. Users as a whole do not sit idle while waiting for a server to respond. They load up new tabs and do something else, or they lose interest and close their browsers altogether. The server doesn't know whether the user is waiting or has gone; it can only make assumptions based on what was in the last transmission from the client browser and how much time has passed.

Deciphering Regular Expressions

> You can't fully appreciate a regular expression until you have read it in the original Klingon.

Many programmers have a love/hate relationship with regular expressions. They love them for their expressive power, and they hate them for being hard to read. They love them for their all-round usefulness, and they hate them for being unforgiving of mistakes. No matter where you stand on the love/hate spectrum, you need to have a good knowledge of regular expressions for the programming interview.

At their most basic, regular expressions are a fancy way of finding strings in a body of text. They are nothing to be scared of, at least not until someone hits you with a regular expression like this one:

```
/^([\w\!\#$\%\&\'\*\+\-\/\=\?\^\`{\|\}\~]+\.)*[\w\!\#$\%\&\'\*\+\-\/\=\?
\^\`{\|\}\~]+@(((([a-z0-9]{1}[a-z0-9\-]{0,62}[a-z0-9]{1})|[a-z])\.)+[a-
z]{2,6})|(\d{1,3}\.){3}\d{1,3}(\:\d{1,5})?)$/i
```

Incidentally, this regex validates an e-mail address, although not perfectly.

One of the first hurdles facing a regex novice is gaining the ability to recognize the constituent parts of a regular expression. It might be composed of literal text, or it might be composed of tokens that represent character classes. It might contain anchors, quantifiers, groups, and assertions. Proficiently reading and writing complex regular expressions takes practice, but the basics are easily mastered, and I cover them here.

Both JavaScript and the .NET framework have adopted a flavor of regular expression syntax that is identical to the syntax found in Perl. Perl predates both JavaScript and .NET, but still survives as a popular language for getting things done. To illustrate some of the basics of regular expressions I have written a Perl script, shown next. It reads from STDIN, creates a case-insensitive regular expression from the first line of input, and evaluates the remaining lines against that regular expression. By feeding a variety of text files to this script you can see how various regular expressions match or don't match the corresponding samples.

```
use strict;
use warnings;

my $re;
my @match;
my @nonmatch;

for (<>) {

    chomp;

    unless ($re) {
        $re = $_;
        print "The regular expression /$_/i matches as follows\n";
        next;
    }

    if (/$re/i) {
        push @match, $_;
    } else {
        push @nonmatch, $_;
    }
}

print "\nMATCHES\n", join ("\n",@match) if @match;
print "\n\nDOES NOT MATCH\n", join ("\n",@nonmatch), if @nonmatch;
```

I then run the script as follows:

```
C:\>perl Regex.pl RegexTest1.txt
```

The file `RegexTest1.txt` contains a list of strings for testing against the regular expression (the first line in this file is interpreted as a regular expression). When run, the script outputs two lists: matching and non-matching lines.

```
The regular expression /great/i matches as follows

MATCHES
!!GreaT!!
GrEaT
great
Great
GrEaT
greatful
ungreatful
UNGREATFUL
UNgreatFUL

DOES NOT MATCH
grate
grated
grea
greet
reat
ungrateful
```

You can see that a regular expression will match a pattern anywhere it can find it. It matches the "great" in "!!Great!!" even though the word is surrounded by exclamation marks. If you want to find the word "great" but not the (misspelled) word "ungreatful" then you need to use *anchors* or *word boundaries*.

Finding content with anchors and word boundaries

You can think of anchors and word boundaries in regular expressions as giving context to a search pattern. In the previous example you saw that searching for `/great/` will match `ungreatful`. There are at least two ways to change that behavior; you can use an anchor to say (for example) that you only want to match the `great` or `greatly` or `great!!`. Here is what that regular expression would look like:

```
^great
```

The caret character (^) is an anchor that tells the regular expression to match only at the start of the string. If you wanted to anchor the pattern at the end of the string you would use the dollar character ($) like so:

```
great$
```

This example would match `!!great` but not `great!!`.

If you want to match text that contains nothing but the word great you can anchor at both the start and at the end.

```
^great$
```

In passing, it is worth noting that these anchors have no "width." In the pattern they are effectively zero characters long, only serving to indicate where the pattern should be matched in a string. Another noteworthy zero-width metacharacter is the *word boundary* represented by \b, as in the following example:

```
\bgreat\b
```

This matches great in both !!great and great!! but not in ungreatful because no word boundaries exist around the pattern great.

Here are some more examples using the Perl script shown previously:

```
The regular expression /^foo\b/i matches as follows

MATCHES
FOO BAR
foo, bar
FOO!

DOES NOT MATCH
FOOBAR
foody
bar foo
foofoo

The regular expression /\bBar$/i matches as follows

MATCHES
Foo bar
!bar
foo-bar
great!bar

DOES NOT MATCH
BAR!
bard's tale
bar's tale
```

Matching character classes

Quite often you will want to match a set of characters rather than one particular character. If you want to find grey and gray then you could use the expression

```
/gr[ea]y/
```

The square brackets and the two characters inside them are a character class that matches either e or a. You can also specify a range of characters in a character class, as follows:

```
/gr[a-z]y/
```

This matches any single character in the alphabet, a, b, c, and so on through to z, but because it only matches one character it will not match greay.

Here are some more examples of matching with character classes:

```
The regular expression /gr[ea]y/i matches as follows

MATCHES
gray
grey
GREY
gray?!
##grey

DOES NOT MATCH
greay
graey
gravy

The regular expression /gr[oa][oe]vy/i matches as follows

MATCHES
groovy
begroovy!

DOES NOT MATCH
gravy
more gravy?
gravy boat!
```

You can also use some predefined character classes. A single dot represents the class of "any character except a newline." Table 5-3 shows some of the most important classes you should know about.

Table 5-3: Important Character Classes

CHARACTER CLASS	INTERPRETATION
.	Any character except a newline
\d	Any digit, including non-ASCII digits (for example, Arabic)
\D	Any non-digit
[A-Za-z0-9]	Any character of the alphabet or any digit
\w	Any alphanumeric character, usually including underscores and periods
\W	Any character not in the class \w

Continued

Table 5-3 *(continued)*

CHARACTER CLASS	INTERPRETATION
\s	Any whitespace character, including spaces, tabs, and sometimes also newlines (depending on which modifiers are used)
\S	Any character not in the class \s

Here is another example showing how the character class \w matches under-scores and numbers in addition to characters of the alphabet:

```
The regular expression /gr\w\wvy/i matches as follows
```

```
MATCHES
groovy
begroovy!
groovyfruits
gra_vy
gr__vy
gr00vy
```

```
DOES NOT MATCH
gravy
more gravy?
gravy boat!
gr!!vy
gr..vy
```

Constraining matches with quantifiers

In addition to specifying characters and character classes, you can also specify how many (or how few) instances of a character or class you want to match.

Here is an example of matching zero or more occurrences of the character "a" in the word gravy:

```
/gra*vy/
```

This matches gravy, but it will also match grvy (zero occurrences) and graaaaaaaaavy (more than zero occurrences).

Table 5-4 lists the quantifiers you should know about.

Table 5-4: Regular Expression Quantifiers

QUANTIFIER	INTERPRETATION
*	Match 0 or more times
+	Match 1 or more times
?	Match 1 or 0 times

QUANTIFIER	INTERPRETATION
{n}	Match exactly *n* times
{n, }	Match at least *n* times
{n,m}	Match at least *n* but not more than *m* times

Here are more examples of how you can use qualifiers:

```
The regular expression /gra*vy/i matches as follows
```

```
MATCHES
grvy
gravy
more gravy?
gravy boat!
```

```
DOES NOT MATCH
groovy
begroovy!
groovyfruits
gra_vy
```

```
The regular expression /gra+vy/i matches as follows
```

```
MATCHES
gravy
more gravy?
gravy boat!
```

```
DOES NOT MATCH
grvy
groovy
begroovy!
groovyfruits
gra_vy
```

Working with groups and captures

Sometimes just matching a pattern isn't enough. Sometimes you need to extract parts of the text in order to do something with them. You might have a log file that contains values you want to capture for analysis, or you might want to find and print all the links in a page that contain the word "Dilbert," or you might want to capture the thing my dog doesn't have:

```
/My dog has no (\w+)/i
```

```
The regular expression /My dog has no (\w+)/i matches as follows
```

```
MATCHES
My dog has no nose (captured 'nose')
```

```
My dog has no canines (captured 'canines')
My dog has no k9s (captured 'k9s')
My dog has no nose, ask me how he smells (captured 'nose')

DOES NOT MATCH
My dog has no !*?#!! (nothing captured)
```

You can supply alternatives in a pattern by using the vertical bar meta-character. If you want to match either `fit` or `fat`, for example, you could use this pattern:

```
/fit|fat/
```

If you want to match these words within a sentence you need to surround the alternatives with parentheses, just to limit the scope of the alternation:

```
/trying to get (fit|fat)/
```

If you don't want to capture anything you can surround the alternation with non-capturing parentheses:

```
/trying to get (?:fit|fat)/
```

Another reason you might want to capture something from a match is to replace it with something else. In Perl you can replace `fit` with `fat` using the substitution operator, like this:

```
s/fit/fat/
```

You could replace either `fit` or `fat` with `paid` using:

```
s/fit|fat/paid/
```

If you want to include the matched word in the replacement text, you can do it with a *backreference*. In Perl, that looks like

```
s/trying to get (fit|fat)/I got $1/
```

and it has the following effect:

```
Before: "trying to get fit"
After: "I got fit"

Before: "trying to get fat"
After: "I got fat"
```

`$1` refers to the first captured group. If you had more groups you would use `$2`, `$3`, and so on.

Avoiding gotchas

A common "gotcha" is failing to account for the greedy nature of regular expression pattern matching. The following regular expression is an attempt at matching any number of characters between two delimiters.

The expression

```
/".*"/
```

when matched against the string

```
I "fail" to "see" the irony
```

might be expected to match

```
"fail"
```

but in fact it matches from the first quotation mark right up to the last quotation mark in the string:

```
"fail" to "see"
```

This (default) behavior of regular expressions is described as *greedy matching*. It can be surprising if you aren't aware of it. One effective way to circumvent this greediness is to avoid using the "any character" class (the dot) and instead specify that after the first delimiter you want to match *anything except* the delimiter, up to the very next occurrence of the delimiter.

To say "anything except" you use the caret character inside a character class, which inverts the class.

So this expression

```
/"[^"]*"/
```

can be interpreted as

- match the first double quotation mark character, followed by

- zero or more instances of *any character except* a double quotation mark, followed by

- a double quotation mark character

Perhaps even more problematic is the fact that scenario where a regular expression that works in one or two cases is assumed to work in all cases. Here are some flawed regular expressions you might see in the wild.

This first one is supposed to ensure a calendar date is valid:

```
The regular expression /\d{1,2}\/\d{1,2}\/\d{4}/ matches as follows
```

```
MATCHES
01/01/1999    # ok
31/02/1999    # invalid
10/10/0000    # invalid
0/0/0000      # invalid
99/99/9999    # invalid
```

This next one tries to validate e-mail addresses, but incorrectly rejects addresses at the 37signals.com domain. It also allows some dodgy e-mails to pass validation:

```
The regular expression /\w+@[A-Za-z_]+?.[A-Za-z]{2,6}/i matches
as follows
```

```
MATCHES
admin@com.org.
a@b@c.com
```

```
DOES NOT MATCH
admin@37signals.com
```

This one tries to match HTML tags, but fails almost instantly:

```
The regular expression /(\</?[^\>]+\>)/ matches as follows
```

```
(The incorrect match is shown emphasized)
```

```
MATCHES
<a title="">>click here!" href="goofy.com">
```

Finally, if you want to see if a number is in the range 1–50, please use the normal comparison operators, and never do this:

```
/^[1-9]$|^[1-4][0-9]$|^50$/  # don't ever do this
```

This regular expression works, but it is far less readable than the equivalent code that uses normal comparison operators:

```
if (number > 0 && number <= 50)
```

More reading

By far the best reference for regular expressions is the book *Mastering Regular Expressions* by Jeffrey Friedl (O'Reilly Media, 2006). Although I have covered some of the basics of regular expressions you will want to refer to Friedl's book for many more interesting examples, along with an in-depth examination of using regular expressions in Perl, Java, .NET, and PHP.

Recognizing Hard Problems

Some types of problems are really hard. You might think reading a complicated regex is difficult, but that is nothing compared to the hardest problems in the domain of computer science. For instance, finding factors for large integers (of say 200 digits) is widely regarded as very difficult, and finding factors that are also large prime numbers is even harder. The best-known algorithms for finding these large prime factors are still impractically slow (think years) to run on even the fastest computers. Starting with two large prime numbers and multiplying them to produce a large integer is easy, but reversing the process is very hard. In fact, the problem of finding these prime factors for a large integer is presumed to be so difficult that it is a key part of modern cryptographic applications. Quite simply, the kind of technology an attacker would need to crack these cyphers does not exist except in theory and in experimental forms of computing that rely on quantum mechanical phenomena.

Finding large prime factors is just one example of the class of problems that have no known solutions that run in *polynomial time*, meaning that for practical purposes they are impossible to solve. These are not the kind of problems you would be given as CS101 homework. More to the point, these are not the problems you would be asked to solve at an interview. At the interview you will only need to recognize this kind of problem so you can avoid the trap of trying to solve it while standing at a whiteboard. Interviews normally last an hour or two; brute-forcing a solution to an *NP-Complete* or *NP-Hard* problem might take several million years.

QUESTIONS

What follows is a list of questions related to the topics in this chapter. You can use these questions to identify areas you need to brush up on. Most programmers will not find these questions too difficult, and you will find that you either know the answer or you don't. Avoid over-thinking the answers.

1. **Linked list versus array**

   What are some important differences between a linked list and an array?

2. **Array versus associative array**

   Describe a common scenario that would lead you to prefer an associative array to a simple array.

3. **Self-balancing binary search tree**

   What is a self-balancing binary search tree?

4. **Representation of a graph**

   Why would you prefer to store a graph as an adjacency matrix? Why would you prefer an adjacency list?

5. **BFS and DFS**

   Describe the key differences between breadth-first search (BFS) and depth-first search (DFS).

6. **Breadth-first search**

   Assuming a binary tree with the following structure, write an implementation of a *breadth-first search* that returns true if a given integer exists in the tree.

Here is the structure of the binary tree:

```
class BinaryTree
{
    public int Value;
    public BinaryTree Left { get; set; }
    public BinaryTree Right { get; set; }
}
```

Here is the signature of the method you will write:

```
bool BreadthFirstSearch(BinaryTree node, int searchFor)
```

7. Depth-first search

Assuming a binary tree with the following structure, write an implementation of a depth-first search that returns true if a given integer exists in the tree.

Here is the structure of the binary tree:

```
class BinaryTree
{
    public int Value;
    public BinaryTree Left { get; set; }
    public BinaryTree Right { get; set; }
}
```

Here is the signature of the method you will write:

```
bool DepthFirstSearch(BinaryTree node, int searchFor)
```

8. Inorder, preorder, postorder traversal

What is the difference between inorder, preorder, and postorder traversal?

9. DFS on a large tree

Write code to perform depth-first traversal on an arbitrarily large tree.

10. String permutations

Write a method that will generate all possible permutations of the characters in a string. The signature of your method should look like this:

```
public static List<string> Permutations(string str)
```

11. Prime numbers

Write a method that will generate N number of primes. Start with a naïve implementation and suggest how it might be optimized.

12. Regular expression for IPv4 addresses

Write a regular expression that can be used to extract IPv4 addresses from a text file.

ANSWERS

1. Linked list versus array

What are some important differences between a linked list and an array?

In most frameworks the memory reserved for an array is pre-allocated before the array is used. This predefined limit constrains how many elements you can add to an array before it overflows. In contrast, linked lists can consume all available memory before overflowing and without any pre-declaration of size.

Reassigning pointers is generally quicker than moving records around in memory, which means that adding elements to a linked list is generally quicker than the equivalent operation on an array.

Each record in an array is generally a fixed length, which means that it is a simple calculation to obtain the address of an array element. This calculation is a fixed number of steps, and so it always takes time $O(1)$. In contrast, accessing the nth element of a linked list requires traversal of $n - 1$ nodes, and therefore takes time $O(n)$. In other words accessing elements in arrays is usually faster than accessing elements in linked lists.

2. Array versus associative array

Describe a common scenario that would lead you to prefer an associative array to a simple array.

An associative array is perfect when you need to quickly look up values based on keys. You don't need to iterate through the collection looking for a key; you use the key directly, as in the following example:

```
var myValue = myHashtable[myKey];
```

You can also easily and quickly test whether a hash table contains a key:

```
bool keyExists = myHashtable.Contains(myKey); // quick!
```

Contrast this with the equivalent code for a simple array where you must iterate to find a given element:

```
foreach (int i=0; i<myArray.Length;i++)
    if (myArray[i] == myKey)
        return true; // Found key

return false; // Did not find key (and took a long time)
```

3. **Self-balancing binary search tree**

   What is a self-balancing binary search tree?

   A self-balancing binary search tree (BST) automatically keeps its nodes arranged so as to minimize the height of the tree. The height of a binary search tree is the distance from the root node to the furthest leaf node in the tree. Keeping the height of a BST small also minimizes the time it takes to perform operations on the tree. The automatic balancing of a BST can take a significant amount of time, so not all implementations are strict about minimizing height, tolerating some deviation in the interest of performance. Two popular implementations of self-balancing BSTs are *red-black tree* and *AVL tree*.

4. **Representation of a graph**

   Why would you prefer to store a graph as an adjacency matrix? Why would you prefer an adjacency list?

   An adjacency list is simply a list of edges between nodes in a graph. An adjacency list takes $O(n)$ time to check whether an edge exists because you potentially must iterate over all elements in the list to check for the existence of an edge.

   An adjacency matrix is often implemented as a two-dimensional array where all nodes appear on each dimension of the array, thus forming a matrix. Edges between nodes are represented by a `true` value (or by a `bit` set to 1). A two-dimensional 10 × 10 graph will therefore require an array of 100 × 100 = 1000 elements. An adjacency matrix for n nodes will take n^2 units of memory, which can be prohibitive for large graphs. The advantage of an adjacency matrix is that testing for the existence of an edge is a simple array lookup that takes $O(1)$ time.

   It is worth noting that if the graph is undirected, where an edge between nodes A → B implies an edge in the reverse direction B → A, then half of an adjacency matrix is wasted space—you don't need to store both edges when one edge implies the other.

   Use a matrix when you have fewer nodes with dense connections and a list when you have many nodes with sparse connections.

5. **BFS and DFS**

   Describe the key differences between breadth-first search (BFS) and depth-first search (DFS).

A breadth-first search (BFS) algorithm visits the immediate children of a node before it goes any deeper. A depth-first search (DFS) goes as deep as it can down a path before visiting sibling nodes (that is, before visiting nodes that share the same parent).

A breadth-first search typically uses a `Queue` (FIFO) to keep track of nodes, whereas a depth-first search typically uses a `Stack` (LIFO).

6. Breadth-first search

Assuming a binary tree with the following structure, write an implementation of a breadth-first search that returns true if a given integer exists in the tree.

Here is the structure of the binary tree:

```
class BinaryTree
{
    public int Value;
    public BinaryTree Left { get; set; }
    public BinaryTree Right { get; set; }
}
```

Here is the signature of the method you will write:

```
bool BreadthFirstSearch(BinaryTree node, int searchFor)
```

Notice that this binary tree consists of nodes that are each also a binary tree (or null). This is a typical arrangement for a binary tree because each node can potentially be a tree in its own right.

```
bool BreadthFirstSearch(BinaryTree node, int searchFor)
{
    Queue<BinaryTree> queue = new Queue<BinaryTree>();

    queue.Enqueue(node);

    int count = 0;

    while (queue.Count > 0)
    {
        BinaryTree current = queue.Dequeue();

        if (current == null)
            continue;

        queue.Enqueue(current.Left);
        queue.Enqueue(current.Right);

        if (current.Value == searchFor)
            return true;
    }

    return false;
}
```

7. **Depth-first search**

Assuming a binary tree with the following structure, write an implementation of a depth-first search that returns true if a given integer exists in the tree.

Here is the structure of the binary tree:

```
class BinaryTree
{
    public int Value;
    public BinaryTree Left { get; set; }
    public BinaryTree Right { get; set; }
}
```

Here is the signature of the method you will write:

```
bool DepthFirstSearch(BinaryTree node, int searchFor)
```

A DFS is often written as a recursive algorithm as follows:

```
bool DepthFirstSearch(BinaryTree node, int searchFor)
{
    if (node == null)
        return false;

    if (node.Value == searchFor)
        return true;

    return DepthFirstSearch(node.Left, searchFor)
        || DepthFirstSearch(node.Right, searchFor);
}
```

Note that this function terminates when it finds the given search term. The answer to question 9 shows an example of a non-recursive DFS.

8. **Inorder, preorder, postorder traversal**

What is the difference between inorder, preorder, and postorder traversal?

Inorder, preorder, and postorder are all depth-first traversals and they all potentially visit every node in a tree. The key difference between these traversals is the order in which nodes are visited.

- Preorder traversal visits nodes in the order *root, left, right*.
- Inorder traversal visits nodes in the order *left, root, right*.
- Postorder traversal visits nodes in the order *left, right, root*.

Perhaps contrasting the difference in code can make things clearer. Assume a tree is constructed of nodes with the following structure:

```
class BinaryTree
{
    public int Value;
    public BinaryTree Left { get; set; }
    public BinaryTree Right { get; set; }
}
```

Here is *preorder* traversal, where each node is visited as soon as it is encountered, before the left and right nodes are visited:

```
static void DFSPreOrder(BinaryTree node)
{
    if (node == null) return;

    visit(node);
    DFSPreOrder(node.Left);
    DFSPreOrder(node.Right);
}
```

Here is *inorder* traversal, where the current node is visited after the left node:

```
static void DFSInOrder(BinaryTree node)
{
    if (node == null) return;

    DFSInOrder(node.Left);
    visit(node);
    DFSInOrder(node.Right);
}
```

Here is *postorder* traversal, where each node is visited after both the left and right nodes are visited:

```
static void DFSPostOrder(BinaryTree node)
{
    if (node == null) return;

    DFSPreOrder(node.Left);
    DFSPreOrder(node.Right);
    visit(node);
}
```

Another helpful way of visualizing the difference is to imagine a line drawn around a tree, starting from the left side of the root node and ending at the right side of the root node.

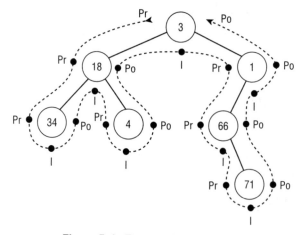

Figure 5-6: Traversal tour

This line visits each node exactly three times, once on the left, once underneath, and once on the right. The order of visitation for a preorder traversal is given by observing the order in which this line passes on the left: inorder when it passes underneath, and postorder when it passes on the right.

Therefore, preorder traversal will visit nodes in this order:

3, 18, 34, 4, 1, 66, 71

Inorder visits in this order:

34, 18, 4, 3, 66, 71, 1

Postorder visits in this order:

34, 4, 18, 71, 66, 1, 3

9. **DFS on a large tree**

Write code to perform depth-first traversal on an arbitrarily large tree.

"Arbitrarily large" in this case prevents you from using the normal recursive DFS algorithm. If you were to try using a recursive function for a large tree you would probably hit a stack overflow exception, because the call stack would need to be at least as big as this arbitrarily large tree. As an alternative you can use an explicit `stack` data structure and a non-recursive algorithm. This avoids using the call stack of the run-time framework and will give you more capacity for tracking nodes. You could also use a database to track nodes, which would give you a virtually unlimited storage capacity, or at least the capacity to scale up as needed.

```
bool DepthFirstSearchIterative(BinaryTree node, int searchFor)
{

    Stack<BinaryTree> nodeStack = new Stack<BinaryTree>();

    nodeStack.Push(node);

    while (nodeStack.Count > 0)
    {
        BinaryTree current = nodeStack.Pop();

        if (current.Value == searchFor)
            return true;

        if (current.Right != null)
            nodeStack.Push(current.Right);

        if (current.Left != null)
            nodeStack.Push(current.Left);
    }

    return false;
}
```

10. String permutations

Write a method that will generate all possible permutations of the characters in a string. The signature of your method should look like this:

```
public static List<string> Permutations(string str)
```

Finding permutations of the characters in a string is a popular interview puzzle. It is a good example of a problem where you can reduce the general case down to a simple base case that is easily solved, and that makes it a perfect candidate for a recursive solution.

Let's look at the base case first.

For characters in the string "A" there is exactly one permutation:

- A

A string of two characters "AB" is nearly as straightforward; there are exactly two permutations:

- AB
- BA

For three characters in the string "ABC" there are six permutations:

- ABC
- ACB
- BAC
- BCA
- CAB
- CBA

If you look closely at the last two permutations for the string "ABC" you will notice that "AB" and "BA" follow the character "C," which is the exact same result gotten for permutations of the previous example "AB." This is the clue that leads you to a generalized algorithm for obtaining permutations of characters in a string:

The permutations of the characters in a string are obtained by joining each character of the string with the permutations of all remaining characters in the string.

So for "ABC" you first list each character:

- A
- B
- C

Then to each character you append permutations of the remaining characters in the string.

For A you need to append the permutations of "BC," giving

- A + BC = **ABC**
- A + CB = **ACB**

For "B" you append the permutations of "AC" as follows:

- B + AC = **BAC**
- B + CA = **BCA**

For "C" you append the permutations of "AB" as follows:

- C + AB = **CAB**
- C + BA = **CBA**

This translates into the following code:

```
public static List<string> Permutations(string str)
{
    // Each permutation is stored in a List of strings
    var result = new List<string>();

    // The base case...
```

```
        if (str.Length == 1)

            result.Add(str);

    else

        // For each character in the string...
        for (int i = 0; i < str.Length; i++)

            // For each permutation of everything else...
            foreach (var p in Permutations(EverythingElse(str,
i)))

                // Add the current char + each permutation
                result.Add(str[i] + p);

    return result;
}

// Return everything in a string except the char at
IndexToIgnore
private static string EverythingElse(string str, int
IndexToIgnore)
{
    StringBuilder result = new StringBuilder();

    for (int j = 0; j < str.Length; j++)
        if (IndexToIgnore != j)
            result.Append(str[j]);

    return result.ToString();
}
```

The number of permutations for a string of *n* characters is equal to *n*!, which makes this function impractical for all but the smallest strings (as you can see from Table 5-5).

Table 5-5: Permutations Generated for Characters in a String

SIZE OF STRING	NUMBER OF PERMUTATIONS
1	1
2	2
3	6
4	24
5	120

Continued

Table 5-5 *(continued)*

SIZE OF STRING	NUMBER OF PERMUTATIONS
6	720
7	5,040
8	40,320
9	362,880
10	3,628,800
11	39,916,800
12	479,001,600
13	6,227,020,800
14	87,178,291,200
15	1,307,674,368,000

Assuming the earlier code was able to generate 100,000 permutations per second (which is probably an optimistic estimate), then for a string of 15 characters it would take around *151 days* to run. Besides the impractical run time, the machine would almost certainly run out of memory before the program finished, unless you took steps to offload the generated permutations to disk.

11. **Prime numbers**

Write a method that will generate N number of primes. Start with a naïve implementation and suggest how it might be optimized.

Writing a method that can generate prime numbers is relatively easy. The challenge in this question is to improve on the naïve implementation. If you start with a very simple algorithm you will produce something like this:

```
public static List<int> GeneratePrimes(int n)
{
    var primes = new List<int>();

    int nextCandidatePrime = 2;

    primes.Add(nextCandidatePrime);

    while (primes.Count < n)
    {
        if (isPrime(nextCandidatePrime))
            primes.Add(nextCandidatePrime);

        nextCandidatePrime += 1;
    }
```

```
    return primes;
}

private static bool isPrime (int n)
{
    for (int i = 2; i < n; i++)
    {
        if (n % i == 0)
            return false;
    }
    return true;
}
```

This is a terrible algorithm, completely unoptimized, but it works. I tested this on my Asus Zenbook laptop (I'm a masochist) and found it took well over seven minutes to find 100,000 primes. You can do a lot better than that!

The first obvious optimization is that you don't need to test so many numbers. When you're testing for numbers that divide evenly into n you need to check only the numbers up to the square root of n. The reason is simple: If n is not a prime then there must be two numbers a and b such that

$a \times b = n$

If both a and b were greater than the square root of n then $a \times b$ would be greater than n; therefore, at least one of these numbers must be less than or equal to the square root of n. Because you only need to find one of these numbers in order to conclude n is not a prime number, you don't need to look any further than the square root.

```
private static bool isPrime(int n)
{
    for (int i = 2; i <= Math.Sqrt(n); i++)
    {
        if (n % i == 0)
            return false;
    }
    return true;
}
```

With this simple modification you now have a much faster algorithm. Testing on the same laptop shows that you have improved from well over seven minutes to about 1.5 seconds:

```
100000 primes generated in 00:00:01.3663523
```

You can still do better. Another optimization is that you don't need to check every divisor in sequence; you can skip all the even numbers. The reason is that if a candidate prime is also an even number then it is obviously not a prime number. If you add a simple test to check for even numbers in the isPrime function, then you can skip all the multiples of 2 in the inner loop:

```
private static bool isPrime(int n)
{
    if (n % 2 == 0) return false;
    for (int i = 3; i <= Math.Sqrt(n); i += 2)
    {
        if (n % i == 0)
            return false;
    }
    return true;
}
```

This approximately halves the run time of the isPrime method:

```
100000 primes generated in 00:00:00.7139317
```

Not only can you skip all the even numbers, you can also skip numbers that are divisible by 3, or by 5 (skipping 4 because it is a multiple of 2), or by 7, and so on, all the way up to the square root of the number being evaluated. In a flash of insight you might realize that the numbers just described are in fact the prime numbers themselves, and further, that because you're building up this set of prime numbers as you go you will have them conveniently available to use when testing each candidate.

```
public static List<int> GeneratePrimesOptimized(int n)
{
    var primes = new List<int>();

    // Prime our list of primes
    primes.Add(2);

    // Start from 3, since we already know 2 is a prime
    int nextCandidatePrime = 3;

    // Keep going until we have generated n primes
    while (primes.Count < n)
    {
        // Assume the number is prime
        bool isPrime = true;

        // Test if the candidate is evenly divisible
        // by any of the primes up to sqrt(candidate)
        for (int i = 0;
            primes[i] <= Math.Sqrt(nextCandidatePrime);
            i++)
        {
            if (nextCandidatePrime % primes[i] == 0)
            {
                isPrime = false;
                break;
```

```
            }
        }
        if (isPrime)
            primes.Add(nextCandidatePrime);

        // We proceed in steps of 2, avoiding the even numbers
        nextCandidatePrime += 2;
    }
    return primes;
}
```

Once again you have approximately halved the run time:

```
100000 primes generated in 00:00:00.3538022
```

This is about as fast as it gets with a naïve algorithm. You may also benefit from investigating alternative algorithms, and a good starting place would be to familiarize yourself with the *sieve of Eratosthenes*, an ancient method that works as follows.

To find all prime numbers up to n:

1. Create a list of integers from 2 to n.
2. Start with the first prime number, $p = 2$.
3. Count up from the start of the list in increments of p and cross out each of these numbers.
4. Find the first available number greater than p in the list. If there is no such number then stop, otherwise, replace p with this number (which is also the next prime) and repeat from step 3.

When this algorithm terminates, all the numbers remaining in the list are prime numbers.

Here is an illustration of how each step refines the list, "sieving" the numbers to leave just primes.

You start with a consecutive sequence of integers:

2, 3, 4, 5, 6, 7, 8, 9, 10, 11, 12, 13, 14, 15, ...

You then remove multiples of 2 (greater than 2):

2, 3, , 5, , 7, , 9, , 11, , 13, , 15, ...

You then remove multiples of 3 (greater than 3) and so on, leaving just prime numbers:

2, 3, , 5, , 7, , , , 11, , 13, , , ...

As a final note, a practical alternative to generating your own prime numbers would be to obtain a pre-calculated list of prime numbers and store this list in a data structure that affords $O(1)$ look-up times. An interviewer won't be happy if you "cheat" this way, but at the same time she will admit that in practice you could reuse an existing list rather than reinvent your own. You might get marks for pragmatism if not lateral thinking.

12. **Regular expression for IPv4 addresses**

Write a regular expression that can be used to extract IPv4 addresses from a text file.

An IPv4 address has the form

```
nnn.nnn.nnn.nnn
```

where *nnn* is a number between 0 and 255.

The simplest pattern that will match an IPv4 address is as follows:

```
(?:[0-9]{1,3}\.){3}[0-9]{1,3}
```

If you can be sure that the source file contains valid IP addresses, then this regex would be sufficient. If you can't be sure then you need to be a bit more paranoid. The preceding pattern would correctly match

```
10.10.1.22
```

but would incorrectly match

```
999.999.999.999
```

Matching a number that is limited to a maximum of 255 is a bit more complicated. The number 249 is permissible but 259 is not, and 199 is permissible but 299 is not. This leads you to use alternations in the matching pattern. Here is the regex that matches a number in the range 0 to 255:

```
(?:25[0-5]|2[0-4][0-9]|[01]?[0-9][0-9]?)
```

You need to allow this pattern to be repeated four times, each part joined by a dot. You should also surround the pattern with word-boundary meta-characters to avoid matching invalid addresses such as this one:

```
1234.255.255.2550    # Invalid, we don't want this
```

So you end up with:

```
\b(?:(?:25[0-5]|2[0-4][0-9]|[01]?[0-9][0-9]?)\.){3}
(?:25[0-5]|2[0-4][0-9]|[01]?[0-9][0-9]?)\b
```

Code Quality

Most technical interviewers have a view on what is important in software development. They universally agree that code quality is vitally important, but the exact definition of quality is a bit less clear. Some put code clarity ahead of efficiency, and some put efficiency first. Others say that correctness is paramount, with clarity and efficiency vying for second place, and some interviewers say none of those things matter if the customer is unhappy.

At another level you will find some interviewers concerned with the layout and consistency of code. Choosing good names for variables and classes is a common concern, and many put their trust in the *SOLID* principles (if you've not heard of SOLID it is explained later in this chapter).

In this chapter you will find questions covering all these angles. These are the questions that technical interviewers use to assess your understanding of what code quality means. It's an opportunity to demonstrate some important things, specifically that you:

- Can read and comprehend someone else's code
- Can spot potentially bad code
- Have a view on what constitutes good code
- Can articulate reasons why code is good or bad

Programmers with any experience will recognize the importance of the first point—reading and comprehending code written by someone else. As a programmer, relatively rarely are you asked to write a lot of code from scratch. Far more commonly, you're asked to maintain or add features to an existing code base. Reading and understanding code, therefore, is a vital skill that every programmer must acquire.

As an interviewer, and as a programmer with strongly held views about code quality, it always surprises and disappoints me when a programmer cannot find fault with code that is clearly substandard. Many interviewers will routinely produce sample code at the interview and ask, "What's wrong with this?" The questions and answers provided in this chapter will ensure you are prepared for this style of questioning.

A natural follow-up to the question, "What's wrong with this code?" is "What could you do to improve it?" In some ways this question is as important as spotting bad code in the first place. After all, the interviewer will reason that, if you, the interviewee, can't improve bad code then you're not going to be much help when you do find it. This is not a new idea.

> "It is easier to criticize than to correct our past errors."
>
> —*Titus Livius, written sometime between 27 and 25 BC*

Finally, after you have identified poor code and formulated ideas about how you might improve it, you need to communicate those ideas. In the same way that identifying poor code but not being able to improve it is of little value, being unable to articulate your opinions is equally unhelpful. Your thoughts might be golden, but they are worthless at the interview unless you can communicate them clearly to the interviewer.

Writing Clear Code

The cost of unclear code is enormous. It costs the programmer at every step—from the initial struggle to make the unclear code compile and work correctly, to the needless complications it causes when testing and debugging, to the abject misery it causes throughout the long years of product maintenance. If you think I'm exaggerating, talk to any experienced maintenance programmer. All this extra effort and stress translates to extra cost for the product owner or the business that relies on or sells that product. The end user of such a product suffers from bugs and quirks caused by the unclear code. Unclear code adds a real and quantifiable cost that is ignored at peril.

If you accept—and I believe you should—that writing code is a special form of communication, where ideas and algorithms are communicated from a programmer to a machine and—in some ways more importantly—to other programmers, then understanding how unclear code comes into existence is easy. It's a basic human failing. If you replace the word *code* with *communication* (as in *unclear communication*) then all the reasons you can think of that contribute to poor communication, such as laziness, misapprehension, and a poor grasp of the language—all these apply equally well to unclear code.

Your job during the interview is to demonstrate that you can recognize unclear code and that you can write clear code. It's all about good communication.

"As simple as possible but not simpler"

—attributed to Albert Einstein

The idea of being as simple as possible but not simpler applies perfectly here; you want the code to be correct and useful, and ideally you want it to be extensible and flexible, but not at the expense of clarity. You should write the minimum code that is necessary to satisfy all the requirements and still be easy to understand. You must avoid sacrificing simplicity for the sake of some hypothetical future requirement.

Of course, if the requirement is more than hypothetical, if you can realistically anticipate a future requirement that forces a complication upon the immediate solution, and you can justify it to yourself (and to whomever reviews your code), then go for it. Don't be too disappointed, however, when the requirement never eventuates and the code remains forever more difficult to maintain than it really ought to have been.

Of course, it is important when designing a system to create abstractions of the problem space, and to generalize the solution so that it can apply to more than just the immediate problem. The danger lies in going too far and (to pick just one unfortunate outcome), ending up with many layers of abstraction that serve no immediate purpose, existing only to satisfy some theoretical future requirement or constraint that might never eventuate. The Extreme Programming movement dismisses this kind of needless embellishment with the acronym YAGNI, "You ain't gonna need it."

Sometimes after a long struggle to get an algorithm working correctly, it might seem appropriate that the resulting code should reflect the effort that went into it. Or, to put it in the words of an anonymous cynic:

"If it was hard to write it should be hard to read."

—Anonymous

That idea is wrong. The next programmer will not thank you. It is much better, and frankly it is good coding manners to spend a little more time making the intent as obvious as possible.

Writing Expressive Code

Expressiveness in code is the quality of being able to convey a lot of information (or intention) in a small amount of code. Expressive code is often succinct—a quality that can help readability in some cases and hurt it in others. One way to think about expressiveness in code is to compare it to your English vocabulary. As your vocabulary grows, you become aware of words that are packed with more meaning. Instead of speaking in long rambling sentences, you can now speak more efficiently, saying more with less. The drawback is that sometimes when you use these words, other people won't understand them. From your point of view, you're communicating more effectively, but from their point of view you're using needlessly complicated words.

Your programming vocabulary is exactly the same. As your proficiency grows, you will tend to take advantage of advanced language or framework features. These advanced features will seem needlessly complicated to the less experienced programmer.

So what is the answer: Should you write code in baby-talk, or should you write code in such a concentrated form that only experts will understand it?

The answer is to write for your audience. A programmer's audience consists of the maintenance programmers who will follow. If you don't know who that might be, then write with some restraint. Think of your own learning experience and show the programmers that follow you some consideration; they may not be as expert as you are. Add code comments where helpful, avoid the tersest expressions, and instead favor simple, clear constructs.

Measuring Efficiency and Performance

Efficiency can be measured in a number of ways. When programmers talk about the efficiency of a function they may be thinking of one or more things, including:

- Speed of function execution; that is, time complexity
- Working-space requirements
- Avoiding needless steps in an algorithm
- The effort required to develop and support the function
- All of the above

As a well-rounded programmer, you should be aware of the different ways that efficiency can be measured. At a standard programming interview you will rarely be quizzed on how much developing a bit of code might cost (in money terms), but you will often be assessed on your ability to assess and compare the efficiency of two alternative functions in terms of time and space complexity. This is particularly true in companies that develop leading-edge software, where performance might be the key to the next generation of solutions in a given domain.

Big-O notation

If you have been formally educated in computer science then the concepts of time-complexity, space-complexity, and big-O notation won't be new to you. But if, like many practicing programmers, you've learned your skills on the job then this book might be the first time you've ever heard of these ideas. Don't be put off by the necessary mathematical references; you don't need an advanced degree to grasp the concepts.

In big-O notation the O stands for *order*, and *n* denotes the size of input given to a function. Big-O is shorthand for describing the performance classification of a function in terms of the number of steps it can be expected to take relative to the size of its input. You might, for example, say *function A is O(n²); it takes on the order of n² steps to execute.*

Slightly more formally, big-O notation characterizes functions according to the asymptotic upper bound of their performance growth rate. Functions that always perform a fixed number of steps (regardless of how long they actually take) are said to perform in *constant time* or *O(1) time*. Functions that perform a number of steps in direct proportion to the size of their input are said to take *linear time* or *O(n) time*.

Note that *inputs* in this context are not necessarily supplied to a function as arguments; they may be read from a database or some other resource pool.

The following are some of the most common classifications, shown in order from best (usually fastest) to worst (usually slowest). Note that the scale of each diagram is far less important than the rate of growth shown.

Constant, O(1)

If a function always performs in the same amount of time, regardless of input, it runs in *O(1)* time, as shown in Figure 6-1. This is not to say that a function that takes constant time will *always* take the *same* amount of time, but that the number of steps it performs (and hence the time it takes) will never grow beyond a constant maximum.

Here is an example:

```
int constantTime(int j, int k) {
    if ((j+k) % 2 == 0)
        return 0;
    int m = j * k;
    int n = m - 42;
    return Math.Max(n,0);
}
```

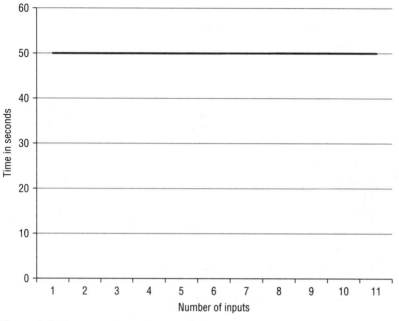

Figure 6-1: Constant time

Logarithmic, O(log n)

Functions that take logarithmic time are usually not much slower than those that take constant time, as illustrated in Figure 6-2. A binary search takes time *O(log n)*, as do most functions that eliminate half of the input at each stage of processing.

Linear, O(n)

If a function will always take time in direct proportion to the size of its input then it is said to take time *O(n)*, as shown in Figure 6-3. Here is an example:

```
int linearTime(int j, int k) {
    if ((j+k) % 2 == 0)
        return 0;
    int m = j * k;
    int n = m - 42;

    for (int index = 0; index < (m + n); index++)
        if (index % 1337 == 0)
            return index;

    return Math.Max(n,0);
}
```

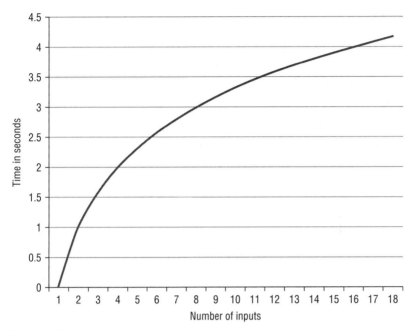

Figure 6-2: Logarithmic time

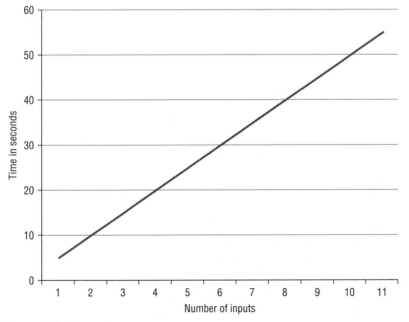

Figure 6-3: Linear time

Quadratic, O(n²)

Functions that take quadratic time generally contain two nested loops over the input, as shown in Figure 6-4 and in the following code example:

```
int quadraticTime(int[] n) {

    int result = 0;
    for (int i = 0; i < n.Length; i++)
        for (int j = 0; j < n.Length; j++)
            result += n[i] + n[j];

    return result;
}
```

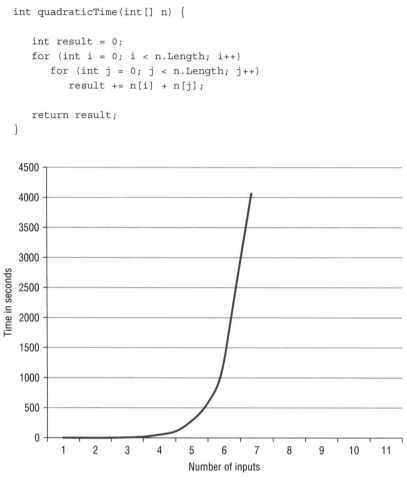

Figure 6-4: Quadratic time

Using big-O

Big-*O* notation is useful when comparing the theoretical performance of alternative functions. It abstracts away the practical difficulties of comparing performance and it intentionally ignores the fixed overhead of a function. For example, it ignores the time a function might require to initialize a hash table prior to processing its input. Big-*O* focuses squarely on the most significant factor that will affect the performance of a function and effectively ignores the rest.

When considering the practical implications of time complexity, you must be familiar with the range of inputs a function will called upon to process. Sometimes the case, usually when inputs are small, is that the big-O classification of two functions suggests relative performance that is contrary to the actual, measured performance. This is counterintuitive and might seem wrong, but consider the performance of two functions, as shown in Figure 6-5.

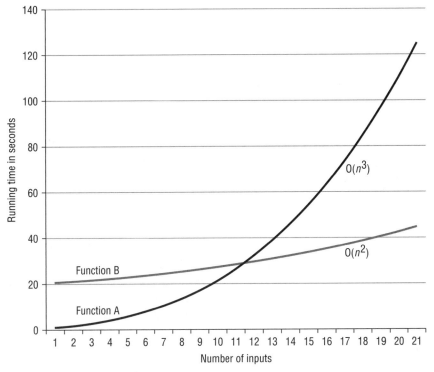

Figure 6-5: Function performance

Function A takes time $O(n^3)$, which is theoretically slower than function B, which takes time $O(n^2)$. As you can see, for small values of n, function A is faster, the opposite of what their big-O classifications would suggest.

Measure performance

The most common reason for measuring the performance of a function or procedure is so it can be optimized. If you don't have a measurement, then you won't know (except perhaps theoretically) whether your "improvement" is an optimization or a pessimization.

NOTE   A pessimization is the opposite of an optimization. "I see Nigel has pessimized the search algorithm."

Wherever possible, you should use CPU time and measures of I/O rather than elapsed (wall-clock) time. CPU time is the time spent by the processor in serving your code, and excludes time spent waiting for I/O operations and other delays caused by the operating system as it multitasks. Measuring a function by timing it with a watch on your wrist is the least sophisticated and most error-prone way of timing a function, and should be done only as a last resort.

Consider context

When considering the real-world performance of a function, context is everything. Will your function be called exactly once per day, or millions of times per hour? What are the typical scenarios that will lead to your function's being called? Will users be waiting for it to finish, or will it be a background process with no dependencies? You want to avoid the embarrassment of benchmarking a function on your machine, declaring it fit for purpose, and then releasing it, only to find everything grinds to a halt and your users have formed an angry mob.

Have a goal

The optimization of a function must be done with a goal in mind. Before you begin measuring and tweaking a function, you must determine exactly what will constitute acceptable performance. Optimization can be fun in a nerdy kind of way, but you won't want to be doing it forever. You need to know the point at which you have finished. If you don't know how to determine performance targets then you should involve your users. Ask them how quickly they expect operations to run, what benchmarks they have (such as other, comparable systems they've used), and so on.

Measure more than once, take an average

When measuring, you should run a function many times and derive an average run time. If you run a function and measure its performance just once then you have only a tiny glimpse of how the function might perform. More often than not you will find that measurements vary, sometimes markedly, depending on what else is running on the machine at the time. By taking many measurements and calculating an average you reduce the significance of these variations.

Divide and conquer

When users report a performance problem, it is usually not obvious where the bottleneck lies. They might complain about the time it takes to produce a monthly report, but you won't know from that complaint whether the performance problem lies in the report itself, or the back-end database, the network, and so on. The problem might be a combination of all these layers.

As a rule, you should first partition the problem and measure each of these partitions in isolation. Sometimes this involves writing a *test harness* to break the interdependence of components and run each part in isolation.

After you see where the majority of time is being spent, you can progressively drill down until you have something concrete that you can improve.

Try the easy things first

Quite often, performance problems are due to something obvious being missed. Does the table have appropriate indexes? Does an unnecessary dependency exist that can be eliminated? Is the server simply overloaded?

Before getting down to any detailed analysis, consider the obvious potential problems. You can resolve many apparently difficult problems by fixing the environment (the server, database, and so on) rather than the code.

Use a profiler

Developers today are fortunate to have many excellent tools available for profiling an application to home-in on performance bottlenecks. It was once the case that the best a developer could do was to introduce logging code and then somehow analyze the log for clues.

Today, a good profiler will let the developer evaluate the performance profile of an application without introducing any logging code. A profiler can show the programmer details of how memory is allocated in an application, and how much time is spent in the parts of the application. It can show object creation and (hopefully) object destruction (if not, you could have a memory leak).

Understanding What "Modular" Means

I recall the first time I was asked to review some code written by another programmer. The most serious problem I noticed was that the programmer had written one enormous subroutine—it must have been many hundreds of lines. At the time I was relatively inexperienced, but I knew this practice wasn't good. I suggested to the programmer that he (it was a he) should break the long subroutine into smaller, more modular subroutines. I assumed he knew what I was talking about.

He didn't.

He had broken the large subroutine into smaller subroutines, but he did it like this:

```
public void mysubroutine() {

    // about 40 lines of code...
```

```
    mysubroutine1();

}

public void mysubroutine1() {

    // 40 more lines of code...

    mysubroutine2();

}

public void mysubroutine2() {

    // 40 more lines of code...

    mysubroutine3();

}

public void mysubroutine3() {

    // 40 more lines of code...

}
```

I remember asking why he had broken the subroutines into chunks of about 40 lines each. He said that was the most he could see on his screen at one time. To my shame, I gave up at that point.

Although this story was, I hope, a rare and unusual take on what "modular" means, it does illustrate the point that programmers don't necessarily understand what modular means.

Here are some characteristics of a modular design:

- Functions and subroutines are small rather than big.
- Each function has a single, specific purpose.
- Functions can be reused in a number of ways.
- Functions are well-named so that the purpose of each one is obvious.
- Functions have little or no side-effects outside the function.
- Functions make little or no assumptions about the state of a system in which they are run.

Note that I've used the word *function* to describe these attributes, but they apply equally to methods, classes, and code libraries.

Understanding the SOLID principles

SOLID is an acronym that stands for five widely accepted principles of object-oriented programming and design. These principles are:

- Single Responsibility Principle
- Open/Closed Principle
- Liskov Substitution Principle
- Interface Segregation Principle
- Dependency Inversion Principle

> **NOTE**   Robert "Uncle Bob" Martin is acknowledged as the first person to iden-
> tify the SOLID principles, although the SOLID acronym was later introduced by
> Michael Feathers.

A recurring theme throughout the SOLID principles is the avoidance of dependencies. It makes intuitive, practical, and theoretical sense to minimize class dependencies: the more things you depend on, the greater the chance something will go wrong.

Single Responsibility Principle

The Single Responsibility Principle (SRP) states that a class should have exactly one responsibility. It should have exactly one reason (or one class of reasons) that cause it to be changed. If you have ever tried to modify a tangled mass of code in which tangential concerns have been mixed up together, where a seemingly innocuous change has unexpected and disastrous consequences, then you might have been a victim of code that ignores this principle.

To illustrate the point, a violation of this principle might look like this:

```
var myReport = new CashflowReport();

formatReportHeader(myReport);

printReport(myReport);

void formatReportHeader(Report report) {

    report.Header.Bold = true;
```

```
    if (report is CashflowReport && report.Content.Profit < 10000) {
        SendAlertToCEO("Profit warning!");
    }

}
```

All well and good—until the CEO asks for the report header to be reset to the default format, without any bold bits. The maintenance programmer (maintenance programmers are usually harassed and short of time) looks at the first few lines of code, and because it appears to be well-structured she innocently deletes the line that calls formatReportHeader. The code now looks like this:

```
var myReport = new CashflowReport();

printReport(myReport);

void formatReportHeader(Report report) {

    report.Header.Bold = true;

    if (report is CashflowReport && report.Content.BankBalance < 1000) {
        SendAlertToCEO("Profit warning!");
    }

}
```

Testing confirms that the report header is no longer emboldened, so the modified system is released to the customer. In this disastrous scenario, warnings about a low bank balance are no longer sent to the CEO and the business quickly becomes insolvent.

I've provided an over-simplified and artificial example that illustrates the point. In real projects it won't be anywhere near as obvious that a small change in one area of the system might affect an unrelated but critical feature in an unrelated part of the system. It isn't hard to see why some programmers develop superstitions about the systems they maintain. *Don't touch the Frobbit module. The last programmer who changed it was blamed for the extinction of pink-frilled lizards.*

Another difficulty many programmers have with following the SRP lies in deciding what *single responsibility* means. This definition can be hard to pin down. You can take a broad view that a single responsibility refers to a group of related business processes (such as invoicing, for example) or you can take a stricter view that invoicing is far too broad and should be broken down in its constituent parts, with each part designated as a responsibility. How far you go depends on your stamina and tolerance. Cross-cutting concerns also muddy the water: Is it consistent with SRP to call logging routines from an invoicing class? (No it isn't, but everyone does it.)

Like many principles, the theory is easier to grasp than the practice. In practice, you must rely on experience and common sense. You really shouldn't remove all your logging from a class, that would be counterproductive, but you really do want to avoid mixing up code for formatting a report with code for enforcing business logic.

Open/Closed Principle

The Open/Closed Principle (OCP) states that a class (or function) should be open for extension but closed for modification. This principle attempts to counter the tendency for object-oriented code to become fragile or easily broken, when base classes are modified in ways that break the behavior of inheriting (child) classes.

It hasn't escaped my attention that one of the key benefits touted for object-oriented programming is the ease with which you can change an entire inheritance chain through modification of the base class. If all your animals (textbook examples of inheritance for some reason seem to favor animals) are to be endowed with a new "panic" behavior, for instance, then you simply add a `panic` method to the base `Animal` class. All animals can now `panic`, even the ones that carry towels and that should therefore be immune to this kind of emotional distress.

> **NOTE** For a better understanding of the towel reference, see: `http://en.wikipedia.org/wiki/Technology_in_The_Hitchhiker%27s_Guide_to_the_Galaxy#Towels`

In a nutshell, adhering to the OCP means that when adding new behavior you should leave base classes alone and instead create new, inheriting classes, adding behavior to these instead of the base class, and thereby avoiding the problem of unintended consequences for classes that inherit from the same base class.

Liskov Substitution Principle

One of the nice things about inheriting from a class is that you can pass this new class to an existing function that has been written to work with the base class, and that function will perform its work just as if you had passed an instance of the base class.

The Liskov Substitution Principle (LSP) is intended to keep that happy working relationship between classes and functions alive and well.

The LSP is similar to the Open/Closed Principle. Both the OCP and the LCP imply that you should avoid modifying the behavior of a base class, but the LSP forbids modification of that behavior through the mechanism of inheritance. LSP states that if type S inherits from type T then both T and S should be interchangeable in functions that expect T.

In other words, if you follow the LSP, you should be free to substitute a child class in a function that expects to deal with the base class. If you can't, you're looking at a violation of the LSP.

But wait! Doesn't this principle undermine one of the key benefits of object-oriented programming? Isn't it a feature of object-oriented programming that you can modify the behavior of a class through inheritance?

Indeed it is. However, experience tells us that changing the behavior of a class in many cases leads to problems elsewhere in a code base. It is another example of how you should strive to minimize dependencies of all kinds in the interest of writing robust and maintainable software.

In many cases, instead of inheritance, programmers should create classes that are *composed* of base classes. In other words, if the programmer wants to use the methods or properties of a class, she can create an instance of that class rather than inheriting from it. By avoiding inheritance, the programmer also avoids violation of the LSP. Functions that expect to deal with a certain base class are guaranteed to remain unaffected by the new class, and the code base of an application is therefore more robust and less likely to break.

In C#, you can prevent the inheritance of a class by using the `sealed` keyword. In Java, you can use the `final` keyword.

Interface Segregation Principle

The Interface Segregation Principle (ISP) is very simple. It says to avoid writing monstrous interfaces that burden classes with responsibilities they don't need or want. You should instead create a collection of smaller, discrete interfaces, partitioning interface members according to what they concern. Classes can then pick and choose what they implement rather than having to swallow all or nothing.

Here is one of these monstrous interfaces:

```
public interface IOneInterfaceToRuleThemAll {
    void DoThis();
    void DoThat();
    void GoHere();
    void GoThere();
    bool MyFavoriteTogglyThing {get; set;}
    string FirstName {get; set;}
    string LastName {get; set;}
}
```

Here is a nicer alternative; a collection of interfaces that segregate different areas of concern:

```
public interface IActionable {
    void DoThis();
    void DoThat();
}
public interface IMovable {
```

```
    void GoHere();
    void GoThere();
}
public interface IToggly {
    bool MyFavoriteTogglyThing {get; set;}
}
public interface INamed {
    string FirstName {get; set;};
    string LastName {get; set;}
}
```

Nothing prevents the programmer from creating a class that implements all of these interfaces, but with smaller interfaces the programmer is free to implement just those parts she needs, ignoring the irrelevant parts. The programmer can now create one class that moves and toggles, and another class that performs actions and has a name.

Dependency Inversion Principle

The Dependency Inversion Principle (DIP) says to "depend upon abstractions, not upon concretions." Somewhat surprisingly it turns out that "concretions" is in fact a real word (I checked). What this principle means is that instead of writing code that refers to actual classes, you should instead write code that refers to interfaces or perhaps abstract classes.

This is consistent with writing code that has minimal dependencies. If class *A* instantiates concrete class *B*, then these two classes are now bound together. If instead of a concrete class you rely on an interface *IB*, then the concrete class that implements *IB* can (in theory) be switched out for a different class through *dependency injection*.

In the following code, class *A* has a dependency on class *B*:

```
class B
{
    // ...
}

class A
{
    public void DoSomething()
    {
        B b = new B(); // A now depends on B
    }
}
```

Here is the same code, rewritten to depend on an interface *IB* rather than the concrete class *B*:

```
interface IB
{
```

```
    // ...
}
class B : IB
{
    // ...
}
class AlternativeB : IB
{
    // ...
}

class A
{
    public void DoSomething(IB b)
    {
        // b can be either B or AlternativeB
    }
}
```

Incidentally, but very conveniently, now that you are free to substitute any class you choose, it becomes trivial to substitute fake or mock classes when writing unit tests, avoiding the overhead of classes that aren't needed for the sake of the test.

A whole class of tools exists for introducing dependency injection to legacy code. If programmers writing this legacy code had created dependencies on interfaces rather than on concrete classes, we wouldn't need these tools.

Avoiding Code Duplication

A respected software architect of my acquaintance once told me—I'm sure it was tongue in cheek—that a valid form of code reuse is to copy and paste code throughout a code project. I probably gave him the reaction he was expecting; I'm easily excited on this topic.

Code reuse, for the record, is achieved through writing code that is modular and suitably generic. It is not achieved through copy and paste. Copy and paste means code duplication, one of the nastier problems you can face as a programmer.

Why is it so awful? It's awful because it injects latent problems into your code project. You won't find them at compile time, and you won't find them through initial testing. The code will work at first, but now you have a bear-trap, set with jaws agape, waiting for the maintenance programmer.

Have you ever fixed a bug in an application only to find that the exact same bug exists in many places other than the one you fixed? That's code duplication in action. To the user it makes you appear careless or dim-witted.

Here's an example related to the adjustment of meeting times:

```
if (start.Hour == 8)
    PostponeOneHour (start);

if (start.Hour == 6)
    PostponeFiveHours (start);

void PostponeOneHour (DateTime start) {

    var time = new TimeSpan(1,0,0);
    start.Add(time);

    // Further delay meetings that start before ten-past
    if (start.Minute <= 10) {
        time = new TimeSpan(0,5,0);
        start.Add(time);
    }
}

void PostponeFiveHours (DateTime start) {

    var time = new TimeSpan(5,0,0);
    start.Add(time);

    // Further delay meetings that start before ten-past
    if (start.Minute <= 10) {
        time = new TimeSpan(0,5,0);
        start.Add(time);
    }
}
```

In this example I've invented some dubious business rules for when meetings should start; meetings scheduled for 8 a.m. should be delayed at least one hour, and meetings scheduled for 6 a.m. should be delayed at least five hours (the delay for early birds is suitably punitive). Meetings should be further delayed by some minutes if they start in the first 10 minutes past the hour.

Code duplication is rife in this example, but the most glaring duplication is of the two nearly identical methods: one that adds five hours and another that adds one hour. These two methods could easily be combined into one:

```
void Postpone (DateTime start, int delayHours) {

    var time = new TimeSpan(delayHours,0,0);
    start.Add(time);

    // Further delay meetings that start before ten-past
    if (start.Minute <= 10) {
```

```
    time = new TimeSpan(0,5,0);
    start.Add(time);
    }
}
```

If you permit duplication like this you commit yourself (and all future main-tenance programmers) to duplicating their efforts. Instead of fixing a bug or adding a feature in one method, now everyone must fix that bug or add that feature in two methods. Not only have you made yourself more work, you now have twice the opportunity to make a mistake.

Suppose you decided that the rule about not starting before ten-past should be removed. You delete the relevant lines of code from the `PostponeOneHour` method, and also from the `PostponeFiveHours` method—if you remember it exists! If you don't remember, you've just sprung the trap.

Imagine these methods are contained within a much larger code base than shown in this example, and you glimpse the potential scale of the problem. In a large code base it is just a matter of time before a maintenance programmer forgets or doesn't realize that this logic has been implemented in two places. Inevitably you will have inconsistency, and you will have users who think their programmers are lazy or feeble-minded.

QUESTIONS

Code quality is one of the more difficult things to detect with automated code review tools. You can find some things, sure, but the best code-review tool I know of is the gaze of a skilled programmer.

Cast your gaze over the sample code in these questions, and see what you think could be improved:

1. **True, False, FileNotFound**

   This C# enumeration has gained some notoriety on the Internet, but what is wrong with it?

   ```
   enum Bool
   {
       True,
       False,
       FileNotFound
   };
   ```

2. **Inheritance**

   Here is a simple example of inheritance in C#. If you take the class names at face value then what, if anything, is wrong with this code?

   ```
   public class Person : PersonCollection
   {
   ```

```
    // [Class definition removed...]
}
```

3. Non-zero values

Is this a good way to check two variables for non-zero values? Can the code be improved?

```
if (new[] { height, width }.Any(c => c != 0))
{
    // Do something with the non-zero value(s) ...
}
```

4. Strange loop

Here's a strange loop. What is it trying to do, and how could you make it clearer?

```
for ( int i=0 ; i < MyControl.TabPages.Count ; i++ )
{
    MyControl.TabPages.Remove (MyControl.TabPages[i] );
    i--;
}
```

5. Expressive code

The following code is an excerpt from a function that is supposed to execute a given subroutine upon detecting a certain condition. If the subroutine was executed, then the next check should be performed a day later; otherwise, the next check should be performed after just six hours have elapsed.

How could you modify this code to be more expressive? What potential maintenance problems could be caused by the code as written?

```
if (conditionExists()) {

    doSomething();

    myTimer.Interval = 86400000;

} else {

    myTimer.Interval = 21600000;

}

myTimer.Start();
```

6. Time complexity of array lookup

What is the time complexity of this function?

```
bool getAnswerLength(int questionId) {
```

```
    return ( (string[]) answers[questionId]).Length;

}
```

7. Time Complexity of array traversal

What is the time complexity of this function?

```
bool stringArraysAreEqual(string[] a, string[] b) {

    if (a.Length != b.Length) return false;

    for (int i = 0; i < a.Length; i++)
        if (!a[i].Equals(b[i])) return false;

    return true;

}
```

8. Optimizing

The following function has been identified as performing poorly. What do you notice about the function that might interfere with efforts to optimize it?

```
bool function ReticulateSplines(List<Splines> splines) {

    foreach (var spline in splines) {

        var length = EvaluateLength(spline.Length);

        if (length > 42) {

            var page = RetrievePageFromPublicInternet(spline.WebPage);

            if (page.RetrievedOk)
                Reticulate(spline, page);

        }

        Reticulate(spline)

    }

    return false;
}
```

9. Parsing

Critique this code snippet. Assume that the variable `ds` is an ADO.Net `DataSet`.

```
if (
    long.TryParse(ds.Tables[0].Rows[0][0].ToString(), out committeId)
    )
{
    committeId = long.Parse(ds.Tables[0].Rows[0][0].ToString());
}
```

10. Boolean expression

Critique this code snippet:

```
if (this.Month == 12)
{
    return true;
}
else
{
    return false;
}
```

11. Code duplication

The following PL/SQL appears to contain two blocks of very similar code. Suggest how you might avoid this duplication.

```
IF P_TYPE IS NOT NULL THEN

    SELECT MEM.BODY_ID AS BODYID,
    MEM.BODY_NAME AS BODYNAME,
    AD.ONE_LINE_ADDRESS AS ONELINEADDRESS,
    AD.TELEPHONE AS TELEPHONE,
    MEM.ACTIVE AS ACTIVE
    FROM
    MEM_BODY MEM, BODY_ADDRESS_DETAIL AD
    WHERE MEM.BODY_ID = AD.BODY_ID(+)
    AND
    MEM.BODY_TYPE LIKE UPPER(P_TYPE) || '%')
    ORDER BY BODYNAME;

ELSE

    SELECT MEM.BODY_ID AS BODYID,
```

```
      MEM.BODY_NAME AS BODYNAME,
      AD.ONE_LINE_ADDRESS AS ONELINEADDRESS,
      AD.TELEPHONE AS TELEPHONE,
      MEM.ACTIVE AS ACTIVE
      FROM
      MEM_BODY MEM, BODY_ADDRESS_DETAIL AD
      WHERE MEM.BODY_ID = AD.BODY_ID(+)
      ORDER BY BODYNAME;

END IF;
```

12. Rambling code

How could you improve this long, rambling, snippet of code?

```
if (length == 1)
{
    return 455;
}
else if (depth == 2)
{
    return 177;
}
else if (depth == 3)
{
    return 957;
}
else if (depth == 4)
{
    return 626;
}
else if (depth == 5)
{
    return 595;
} else if (depth == 6)
{
    return 728;
}
```

13. Unique characters

Write a function that will count the number of unique characters in a string. Optimize the function for clarity.

14. Swiss Army enumeration

Critique this enumeration with reference to the SOLID principles.

```
public enum SwissArmyEnum
{
```

```
        Create,
        Read,
        Update,
        Delete,
        Firstname,
        Lastname,
        Dateofbirth,
        Statusok,
        Statuserror,
        Statusfilenotfound,
        Small,
        Medium,
        Large
}
```

15. Odd function

What is this function trying to do, and how could you write it more clearly?

```
public bool StrangeFunction(int n)
{
    for (int i = 0; i <= 13; i++)
    {
        if ((i == 1) || (i == 3) || (i == 5)
            || (i == 5) || (i == 7) || (i == 9)
            || (i == 11))
        {
            return true;
        }
    }
    return false;
}
```

16. Overlapping dates

Write a function that returns `true` if two given date ranges overlap. Make this function as clear and concise as possible.

Assume that each date range is an `IDateRange` as per the following definition:

```
public interface IDateRange
{
    DateTime? Start { get; set; }
    DateTime? End { get; set; }
}
```

ANSWERS

1. True, False, FileNotFound

This C# enumeration has gained some notoriety on the Internet, but what is wrong with it?

```
enum Bool
{
    True,
    False,
    FileNotFound
};
```

It might surprise you that this code actually compiles without any warnings. At first glance it looks like it attempts to redefine several C# reserved words: `Bool`, `True`, and `False`. In fact, C# reserves `bool`, `true`, and `false` (all lowercase) and this code compiles just fine.

The real problem lies in the confusion of thought that led to this code, and the consequent burden it will place on the maintenance programmer—not to mention the burden carried by the original programmer.

First, why would anyone want to mimic a built-in type, especially one as fundamental as Boolean? This appears to be a poorly reinvented wheel.

Second, if the intention was to create an enumeration that mimics the built-in Boolean type, which by definition has two possible values (`true` and `false`) then it makes no logical sense to add a third value of `FileNotFound`. Note that C# supports a nullable Boolean `bool?`, which in addition to `true` and `false` allows the possibility of null, meaning "the value is unknown." This is quite different to the strange inclusion of "file not found."

Third, any reasonable scenario in which you might imagine `FileNotFound` is a valid member of the enumeration will lead you directly to the conclusion that `Bool` is a poor choice of name. It tells you nothing useful about the enumerated set of values and in fact appears to be quite misleading. Should it be called `FileStatus`? It's unclear. Either the enumeration is a set of Boolean values, or it isn't. If it is not Boolean then it should be called something else. If it is Boolean then `FileNotFound` does not belong in the list.

2. Inheritance

Here is a simple example of inheritance in C#. If you take the class names at face value then what, if anything, is wrong with this code?

```
public class Person : PersonCollection
{
    // [Class definition removed...]
}
```

The question instructs you to take the class names at face value, so you should assume that the `Person` class represents a person and the `PersonCollection` class represents a collection of persons. You don't have enough information to decide what kind of collection this might be; it could be an arbitrary list of people, a membership list, and so on.

Does it make sense for `Person` to inherit from `PersonCollection`? No, it really doesn't. What possible sense could be made of a singular object inheriting the properties and methods of a collection of the same object?

Suppose you questioned the author of this code and the explanation was simply, "I needed to use some of the methods of the `Collection` class in the `Person` class." If that were the case it would have been better to factor out the common methods into a new class that both `Person` and `PersonCollection` could reference. Setting up an inheritance relationship between classes purely for the sake of making methods available to inheriting classes is poor design and should trigger alarm bells at code review.

To brush up on object-oriented programming look at Chapter 6 in Part II, which covers the fundamentals.

3. Non-zero values

Is this a good way to check two variables for non-zero values? Can the code be improved?

```
if (new[] { height, width }.Any(c => c != 0))
{
    // Do something with the non-zero value(s) ...
}
```

Consider what this code is doing. First, an anonymous type is being created:

```
if (new[] { height, width }.Any(c => c != 0))
```

Next, the LINQ `Any()` method determines whether any of the properties of this newly created object are non-zero:

```
if (new[] { height, width }.Any(c => c != 0))
```

So in effect, each variable is in turn tested to see whether it is non-zero. If any variable is non-zero then the conditional code block is executed:

```
if (new[] { height, width }.Any(c => c != 0))
{
    // Do something with the non-zero value(s) ...
}
```

How else could this be written?

If you think of the most straightforward way to test the value of a variable you could write this test of two variables as follows:

```
if (height != 0 || width != 0)
{
    // Do something with the non-zero value(s) ...
}
```

Is this better? Yes! It is simpler, easier to understand, and therefore easier to maintain. Even if you are familiar with anonymous types and LINQ you will spend a longer time understanding the original version of this code than the second, simpler version.

You might imagine that this code was written to make it easy to add more variables to the list of "things to check for non-zero values." I doubt that was the motivation. It looks like a result of over-enthusiasm for fancy language features. Also consider that if there were more than a few variables involved it would be more appropriate (i.e., more extensible, easier to understand) to use a collection of variables rather than individual variables, so even then this would still not be the best approach.

4. **Strange loop**

   Here's a strange loop. What is it trying to do, and how could you make it clearer?

   ```
   for ( int i=0 ; i < MyControl.TabPages.Count ; i++ )
   {
       MyControl.TabPages.Remove (MyControl.TabPages[i] );
       i--;
   }
   ```

The first thing you should notice about this loop is that the index variable i is modified inside the loop. If you think back to when you first learned about for loops, you might remember that the hardest thing to get right was the correct handling of the loop index variable.

The reason the loop index variable is relatively tricky to understand and get right is because you need to understand the flow of the loop—exactly when the loop index will be initialized, the value it will have within the loop block during the first iteration, the second iteration and so on—all the way through to the final iteration. You need to understand when the loop will exit according to the conditional expression. You also need to know at which point the loop index variable will be modified.

If you modify the loop variable within the body of the loop you make it much harder to understand the flow of the loop.

"Don't monkey with the loop index"

—Steve McConnell, Code Complete 2

These days you almost never need this kind of loop because most languages, including C# and Java, have language constructs that iterate over collections without the need for an index variable. For example, C# has foreach:

```
foreach (var t in MyControl.TabPages)
{
    // ...
}
```

Back to the question of what the loop is trying to do. This is actually quite hard to figure out without tracing the loop for collections of different sizes. You might guess that it removes one element, or some elements, or all elements. In fact, it removes all elements of the collection, leaving the collection empty. It does this by keeping the loop index variable at zero until all items in the collection are removed. It's unusual, but it works.

Knowing this, you can now think of how you might improve the code. If you stay with a loop you could try a simple "loop until all tab pages are removed" construct.

```
while(MyControl.TabPages.Count > 0)
{
```

```
    MyControl.TabPages.Remove(MyControl.TabPages[0]);
}
```

This works, but you could make it even simpler:

```
while(MyControl.TabPages.Count > 0)
{
    MyControl.TabPages.RemoveAt(0);
}
```

And simpler still:

```
MyControl.TabPages.Clear();
```

Most collections have a `Clear()` method. If not, then you should write one. The intention of this single line of code is clear and unmistakable; therefore, this is the best solution.

5. **Expressive code**

   The following code is an excerpt from a function that is supposed to execute a given subroutine upon detecting a certain condition. If the subroutine was executed then the next check should be performed a day later; otherwise, the next check should be performed after just six hours have elapsed.

   How could you modify this code to be more expressive? What potential maintenance problems could be caused by the code as written?

```
if (conditionExists()) {

    doSomething();

    myTimer.Interval = 86400000;

} else {

    myTimer.Interval = 21600000;

}

myTimer.Start();
```

   The obvious first answer is simply to add some code comments explaining why you have used these particular numbers. So you might have

```
myTimer.Interval = 86400000; // 24 hours, in milliseconds
```

   and

```
myTimer.Interval = 21600000; // 6 hours, in milliseconds
```

Although this looks to be a big improvement—it certainly makes it clear what those numbers mean—it also introduces another potential problem.

Suppose you added these comments and then some time later it was decided that the six-hour delay should be just four hours? You calculate that four hours is equal to 14,400,000 milliseconds and so you end up with

```
myTimer.Interval = 14400000; // 6 hours, in milliseconds
```

Notice the problem I just introduced? The code will correctly delay for 4 hours but I forgot to update the code comment! The next person to look at this code might notice that 6 hours is not 14,400,000 milliseconds, or—much more likely—he might not notice. If he needs to add a six-hour delay elsewhere in code he might even copy this buggy line (or just the buggy number) without bothering to check. If he realizes he has inherited this buggy line of code he won't be very thankful. The possibility exists that this buggy line could cause a problem for you while you are still working on it.

If the value of this delay is to be frequently adjusted, then you could store it in a configuration file along with a suitable user interface for editing it.

Obviously, the programmer who changed the interval from six hours to four hours should have been more careful and updated the code comment, but something even more powerful could have been done, something that would greatly improve this code.

First, notice that although the code comment is supposed to be helpful, it actually isn't. Because the same thing is being expressed in code as well as in the comment it is technically a form of code duplication. Adding such a comment obliges all future programmers to make a change in two places rather than just one. It also introduces the possibility of an inconsistency between the code and the comment, which is exactly what happened in this example.

So if code comments, which at first looked like a good idea, are actually introducing a potentially more serious problem, what else can you do?

Think about the context of this question. You're trying to improve the code by making it more expressive. Another option, instead of code comments, is to replace the numbers with some well-named constants.

You might rewrite the code as

```
const int FOUR_HOURS_IN_MS        = 14400000;
const int SIX_HOURS_IN_MS         = 21600000;
const int TWENTYFOUR_HOURS_IN_MS = 86400000;

if (conditionExists()) {

    doSomething();

    myTimer.Interval = TWENTYFOUR_HOURS_IN_MS;

} else {

    myTimer.Interval = FOUR_HOURS_IN_MS;

}
```

This is a vast improvement over adding comments. You've avoided code duplication and the risk that your code might become inconsistent. The intention is now crystal clear—you've even managed to make it clear that these values are in milliseconds, avoiding the problem of someone mistakenly assuming the values are seconds rather than milliseconds.

Notice that in making this code clearer, you've sacrificed brevity. You added some code and now there is more to read. The principle of being succinct took second place to the principle of being clear.

Whenever you are forced to choose between brevity and clarity, clarity should always win.

You could make one more potential improvement to this code. Those numbers are still somewhat inscrutable. You can double-check them easily enough with a calculator or with some mental arithmetic but here's a thought—why not let the compiler do the hours-to-milliseconds calculation while you make our intentions even clearer?

```
const int FOUR_HOURS_IN_MS        = 4 * 60 * 60 * 1000;
const int SIX_HOURS_IN_MS         = 6 * 60 * 60 * 1000;
const int TWENTYFOUR_HOURS_IN_MS = 24 * 60 * 60 * 1000;
```

This doesn't cost you anything at runtime because the compiler will perform the calculation and generate the same code as if you had written the calculated results for each constant. By explicitly showing each part of the calculation you can see where the numbers came from, and mistakes are more likely to be noticed.

You can eliminate one more aspect of duplication, and at the same time make your const definitions even more useful—by adding a "unit" of one hour in milliseconds:

```
const int ONE_HOUR_IN_MS        = 60 * 60 * 1000;
```

Now you can base other constants on this "unit."

```
const int FOUR_HOURS_IN_MS       = 4  * ONE_HOUR_IN_MS;
const int SIX_HOURS_IN_MS        = 6  * ONE_HOUR_IN_MS;
const int TWENTYFOUR_HOURS_IN_MS = 24 * ONE_HOUR_IN_MS;
```

Now that the code has been rewritten to make it expressive, anyone who misinterprets or manages to break it just isn't paying attention. Notice that in keeping with the principle of brevity you can now dispense with some of the const definitions while still retaining clarity. Here's the final version:

```
const int ONE_HOUR_IN_MS = 60 * 60 * 1000; // 60 min * 60 sec

if (conditionExists()) {

    doSomething();

    myTimer.Interval = 24 * ONE_HOUR_IN_MS;

} else {

    myTimer.Interval = 4 * ONE_HOUR_IN_MS;

}

myTimer.Start();
```

6. Time complexity of array lookup

What is the time complexity of this function?

```
bool getAnswerLength(int questionId) {

    return ( (string[]) answers[questionId]).Length;

}
```

This function executes in *O(1)* time, or constant time.

This function simply performs a collection lookup using questionId as the key. It doesn't matter what value of questionId is supplied to this function because it will always take up to a fixed and constant limit of time to look up and return the answer (or to throw an exception if the key is not found).

7. **Time complexity of array traversal**

What is the time complexity of this function?

```
bool stringArraysAreEqual(string[] a, string[] b) {

    if (a.Length != b.Length) return false;

    for (int i = 0; i < a.Length; i++)
        if (!a[i].Equals(b[i])) return false;

    return true;

}
```

This function has running time of $O(n)$.

After checking that both arrays have the same length this function iterates over each item in the first array and compares it to the corresponding item in the second array. If any items are different it immediately returns false. Finally, because the arrays are identical in all the ways that matter to the author of this function (though other differences might exist between the arrays), it returns true.

In the fastest case this function will terminate as soon as it discovers that the arrays have different lengths. Also you can reasonably expect that in many cases, this function will return false without iterating over all items in the first array. These cases don't change the performance classification of this function, which is based on the worst-case performance—which increases linearly depending of the length of the arrays.

In general, a function that iterates once through its input will have a running time of $O(n)$.

8. **Optimizing**

The following function has been identified as performing poorly. What do you notice about the function that might interfere with efforts to optimize it?

```
bool function ReticulateSplines(List<Splines> splines) {

    foreach (var spline in splines) {

        var length = EvaluateLength(spline.Length);

        if (length > 42) {
```

```
    var page = RetrievePageFromPublicInternet(spline.WebPage);

    if (page.RetrievedOk)
        Reticulate(spline, page);

}

    Reticulate(spline)

}

    return false;
}
```

In the worst case, a call to retrieve a `page` (presumably a web page) will be made for every `spline` given as input to this function. The timing of this function will depend on how long it takes to retrieve these web pages from the Internet, and this might vary enormously depending on factors outside the control of the programmer. For example, the programmer will not be able to control the response time of the site serving the requested page.

To optimize this function it will be necessary to eliminate this variable so that consistent measurements can be taken and so that the rest of the function can be evaluated. One way of achieving this is to write a "fake" `RetrievePageFromPublicInternet` method that returns a static page without using the public Internet (or any network at all).

The size of the `page` returned from this method is also a factor. The programmer must consider how this method performs for the range of possible sizes that it might retrieve, which might include some extremely large pages. Measurements must be taken for a representative sample of `page` sizes.

Finally, it isn't clear from the question exactly what the `Reticulate` function does. It might be the case that this function also involves a call to retrieve information from the Internet, in which case you would need to treat it similarly.

9. **Parsing**

Critique this code snippet. Assume that the variable `ds` *is an* ADO.Net *DataSet.*

```
if (
    long.TryParse(ds.Tables[0].Rows[0][0].ToString(), out committeId)
    )
{
    committeId = long.Parse(ds.Tables[0].Rows[0][0].ToString());
}
```

This code attempts to parse a `long` value from the first column in a row of a table. The first line checks whether a `long` can be parsed, and if so it then (in the third line) parses the value and stores it in variable `committeId`.

A few things are wrong with this snippet.

Probably most importantly, this code relies on the fact that the `Tables` property of the `DataSet` does contain at least one table, and that the table does contain at least one row, and that the row does contain at least one column. You might assume that the code to check these preconditions has been omitted from the code snippet, but at face value this code risks throwing a `NullReferenceException` at run time.

Another problem is that the third line is completely redundant. It is executed only if the expression in the first line evaluates to `true`. The only way this expression will evaluate to `true` is if the attempt to parse a `long` succeeds. If the parse succeeds, the `long` value is stored in `committeId`. Then, if the parse succeeds, the third line redundantly parses the `long` and redundantly stores the value in `committeId`. It is perhaps also an error that the programmer does not handle the case of `TryParse` returning `false`, which leaves `committeId` undefined.

To make this code more readable, the programmer might have used constants in place of hard-coded references to the table and column indexes. So, for example, instead of `ds.Tables[0].Rows[0][0]` the programmer might have written

`ds.Tables[INVOICE_TABLE].Rows[0][COMMITTE_ID].`

Alternatively the programmer could have used the actual name (as a string) instead of integers or even constants. Both of these options would be better than the uninformative index reference `[0]`.

Finally, it looks like "committee" has been spelled incorrectly in the variable `committeId`.

10. Boolean expression

Critique this code snippet:

```
if (this.Month == 12)
{
    return true;
}
else
{
    return false;
}
```

There are two things that could be improved. First, the hard-coded number 12 could be replaced with a more meaningful constant or enum. You can reasonably assume that 12 refers to calendar month, in which case instead of

```
if (this.Month == 12)
```

you could write

```
if (this.Month == DECEMBER)
```

Of course, this assumption would need to be confirmed—it could be a financial year, or the Month property might be zero-based (that is, in the range 0–11) in which case the value 12 would be invalid.

Another issue is that this snippet is seven lines longer than it needs to be. Ignoring exceptions, this expression will always return either true or false. If the expression evaluates to true then it will return true. If it evaluates to false it will return false. Do you see where I'm heading with this?

Instead of evaluating the expression to a Boolean, wrapping it with an if-else construct, and returning a Boolean value that is the same as the expression, you can simply return the expression itself.

So rather than:

```
if (this.Month == 12)
{
    return true;
}
else
{
    return false;
}
```

you can simply write

```
return (this.Month == 12);
```

11. **Code duplication**

The following PL/SQL appears to contain two blocks of very similar code. Suggest how you might avoid this duplication.

```
IF P_TYPE IS NOT NULL THEN

    SELECT MEM.BODY_ID AS BODYID,
    MEM.BODY_NAME AS BODYNAME,
    AD.ONE_LINE_ADDRESS AS ONELINEADDRESS,
    AD.TELEPHONE AS TELEPHONE,
    MEM.ACTIVE AS ACTIVE
```

```
    FROM
    MEM_BODY MEM, BODY_ADDRESS_DETAIL AD
    WHERE MEM.BODY_ID = AD.BODY_ID(+)
    AND
    MEM.BODY_TYPE LIKE UPPER(P_TYPE) || '%')
    ORDER BY BODYNAME;

ELSE

    SELECT MEM.BODY_ID AS BODYID,
    MEM.BODY_NAME AS BODYNAME,
    AD.ONE_LINE_ADDRESS AS ONELINEADDRESS,
    AD.TELEPHONE AS TELEPHONE,
    MEM.ACTIVE AS ACTIVE
    FROM
    MEM_BODY MEM, BODY_ADDRESS_DETAIL AD
    WHERE MEM.BODY_ID = AD.BODY_ID(+)
    ORDER BY BODYNAME;

END IF;
```

This code snippet has two very similar SELECT statements separated
by an IF-THEN-ELSE construct. If you look closely you can confirm
they are identical except for the additional expression in the WHERE
clause, highlighted as follows:

```
IF P_TYPE IS NOT NULL THEN

    SELECT MEM.BODY_ID AS BODYID,
    MEM.BODY_NAME AS BODYNAME,
    AD.ONE_LINE_ADDRESS AS ONELINEADDRESS,
    AD.TELEPHONE AS TELEPHONE,
    MEM.ACTIVE AS ACTIVE
    FROM
    MEM_BODY MEM, BODY_ADDRESS_DETAIL AD
    WHERE MEM.BODY_ID = AD.BODY_ID(+)
    AND
    MEM.BODY_TYPE LIKE UPPER(P_TYPE) || '%')
    ORDER BY BODYNAME;

ELSE

    SELECT MEM.BODY_ID AS BODYID,
    MEM.BODY_NAME AS BODYNAME,
    AD.ONE_LINE_ADDRESS AS ONELINEADDRESS,
    AD.TELEPHONE AS TELEPHONE,
    MEM.ACTIVE AS ACTIVE
    FROM
    MEM_BODY MEM, BODY_ADDRESS_DETAIL AD
    WHERE MEM.BODY_ID = AD.BODY_ID(+)
    ORDER BY BODYNAME;

END IF;
```

How could you rewrite this to avoid code duplication? The simplest solution might be to incorporate the IF-THEN-ELSE construct into the WHERE clause as follows:

```
SELECT MEM.BODY_ID AS BODYID,
MEM.BODY_NAME AS BODYNAME,
AD.ONE_LINE_ADDRESS AS ONELINEADDRESS,
AD.TELEPHONE AS TELEPHONE,
MEM.ACTIVE AS ACTIVE
FROM
MEM_BODY MEM, BODY_ADDRESS_DETAIL AD
WHERE MEM.BODY_ID = AD.BODY_ID(+)
AND
(P_TYPE IS NULL OR MEM.BODY_TYPE LIKE UPPER(P_TYPE) || '%'))
ORDER BY BODYNAME;
```

With this simple change, you have halved the amount of code, reducing your maintenance burden, and eliminated the future possibility of inconsistent code modifications.

12. **Rambling code**

    How could you improve this long, rambling, snippet of code?

```
if (length == 1)
{
    return 455;
}
else if (depth == 2)
{
    return 177;
}
else if (depth == 3)
{
    return 957;
}
else if (depth == 4)
{
    return 626;
}
else if (depth == 5)
{
    return 595;
} else if (depth == 6)
{
    return 728;
}
```

This snippet has a collection of Boolean expressions that result in an apparently random number being returned should one of them evaluate to true.

The key to identifying an improved version of this code is to consider what it is trying to do. It is returning an integer based on a key. Is there a data structure that could be used to store these keys and values?

Yes, you should use a hash table, or even better, a dictionary of integer values with integer keys:

```
var lookupTable = new Dictionary<int,int>();
lookupTable.Add(1, 455);
lookupTable.Add(2, 177);
lookupTable.Add(3, 957);
lookupTable.Add(4, 626);
lookupTable.Add(5, 595);
lookupTable.Add(6, 595);
```

Now, thanks to your dictionary, you can condense this code …

```
if (length == 1)
{
    return 455;
}
else if (depth == 2)
{
    return 177;
}
else if (depth == 3)
{
    return 957;
}
else if (depth == 4)
{
    return 626;
}
else if (depth == 5)
{
    return 595;
} else if (depth == 6)
{
    return 728;
}
```

…to a single line:

```
return lookupTable[length];
```

The revised code is shorter, more readable, and much easier to maintain than the original.

Consider this kind of alternative whenever you see a long list of `if-then-else` statements.

13. **Unique characters**

   Write a function that will count the number of unique characters in a string. Optimize the function for clarity.

   This problem isn't hard; the challenge is to write the clearest implementation.

   If you start with a naïve, loop-based approach you might have something like this:

```
public int countDistinctChars(string input)
{
    // *This is not the ideal solution*

    // Obtain the number of unique characters
    // in a string by looping over the input,
    // looking at each character in turn.
    //    If we have seen it before then ignore it,
    //    otherwise add it to our derived string
    //
    // Once we have finished, the length of the
    // derived string equals the number of unique
    // characters in the input string.

    string distinctChars = string.Empty;

    for (int i = 0; i <= input.Length; i++)
        if (distinctChars.IndexOf(input[i]) < 0)
            distinctChars += input[i];

    // The number of characters in our derived string equals
    // the number of unique characters in the input string
    return distinctChars.Length;
}
```

   This code is fairly clear. On the positive side, it contains helpful code comments to explain the algorithm.

   On the negative side, it doesn't work. In fact, it throws an `IndexOutOfRangeException` due to the loop continuation expression containing a less-than-or-equal operator (`<=`) when it should be a less-than operator (`<`).

   I made a deliberate mistake in that code, but I could easily have made the same mistake by accident. An alternative construct sidesteps the risk: the `foreach` statement. Also, why use an inefficient `string` to accumulate unique characters when you could use a `List<char>`?

Here's version two of the same function:

```
static int countDistinctChars2(string input)
{
    List<char> distinctChars = new List<char>();

    foreach (char c in input)
        if (!distinctChars.Contains(c))
            distinctChars.Add(c);

    return distinctChars.Count();

}
```

I've removed the comments from my first attempt. The function is now small enough that I don't need them. They add bulk and in this case I've made the judgment that the code is clearer without them.

Importantly, you can see that the code has been made clearer by adopting a data structure that is better suited to my purposes. I can take this improvement one more step. All I care about are unique characters in the string, and I don't care about the order in which I store these characters. Which data structure is good for storing unsorted unique values? A hashset!

14. **Swiss Army enumeration**

Critique this enumeration with reference to the SOLID principles.

```
public enum SwissArmyEnum
{
    Create,
    Read,
    Update,
    Delete,
    Firstname,
    Lastname,
    Dateofbirth,
    Statusok,
    Statuserror,
    Statusfilenotfound,
    Small,
    Medium,
    Large
}
```

This enumeration appears to contain values from several different domains. This is violation of the "S" in SOLID, the *single responsibility principle*, which requires that a class (or in this case an enum) should have exactly one reason to change. This enum should be broken down into several domain-specific enumerations.

```
public enum CRUD
{
    Create,
    Read,
    Update,
    Delete
}
public enum PersonAttributes
{
    Firstname,
    Lastname,
    Dateofbirth,
}
public enum Status
{
    Ok,
    Error,
    Filenotfound
}
public enum Sizes
{
    Small,
    Medium,
    Large
}
```

15. Odd function

What is this function trying to do, and how could you write it more clearly?

```
public bool StrangeFunction(int n)
{
    for (int i = 0; i <= 13; i++)
    {
        if ((i == 1) || (i == 3) || (i == 5)
            || (i == 5) || (i == 7) || (i == 9)
            || (i == 11))
        {
            return true;
        }
    }
    return false;
}
```

One can't be sure of the motivation for writing this strange function, but it's not hard to see what it does. It returns `true` if a number is less than 13 and odd; otherwise, it returns `false`.

A universally applicable method for testing whether a number is odd or even is to use the modulus operator:

```
bool isOdd = (n % 2 != 0);
```

So you could rewrite this function as follows:

```
bool IsOddAndLessThan13(int n)
{
    return (n < 13 && n % 2 != 0);
}
```

If you were concerned with maximizing code reuse, you could factor out the test for oddness from the test for "less than 13," which is far less likely to be a common requirement, leaving you with

```
bool IsOdd(int n)
{
    return (n % 2 != 0);
}
```

16. Overlapping dates

Write a function that returns true *if two given date ranges overlap. Make this function as clear and concise as possible.*

Assume that each date range is an IDateRange *as per the following definition:*

```
public interface IDateRange
{
    DateTime? Start { get; set; }
    DateTime? End { get; set; }
}
```

This problem comes up surprisingly often in the development of line-of-business software. It is a deceptively hard problem, not because the code is complicated (it isn't) but because pinning down the logic of this function without a clear mental model of the possible scenarios is tricky.

You can simplify the problem by making an assumption that the two given dates are not null. The question did not specify whether these dates could be null, but because checking for nulls is easy you can add this after you have a working function.

Also assume that in each date range, the start date of the range is earlier than the end date. Again, you can make this assumption to simplify the problem and then add assertions or code later when you have a working solution.

Drawing a diagram of all the possible scenarios results in something like Figure 6-6.

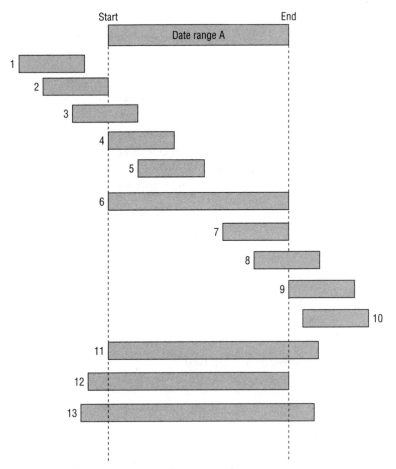

Figure 6-6: Date range comparison scenarios

You can see that 13 possible scenarios exist. You could start writing code to cover each scenario; for instance:

```
if (B.Start < A.Start && B.End < A.Start) {
    return false; // Case 1, no overlap
}
if (B.Start < A.Start && B.End == A.Start) {
    return true; // Case 2, overlap
}
if (B.Start < A.Start && B.End > A.Start && B.End < A.End) {
    return true; // Case 3, overlap
```

```
    }
    if (B.Start == A.Start && B.End > A.Start && B.End < A.End) {
        return true; // Case 4, no overlap
    }
    // and so on, etc...
```

This approach works, but it is not very clear or concise and is unlikely to impress an interviewer.

If you study Figure 6-6 carefully you can see exactly two cases where the dates do not overlap; case 1 (which is entirely before the start of A) and case 10 (which is entirely after the end of A). Because all the other cases *do* overlap date range A then you can greatly simplify the problem by writing logic that detects either of these two cases, returning `false` (no overlap) if either is found, and otherwise concluding that the ranges do overlap and returning `true`.

To test for the first case, you can check that the end of B is earlier than (or equal to) the start of A:

```
(B.End <= A.Start)
```

Similarly, you can check that the start of B is later than (or equal to) the end of A:

```
(B.Start >= A.End)
```

Putting these together you have:

```
if (B.End <= A.Start || B.Start >= A.End) {
    return false; // dates do not overlap
} else {
    return true; // dates overlap
}
```

Or even more simply (but less clear):

```
    return !(B.End <= A.Start || B.Start >= A.End);
```

Now that you have a functioning solution you can return to the question of `null`s. This example assumed that `null`s would not make an appearance, but what if they did? You can't ignore `null`s in that case, or you risk `null` the dreaded `NullReferenceException`.

NOTE   `DateTime`? in .NET is actually a non-nullable value type, but the following example uses the nullable `DateTime`?.

Assume you should interpret a `null` start date as meaning "the beginning of time" and similarly interpret a `null` end date as "the end of time." So a date range of (1/1/2012, null) would be interpreted as "the first day of 2012 until the end of time." A date range of (null, 1/1/2012) would be interpreted as "all of time up to the first day of 2012." A date range of (null, null) would be interpreted as "all of time." The latest version of .NET does not provide constants for the beginning or the end of time, so you have to be content with `DateTime.MinValue` and `DateTime.MaxValue`.

```
DateTime? AStart = A.Start ?? DateTime.MinDate;
DateTime? AEnd = A.End ?? DateTime.MaxDate;
DateTime? BStart = B.Start ?? DateTime.MinDate;
DateTime? BEnd = B.End ?? DateTime.MaxDate;

return !(BEnd <= AStart || BStart >= AEnd);
```

In production code, you would also need to ensure that the start date is earlier than the end date for each range.

The Usual Suspects

Every programmer will eventually face a bug that defies their attempts at fixing it. The bug might seem impossible to reproduce, or it might show up only occasionally on a remote customer's machine. Some bugs are so difficult and time consuming to investigate that living with them can be cheaper than trying to fix them. On the other end of the scale, some bugs are so costly that no option exists but to fix them. Struggling with hard bugs is such an important programming experience that I am skeptical of any programmer who claims to be an expert, but who cannot tell at least one or two bug-fixing horror stories.

Here is one of my horror stories: I was asked to help a team who had been struggling for about a week with an elusive bug. This bug had a particularly high profile because it involved the loss of data in a system that managed the personal information of children and families. The team could not reproduce the problem despite daily reports of data loss.

Compounding the difficulty, the support team was given access to the problematic customer database for only a few hours daily and only after obtaining written authorization from the client each day. There was also uncertainty about which version of the database was being used by the customer. All the stored procedures, functions, and views in the database (hundreds of them) were encrypted and the database had no proper version information so the support team was forced to guess or experiment to find out which version of each object was deployed in the database.

We eventually fixed the bug after two stressful weeks of investigating. It turned out the problem was not just one bug but at least three related bugs, on top of which several serious design problems existed. The worst three issues were:

- A database-update race condition that meant some records were assigned incorrect index keys; in some cases this meant that family members were being associated with the wrong families
- A confusing and misleading user interface that allowed users to delete data without realizing they had done so
- A buggy diagnostic subroutine that sent the team on several time-wasting wild goose chases

The buggy system was a victim of its own success. It had never been tested at the scale in which these bugs occurred.

Experiences like this are shared daily by programmers around the world. They are unpleasant while you suffer through them, but from them we learn invaluable lessons. If a new programmer goes to a skilled programmer for help, the first question the skilled programmer will ask is likely to be *have you checked the usual suspects?*

This chapter is all about some of these *usual suspects,* including issues related to concurrency, poor design, and various bad habits that lead to buggy code.

Concurrent Programming

Many complicated problems stem from a common scenario: Software that was written for and tested by a single user, or perhaps a handful of users, is then expected without modification to support a far greater number of concurrent users. The application goes from being successful and stable to being bug-ridden and unstable, crashing and corrupting data like never before. As a simple demonstration of how programs can go from stable to unstable when threads are introduced, consider the following code:

```
static void Main()
{
    Step1();
    Step2();

    if (Debugger.IsAttached)
        Console.ReadLine();
}

static void Step1()
{
```

```
        for (int i = 200; i > 0; i--)
        {
            Console.Write("ONE");
            Thread.Sleep(random.Next(50));
        }
    }
    static void Step2()
    {
        for (int i = 200; i > 0; i--)
        {
            Console.Write("TWO");
            Thread.Sleep(random.Next(50));
        }
    }
}
```

When this program is run, it writes 100 instances of ONE to the output console, followed by 100 instances of TWO, shown in Figure 7-1:

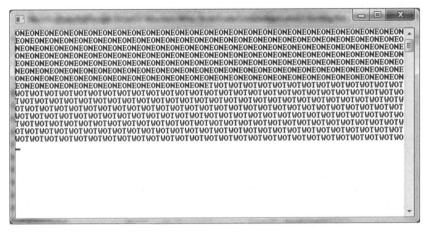

Figure 7-1: A predictable output

Technically, this program already has a thread because every Windows process creates at least one thread (the main thread) when it is run. The following code shows the addition of two more threads.

```
static void Main()
{
    new Thread(Step1).Start();
    new Thread(Step2).Start();
}
```

Immediately you can see a difference in the output from this program (see Figure 7-2). Predicting the output sequence of ONE and TWO is no longer easy, and the output is likely to be different every time this program is run.

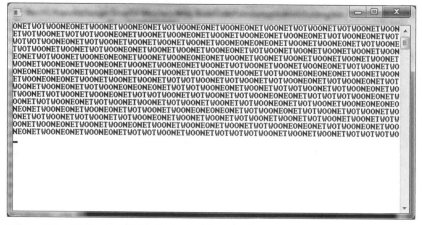

Figure 7-2: An unpredictable output with threads

Race conditions

A *race condition* occurs when two threads access a shared item of data at the same time. The outcome depends on a kind of race between these threads. Remember that all multitasking operating systems have the power to interrupt and switch threads at (almost) any point during their execution, and this means that a race condition can occur in even a single line of C# or Java code. (All high-level languages must be translated to native instructions before they can be run, so a single line of C# code might be translated to many instructions and the thread might be interrupted before all these instructions are completed.)

When two threads simultaneously attempt to access a shared item of data, both with the aim of updating and reading the value of the item, the outcome can be unpredictable. Consider the example of two threads attempting to deduct an amount of money from a bank balance. Depending on the exact timing of events, one of the threads might withdraw an amount that puts the account into overdraft, something that would be prevented if the balance were properly synchronized between threads.

Locks

All modern Relational Database Management Systems (RDBMSs) provide mechanisms for synchronizing access to data, and all modern programming languages provide mechanisms for synchronizing or serializing the execution of code sections. Some frameworks go even further and provide tools such as the .NET *Task Parallel Library* (*TPL*), which makes adding parallelism and concurrency to applications much easier for programmers. Whatever the level of support offered by the framework, a sound understanding of the fundamentals of programming for concurrency is very important, especially when things go wrong. One of the most fundamental tools for managing access to a shared item of data is the *lock*.

In a very real sense, obtaining a lock is like obtaining a unique token that gives you permission to perform an action or to access an item of data. While you hold that token, no other process has permission to perform that action or to access that data. They have to wait until you let go of the token, and then they have to obtain the token before they can proceed. If a lot of threads are competing to obtain a token, or if a thread is slow to release a lock, then an application might grind to a halt while each thread waits for its turn. From this simple observation it follows that threads should be written to release locks as quickly as possible to avoid causing a buildup of blocked threads. Similarly, locks should be used to protect only data that is genuinely shared between processes. Little point exists in protecting data that is at no risk of contention; indeed, indiscriminate locking is wasteful and adds unwanted complexity to a program.

The following is another example of how a simple program can go terribly wrong when concurrency is introduced. The goal of this contrived program is to withdraw small amounts of money from an initial balance of 100 until finally it attempts to withdraw more money than is available. At no point should the balance go overdrawn. The core class of this program is shown in the following code, a class named `BigSpender`:

```
public class BigSpender
{
    public decimal Balance = 100m;
    Random rand = new Random();

    public void spendAll()
    {
        while (withdraw((rand.Next(5, 11))));
    }

    bool withdraw(decimal amount)
    {
        if (Balance - amount < 0)
        {
            Console.WriteLine(string.Format(
                "Balance is {0}, unable to withdraw {1}",
                Balance, amount));
            return false;
        }

        Console.WriteLine(string.Format(
            "Balance is {0}, withdrawing {1}", Balance, amount));

        Balance -= amount;

        if (Balance < 0) // Can't happen! (famous last words)
```

```
Console.WriteLine(string.Format(
    "Balance is {0}, this should never happen...",
    Balance));

return true;
}

}
```

You can test this class with the following code:

```
var b = new BigSpender();
b.spendAll();

if (b.Balance < 0)
    throw new OverdrawnException();
```

Running this test shows a nice orderly sequence of spending, as shown in Figure 7-3.

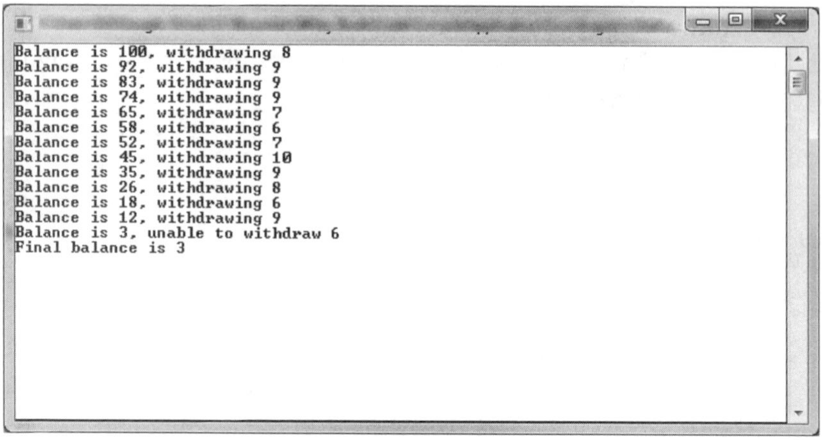

Figure 7-3: Orderly spending, no errors

Notice how the `withdraw` method in the `BigSpender` class checks that the `Balance` is sufficient for the amount to be withdrawn. In a single-threaded program this method will always work. In a multi-threaded program it will sometimes work, but will fail more often than not. Let's make a naïve switch to using threads for withdrawals and see what happens.

```
public void spendAllWithThreads()
{
    for (int i = 0; i < 5; i++)
        new Thread(spendAll).Start();
}
```

This program now has serious problems; see Figure 7-4 for an example of the ensuing mayhem.

```
Balance is 100, withdrawing 5
Balance is 100, withdrawing 7
Final balance is 100
Balance is 67, withdrawing 7
Balance is 60, withdrawing 10
Balance is 50, withdrawing 10
Balance is 40, withdrawing 5
Balance is 35, withdrawing 7
Balance is 28, withdrawing 9
Balance is 19, withdrawing 9
Balance is 10, withdrawing 5
Balance is 5, unable to withdraw 7
Balance is 79, withdrawing 9
Balance is -4, this should never happen...
Balance is 88, withdrawing 7
Balance is -11, this should never happen...
Balance is -11, unable to withdraw 10
Balance is 74, withdrawing 7
Balance is -18, this should never happen...
Balance is -18, unable to withdraw 9
Balance is -4, unable to withdraw 5
Balance is 88, withdrawing 9
Balance is -27, this should never happen...
Balance is -27, unable to withdraw 7
```

Figure 7-4: Disorderly spending

To understand what has happened, it is helpful to show the thread ID of each thread as it reports progress, as shown in Figure 7-5.

file:///C:/Users/Ed/Google Drive/CV Mountain/Wiley Book/Code/ConsoleApplication1/Locking/bin...

```
Thread 13: Balance is 100, withdrawing 9
Thread 13: Balance is 91, withdrawing 9
Thread 13: Balance is 82, withdrawing 10
Thread 12: Balance is 100, withdrawing 7
Thread 12: Balance is 65, withdrawing 5
Thread 12: Balance is 60, withdrawing 7
Thread 13: Balance is 72, withdrawing 9
Thread 13: Balance is 44, withdrawing 9
Thread 13: Balance is 35, withdrawing 9
Thread 13: Balance is 26, withdrawing 9
Thread 13: Balance is 17, withdrawing 8
Thread 13: Balance is 9, withdrawing 7
Thread 13: Balance is 2, unable to withdraw 9
Thread 14: Balance is 82, withdrawing 8
Thread 14: Balance is -6, this should never happen...
Thread 14: Balance is -6, unable to withdraw 5
Thread 11: Balance is 100, withdrawing 6
Thread 11: Balance is -12, this should never happen...
Thread 11: Balance is -12, unable to withdraw 9
Thread 12: Balance is 53, withdrawing 9
Thread 12: Balance is -21, this should never happen...
Thread 12: Balance is -21, unable to withdraw 8
Thread 15: Balance is -21, unable to withdraw 10
```

Figure 7-5: Which thread said that?

Figure 7-5 shows that the actions of each thread are interleaved in an unpredictable way. The full picture is still unknown, but it is clear that the shared variable Balance does not stay constant in the time between when a thread reads its value and when that same thread updates its value. Other threads are updating it at the same time and the balance is changing in an unpredictable way as each thread executes this section of code.

A simple (but again naïve) fix for this program would be to ensure that no other thread can change the value of Balance while a thread is operating on it. Blocking each thread until it can obtain a lock before allowing the thread to make a withdrawal at least ensures that threads do not run into conflict.

```
public void spendAll()
{
    lock(lockToken)
        while (withdraw((rand.Next(5, 11)))) ;
}
```

Unfortunately, this also means that all other threads are completely blocked until the first one has finished, which negates the benefit of having multiple threads. All threads must wait for the first one to finish, as shown in Figure 7-6.

```
file:///C:/Users/Ed/Google Drive/CV Mountain/Wiley Book/Code/ConsoleApplication1/Locking/bin...
Thread 12: Balance is 100, withdrawing 9
Thread 12: Balance is 91, withdrawing 8
Thread 12: Balance is 83, withdrawing 10
Thread 12: Balance is 73, withdrawing 10
Thread 12: Balance is 63, withdrawing 5
Thread 12: Balance is 58, withdrawing 5
Thread 12: Balance is 53, withdrawing 9
Thread 12: Balance is 44, withdrawing 7
Thread 12: Balance is 37, withdrawing 8
Thread 12: Balance is 29, withdrawing 9
Thread 12: Balance is 20, withdrawing 5
Thread 12: Balance is 15, withdrawing 5
Thread 12: Balance is 10, withdrawing 7
Thread 12: Balance is 3, unable to withdraw 5
Thread 13: Balance is 3, unable to withdraw 10
Thread 14: Balance is 3, unable to withdraw 5
Thread 15: Balance is 3, unable to withdraw 10
Thread 16: Balance is 3, unable to withdraw 7
```

Figure 7-6: Threads, form a queue!

A better locking strategy is to allow each thread to begin executing and lock just the section of code that depends on Balance remaining constant while it is being checked and then updated. You could wrap the relevant lines in the withdraw method in a lock as follows:

```
bool withdraw(decimal amount)
{
    lock (lockToken)
    {
        if (Balance - amount < 0)
        {
            WriteLineWithThreadId(string.Format(
```

```
            "Balance is {0}, unable to withdraw {1}",
            Balance, amount));
        return false;
    }

    WriteLineWithThreadId(string.Format(
        "Balance is {0}, withdrawing {1}",
        Balance, amount));

    Balance -= amount;

    if (Balance < 0) // Can't happen! (famous last words)
        WriteLineWithThreadId(string.Format(
            "Balance is {0}, this should never happen...",
            Balance));
    }
    return true;
}
```

In Figure 7-7 you can now see that the threads are all making progress concurrently, and without the chaos and unpredictability of the naïve first attempt.

```
Thread 10: Balance is 100, withdrawing 10
Thread 11: Balance is 90, withdrawing 9
Thread 12: Balance is 81, withdrawing 10
Thread 12: Balance is 71, withdrawing 7
Thread 12: Balance is 64, withdrawing 5
Thread 14: Balance is 59, withdrawing 9
Thread 14: Balance is 50, withdrawing 10
Thread 14: Balance is 40, withdrawing 5
Thread 14: Balance is 35, withdrawing 9
Thread 14: Balance is 26, withdrawing 8
Thread 14: Balance is 18, withdrawing 5
Thread 14: Balance is 13, withdrawing 10
Thread 14: Balance is 3, unable to withdraw 6
Thread 10: Balance is 3, unable to withdraw 10
Thread 11: Balance is 3, unable to withdraw 9
Thread 13: Balance is 3, unable to withdraw 5
Thread 12: Balance is 3, unable to withdraw 5
```

Figure 7-7: Multi-threaded spending

Deadlocks

A deadlock can occur when two locks (let's call these locks "X" and "Y") are required by a thread. A thread might obtain a lock on X, but before it can obtain lock on Y, suppose another thread has jumped in and locked Y and is now waiting for a lock on X. Because the first thread does not release X until it has Y and the second thread does not release Y until it has X, both threads are blocked until one of them terminates. This is a classic deadlock scenario.

You should be aware of the *Coffman conditions,* a list of conditions that are required for a deadlock to occur:

- *Mutual exclusion*: Lock resources are non-shareable, meaning that if a resource is held by a process then no other process may hold the same resource.

- *Hold and wait*: A thread holds on to a lock while waiting to acquire another.

- *No preemption*: A thread holding a lock cannot be forced to release it (for example, forced by another thread or by the operating system).

- *Circular wait*: For example, process A is waiting for a resource held by process B, while B is waiting for a resource held by C, and C is waiting for a resource held by A.

In practice and in programming frameworks such as .NET, the first three conditions listed in the preceding list are largely pre-determined; locks are not shareable, multiple locks are often required, and forcing processes to release their locks can be difficult and can lead to instability. Programmers tend to focus on the fourth condition, avoiding the *circular wait*. It turns out that circular waits can be avoided by following a simple rule: *When multiple locks are required they should always be acquired in a fixed order.* For example, if a process requires three locks A, B, and C then each process should first acquire a lock on A and only then lock on B, then C, and no process should start by locking on B or C. This makes intuitive sense because a fixed lock order prevents other processes from first locking on B or C and therefore prevents a circular wait-graph from forming.

Livelocks

One of the many strategies devised for avoiding deadlock is as follows. If a thread cannot obtain all the locks it requires then it releases all the locks it has so far obtained and then waits for a fixed amount of time before trying again. This strategy works to prevent a deadlock, but it can lead to a *livelock*.

If you've ever performed an awkward corridor dance with someone, hopping from side to side to let them pass while they do the same, then you have experienced a form of livelock.

In a livelock, doomed threads that try and fail to obtain a lock will clash again and again at fixed intervals, forever trying and failing to obtain the locks they need. Sometimes a livelock can be worse than a deadlock, especially if threads consume CPU and RAM while they thrash about.

An obvious refinement to the basic wait-and-retry approach is to instruct each thread to wait for a random interval before retrying lock acquisition. This reduces the chance of repeated conflict at the cost of time spent waiting beyond the minimum necessary.

Relational Databases

In recent times a great deal of effort has been invested in the idea that a database should be either a place to store data (and nothing more) or it should be a distributed, "web-scale" and "eventually consistent" collection of key-value pairs stored in the cloud. *Object-relational mapping* (ORM) techniques have been developed to enable programmers to perform *CRUD* (*create, read, update, delete*) operations almost entirely without reference to a database of the traditional (relational) kind, and the rise in popularity of NoSQL has seen the term *relational database* become almost a synonym for regressive thinking in some circles. Advocates against relational databases point to the needless overhead for certain kinds of applications while advocates for relational databases point out that modern alternatives lack proper support for important features such as *declarative referential integrity* (*DRI*). The truth is probably somewhere in between.

The thoughtful programmer will know why he chose one database platform over another, and will understand the trade-offs of his decision. Sometimes, persisting objects without the overhead of a full-blown database can be expedient but sometimes taking advantage of RDBMS features such as DRI and server-based query performance is much more important.

All programmers should understand the principles of relational databases if only so they can discern where RDBMS is a good fit.

Another important point to remember is that the glamorous advances in new technologies do not always reflect the reality of programmers working in typical corporate and "enterprise" programming environments. In these environments programmers will need expertise in Oracle or SQL Server much more often than they will need expertise in MongoDB, Redis, Memcached, and the like. Core enterprise systems tend to run on traditional RDBMSs, and that, for better or for worse, is where the majority of programmers will find employment throughout their careers.

Database design

One entire class of difficult problems arises from poor database design. If your application stores data in one enormous multi-valued table, or if you have two tables that are so similar that each is consistently mistaken for the other, then you have a database design problem. If you find your code is riddled with clauses to handle strange edge cases, or if your code deals with nothing but "edge cases" (meaning they probably aren't edge cases) then you have a design problem.

Many design issues are avoided by following the rules of normalization. They really do work, and if you've been avoiding them with the idea that they are old-fashioned or work against agile development (they don't) then I strongly encourage you to take another look.

Normalization

Database normalization is the process of ensuring that a database design (by which I mean the tables, the columns within those tables, and the declared relationships between the tables) adhere to a set of rules. By adhering to these rules your design will be flexible (easily adaptable), and you will avoid or minimize redundancy, which in turn reduces or eliminates the possibility of inconsistencies in your data.

It is often said of formal normalization that a sensible and conformant database design can be obtained more easily by using simple common sense. Some truth exists in this, though I believe the common sense of an experienced database designer, one fully versed in normalization theory, will be more reliable and produce better results than the common sense of an inexperienced designer.

The rules of normalization in themselves are not too difficult to grasp, and I present an informal summary of them next. Normalization aside, choosing between alternative designs can be much more difficult when they all appear to be equally robust and flexible. Choosing a design from a number of valid alternatives can sometimes be helped by a short period of testing each design, and a good way to test a design is to write code that builds on top of it. If a team is divided into opposing camps over a design, then having each side set the other a time-limited coding challenge to prove or disprove the perceived difficulties can be helpful. If the new design is intended to replace a legacy system, or if it is a major upgrade to an existing system, then a data-migration exercise might be even more enlightening. Ultimately, if a decision cannot be reached by consensus then the team leader must decide.

First normal form: "No repeated values"

An informal definition of *first normal form* (1NF) is that each attribute in a row should contain no more than one value. You shouldn't, for instance, store more than one telephone number against the "home number" attribute in a "person" table. If you ever see a value with commas (or other separation characters) then you are probably looking at a violation of 1NF.

Sometimes this rule is not quite so easy to interpret; for example, an attribute called name (used to store a person's name) could be used to store all parts of a person's name, such as the name "Inigo Montoya." It could be argued that this violates 1NF because two names—"Inigo" and "Montoya"—are stored in the one attribute. Indeed, most databases would have at least two attributes for a person's name: first name and last name. The question of whether or not this violates 1NF tends to be academic, because in most systems searching for a person by surname will be necessary, which makes it necessary to store surname as a distinct field. This requirement has nothing to do with normalization, and yet it clearly forces a design that splits "name" into at least two parts in the database. Quite often the case is that a database follows the rules of 1NF for reasons that are unrelated to normalization.

Second normal form: "No partial dependencies"

For a table to be in *second normal form* (2NF) it must first be in 1NF.

If you take a look at the attributes of the table, sometimes you will notice that a few of those attributes, when combined, could be used as a unique identifier for each row. For example, you might notice that a combination of `employee number`, `department`, and `start date` might serve to uniquely identify rows in a `job history` table. Those three attributes are therefore a *candidate composite key*.

If the table doesn't have a candidate composite key, the table is deemed to be in 2NF and you need look no further. Note that there may be more than one candidate composite key in a table. Also note that a candidate composite key could potentially be used as the *primary key* for the table, although by far the most common preference is to use *surrogate keys* instead of these *natural keys*.

If the table in question has a candidate composite key then you need to ask another question: Does every other non-key attribute in the table depend on the whole of that key? If not, then the table is not in 2NF.

For example, if the job history table has an attribute of `emergency contact name` then this clearly depends on `employee number` but does not depend in any way on the department in which that employee works or their start date within that department (the other parts of the composite key). This is a *partial dependency*, and it violates 2NF. You can make this table comply with 2NF by moving the `emergency contact` name attribute to another table; for instance, you could move it to the employee table and link to it via a *foreign key*.

Third normal form: "No transitive dependencies"

For a table to be in *third normal form* (3NF), it must first be in 2NF.

Suppose in addition to `emergency contact name` in the "employee history" table you also have `emergency contact number`. This contact number depends on `emergency contact name`, but it does not directly depend on the employee. This is a *transitive dependency*, and if you have any of these in a table, the table violates 3NF. To resolve this violation you would move both `emergency contact name` and `emergency contact number` to a new table, linking to this new table via a new foreign key in the employee history table.

Boyce-Codd normal form

Boyce-Codd normal form (BCNF) is very similar to 3NF, so much so that it is sometimes referred to as *3.5NF*.

The difference between 3NF and BCNF is that although 3NF is a rule about non-key attributes, BCNF is a rule for all attributes in the table regardless of whether they form part of a candidate key.

Beyond BCNF

In practice normalizing to BCNF is usually sufficient because the effort of checking each table against the more esoteric normal forms usually outweighs the benefit obtained. It is unlikely that you will be quizzed on the more advanced normal forms during an interview.

Denormalization

Some situations exist in which designing a database without following all the rules of normalization is perfectly acceptable. One of the most obvious exceptions is when the primary purpose of the database is to serve as a read-only repository of information, such as for a *data warehouse* or an *online analytical processing (OLAP)* application. If a database is read-only no chance exists of update anomalies occurring, and deliberate redundancy can be useful when (for instance) calculated values need not be recalculated every time they are requested. In these cases a denormalized database can perform better than the normalized equivalent.

One of the key benefits (if not the key benefit) of database normalization is data integrity. If a database is properly normalized then the RDBMS will prevent update anomalies, orphaned rows, and other kinds of inconsistency. It will protect the data no matter what happens at the application level. It therefore follows that considering denormalization is valid when data integrity is not the highest priority.

Normalization is not necessarily an all-or-nothing affair. You can have a fully normalized database with some extra, denormalized tables for the sake of a specific performance requirement. Ideally, you would partition these tables in a way that future programmers would be aware of the denormalization, the intentional redundancy, and thereby avoid update potential anomalies and inconsistencies associated with the denormalization.

Populating a normalized database

When a database is being developed or first populated with data, normalization—or more generally, *database constraints*—can get in the way. You might be working on a function to handle data in a table, but because the table is related in some way to other tables, you find yourself dealing with those tables as well. You might find that some of the database constraints prevent you from populating the table with data in order to write or test code to handle certain edge cases. If the related tables are simple lookup tables, you should consider populating those first; but if the situation is more complicated, you might consider *temporarily* disabling database constraints during development—provided, of course, you enable these constraints for testing long before the product is staged for release. Never be tempted to permanently abandon database constraints for the sake of development expediency. It will come back to bite you in the form of corrupted data and endless bug-hunting.

Pointers

When I was a young programmer, a wise old programmer with a luxuriant beard told me that programmers either understand pointers right away or they will never truly understand them. If you know in advance that your interviewer has a beard then you might expect to read or write some tricky pointer code during their interview. Be warned: Even beardless interviewers have been known to test candidates along the lines of "decipher this pointer code." For the record, I don't think that bearded programmer was right; I think you can come to understand pointers just fine even if you don't get them at first.

Pointers are usually associated with C and C++, and every programmer will benefit from understanding the basic syntax in these languages. Apart from anything else, programmers who understand pointers usually have broader and deeper knowledge and experience than those who don't. I'm not suggesting you study up on pointers in order to fake it at the interview—other programmers can smell fakery. Think of this section as a checklist of things you should already know. If you find that you don't understand some or all of the following notes then you probably need to study up. Start by testing yourself with the C-specific questions later in this chapter.

Let's start with a definition: A *pointer* is a variable that contains the address of another variable. Consider the representation of a pointer in Figure 7-8. This is a pointer ptr that contains the address of variable i. In other words ptr *points to* i.

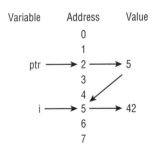

Figure 7-8: A pointer

In the C language, a pointer is declared and used as follows:

```
int *ptr;   // A pointer to an integer
ptr = malloc(10);   // Allocate some memory and store the address in ptr
```

All C compilers disregard insignificant whitespace, so the following declarations are equivalent:

```
int *ptr;
int* ptr;
int * ptr;
int*ptr;
int     *     ptr;
```

Notice that assigning p like this is a mistake:

```
int *ptr;
*ptr = malloc(10);   // oops!
```

The problem with this assignment is that it attempts to store the address returned from malloc into the location that is "pointed at" by ptr. Because ptr has not yet been initialized with an address, this doesn't work. Assigning a value to a pointer is the same as any other variable:

```
ptr = malloc(10);
```

You can obtain the address of a variable with the ampersand operator.

```
// set ptr to contain the address of i
ptr = &i;
```

You can assign a value to a variable by using its address instead of assigning the value directly.

```
int *ptr;
int i;

i = 100;

// get the address of i into ptr
ptr = &i;

// this sets the value of i to 99
*ptr = 99;

printf("The value of i is %d\n",i);
```

So far, I've shown only pointers to integers, but you can have pointers to other types including chars and structs. You can point to other pointers and you can even point to functions. There is also the untyped pointer `void *`, which can point to anything.

Functions in C receive arguments by value

Functions in C and C++ accept arguments by value. When a function is called with an argument it receives a copy of the original variable. If the function modifies this local copy it has no effect on the original variable.

```
void tryTomodifyArgument(int i) {

    // this doesn't work as expected

    i = 99;  // modifies local copy only
}

void main() {

    int i = 100;

    printf("i = %d\n",i);  // 100

    tryTomodifyArgument(i);  // does not modify

        printf("i = %d\n",i);  // still 100

}
```

To modify a variable in a function, it must be passed by reference. In C this is done by passing a pointer to the variable.

```
void tryTomodifyArgument(int *i) {

    *i = 99;  // modifies original by dereferencing the pointer
}

void main() {

    int i = 100;

    printf("i = %d\n",i);  // 100

    tryTomodifyArgument(&i);  // modifies by passing pointer to i

    printf("i = %d\n",i);  // now 99

}
```

Arrays in C are handled like pointers

C compilers handle array references as if they were pointers. They aren't quite the same, but when you reference an array the compiler generally interprets the reference as if you had explicitly used the ampersand operator to obtain the address of the variable. The following two `printf` lines both print the same thing: the address of array variable `myArray`.

```
int myArray[10];
printf("myArray = %p\n",(void*) myArray);
printf("&myArray = %p\n",(void*) &myArray);
```

One subtle difference exists between *myArray* and *&myArray*. Both are interpreted as a pointer, but the first is a pointer to an integer whereas the second is interpreted as a pointer to an array of 10 integers. This can sometimes cause confusion (and compiler warnings) when a function expects a pointer to an array of integers and is given a pointer to an integer (or vice versa). The following code generates a compiler warning:

```
/* This code generates a compiler warning
      expected 'int *' but argument is of type 'int (*)[10]'
*/
void handleArray(int * theArray) {
    // do something with the array pointer…

}

void main() {
    int myArray[10];

    handleArray(&myArray);
}
```

Another "gotcha" occurs when an array is passed as an argument to a function. The compiler interprets the argument as a pointer to an integer rather than an array (or a pointer to an array of integers) and reports the size of an `int`, always 4 bytes.

```
int sizeOfArray(int a[10])
{
    return sizeof(a);
}

void main() {
```

```
int myArray[10];

/* Each int in this array is 4 bytes, so the
   size of this array is 4 * 10 = 40 */
printf("sizeof(myArray) = %d\n",sizeof(myArray));   // 40

/* However .. the function does not receive the array,
   it receives a pointer to an int, which is 4 bytes */
printf("sizeOfArray(myArray) = %d\n",sizeOfArray(myArray));   // 4

}
```

Passing values and references

In the section on pointers I noted that functions in C receive their arguments by value. It is the same in .NET and Java. When an object is passed to a method, the method receives an object reference, but by default—and somewhat confusingly—*the object reference itself is passed by value.* That might seem counterintuitive because you probably know that when you pass an object to a method in .NET and Java you are, indeed, able to modify the properties of the original object. What you can't modify is the object reference; you can't replace it with another object, for instance. What you have is effectively a copy of the reference. It is the same as receiving a pointer in C—you can change the value that the pointer "points at," but you can't replace the value of the pointer itself. An example will make this concept clearer.

```
namespace ValuesAndReferences
{
    class Program
    {
        static void Main()
        {
            int newValue = 100;

            Foo foo1 = new Foo();
            foo1.Bar = newValue;
            CheckItWorked(newValue, foo1);

            // We can change a property of Foo in a method
            newValue = 99;
            replaceFooProperty(foo1,newValue);
            CheckItWorked(newValue, foo1);

            // But we can't replace the object itself - this will fail
```

```
            newValue = 98;
            replaceFoo(fool, newValue); // Fails!
            CheckItWorked(newValue, fool);

            // ...unless we pass the object as an explicit
            // reference using the ref keyword

            newValue = 97;
            replaceFoo(ref fool, newValue);
            CheckItWorked(newValue, fool);

            Console.ReadLine();
        }

        private static void CheckItWorked(int newValue, Foo foo)
        {
            Console.WriteLine(string.Format(
                "Attempt to change foo.Bar to {0} {1}",
                newValue, newValue == foo.Bar
                    ? "succeeded" : "**FAILED**"));
        }

        private static void replaceFooProperty(Foo foo, int value)
        {
            // This works
            foo.Bar = value;
        }

        private static void replaceFoo(Foo foo, int value)
        {
            // This doesn't work! The original foo won't be changed
            foo = new Foo();
            foo.Bar = value;
        }

        private static void replaceFoo(ref Foo foo, int value)
        {
            // This works by replacing the object (only in .NET)
            foo = new Foo();
            foo.Bar = value;
        }
    }
}
```

When run, this program shows the success or failure of each attempt at changing the property foo.Bar. Figure 7-9 shows the output.

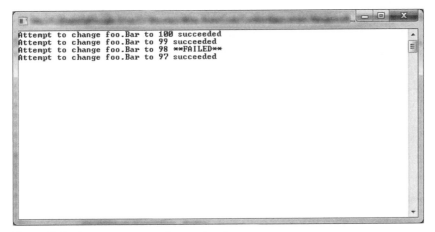

Figure 7-9: Arguments are values not refs.

Design Issues

In a chapter about the "usual suspects," ignoring *design issues* would be a grave omission. Programmers face many difficult challenges while writing code and while maintaining code written by others, but design problems (and here I'm talking about system design, not user-interface design) are among the most persistent and intractable sources of difficult bugs. Product owners might occasionally despair at a seemingly endless stream of bugs being discovered in their products, and they might at times be tempted to blame poor programming. Sometimes they will be right, but quite often it is closer to the truth that the product suffers from *poor design* rather than poor programming per se. Programmers have a duty to produce the best design they can, but quite often programmers are constrained by ill-conceived requirements and shallow thinking around product features. The best a programmer can do in these circumstances is to challenge product owners and work with them to overcome weaknesses in design. What follows are some hard-won bits of advice so that you might reflect on your own experiences, and be ready to relate them at the interview. "Hard won" means that I've either suffered this problem, inflicted it on others, or both.

YAGNI is not an excuse to take shortcuts

Almost every programmer (certainly those involved with Agile projects) has heard of *YAGNI*, short for *You Ain't Gonna Need It*. This pithy admonition has its roots in the Agile movement and it is a reaction to the problem of over-engineering or adding fancy embellishments in the hope that they will, someday, be useful.

The principle of YAGNI encourages programmers to pare down their design to the minimum necessary to get the immediate job done and then to stop. I am inclined to think of this as a valuable correction to the problem of over-engineering but I also think that people should be wary of overcorrecting. In other words you should be careful to avoid reducing the requirements beyond the minimum necessary for producing maintainable software. You should, for instance, never compromise established coding best practices in the name of YAGNI. Keep in mind the saying, "the longest distance between two points is a hasty shortcut."

Design for performance

Deferring thinking about the performance of a product until tests show that some aspect of performance is unacceptable is a common mistake. The difficulty of improving the performance of a product increases throughout development and is most difficult after a product has been released. Good performance and good quality are attributes that emerge from solid design. You can't add them after the fact except through significant or prolonged effort. You can't, for instance, plug in a component that will automatically enable a product to perform distributed processing of its core functionality.

The maxim that "hardware is cheap" (when compared to the cost of development) should not be interpreted as license to ignore performance issues. Additional hardware will not, for instance, overcome the limitations of a function with $O\left(2^n\right)$ performance or enable concurrency in an application that does not correctly handle shared state.

You might also have heard the advice to "get it working and then (if needed) make it faster." This is good advice when trying to solve a problem or invent an algorithm, but terrible advice when building a product unless you have the luxury of throwing away the first version and starting again.

Do not trade common sense for a methodology

One can easily get the impression that some software development or project management methodologies can be applied to overcome many of the well-known obstacles to developing good software. In a limited sense this is true, but some things remain difficult no matter how you approach them. No one would suggest, for instance, that hard mathematical problems can be solved by the diligent application of a project-management methodology, or that you could produce a fine work of art by holding daily stand-up meetings. The same is true of developing high-quality software: It takes concerted effort by skilled and suitably experienced professionals working in an appropriate environment. Naturally, some project-administration difficulties are overcome by following a disciplined approach, but these are tangential to the essential work of software development. A sound methodology will enable and facilitate quality software development, but that is the extent of it. After a software development project is "enabled and facilitated," the quality of the software produced is a consequence of the talent and application of the programmers. It is orthogonal to the choice of project-management discipline.

In short, no methodology is a substitute for effective and critical thinking. You cannot produce a quality product without some kind of a design blueprint. You cannot add "performance" in a single sprint. You certainly cannot add quality to a product by testing it just prior to a release.

Whatever methodology you and your team follow—and Agile is at least as good as any of its predecessors—be sure that no one in the team is under any illusion that the approach guarantees good software. A project management methodology can only guarantee that mediocre software is delivered on time and to budget.

Bad Habits

A lot of books are available on coding style, coding conventions, good and bad practices, and how to write code like a boss. My top two book recommendations are *The Pragmatic Programmer* and *Code Complete (2nd edition)*. Both of these books are inspirational, always reviving my enthusiasm for writing good code, and both of them are practical and specific, pairing solid advice with concrete examples.

This section of bad coding habits is not a comprehensive list; it is a short list of things that set my alarms bells ringing while interviewing candidates.

Mishandling exceptions

If you can't handle an exception in your catch block you should allow it to bubble up. If you don't, then the possibility exists you will be hiding errors that cause data corruption and other unpleasant outcomes. If an exception is thrown part way through an operation it can leave data in an inconsistent state, or it can leave it just plain corrupt.

Very few valid reasons exist to ignore an exception in a catch block, and by ignoring it you might be masking a problem that causes a subsequent failure, hindering the debugging process by obscuring the source of a problem.

Also, if you catch and re-throw an exception, take care to avoid interfering with the exception when you re-throw it. For instance, in .NET you can inadvertently reset the call stack by re-throwing an exception like this:

```
void MyMethod() {
    try
    {
        RiskyOperation();
```

```
        // ...
    }
    catch (InvalidOperationException ex)
    {
        if (!TryToHandle(ex))
            throw ex;  // oops, just reset the call stack.
    }
}
```

If the exception was thrown in the `RiskyOperation()` method then re-throwing it this way will make it appear to have originated in `MyMethod()`. If you want to re-throw an exception you should do so as follows:

```
try
{
    SomethingThatMightRaiseAnException();
    // ...
}
catch (InvalidOperationException ex)
{
    if (!TryToHandle(ex))
        throw;  // this preserves the call stack
}
```

Finally, never write an empty catch-block, not even if you intend to come back and finish it later. You might not.

Don't do this, it's a potential disaster:

```
catch (Exception ex)
{
    // not sure how to handle this
}
```

Instead, if you really want a "placeholder" in your catch block, you should write something like this, at least ensuring that the exceptional condition will be noticed if not properly handled:

```
catch (Exception ex)
{
    throw new NotImplementedException();
}
```

Not being paranoid enough

If I had to choose the bug I've seen most often it would be the `NullReferenceException` and variations on the same theme. Unsurprisingly, a null reference exception happens when you reference a nullable object (most objects are nullable) without first checking that the object you're referencing has been initialized.

Instead of this...

```
if (myObject.Foo == null)
    DoSomething();
```

...you should do something like this:

```
if (myObject != null)
    if (myObject.Foo == null)
        DoSomething();
```

As with all advice of this sort, you need to take a pragmatic view. Excessive paranoia can lead to bloated code, with needless tests for null littered redundantly throughout your project. If you can reasonably expect that an object has been initialized then you might omit the test for null but in most cases you can't assume that the object has been initialized. The normal and exception-free path of code execution might always result in objects that are initialized, but what about the case where an exception has occurred and objects were not properly initialized? You need to decide which is more important: avoiding the clutter of testing for null or writing code that is robust and defensive.

In an interview, being too paranoid when writing code is nearly impossible. Always include defensive tests for null, or at least mention that production code would ("of course") include additional tests for null for the sake of a robust product. Make sure that you write at least one test for null so that your interviewer knows you are aware of the issue.

Being superstitious

I'm not going to lecture you about superstition. If you have rituals and rites that help you produce good code then carry on as you please. On the other hand, most programmers don't overtly rely on magic to write software, unless you count regular expressions as magic. Ask any programmer whether he is superstitious and nine out of ten will say "no." Yet over and over I have discovered inexplicable artifacts during code reviews, bits of code that can't be explained by the author of the code. Bits of code that the programmer consciously added without knowing exactly why he added it. Apparently this psychological phenomenon is a common one. Do a web search for "cargo cult" for a fascinating backstory about how superstitions evolve.

Let me give you some examples of coding superstition:

- Believing that your code is automatically bad unless you add comments in between every line

- Commenting out (rather than deleting) lines of code for fear of irretrievably losing them, despite having source control in place with a full version history of the file

- Adding type suffixes after all numeric literals for no good reason
- Avoiding certain features of a platform for no good reason
- Repeating a line of code to "ensure it happens"

Working against the team

You might have strong views about the form in which code should be written; for instance, you might think that anyone who formats her code with tabs instead of spaces should be publically humiliated. You might be right, but here's the catch: If you are working in a team then you are duty-bound to follow the established conventions. If you don't, if you format your code and name your variables different from everyone else then you don't belong on the team. You aren't helping the team; you're working against it. It's like the cyclist who has the right-of-way at an intersection and in exercising his right to proceed is run over. He might have been in the right but now will spend six months eating soft food. In other words the precedent set by a team should override the preferences of an individual programmer regardless of whether that programmer is "right." By all means debate the right and wrong of a convention, but don't be that annoying programmer who everyone secretly wishes would find a job somewhere else.

The reason conventions are so important is simple: They are all about making the maintenance programmer's life easier. Every person who doesn't follow the conventions of the team *adds another convention* that the maintenance programmer has to learn (or decipher) to do his job.

There will be times where the team is wrong, and where you should stand up for what is right. Some frameworks, especially those developed by confident but inexperienced "architects," are more trouble than they are worth. When you encounter one of these then you should try to fix it, or more realistically you should try to convince the team it needs fixing, even if it can't be done right away. Never let yourself get into a situation where you try to covertly fix the broken framework or architecture to "surprise" the team. It always takes longer than you think, and the whole time you're working on it a chance exists that something will go wrong and you'll break something you had no business tampering with. The team won't thank you at that point. It will be much better and much less stressful if you work with the team rather than against them.

Copying and pasting too much

The main problem with duplicating code is that every change you make, every bug fix, every performance tweak, every new feature that is added to that code must be repeated in each occurrence of that duplicated code. This increases the cost of maintaining the product, and it greatly increases the risk that mistakes will be made in the future. It encourages a subtle class of bugs to creep in to the project, including things such as:

- A bug fix is made to one of the clones but not to the other, making the maintenance programmer look a bit backward. ("You said it was fixed, but it clearly isn't.")

- A cloned function is changed in some important way and is then mistaken for the original by a subsequent programmer, who overlooks the important difference, merges the two functions together (losing the difference) and, again, ends up looking a dunce.

Whenever you feel the temptation to copy and paste more than (say) five lines of code, always consider how you will avoid these problems. Comments in code ("If you change X, don't forget to change Y") are usually not good enough. They are too easy to overlook, and they tend to become less relevant (and less correct) over time as changes accumulate in the various copies lying around the code base.

Eager loading

Lazy loading is a technique where the actual loading (or resource-intensive processing) of data from disk or from a database is deferred to the time when it is actually needed. This can give a massive performance boost because it completely eliminates the overhead unless it is absolutely necessary. Naïvely loading data that is never used is one of the most common performance-inhibiting mistakes a programmer can make.

Lazy loading in its most basic form it looks like this:

```
public class LazyLoader
{
    private List<string> _filenames = null;
    public List<string> GetFileNames
    {
        get
        {
            if (_filenames == null)
                LoadFileNames();

            return _filenames;
        }
    }

    private void LoadFileNames()
    {
        // Iterate over a folder and obtain some file names
        // time-consuming! Don't call this needlessly!
```

```
    // etc...

    }
}
```

Sometimes it is easy to write "eager loading" code without realizing it. If you have ever written a class constructor that populates class members with data then you might have fallen for this trap. It *might* be necessary to front-load all the work by putting it into the class constructor, but did you consider how the class might be used in practice by future programmers? Will that loaded data *always* be used, or will it sometimes be wasted effort? Class constructors that take more than the minimum execution time are extremely unfriendly to performance-sensitive applications, and the problem is compounded if these classes are instantiated many times through the run time of the application.

QUESTIONS

This chapter discussed the kinds of situations you might face when fixing a bug. The following questions test your knowledge:

1. **Lock ordering**

   Explain the importance of obtaining locks in a fixed order; that is, why is lock ordering important?

2. **Locking on "this"**

   Explain why it might be considered bad practice to lock on a reference to the current instance of a class as per the following C# code:

   ```
   lock (this)
   {
       this.Name = "foo";
       this.Update();

       // etc...
   }
   ```

3. **Locking on a string**

   Explain why it might be considered bad practice to lock on a string as per the following C# code:

   ```
   lock ("my lock")
   {
       this.Name = "foo";
       this.Update();

       // etc...
   }
   ```

4. **Modify an object passed by value**

    If all arguments are passed to methods by value (not by reference) explain how it is possible to modify the properties of an object that is passed as an argument to a method.

5. **Difference between ref and out**

    In C#, what is the difference between the ref modifier and the out modifier?

6. **Normalize this**

    Table 7-1 contains the details of every employee in Acme Widgets, Inc. Normalize this table into BCNF.

Table 7-1: Employees Table

COLUMN NAME	DESCRIPTION
employee number	Employee number. Every employee has a unique number that is never shared with any other employee. If an employee leaves and returns he is assigned a new number.
name	An employee's name; for example, "Inigo Montoya."
numbers	All of an employee's telephone numbers including departmental extension, mobile/cell numbers, fax number, home phone number.
emergency contact name	The name of who to contact in an emergency.
emergency contact number	The telephone number of the emergency contact.

7. **Denormalizing**

    Describe denormalization. Describe one reason why you might denormalize a database.

8. **Catching exceptions**

    Why is it almost always a bad to catch the base Exception as in the following code?

```
try
{
    DoSomething();
}
catch (Exception ex)
{
    if (ex is MyCustomException)
    {
        Panic();
    }
}
```

ANSWERS

1. Lock ordering

Explain the importance of obtaining locks in a fixed order; that is, why is lock ordering important?

Obtaining locks in a fixed order defeats the *Coffman condition* known as *circular wait,* where threads wait on each other for mutually held lock resources. This prevents *deadlock* from occurring.

2. Locking on "this"

Explain why it might be considered bad practice to lock on a reference to the current instance of a class as per the following C# code:

```
lock (this)
{
    this.Name = "foo";
    this.Update();

    // etc...
}
```

The best resources on which to obtain a lock are those that your code controls and that are private to the class. If a resource is public then it is possible for some code outside of your control to lock the resource and create potential deadlock situations.

Note that locking an object reference prevents other threads from locking the same reference but it has no other effect. The object can still be accessed and its properties can still be updated.

3. Locking on a string

Explain why it might be considered bad practice to lock on a string as per the following C# code:

```
lock ("my lock")
{
    this.Name = "foo";
    this.Update();

    // etc...
}
```

Recall that strings in .NET and Java are immutable. One of the benefits of string immutability to the Java and .NET compilers is that each string can be *interned*, meaning that a single copy of each unique string is stored in memory and all references to that same literal string point to the same location.

The implication for locking is that references to string literals can be and are shared widely, even across AppDomains. This makes them unsuitable for use in locking for the same reasons that public variables are unsuitable (see Question 2 for more explanation).

4. **Modify an object passed by value**

   If all arguments are passed to methods by value (not by reference) explain how modifying the properties of an object that is passed as an argument to a method is possible.

   Although an object reference is passed by value it is still possible to modify its properties because each of the object's properties is accessed by reference. For instance, the following code compiles and runs and has the expected result of replacing the value of Bar with the value of newValue:

   ```
   private static void replaceFooProperty(Foo foo, int newValue)
   {
       // This works
       foo.Bar = value;
   }
   ```

   The key to answering this question is to understand that an object reference is itself passed by value. You cannot, for example, replace an object reference in a method like this:

   ```
   private static void replaceFoo(Foo foo, int value)
   {
       // This doesn't work! The original foo won't be changed
       foo = new Foo();
       foo.Bar = value;
   }
   ```

   Note that you can replace an object reference in a .NET method, but it requires the ref modifier as follows:

   ```
   private static void replaceFoo(ref Foo foo, int value)
   {
       // This works by replacing the object (only in .NET)
       foo = new Foo();
       foo.Bar = value;
   }
   ```

5. **Difference between *ref* and *out***

   In C#, what is the difference between the ref modifier and the out modifier?

Both of these modifiers permit a called method to modify the value of the variable that is passed as an argument. Both of the following methods are equivalent in this respect:

```
void update(ref int a) {
    a = 99;
}
```

```
void update(out int a) {
    a = 99;
}
```

Both `out` and `ref` indicate that the argument to a function should be passed by reference, allowing for modification inside the called method.

If you try to pass a variable to a method by reference (using the `ref` modifier) without first initializing it you will get a compilation error "Use of unassigned variable." The `out` modifier removes the requirement that a reference parameter be initialized before it is passed to a method.

This is legal:

```
int i;  // not initialized
replaceOutArg(out i, 99);  // no problem!
```

This generates a compilation error:

```
int i;  // not initialized
replaceOutArg(ref i, 99);  // does not compile!
```

Conversely if you forget to assign a value to an argument passed with the `out` modifier you will also get a compilation error.

```
private static void replaceOutArg(out int foo, int value)
{
    // oops - forgot to assign a value to foo!
}
```

```
int i;  // not initialized
replaceOutArg(out i, 99);  // does not compile!
```

6. Normalize this

Table 7-1 contains the details of every employee in Acme Widgets, Inc. Normalize this table into BCNF.

Table 7-1: Employees Table

COLUMN NAME	DESCRIPTION
employee number	Employee number. Every employee has a unique number that is never shared with any other employee. If an employee leaves and returns they are assigned a new number.
name	An employee's name; for example, "Inigo Montoya."
numbers	All of an employee's telephone numbers including departmental extension, mobile/cell numbers, fax number, home phone number.
emergency contact name	The name of who to contact in an emergency.
emergency contact number	The telephone number of the emergency contact.

The way to approach any normalization task is to work through the normal forms starting with 1NF and evaluate the rules of normalization against the table at each step.

The rule for 1NF is *no repeated values*. Table 7-1 shows that you have a column containing all the employee's telephone numbers, so this is a violation of 1NF. To resolve this violation you move these numbers to a new table and establish a *foreign key relationship* between the employee table and the new table as shown in Figure 7-10.

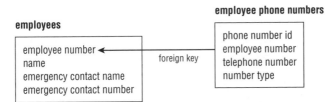

Figure 7-10: First normal form

The rule for 2NF is *no partial dependencies*. A partial dependency exists when an attribute (a column) in the table depends on part of a candidate key. The only candidate key in this table is employee number (employee name is almost certainly not unique therefore not a suitable key), which means that it is not possible for any other attribute to have a partial dependency. Therefore, this table is automatically in 2NF.

The rule for 3NF is *no transitive dependencies*. This example does have a violation of 3NF because emergency contact number depends on emergency contact, which in turn, depends on employee. To resolve this 3NF violation you should move emergency contact name and number to a new table, establishing a new foreign key relationship between employee and emergency contact as shown in Figure 7-11.

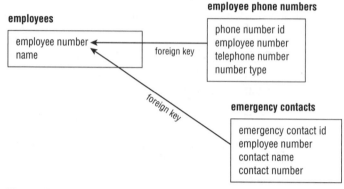

Figure 7-11: Third normal form

The rule for BCNF is *the same as 3NF but specifically includes key attributes*. The only key attribute to consider is employee number. This is obviously not a transitive dependency so the table is automatically in BCNF.

7. Denormalizing

Describe denormalization. Describe one reason why you might denormalize a database.

Denormalization is the process of moving away from a normalized database schema in the interest of read performance or scalability.

Denormalization is not generally recommended except in situations where data integrity is either not important or is covered by some other factor. Data warehouses are typically read-only databases or they are discarded and recreated periodically, and so the usual priority of normalization and data integrity takes a backseat to performance concerns.

A database that has not been normalized does not qualify as a denormalized database.

8. Catching exceptions

Why is it almost always a bad to catch the base Exception *as in the following code?*

```
try
{
    DoSomething();
}
catch (Exception ex)
{
    if (ex is MyCustomException)
    {
        Panic();
    }
}
```

In general it is a bad idea to catch the base Exception unless you really do intend to handle all the possible exceptions that might be thrown by the DoSomething method. Although you might write the DoSomething method in such a way that it only throws one kind of exception, it might still be modified by another programmer (or even by you) at some future point in time. By catching all possible exceptions and then ignoring all of them except MyCustomException, you potentially bury exceptions that would otherwise bubbled up to another catch block or surface as an unhandled exception.

The following code would not be quite so bad if the catch block were to re-throw the exceptions it doesn't handle:

```
try
{
    DoSomething();
}
catch (Exception ex)
{
    if (ex is MyCustomException)
    {
        Panic();
    }
    else
    {
        throw;
    }
}
```

Quirks and Idioms

Just like languages spoken around the world, every programming language has its own idioms and quirks. These quirks make a language interesting and are powerfully expressive, just as much as they might infuriate the language student. A clever trick such as the *Schwartzian Transform* might seem unmaintainable madness to the uninitiated, but knowledge of the Schwartzian Transform is one of the hallmarks of fluency in Perl. A programmer fluent with .NET will generally prefer LINQ over looping constructs. A fluent C programmer will not overheat at the semantic implications of a pointer-to-a-pointer-to-a-pointer. The list goes on.

An interviewer who tests you on the quirks of a language will generally not be testing your ability to remember programming language trivia. The interviewer will be testing your familiarity and fluency with a language or a framework. The assumption is that if you are proficient with a language, then you will know most of its idioms and many of its quirks.

In this chapter I barely scratch the surface of the many, many quirks and idioms you will find in the wild as a practicing programmer. If, after attempting these questions, you find that you aren't as familiar with a language as you would like, the best way to improve is to study the code of others and focus on anything that isn't obvious. You won't improve your knowledge by sticking to what you already know.

I have divided this chapter into sections based on language so that you can jump to what interests you. Floating point numbers are in a section of their own because they can affect every programmer no matter which language is used.

Perhaps the world's most common coding question is, "Write code that reverses a string." As a tribute to this popular question, I have included a variation of it in each language section, including the section on T-SQL.

Binary Fractions and Floating Point Numbers

You might remember from school that some fractions can't be accurately represented by a decimal number. The fraction $\frac{1}{2}$ is exactly 0.5 in decimal, but the fraction $\frac{1}{3}$ is not exactly 0.3, nor is it exactly 0.33 or 0.333 or 0.3333333333. No matter how many 3s you use, you can't represent $\frac{1}{3}$ as an exact decimal number without resorting to special notation. Irrational numbers like π cannot be exactly represented in *any* number system. The best you can do is an approximation of π (even if that approximation is trillions of digits long). The inability to represent some numbers exactly is not a significant problem in practice because, for all practical (and most theoretical) purposes, you never need a degree of accuracy more than around 20 decimal places. Even the infinitesimally small unit of *Planck Time* can be written using around 50 decimal places. For all practical purposes, a super-high degree of accuracy is simply not that important.

It is the exact same thing with computers and binary numbers. Some fractions can be represented accurately in binary and other fractions cannot. The degree of accuracy you need depends entirely on your application.

A quick word on terminology: You will be familiar with the *decimal point* when discussing decimal fractions. When discussing binary fractions, the correct terminology is *binary point*, or more generally *radix point*.

The term *floating point* refers to how the position of the radix point varies depending on the scale of the number. Large numbers will have more digits to the left of the radix point, and small numbers have more to the right. This allows a computer to use a fixed-width data type (like an `int`) to store both very large and very small numbers.

In addition to the flexibility of floating point numbers, programming frameworks often provide extensions to overcome hardware limitations; Java has `java.math.BigInteger`, Perl has `bigint`, and C# has `System.Numerics.BigInteger`. These extensions allow numbers to exceed the usual limitation of $\pm10^{127}$ in exchange for reduced performance in some operations.

Quite often, the simplest and most effective way to avoid inaccuracies caused by floating point calculations is to use an alternative data type such as decimal. Most (if not all) built-in decimal data types will use a floating point representation internally, but they provide the programmer with a predictable façade of accuracy, making it more suitable for storing (for instance) currency values where accuracy (or at least predictable inaccuracy) is desirable. If your framework has a currency data type, then that will be the best data type for storing currency values. You can also sometimes skirt around the issue by using integer data types to perform arithmetic and then inserting your decimal point for display after the arithmetic is done.

QUESTIONS

1. **Write 0.1 as a binary fraction**

   The decimal fraction $\frac{3}{4}$ (0.75) can be written as a binary number 0.11. Convert the decimal fraction $\frac{1}{10}$ to a binary number by hand on paper or on a whiteboard.

2. **Simple addition, surprising results**

   Why does the following JavaScript give the unexpected result of 0.30000000000000004?

   ```
   var n = 0.1;
   n += 0.2;
   document.writeln('0.1 + 0.2 = ' + n); // 0.30000000000000004
   ```

JavaScript

Love it or hate it, JavaScript is here to stay. The last decade has seen JavaScript rise from a language that was often confused for "Java" to the number one language of client-side web developers around the world. I know many programmers who love JavaScript, many programmers who hate it, and a few who both love it and hate it.

If you write code for the World Wide Web, then sooner or later you will find yourself confronted with what looks like strange behaviour in JavaScript. Take a look at the second question in this section (the one about expressions that evaluate to `true` or `false`) to see a good example of "strange" behaviour that a lot of JavaScript programmers take for granted.

QUESTIONS

3. **Reverse the words in a string**

   Write a short program in JavaScript to reverse the order of words in the following string:

   ```
   var dwarves = "bashful doc dopey grumpy happy sleepy sneezy";
   ```

Your output should look like this:

```
sneezy sleepy happy grumpy dopey doc bashful
```

4. Some expressions are more equal than others

To what does each of the following JavaScript expressions evaluate?

```
'' == '0'
```

```
'' == 0
```

```
false == 'false'
```

```
false == 0
```

```
false == '0'
```

```
null == undefined
```

```
'\t\r\n  ' == 0
```

```
undefined == undefined
```

```
NaN == NaN
```

```
1 == true
```

```
1 === true
```

5. Block scope

What is the output of the following JavaScript code?

```
x();

function x() {

    var x = 1;

    document.writeln("1: " + x);

    {
        var x = 4;
    }

    document.writeln("2: " + x);

    var f = function ()
    {
        document.writeln("3: " + x);
        var x = 3;
```

```
    };

    f();

    document.writeln("4: " + x);
}
```

6. Let me help you with that...

What is the value returned from this function?

```
function returnTrue()
{
    return
    {
        result: true;
    };
}
```

7. NaN

What is wrong with this test for NaN?

```
if (dubiousNumber === NaN)
{
    // ...
}
```

8. What is the meaning of this!

To what does this refer in each occurrence of document.writeln()?

```
document.writeln("A: " + this);

var o = {
    f: function() {
        return this;
    }
};

document.writeln("B: " + o.f());

var f = o.f;
document.writeln("C: " + f());

var obj = {};
document.writeln("D: " + f.call(obj));

var o = {
    f: function() {
        var ff = function() {
            return this;
        };
```

```
                return ff();
        },
        g: {
                h: function() {
                        return this;
                }
        }
};

document.writeln("E: " + o.f());

document.writeln("F: " + o.g.h());
```

C#

The popularity of C# is not really surprising. The C# language combines some of the best features from Java and C, but without the pain associated with pointer manipulation. C# has a gentle learning curve and recent releases have added some very cool features to the language such as lambda expressions and built-in support for asynchronous and concurrent programming constructs.

Trivia: If it were not for potential trademark concerns, the language we know as C# might have been released to the world with the name "Cool," which stood for "C-like Object Oriented Language." This was its internal code-name while it was in development at Microsoft. I will leave it up to you to decide if that name would have made any difference to the popularity the language presently enjoys.

QUESTIONS

9. **Reverse the words in a string**

   Write a short program in C# to reverse the order of words in the following string:

   ```
   string dwarves = "bashful doc dopey grumpy happy sleepy sneezy";
   ```

   Your output should look like this:

   ```
   sneezy sleepy happy grumpy dopey doc bashful
   ```

10. **Avoid Magic Numbers**

    The following method was written to calculate the difference between two years. If it receives a "year of birth" that is greater than the supplied "current year" then it returns 999 to signify an invalid year of birth. Suggest three alternative ways this method could be improved so that it doesn't involve the "magic number," 999.

Hint: Consider how you might indicate failure without returning a specific integer.

```
static int CalculateAge(int yearOfBirth, int currentYear)
{
    if (yearOfBirth > currentYear)
        return 999; // invalid year of birth

    return currentYear - yearOfBirth;
}
```

11. **A path on any platform**

    The following code does not work properly when run on Linux (compiled with Mono!) Suggest a way to improve this snippet so that it will produce a path that is compatible on other platforms while still retaining compatibility with Windows.

    ```
    string path = folder + "\\" + file;
    ```

12. **Debugging helper**

    What is the effect of applying the DebuggerDisplay attribute as per the following code?

    ```
    [DebuggerDisplay("X = {X}, Y = {Y}")]
    public class LittleHelp
    {
        private int x;

        public int X { get { return x; } set { x = value; Y = -value; } }
        public int Y { get; set; }

    }
    ```

13. **The "as" keyword**

    What does the as keyword do, and how is it helpful?

14. **Verbatim String Literals**

    What is a *verbatim string literal* and how is it helpful?

15. **Immutable Strings**

    If strings are immutable, meaning that strings cannot be altered, what happens to myString when you append to it as in the following code?

    ```
    string myString = "prince";
    myString += "ss"; // How can I do this if strings are immutable?
    ```

Java

Java is one of the most popular languages in the world. It has evolved more slowly than languages like C# but it still dominates in the corporate world, and it is particularly dominant in server-side development.

Java is notorious for its verbosity, although this is perhaps more the fault of Java libraries and frameworks rather than the language itself. Java assumes very little and provides nearly no syntactic shortcuts. This can be annoying for programmers familiar with less formal languages (like Perl), but on the positive side it encourages a consistent and uniform style of programming that greatly assists the maintenance programmer.

QUESTIONS

16. **Reverse the words in a string**

    Write a short program in Java to reverse the order of words in the following string:

    ```
    String dwarves = "bashful doc dopey grumpy happy sleepy sneezy";
    ```

    Your output should look like this:

    ```
    sneezy sleepy happy grumpy dopey doc bashful
    ```

17. **Double brace initialization**

    The following code declares, creates, and initializes an instance of List<String> using what is often called *double brace initialization*.

    Explain how double brace initialization works and rewrite this code to initialize the instance without using double brace initialization.

    ```
    List<String> list = new ArrayList<String>() {{
        add("Lister");
        add("Rimmer");
        add("Kryten");
    }};
    ```

18. **Labelled blocks**

    Although Java does not have a goto statement it does have a similar construct that uses *labeled blocks* in combination with break and continue statements.

    Explain what happens when the break statement is executed in the following code excerpt:

    ```
    int i;
    int j = 0;
    ```

```
        boolean found = false;
        int[][] arr = {
            { 4, 8, 15, 16, 23, 42 },
            { 11, 23, 29, 41, 43, 47 },
            { 757, 787, 797, 919, 929, 10301 }
        };
        int find = 41;


iterate:
        for (i = 0; i < arr.length; i++) {
            for (j = 0; j < arr[i].length; j++)
            {
                if (arr[i][j] == find) {
                    found = true;
                    break iterate;
                }
            }
        }

        if (found) {
            System.out.println("Found");
        } else {
            System.out.println("Not found");
        }
```

19. **There can be only one**

    Describe the *design pattern* that is being implemented in the following code:

```
public enum Highlander {
        INSTANCE;
        public void execute () {
                //... perform operation here ...
        }
}
```

Perl

Perl was created in 1987, which makes it the oldest language covered in this chapter. It is widely regarded as a flexible and powerful language although these qualities have earned it the dubious nickname of "the Swiss army chainsaw of scripting languages." Some programmers go so far as to refer to Perl as a "write-only" language, unkindly implying that Perl code is uniformly difficult to read. These unkind programmers point to Perl's numerous special variables and shortcuts, and, in particular, to the way that Perl is not only forgiving of ambiguous code but also tries to guess what the programmer intended.

Many of these criticisms are also the reasons why some programmers fall in love with Perl. Here's an example of Perl trying very hard to do what the programmer probably intends, even when most other languages would throw an exception and refuse to run at all:

```
C:\code>perl -d -e 1

Loading DB routines from perl5db.pl version 1.37
Editor support available.

Enter h or 'h h' for help, or 'perldoc perldebug' for more help.

main::(-e:1):    1
  DB<1> $i=1; print ++$i;   # Normal increment
2

  DB<2> $i='A'; print ++$i; # Alpha increment
B

  DB<3> $i='AA'; print ++$i; # Alpha sequence increment
AB

  DB<4> $i='A1'; print ++$i; # Alpha numeric sequence increment
A2

  DB<5> $i='ZZ'; print ++$i; # Alpha sequence increment with rollover
AAA

  DB<6> $i='Z9'; print ++$i; # Alpha num sequence increment
                             # with rollover
AA0

  DB<7>
```

Depending on your programming experiences to date, you might find this "do what I mean" behavior to be somewhat liberating or somewhat scary.

QUESTIONS

20. **Reverse the words in a string**

    Write a short program in Perl to reverse the order of words in the following string:

    ```
    my $dwarves = "bashful doc dopey grumpy happy sleepy sneezy";
    ```

    Your output should look like this:

    ```
    sneezy sleepy happy grumpy dopey doc bashful
    ```

21. Sorting 101

The following Perl code is an attempt to sort a list of numbers into numerical order, but it does not work correctly. Explain what might be wrong and suggest an improvement that will properly sort these numbers into ascending numerical order.

```
my @list = ( 1, 4, 1, 5, 9, 2, 6, 5, 3, 5, 10, 20, 30, 40 );
print join ",", sort @list;
```

22. Sorting 201

Suppose you have a list of characters as follows. Write code to produce two lists: the first sorted by race, the second sorted by age then race.

```
my @list = (
        [qw(Pippin   Hobbit  29)],
        [qw(Merry    Hobbit  37)],
        [qw(Frodo    Hobbit  51)],
        [qw(Legolas  Elf     650)],
        [qw(Gimli    Dwarf   140)],
        [qw(Gandalf  Maiar   2021)],
        [qw(Aragorn  Man     88)],
        [qw(Sam      Hobbit  36)],
        [qw(Boromir  Man     41)],
);
```

23. Sorting 301: The Schwartzian Transform

The *Schwartzian Transform* is a particularly idiomatic (you could say *Perlish*) way of sorting a list. It is an excellent illustration of how Perl operators can be combined to perform complex transformations with just a small amount of code. Here is a transform that sorts a list of integers by the number of characters in each integer:

```
my @list = (111111111,22222222,3333333,444444,55555,6666,777,88,9);

my @sorted =
    map { $_->[1] }
    sort { $a->[0] <=> $b->[0] }
    map { [length $_, $_] } @list;

print join ',', @sorted
```

When run, this program prints:

```
9,88,777,6666,55555,444444,3333333,22222222,111111111
```

Here is another list, this time with numbers represented by English words:

```
my @list = qw/three two one six five four nine eight seven/;
```

Write a Schwartzian Transform that will sort this list into numeric order, from "one" to "nine."

24. It depends...

Built-in functions such as `sort` are sensitive to the context in which they are called. If you call `sort` in a list context you will get back a list. If you call `sort` in a scalar context you will get back `undefined`.

Write a `sensitiveSort` subroutine that sorts `@_` and returns a string if called in scalar context. In other words, wrap the built-in `sort` routine so that `sort` no longer returns `undefined` in scalar context.

25. The branch you're standing on

The following code is intended to loop over an array of numbers and print the square of each number and the total of all squares. This code works but it has unintended consequences. What are these unintended consequences and how can they be avoided?

```
use strict; use warnings;

my @array = (1 .. 9);
my $sum = 0;

foreach my $num (@array) {
    print "$num^2=";
    $num = $num * $num;
    print "$num\n";
    $sum += $num;
}

print "Sum of squares is $sum\n";
```

The output is:

```
1^2=1
2^2=4
3^2=9
4^2=16
5^2=25
6^2=36
7^2=49
8^2=64
9^2=81
Sum of squares is 285
```

26. Perl isn't Java

This Perl code does not behave as the programmer intended. What is wrong with it? Rewrite it so that it will behave as the programmer probably intended.

```
my $dwarves = "bashful doc dopey grumpy happy sleepy sneezy";
```

```
print &ReverseWords($dwarves);

sub ReverseWords {
    my $arg = shift;

    if ($arg != null) {
        return join ' ', reverse split ' ', $dwarves;
    }
}
```

Ruby

Ruby is considered by some programmers to be just like Perl, only with better support for object-oriented programming and with fewer idiosyncrasies.

QUESTIONS

27. Reverse the words in a string

Write a short program in Ruby to reverse the order of words in the following string:

```
dwarves = "bashful doc dopey grumpy happy sleepy sneezy";
```

Your output should look like this:

```
sneezy sleepy happy grumpy dopey doc bashful
```

28. Swap variable values without a temp variable

Write code to swap the values of two variables without using a temporary variable.

In other words, start with

```
x == 1
y == 2
```

and write code to obtain

```
x == 2
y == 1
```

29. &&= operator

What does the following code do, and how is it potentially helpful?

```
myString &&= myString + suffix
```

Transact-SQL

Transact-SQL (T-SQL, Microsoft's version of SQL) is unlike any other language covered in this chapter. It is primarily a language for querying and processing data in a relational database (specifically SQL Server) and it builds on the standard SQL language. SQL is sometimes described as a *declarative* language, meaning that the programmer will write code that describes *what* results to obtain rather than writing code that describes *how* to obtain those results. Despite being called a declarative language, SQL (and especially T-SQL) does contain procedural elements such as looping constructs, IF statements, and text-manipulation functions. These constructs can be very convenient, but they can also mislead the inexperienced SQL programmer into thinking that SQL is just like any other language, only uglier.

Programmers who learn other languages before learning SQL often find themselves struggling to reproduce the idioms of those other languages in SQL. These programmers are almost without exception disappointed and frustrated. You *can* write procedural SQL code just as you *can* bang in a nail with a screwdriver. With effort and creativity you can do just about anything in T-SQL that you can do in other languages, but that does not mean that you should. Writing code to reverse the order of words in a string using T-SQL (see the first question in this section) is most certainly possible, but I would prefer to use almost any other language for this kind of purpose.

The power of SQL lies in its ability to query and filter large amounts of data with relatively few lines of code. Just as Perl and JavaScript enable the programmer to do a lot with very little code, SQL enables the programmer to perform complex operations on *sets* of data with very little code. If you think SQL is verbose, try writing the equivalent code without a database engine.

Writing SQL code that iterates over rows in a table instead of performing a set-based operation is a common newbie mistake. Quite often the SQL novice will write many hundreds of lines of complicated and bug-ridden code without realizing that they can obtain better (meaning faster, more efficient, and easier to debug) results with far fewer lines of set-based SQL.

Just because an interviewer might encourage you to stretch the limits of SQL in an interview question does not mean that this should be standard practice. Use SQL for what it was intended and leave these shenanigans to eccentric interviewers and oddball websites.

QUESTIONS

30. Reverse the words in a string

Write a short T-SQL script to reverse the order of words in the following string:

```
DECLARE @dwarves VARCHAR(MAX)
SET @dwarves = 'bashful doc dopey grumpy happy sleepy sneezy'
```

Your output should look like this:

```
sneezy sleepy happy grumpy dopey doc bashful
```

31. Correlated subquery

Consider the following table, which contains a list of users, each with a reputation and a location:

```
CREATE TABLE [dbo].[Users](
            [Id] [int] NOT NULL,
            [Reputation] [int] NULL,
            [DisplayName] [nchar](40) NULL,
            [Location] [nchar](100) NULL,
            [JoinDate] [smalldatetime] NULL
)
```

Write a SELECT statement that uses a *correlated subquery* to obtain a list of users with a higher-than-average reputation within that user's location.

32. Which date is that?

The following two lines of SQL are supposed to insert a new row into the Users table. Assuming that this SQL worked correctly at least once (when the developer wrote and tested it) what could potentially go wrong it, and how could you rewrite it to avoid this problem?

```
INSERT INTO Users (Id, DisplayName, JoinDate)
VALUES (1, 'Ted', CONVERT(smalldatetime,'12/01/2015'))
```

33. Collation order

Consider a scenario where your SQL Server database is deployed to a customer site and to an existing SQL Server instance alongside other databases that you don't control or know anything about. In that circumstance, what is potentially wrong (or perhaps missing) in this CREATE TABLE statement, and how should you rewrite it to avoid this potential problem?

```
CREATE TABLE #temp
(
    [Id] int     identity(1,1) NOT NULL,
    [Name] nvarchar(100) NULL,
    [DateJoined] smalldatetime NULL
)
```

34. Selecting a random row from a table

Write a SELECT statement that will select a single row at random from the Users table. Assume the table has between 10 and 10,000 rows.

ANSWERS

This section contains answers to questions asked previously in this chapter.

1. Write 0.1 as a binary fraction

The decimal fraction $\frac{3}{4}$ (0.75) can be written as a binary number 0.11. Convert the decimal fraction $\frac{1}{10}$ to a binary number by hand (on paper or on a whiteboard).

An interviewer might ask a question like this to test your understanding of how decimal fractions numbers are stored in binary. This particular question is a bit of a trick because it is impossible to convert the decimal fraction $\frac{1}{10}$ to an exact binary equivalent. It is possible to store a number that is very close to $\frac{1}{10}$ and that is what a computer does. It stores an approximation and leaves it up to programming frameworks to "pretend" (or not, in many cases) that they are storing an exact number.

Just knowing that it is impossible to represent 0.1 exactly in binary might not be enough for some interviewers. You might be pressed to "show your work." Here is an example of how you would try to convert 0.1 to binary by hand:

First, write a 0 followed by the binary point, followed by nine or ten place holders as shown in Figure 8-1.

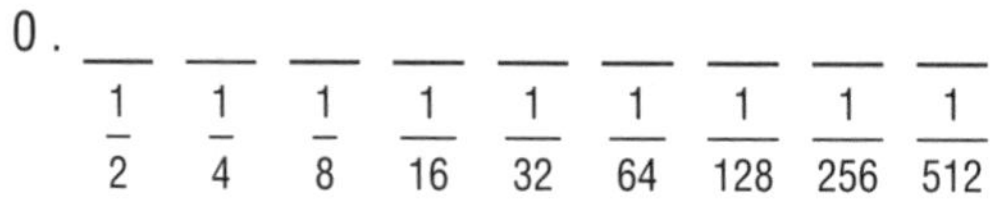

$$0 . \; \underline{\frac{1}{2}} \; \underline{\frac{1}{4}} \; \underline{\frac{1}{8}} \; \underline{\frac{1}{16}} \; \underline{\frac{1}{32}} \; \underline{\frac{1}{64}} \; \underline{\frac{1}{128}} \; \underline{\frac{1}{256}} \; \underline{\frac{1}{512}}$$

Figure 8-1: Converting 0.1 to binary

Next, draw in the value of each place as shown in Figure 8-2. If you weren't already aware, notice how the value of each place after the binary point is a progression of the sequence 2^{-1}, 2^{-2}, 2^{-3}, and so on.

You might not be able to remember values beyond $\frac{1}{16}$, in which case you could ask your interviewers whether they remember, or borrow a calculator just for working out $\frac{1}{32}$ and so on as decimal numbers. It is unlikely you will be penalized for this; not many people walk around with these decimal numbers in their head, I certainly don't. By this point your interviewer will see you are heading in the right direction.

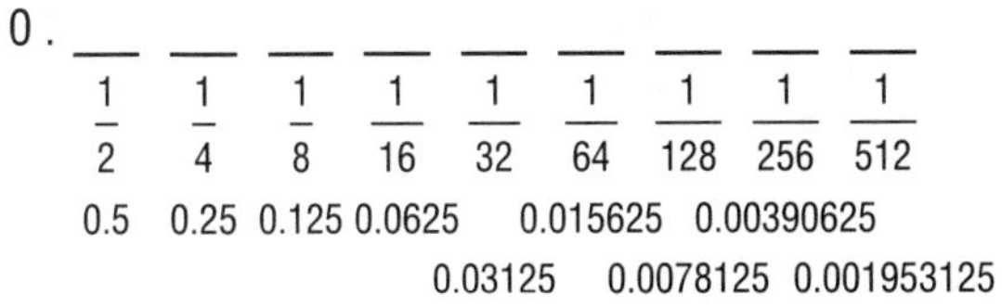

0 . __ __ __ __ __ __ __ __ __

$\frac{1}{2}$	$\frac{1}{4}$	$\frac{1}{8}$	$\frac{1}{16}$	$\frac{1}{32}$	$\frac{1}{64}$	$\frac{1}{128}$	$\frac{1}{256}$	$\frac{1}{512}$

0.5   0.25 0.125 0.0625   0.015625   0.00390625
                        0.03125   0.0078125 0.001953125

Figure 8-2: Convert fractions to decimal

Now you are ready to start the conversion of 0.1 to a binary fraction. The process is quite mechanical:

1. Start at the binary point.

2. Move (that is, look at) one place to the right.

3. If the current place value is greater than your decimal fraction, then write a "0" in that place and repeat from step 2.

4. If the current place value is less than or equal to your decimal fraction then write a "1" in that place and subtract the place value from your decimal fraction.

5. If the subtraction in step 4 gives 0 then you are finished.

6. Otherwise, repeat from step 2.

   Following this process for 0.1, start at the binary point and move one place to the right. You should be looking at the value of this place, which is 0.5, as shown in Figure 8-3.

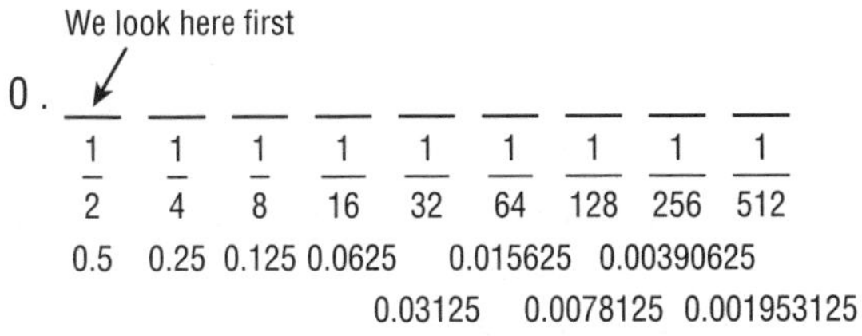

We look here first

0 . __ __ __ __ __ __ __ __ __

$\frac{1}{2}$	$\frac{1}{4}$	$\frac{1}{8}$	$\frac{1}{16}$	$\frac{1}{32}$	$\frac{1}{64}$	$\frac{1}{128}$	$\frac{1}{256}$	$\frac{1}{512}$

0.5   0.25 0.125 0.0625   0.015625   0.00390625
                        0.03125   0.0078125 0.001953125

Figure 8-3: The value of the first binary place is 0.5.

Step 3 indicates that you write a "0" in this place. Figure 8-4 shows the work so far.

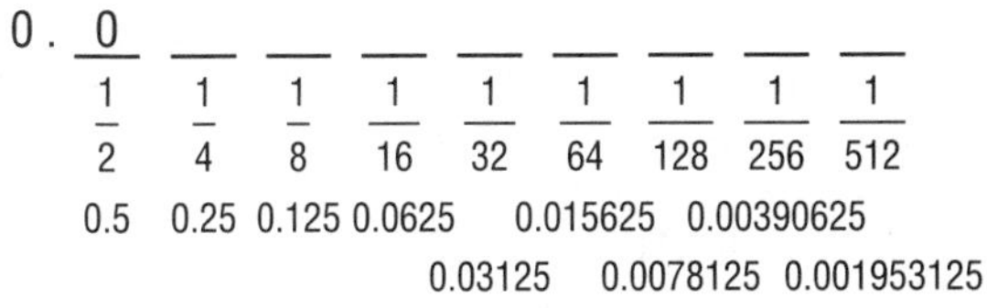

0 . 0 __ __ __ __ __ __ __ __

$\frac{1}{2}$	$\frac{1}{4}$	$\frac{1}{8}$	$\frac{1}{16}$	$\frac{1}{32}$	$\frac{1}{64}$	$\frac{1}{128}$	$\frac{1}{256}$	$\frac{1}{512}$

0.5   0.25 0.125 0.0625   0.015625   0.00390625
                        0.03125   0.0078125 0.001953125

Figure 8-4: Write a "0" in the first place.

Now repeat steps 2 and 3, writing "0" in each place until you come to the fourth place, which has a value of 0.0625, as shown in Figure 8-5.

The value of this place is less than 0.1

$$0 . \underline{0} \quad \underline{0} \quad \underline{0} \quad \swarrow \quad \underline{} \quad \underline{} \quad \underline{} \quad \underline{} \quad \underline{}$$

| $\frac{1}{2}$ | $\frac{1}{4}$ | $\frac{1}{8}$ | $\frac{1}{16}$ | $\frac{1}{32}$ | $\frac{1}{64}$ | $\frac{1}{128}$ | $\frac{1}{256}$ | $\frac{1}{512}$ |

0.5   0.25 0.125 0.0625   0.015625   0.00390625
                    0.03125   0.0078125 0.001953125

Figure 8-5: Finding a value less than 0.1.

Following the instruction at step 4, write a "1" in the fourth place, and subtract the value of this place from your value. Figure 8-6 shows the progress so far and the subtraction performed.

$$0 . \underline{0} \quad \underline{0} \quad \underline{0} \quad \underline{1} \quad \underline{} \quad \underline{} \quad \underline{} \quad \underline{} \quad \underline{}$$

| $\frac{1}{2}$ | $\frac{1}{4}$ | $\frac{1}{8}$ | $\frac{1}{16}$ | $\frac{1}{32}$ | $\frac{1}{64}$ | $\frac{1}{128}$ | $\frac{1}{256}$ | $\frac{1}{512}$ |

0.5   0.25 0.125 0.0625   0.015625   0.00390625
                    0.03125   0.0078125 0.001953125

Subtracting this value from 0.1 ...
```
 0.1000
-0.0625
 0.0375
```

Figure 8-6: Subtracting a place value.

Having performed the subtraction you are left with a value of 0.0375. Steps 5 and 6 say to repeat the process from step 2. Continue with the next binary place, writing a "1" because the value of 0.0375 is greater than the place value of 0.03125.

By this point your interviewer should have interrupted to either stop you (because you clearly know what you are doing) or to ask (perhaps sarcastically) how many places you intend to calculate. If the interviewer doesn't stop you I recommend stopping yourself after the first few digits to explain that the sequence doesn't end at nine binary places but continues indefinitely like this:

0.00011001100110011001100110011001100110011...

Trying to derive an exact representation in this fashion would require an infinite sequence of digits, which makes representing the decimal value exactly as a binary fraction impossible.

By the way, I hope you never need to do this kind of conversion by hand outside of an interview.

2. Simple Addition, Surprising Results

Why does the following JavaScript give the unexpected result of 0.30000000000000004?

```
var n = 0.1;
n += 0.2;
document.writeln('0.1 + 0.2 = ' + n); // 0.30000000000000004
```

Results like this are less surprising when you appreciate the inherent limitations of representing floating point numbers in binary. Recall that 0.1 is stored internally as an approximation rather than an exact number. The surprising result is a consequence of performing addition with an approximate number.

Also recall that although many fractions cannot be represented exactly, many others can. If you aren't aware of this limitation then you might incorrectly conclude that JavaScript (or another language) is returning inconsistent results.

This same question could have been phrased as:

What is the result of the following JavaScript expression, true or false?

```
(0.1 + 0.2) === 0.3
```

This isn't quite as obvious as the answer to the previous question. The answer here is "false," and again, the key is to appreciate the inexact binary representation of decimal fractions.

3. Reverse the words in a string

Write a short program to reverse the order of words in the following string.

```
var dwarves = "bashful doc dopey grumpy happy sleepy sneezy";
```

Your output should look like this:

```
sneezy sleepy happy grumpy dopey doc bashful
```

For brevity, JavaScript is sometimes on a par with Perl. Just like Perl, JavaScript has a `join` function, a `split` function, and a `reverse` function that works on arrays.

```
var sevrawd = dwarves.split(' ').reverse().join(' ');
document.writeln(sevrawd);
```

4. **Some expressions are more equal than others**

To what does each of the following JavaScript expressions evaluate?

```
'' == '0'

'' == 0

false == 'false'

false == 0

false == '0'

null == undefined

'\t\r\n   ' == 0

undefined == undefined

NaN == NaN

1 == true

1 === true
```

The result of some of these comparisons might surprise you. You should appreciate that the equals operator `==` will generally attempt to coerce each value to have the same type before it does the comparison. Sometimes this does what you might expect, and sometimes it doesn't. The strict-equals operator `===` returns `false` if the values do not have the same type and is therefore more predictable in most cases. One notable exception to the usual rules is that `NaN === NaN` will always return `false`.

```
'' == '0'              // false

'' == 0                // true

false == 'false'       // false

false == 0             // true
```

```
false == '0'            // true

null == undefined       // true

'\t\r\n  ' == 0         // true

undefined == undefined  // true

NaN === NaN             // false

1 == true               // true

1 === true              // false
```

5. Block scope

What is the output of the following JavaScript code?

```javascript
x();

function x() {

    var x = 1;

    document.writeln("1: " + x);

    {
        var x = 4;
    }

    document.writeln("2: " + x);

    var f = function ()
    {
        document.writeln("3: " + x);
        var x = 3;
    };

    f();

    document.writeln("4: " + x);

}
```

The output of this code is:

```
1: 1
2: 4
3: undefined
4: 4
```

The first step in understanding the answer to this question is to appreciate that JavaScript does not have block scope like other languages. In most other languages this block...

```
{
    var x = 4;
}
```

...would declare a new variable confined to the scope of the block (or else it would generate a compiler error). In JavaScript this variable replaces the original, changing the value of x.

So why doesn't the second "block" change the value of x?

Even though JavaScript doesn't have block scope it does have what is known as *function scope*. Function scope is a bit one sided; it means that a function inherits the scope in which it is declared (which in this case is the scope of the function x) but it cannot change any of these variables. Functions also have their own "private" (or "inner") scope that overrides the inherited scope within the function block. If a variable name conflicts then the innermost scope wins.

But if the function inherits the scope of its context, why does x *show as undefined when calling* f ()?

Variable declarations are always *hoisted* to the top of the declaring block regardless of where the var declaration appears inside the block. The following function

```
function () {
    document.writeln(x);
    var x = 1;
}
```

is interpreted as

```
function () {
    var x = undefined;
    document.writeln(x);
    x=1;
}
```

Notice that while variable declarations are hoisted, variable assignments are not.

Returning to the original question this means that the function expression

```
    var f = function ()
    {
        document.writeln("3: " + x);
        var x = 3;
    };
is interpreted as
    var f = function ()
    {
        var x = undefined;
        document.writeln("3: " + x);
        x = 3;
    };
```

Variables declared and assigned within the scope of this inner (anonymous) function do not affect variables in the scope of the outer function, so the assignment x = 3 does not change x as shown in the final line of output.

As you can see, JavaScript is fertile ground for the creative interviewer.

6. **Let me help you with that...**

What is the value returned from this function?

```
function returnTrue()
{
    return
    {
        result: true;
    };
}
```

Somewhat surprisingly (or perhaps somewhat predictably given the nature of this chapter) the return value is not what it might seem. At first glance this function appears to return an object with a result property set to true. Actually, this function returns undefined. Here's a hint: The function works as expected if you rewrite at as follows:

```
function returnTrue()
{
    return {
        result: true;
    };
}
```

The difference is in the line containing the `return` statement. JavaScript expects return values to be on (or to start on) the same line as the `return` statement; otherwise, JavaScript assumes you missed a semicolon and adds one for you. In other words, a line like this...

```
return
    5;
```

...is interpreted as

```
return;
    5;
```

The automatic insertion of semicolons in certain statements is not a bug in JavaScript; it is according to the EMCAScript Language Specification (ECMA-262 section 7.9), which says (emphasis added):

Certain ECMAScript statements (*empty* statement, *variable* statement, *expression* statement, *do-while* statement, *continue* statement, *break* statement, *return* statement, and *throw* statement) must be terminated with semicolons. Such semicolons may always appear explicitly in the source text. For convenience, however, *such semicolons may be omitted from the source text in certain situations.*

---

7. **NaN**

   What is wrong with this test for NaN?

   ```
   if (dubiousNumber === NaN)
   {
       // ...
   }
   ```

   `NaN` is the only value in JavaScript that always returns `false` when compared to itself. This means the preceding test will always evaluate to `false`, even if `dubiousNumber` is `NaN`.

   Fortunately, JavaScript provides a built-in function to test for `NaN`.

   ```
   isNaN(NaN) === true
   ```

8. **What is the meaning of this!**

   To what does `this` refer in each occurrence of `document.writeln()`?

   ```
   document.writeln("A: " + this);

   var o = {
   ```

```
        f: function() {
            return this;
        }
};

document.writeln("B: " + o.f());

var f = o.f;
document.writeln("C: " + f());

var obj = {};
document.writeln("D: " + f.call(obj));

var o = {
    f: function() {
        var ff = function() {
            return this;
        };
        return ff();
    },
    g: {
            h: function() {
                    return this;
            }
        }
};

document.writeln("E: " + o.f());

document.writeln("F: " + o.g.h());
```

When run, this JavaScript produces the following output:

`A: [object Window]`

By default, this refers to the global object (window).

`B: [object Object]`

The function f() is a property of object o. When a function is called via an object as in o.f(), this refers to the parent object o.

`C: [object Window]`

When the function f is called directly (without referencing an object) this refers to the global object (window).

`D: [object Object]`

When a function is called via call(), the value of this refers to the first argument supplied. If the first argument is not an object, or if it is null then this refers to the global object (window). Here I supplied object obj so this is an object:

```
E: [object Window]
```

The function ff() is not a property of object o, so this refers to the global object (window).

```
F: [object Object]
```

The function h() is a function of nested object g, so this refers to the parent object g.

9. Reverse the words in a string

Write a short program in C# to reverse the order of words in the following string:

```
string dwarves = "bashful doc dopey grumpy happy sleepy sneezy";
```

Your output should look like this:

```
sneezy sleepy happy grumpy dopey doc bashful
```

This C# program splits the sentence with String.Split(). It then uses Enumerable.Reverse() to reverse and String.Join() to reconstruct the list of words

```
using System;
using System.Linq; // For the Reverse() method

namespace Ace
{
    public class ReverseWords
    {
        public static void Main(string[] args)
        {
            string dwarves =
                "bashful doc dopey grumpy happy sleepy sneezy";
            string sevrawd = String.Join(" ",
                dwarves.Split(' ').Reverse() );
            Console.WriteLine(sevrawd);
        }
    }
}
```

10. Magic numbers, avoiding

The following method was written to calculate the difference between two years. If it receives a "year of birth" that is greater than the supplied "current year" then it returns 999 to signify an invalid year of birth. Suggest three alternative ways this method could be improved so that it doesn't rely on a magic number 999.

Hint: Consider how you might indicate failure without returning a specific integer.

```
static int CalculateAge(int yearOfBirth, int currentYear)
{
    if (yearOfBirth > currentYear)
        return 999; // invalid year of birth

    return currentYear - yearOfBirth;
}
```

Magic numbers are generally best avoided. In the example shown, the number 999 is used as an indicator that the calculation failed. This is a magic number, and it puts the onus on the maintenance programmer to be aware of this number forever after. Also, if the number 999 should one day become a valid age (it is conceivable!) then this code would stop working.

One way of avoiding the problem would be to have the method return a nullable integer instead of an integer, so that if the calculation failed then the function could simply return `null` instead of an integer. This way there can be no confusion about the return value—you get an `int` if it works and a `null` if it fails, and because `null` is not even a valid integer it can never be confused for a valid age.

```
static int? CalculateAge(int yearOfBirth, int currentYear)
{
    if (yearOfBirth > currentYear)
        return null; // invalid year of birth

    return currentYear - yearOfBirth;
}
```

Another possibility would be to use an `out` parameter to return the calculated age, and change the method type to `bool` so that if the calculation fails the method will return `false`. The caller would need to check the return value before using the calculated age.

```
static bool CalculateAge(
                        int yearOfBirth,
                        int currentYear,
                        out int Age)
{
    Age = currentYear - yearOfBirth;

    return Age >= 0;
}
```

One more possibility would be to throw an exception if the calculation fails, perhaps an `ArgumentOutOfRangeException`. The caller would need to catch and handle this exception, but there is no chance of an invalid date leaking out of this function. The invalid result is unambiguous.

```
static int CalculateAge(int yearOfBirth, int currentYear)
{
    if (yearOfBirth > currentYear)
        throw new ArgumentOutOfRangeException();

    return currentYear - yearOfBirth;
}
```

11. A path on any platform

The following code does not work properly when run on Linux (compiled with Mono!) Suggest a way that this snippet could be improved so that it will produce a path that is compatible on other platforms while still retaining compatibility with Windows.

```
string path = folder + "\\" + file;
```

After you've discovered `Path.Combine()` you will never combine parts of a path with string concatenation ever again. (Will you promise?)

```
string path = Path.Combine(folder, file);
```

12. Debugging helper

What is the effect of applying the DebuggerDisplay attribute as per the following code?

```
[DebuggerDisplay("X = {X}, Y = {Y}")]
public class LittleHelp
{
    private int x;

    public int X { get { return x; } set { x = value; Y = -value; } }
    public int Y { get; set; }

}
```

This is an extremely useful attribute during development and debugging with Visual Studio. When you've interrupted an executing program (Debug ➤ Break All) you can then simply hover over the object instance and get a nicely formatted display of whatever you have put into the `DebuggerDisplay` attribute, as illustrated in Figure 8-7.

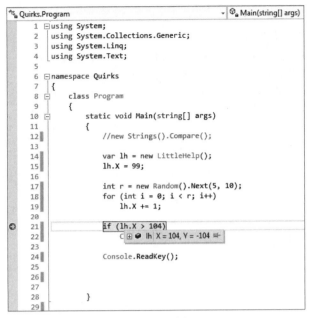

Figure 8-7: DebuggerDisplay tooltip

Figure 8-8 shows what you get by default, without using `DebuggerDisplay` attribute.

Figure 8-8: Debugging without DebuggerDisplay

13. The "as" keyword

What does the as keyword do, and how is it helpful?

The as keyword is like a cast operation, it attempts to convert a variable to a specified type. Unlike cast however, if the conversion is not possible it will return null instead of throwing an exception. This is useful when the cast might fail because it avoids the need to catch and handle an Exception. It is equivalent to the following expression:

```
expression is type ? (type)expression : (type)null
```

The following code illustrates the difference:

```
public class Foo
{
}

public class Bar : Foo
{
}

public class TestFooBar
{
    public void test()
    {
        Foo foo = new Foo();
        Bar bar = new Bar();

        Object list = new List<string>();

        var test = bar as Foo;   // OK, casts bar as Foo

        var test1 = list as Foo;  // OK, but test1 is null

        var test2 = (Foo)list;  // Throws an exception
    }
}
```

14. Verbatim string literals

What is a verbatim string literal and how is it helpful?

String literals in C# can contain escape sequences like \t (tab) and \n (newline) and \u00BB (Unicode symbol »).

```
string s = "My \t string \n contains \u00BB symbols";
```

When output to the console, this string is shown as in Figure 8-9.

Figure 8-9: String containing symbols

If you want to avoid this interpretation of escape sequences, you can use a verbatim string literal by prefixing the string with an @ symbol, as follows:

```
string s = @"My \t string \n contains \u00BB symbols";
```

When output to the console this string is shown as in Figure 8-10.

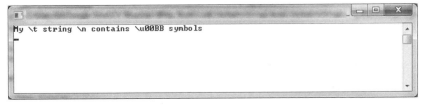

Figure 8-10: Verbatim string literal

If you want to include a quote character inside a verbatim string literal you need to escape it by using two consecutive quotes.

```
string s = @"My \t string \n ""contains"" \u00BB symbols";
```

When output to the console, this string is shown as in Figure 8-11.

Figure 8-11: Quotes in a verbatim literal string

15. Immutable strings

If strings are immutable, meaning that strings cannot be altered, what happens to myString *when you append to it as in the following code?*

```
string myString = "prince";
myString += "ss"; // How can I do this if strings are immutable?
```

Strings in .NET (and Java) are truly immutable. After they come into existence they can't be changed without resorting to unsafe code. Examples like the one in this question appear to contradict this fact, but looks are deceptive.

The syntax used to manipulate strings gives the appearance of modification but under the hood the object that myString references is actually being replaced with a new string object. This can be confirmed easily using the Object.ReferenceEquals() method, which returns true if two object instances are the same instance.

```
public void Compare()
{
    string a = "prince";
    string b = a;

    Console.WriteLine(string.Format("a == '{0}', b=='{1}'", a,  b));
    Console.WriteLine(string.Format("(a == b) == {0}",  (a == b)));
    Console.WriteLine("Object.ReferenceEquals(a,b) == " +
        Object.ReferenceEquals(a, b));

    // Now "modify" a, the reference changes!
    a += "ss";

    Console.WriteLine(string.Format("a == '{0}', b=='{1}'", a, b));
    Console.WriteLine(string.Format("(a == b) == {0}", (a == b)));
    Console.WriteLine("Object.ReferenceEquals(a,b) == " +
        Object.ReferenceEquals(a, b));

    // Restore the original value, the original reference returns!
    a = "prince";

    Console.WriteLine(string.Format("a == '{0}', b=='{1}'", a, b));
    Console.WriteLine(string.Format("(a == b) == {0}", (a == b)));
    Console.WriteLine("Object.ReferenceEquals(a,b) == " +
        Object.ReferenceEquals(a, b));
}
```

16. Reverse the words in a string

Write a short program to reverse the order of words in the following string:

```
String dwarves = "bashful doc dopey grumpy happy sleepy sneezy";
```

Your output should look like this:

```
sneezy sleepy happy grumpy dopey doc bashful
```

This answer splits the string on whitespace and then uses a LIFO (last in, first out) stack to reverse the list:

```
import java.util.*;
import java.lang.*;

public class Main
{
    public static void main (String[] args)
        throws java.lang.Exception
    {
        String dwarves =
            "bashful doc dopey grumpy happy sleepy sneezy";

        List<String> list = Arrays.asList(dwarves.split(" "));
        Stack<String> s = new Stack<String>();
        s.addAll(list);

        String sevrawd = "";

        while (!s.empty()) {
            sevrawd += s.pop() + " ";
        }

        System.out.println(sevrawd);
    }
}
```

17. Double brace initialization

The following code declares, creates, and initializes an instance of List<String> *using what is often called double brace initialization.*

Explain how double brace initialization works and rewrite this code to initialize the instance without using double brace initialization.

```
List<String> list = new ArrayList<String>() {{
    add("Lister");
    add("Rimmer");
    add("Kryten");
}};
```

Quite a lot is going on within these two braces. The first brace creates a new *anonymous inner class*. The second brace declares an *instance initializer* block. This initializer block is run when the anonymous inner class is instantiated, adding three strings to the new list. This style of initialization does not work for final classes because it relies on the creation of an anonymous subclass.

The code shown in the question could have been written as:

```
List<String> list = new ArrayList<String>();
list.add("Lister");
list.add("Rimmer");
list.add("Kryten");
```

18. Labelled blocks

Explain what happens when the break *statement is executed in the following code excerpt*:

```
int i;
int j = 0;
boolean found = false;
int [] [] arr = {
    { 4,  8,  15,  16,  23,  42 },
    { 11,  23,  29,  41,  43,  47 },
    { 757,  787,  797,  919,  929,  10301 }
};
int find = 41;


iterate:
for (i = 0; i < arr.length; i++) {
    for (j = 0; j < arr[i].length; j++)
    {
        if (arr[i][j] == find) {
            found = true;
            break iterate;
        }
    }
}

if (found) {
    System.out.println("Found");
} else {
    System.out.println("Not found");
}
```

This excerpt searches a two-dimensional array of integers for the integer 41. It does this by iterating over each dimension and comparing each element to the value of find. When it finds a match it sets found to true and then executes a break statement. The break statement terminates the loop that is labelled iterate. Execution continues at the if (found) statement.

19. There can be only one

Describe the design pattern that is being implemented in the following code:

```
public enum Highlander {
        INSTANCE;
        public void execute () {
                //... perform operation here ...
        }
}
```

The *singleton pattern* is a design pattern that is intended to limit the number of instances of a class to exactly one. This can useful when an object is responsible for coordinating access to a unique resource such as a system queue or an item of hardware. There are a number of different ways of implementing this pattern but this implementation using enum is said to be the best (by Joshua Bloch in *Effective Java, Second Edition*).

20. Reverse the words in a string

Write a short program to reverse the order of words in the following string:

```
my $dwarves = "bashful doc dopey grumpy happy sleepy sneezy";
```

Your output should look like this:

```
sneezy sleepy happy grumpy dopey doc bashful
```

A simple algorithm that works well with Perl is

1. Split the string into words.

2. Reverse the list of words obtained in step 1.

3. Join the words obtained in step 2 using a single space between them.

   You accomplish step 1 with the split operator.

   ```
   my @words = split ' ', $dwarves;
   ```

   When a single space is used as the separator character, split looks for any contiguous whitespace (not just a single space). The split operator discards leading spaces, trailing spaces, and extra spaces between words, so it works well regardless of spacing in the string.

   Step 2 is to reverse the list of words.

   ```
   my @reverse = reverse @words;
   ```

Step 3 is to put the reversed words back together, joining them with a single space.

```
my $sevrawd = join ' ', @reverse;
```

Mission accomplished in three lines. It could be done in one:

```
my $sevrawd = join ' ', reverse split ' ', $dwarves;
```

21. Sorting 101

The following Perl code is an attempt to sort a list of numbers into numerical order, but it does not work correctly. Explain what might be wrong and suggest an improvement that will properly sort these numbers into ascending numerical order.

```
my @list = ( 1, 4, 1, 5, 9, 2, 6, 5, 3, 5, 10, 20, 30, 40 );
print join ",", sort @list;
```

By default, the sort operator sorts values alphabetically using the cmp operator. The sort in this question is equivalent to

```
sort { $a cmp $b } @list;
```

This results in an alphabetically sorted list of numbers:

```
1,1,10,2,20,3,30,4,40,5,5,5,6,9
```

To sort values numerically you must use the numeric comparison operator as follows:

```
sort { $a <=> $b } @list;
```

This returns a numerically sorted list:

```
1,1,2,3,4,5,5,5,6,9,10,20,30,40
```

To sort the list in descending numeric order you simply reverse the arguments in the sort block.

```
sort { $b <=> $a } @list;
```

This returns a numerically descending sorted list:

```
40,30,20,10,9,6,5,5,5,4,3,2,1,1
```

22. Sorting 201

Suppose you have a list of characters as follows. Write code to produce two lists; the first sorted by race, the second sorted by age then race.

```
my @list = (
        [qw(Pippin   Hobbit   29)],
        [qw(Merry    Hobbit   37)],
        [qw(Frodo    Hobbit   51)],
        [qw(Legolas  Elf      650)],
        [qw(Gimli    Dwarf    140)],
        [qw(Gandalf  Maiar    2021)],
        [qw(Aragorn  Man      88)],
        [qw(Sam      Hobbit   36)],
        [qw(Boromir  Man      41)],
);
```

Sorting by race is relatively simple; you just need to refer to the race column in each list item as follows:

```
my @race = sort { $a->[1] cmp $b->[1] } @list;
```

Sorting by age and then by race requires a bit more logic. Because Perl comparison operators return 0 when two items are equal you can use the logical-or operator || to introduce a "tie break" comparison, as follows:

```
my @race = sort {     $a->[2] <=> $b->[2]
                  || $a->[1] cmp $b->[1] } @list;
```

Putting this together, here is a complete Perl program to produce the two lists as required by the question:

```
use strict; use warnings;

my @list = (
        [qw(Pippin   Hobbit   29)],
        [qw(Merry    Hobbit   37)],
        [qw(Frodo    Hobbit   51)],
        [qw(Legolas  Elf      650)],
        [qw(Gimli    Dwarf    140)],
        [qw(Gandalf  Maiar    2021)],
        [qw(Aragorn  Man      88)],
        [qw(Sam      Hobbit   36)],
        [qw(Boromir  Man      41)],
);

my @race = sort { $a->[1] cmp $b->[1] } @list;
print "Sorted by race:\n";
&printCompany(@race);

print "Sorted by age then race:\n";
@race = sort {     $a->[2] <=> $b->[2]
               || $a->[1] cmp $b->[1] } @list;

&printCompany(@race);
```

```
sub printCompany() {

    foreach my $i (@_) {
        print "$i->[0]\t$i->[1]\t$i->[2]\n";
    }

    print "---\n";
}
```

This program produces the following output:

```
Sorted by race:
Gimli    Dwarf    140
Legolas  Elf      650
Pippin   Hobbit   29
Merry    Hobbit   37
Frodo    Hobbit   51
Sam      Hobbit   36
Gandalf  Maiar    2021
Aragorn  Man      88
Boromir  Man      41
---

Sorted by age then race:
Pippin   Hobbit   29
Sam      Hobbit   36
Merry    Hobbit   37
Boromir  Man      41
Frodo    Hobbit   51
Aragorn  Man      88
Gimli    Dwarf    140
Legolas  Elf      650
Gandalf  Maiar    2021
---
```

23. Sorting 301: The Schwartzian Transform

Write a Schwartzian Transform that will sort the following list into numeric order, from "one" to "nine."

```
my @list = qw/three two one six five four nine eight seven/;
```

This problem becomes much easier if you introduce a hash to map the English words to their integer equivalents. Then, you can simply sort on the integer value of each word using the hash to look up values for each word.

```
my @numbers = qw/three two one six five four nine eight seven/;

my %values = (
    'one' => 1,
    'two' => 2,
```

```
        'three' => 3,
        'four' => 4,
        'five' => 5,
        'six' => 6,
        'seven' => 7,
        'eight' => 8,
        'nine' => 9
);

# Here is the ST, taking advantage of the %values hash
my @sorted =
    map { $_->[1] }
    sort { $a->[0] <=> $b->[0] }
    map { [$values{$_}, $_] } @numbers;

print join ',', @sorted;
```

24. Context matters

Built-in functions such as sort *are sensitive to the context in which they are called. If you call* sort *in a list context you will get back a list. If you call* sort *in a scalar context you will get back* undefined.

Write a sensitiveSort *subroutine that sorts* @_ *and returns a string if called in scalar context. In other words, wrap the built-in* sort *routine so that* sort *no longer returns* undefined *in scalar context.*

The key to this answer is being aware of the wantarray operator. This is the only reliable way to determine whether a subroutine (or eval block) has been called in list or scalar (or void) context. Here is one possible solution that uses wantarray:

```
use strict; use warnings;

sub sensitiveSort {
    return wantarray ? sort @_ : join ',', sort @_;
}

my @list = ( 1, 4, 1, 5, 9, 2, 6, 5, 3, 5, 10, 20, 30, 40);

# list context
print "The first element is: " . (sensitiveSort (@list))[0];

# scalar context
print "\nThe sorted list: " . sensitiveSort(@list);
```

25. The branch you're standing on

The following code is intended to loop over an array of numbers and print the square of each number and the total of all squares. This code works but it

*has unintended consequences. What are these unintended consequences and
how can they be avoided?*

```
use strict; use warnings;

my @array = (1 .. 9);
my $sum = 0;

foreach my $num (@array) {
    print "$num^2=";
    $num = $num * $num;
    print "$num\n";
    $sum += $num;
}


print "Sum of squares is $sum\n";
```

The output is:

```
1^2=1
2^2=4
3^2=9
4^2=16
5^2=25
6^2=36
7^2=49
8^2=64
9^2=81
Sum of squares is 285
```

In this question you have a loop that iterates over an array, using
the variable $num as the iterator variable. You modify this iterator
variable to obtain the square of each number. The mistake is that by
modifying this variable, you are also modifying each element of the
original array. This is almost certainly an unintended consequence.
You can see the modified array by printing it after your loop.

```
print join "\n", @array;
```

You can see that the array now contains squares instead of the original values 1 to 9.

```
1
4
9
16
25
36
```

```
49
64
81
```

Making this mistake without realizing that the original data is being changed is easy. The best way to avoid this unintended consequence is to avoid modifying an iterator variable within a loop, as shown next.

```perl
use strict; use warnings;

my @array = (1 .. 9);
my $sum = 0;

foreach my $num (@array) {
    my $square = $num * $num;
    print "$num^2=" . $square . "\n";
    $sum += $square;
}

print "Sum of squares is $sum\n";

print join "\n", @array;
```

Now, when you run this improved program you get the same result, but this time you avoid modification of the original array.

```
1^2=1
2^2=4
3^2=9
4^2=16
5^2=25
6^2=36
7^2=49
8^2=64
9^2=81
Sum of squares is 285

The original array remains as first initialised:

1
2
3
4
5
6
7
8
9
```

26. Perl isn't Java

This Perl code does not behave as the programmer intended. What is wrong with it? Rewrite it so that it will behave as the programmer probably intended.

```
my $dwarves = "bashful doc dopey grumpy happy sleepy sneezy";

print &ReverseWords($dwarves);

sub ReverseWords {
    my $arg = shift;

    if ($arg != null) {
        return join ' ', reverse split ' ', $dwarves;
    }
}
```

If you spend much time programming in languages such as Java and C#, then you might develop a habit of checking that arguments are not null before performing operations on them. This is generally a good habit to have.

If you haven't already realized, the code in this question fails because Perl does not have a built-in value of null. The closest equivalent is undef. Perl interprets the null (without any quotes) as a *bareword* (a string) meaning that this line

```
if ($arg != null) {
```

is interpreted as if it had been written as

```
if ($arg != 'null') {   # Bareword interpreted as string
```

But that is not all. Another problem is that the numeric comparison operator != has been used instead of the string comparison operator cmp. This leads Perl further astray, as if this line had been written as

```
if ($arg != 0) {   # Numeric interpretation of the string 'null'
```

Now when the seven dwarves are passed as an argument, Perl will also interpret that dwarfish string as a number; that is, 0, meaning that you end up with an expression that will never evaluate to true.

```
if (0 != 0) {   # Will never be true
```

Seasoned Perl programmers will have noticed that this code is missing two useful pragma directives:

```
use warnings;
use strict;
```

When these are added Perl complains loudly about the mistaken code.

```
C:\code>PerlIsNotJava.pl
Bareword "null" not allowed while "strict subs" in use
at C:\code\PerlIsNotJava.pl line 11.
Execution of C:\code\PerlIsNotJava.pl aborted due to
compilation errors.
```

The programmer who wrote this probably intended simply to check that an argument is supplied before attempting to operate on it. The following code works correctly:

```
use warnings;
use strict;

my $dwarves = "bashful doc dopey grumpy happy sleepy sneezy";

print &ReverseWords($dwarves);

sub ReverseWords {
    my $arg = shift;

    if ($arg) {
        return join ' ', reverse split ' ', $dwarves;
    }
}
```

27. Reverse the words in a string

Write a short program to reverse the order of words in the following string:

```
dwarves = "bashful doc dopey grumpy happy sleepy sneezy";
```

Your output should look like this:

```
sneezy sleepy happy grumpy dopey doc bashful
print dwarves.split.reverse.join(' ')
```

28. Swap variable values without a temp variable

Write code to swap the values of two variables without using a temporary variable.

In other words, start with

```
x == 1
y == 2
```

and write code to obtain

```
x == 2
y == 1
```

Swapping the values of two variables was one of the first programming techniques I was ever taught. The pattern I was shown was to use a temporary variable to hold one of the values while you replace that variable.

```
initialize two variables...
x = 1
y = 2

now swap them...
temp = x
x = y
y = temp
```

Ruby (and Perl) removes the need for a temporary variable by supporting a language feature called *parallel assignment*:

```
x = 1
y = 2

x,y = y,x  # Parallel assignment, swapping values
```

You should also be aware of the technique known as the *XOR swap*. This is a "clever" bit of code that I would never recommend for real production code simply because understanding it is hard unless you happen know the trick.

```
# initialize two variables
x = 1
y = 2

# now swap them with xor
x = x ^ y
y = x ^ y
x = x ^ y
```

To understand this magical swap it helps to remember how the bitwise XOR operator works. The rule for XOR is "one or the other, but not both." Here is the XOR truth table:

```
0 xor 0 = 0
0 xor 1 = 1
1 xor 0 = 1
1 xor 1 = 0
```

If you step through the XOR swap with binary numbers (in place of decimal) then seeing how it works is a bit easier.

```
# Binary numbers
x = 01  # = decimal 1
y = 10  # = decimal 2
```

```
# swap them
x = x ^ y  # 01 ^ 10 = 11 = decimal 3
# (x accumulates the value of y)
y = x ^ y  # 11 ^ 10 = 01 = decimal 1 (swapped!)
x = x ^ y  # 11 ^ 01 = 10 = decimal 2 (swapped!)
```

29. &&= operator

What does the following code do, and how is it potentially helpful?

```
myString &&= myString + suffix
```

You are probably familiar with the | | and && operators, the Boolean OR and Boolean AND operators. You might also be aware of the Boolean OR EQUALS operator | |=, which assigns a value to variable if it doesn't already have one. It is handy when you want to assign a default value.

```
a ||= 1  # If a has no value, give it a value of 1
```

The AND EQUALS operator works similarly, but it will assign a value only if the variable already has one. It is handy when you want to append a string (like a suffix, for example), but only if the variable already has a value.

30. Reverse the words in a string

Write a short program to reverse the order of words in the following string:

```
DECLARE @dwarves VARCHAR(MAX)
SET @dwarves = 'bashful doc dopey grumpy happy sleepy sneezy'
```

Your output should look like this:

```
sneezy sleepy happy grumpy dopey doc bashful
```

If you contrast the code for this answer with the equivalent code in other languages (most of which are one-liners) you will, I hope, come to the conclusion that T-SQL is not the best language for this kind of operation.

```
DECLARE @dwarves VARCHAR(MAX)
SET @dwarves = 'bashful doc dopey grumpy happy sleepy sneezy'

DECLARE @sevrawd VARCHAR(MAX)
SET @sevrawd = ''

WHILE LEN(@dwarves) > 0
BEGIN
    IF CHARINDEX(' ', @dwarves) > 0
```

```
        BEGIN
            SET @sevrawd =
                SUBSTRING(@dwarves,0,CHARINDEX(' ', @dwarves))
                + ' ' + @sevrawd
            SET @dwarves =
                LTRIM(RTRIM(SUBSTRING(@dwarves,CHARINDEX(' ',
                @dwarves)+1,LEN(@dwarves))))
        END
        ELSE
        BEGIN
            SET @sevrawd = @dwarves + ' ' + @sevrawd
            SET @dwarves = ''
        END
    END

    SELECT @sevrawd
```

31. Correlated subquery

Consider the following table. This table contains a list of users, each with a reputation and a location.

```
CREATE TABLE [dbo].[Users](
            [Id] [int] NOT NULL,
            [Reputation] [int] NULL,
            [DisplayName] [nchar](40) NULL,
            [Location] [nchar](100) NULL,
            [JoinDate] [smalldatetime] NULL
)
```

Write a select *statement that uses a correlated subquery to obtain a list of users with a higher-than-average reputation within that user's location.*

A *correlated subquery* is a nested (or inner) query that references one or more values in the parent (or outer) query. In the following answer, the inner query references the location of the user from the parent query. Notice that table aliases are used to uniquely identify each table.

```
SELECT DisplayName, Reputation, Location
FROM Users u
WHERE Reputation >
(SELECT AVG(Reputation)
FROM Users u1
WHERE u1.Location = u.Location)
```

Now that you know what a correlated subquery actually is, you can write the SQL *and* you can casually mention its fancy name. The bonus points are all yours.

It is also worth being aware (and mentioning at the interview) that most correlated subqueries can be written using joins. For instance, you could have written the answer to this question as follows:

```
SELECT u.DisplayName, u.Reputation, u.Location
FROM Users u
INNER JOIN
(SELECT Location, AVG(Reputation) as AvgRep
FROM Users
GROUP BY Location) as u1
ON u.Location = u1.Location
AND u.Reputation > AvgRep
```

The query optimizer (most RDBMSs have one) will usually work out an optimal execution plan regardless of the presence or absence of a correlated subquery. If performance is important (it isn't always the most important thing) then you would benchmark and compare alternative queries to determine the most efficient. Very few hard-and-fast rules exist about the efficiency of correlated subqueries versus joins.

32. Which date is that?

The following two lines of SQL are supposed to insert a new row into the Users table. Assuming that this SQL worked correctly at least once (when the developer wrote and tested it) what could potentially go wrong with it, and how could you rewrite it to avoid this problem?

```
INSERT INTO Users (Id, DisplayName, JoinDate)
VALUES (1, 'Ted', CONVERT(smalldatetime,'12/01/2015'))
```

The potential problem with this SQL is that the date literal might be interpreted incorrectly. The date `'12/01/2015'` is ambiguous because it could mean the first day of December or the twelfth day of January, depending on the active date format.

If you think that the date format on server or in a database will never change, you join a very large group of programmers to whom the inevitable is yet to happen. If it doesn't happen on the server-side, it will happen on the client-side, in a third-party component, or in some data provided by a customer. Sooner or later it will happen.

The correct handling of dates is not difficult, provided you follow a few simple rules. Foremost of these rules is that whenever you write a date literal you should use an unambiguous date format.

You can easily see the impact of different language settings in T-SQL by converting a string containing a date to a `smalldatetime` as demonstrated in the following lines of SQL:

```
set language us_english
select CONVERT(smalldatetime,'12/01/2015') as [Date]
```

```
Output:

Changed language setting to us_english.
```

```
Date
----------------------
2015-12-01 00:00:00
```

When the language is set to `british`, SQL Server interprets this as a completely different date.

```
set language british
select CONVERT(smalldatetime,'12/01/2015') as [Date]
```

```
Output:

Changed language setting to British.
Date
----------------------
2015-01-12 00:00:00
```

A date that is misinterpreted this way can be disastrous; for example it could be the expiry date of an immigration visa, or of a life insurance policy. To avoid ambiguity in date literals you should always use one of the following two formats:

```
// Format 1
YYYYMMDD  // For a date-only (no time), notice no hyphens!

20121210  // 10th of December, 2012
19011111  // 11th of November, 1901

// Format 2
YYYY-MM-DDTHH:MM:SS  // For specifying a time + date, notice the 'T'

1920-08-18T00:00:00  // 18th of August, 1920
2012-01-10T01:02:03  // 10th of Jan, 2012, at 3 seconds past 1:02am
```

These two formats are from the ISO 8601 standard for calendar dates, and SQL Server will always interpret these dates in a predictable way regardless of language or date-format settings. Note that you should avoid a few "close but not quite" date formats because they are also ambiguous.

```
YYYY-MM-DD  // Ambiguous!
YYYY-MM-DD HH:MM:SS  // Ambiguous! (Missing the 'T')
```

33. Collation order

Consider a scenario where your SQL Server database is deployed to a customer site and to an existing SQL Server instance alongside other databases that you don't control or know anything about. In that circumstance, what is potentially wrong (or perhaps missing) in this CREATE TABLE *statement, and how should you rewrite it to avoid this potential problem?*

```
CREATE TABLE #temp
(
    [Id]  int     identity(1,1) NOT NULL,
    [Name] nvarchar(100) NULL,
    [DateJoined] smalldatetime NULL
)
```

When a table is created, all the text columns in that table (for example, varchar, nvarchar, and so on) will, by default assume the same *collation* as the database in which the table is created. However, the same is not true of temporary tables (indicated by the #) which, by default, take on the collation of the tempdb database (this is the database in which temporary tables are created by SQL Server). The collation of the tempdb database can be different to the collation of your database and this can lead to runtime errors such as "cannot resolve the collation conflict." Depending on the nature of the problem, one solution is to add COLLATE DATABASE_DEFAULT to all text columns when creating a temporary table.

```
CREATE TABLE #temp
(
    [Id]  int     identity(1,1) NOT NULL,
    [Name] nvarchar(100) COLLATE DATABASE_DEFAULT NULL,
    [DateJoined] smalldatetime NULL
)
```

Another possible solution is to add the same collation modifier to the join clause.

```
SELECT * from #temp
INNER JOIN Users ON
  [name]=[DisplayName] COLLATE DATABASE_DEFAULT
```

34. Selecting a random row from a table

Write a SELECT *statement that will select a single row at random from the Users table. Assume the table has between 10 and 10,000 rows.*

At least two solutions exist to this problem. The first takes advantage of the TABLESAMPLE clause, introduced with SQL Server 2005.

```
SELECT TOP 1 *
FROM Users
TABLESAMPLE (1 ROWS)
```

This solution is not ideal for several reasons. First, the TABLESAMPLE clause works on a page level, not a row level. It will pick a random page from the table and return all rows in that page. If you want just one row (or *n* rows), you need to add the TOP 1 (or TOP *n*) clause to your select statement. Unfortunately, if you restrict the number of rows this way, then some rows might never be selected. For example, if a page contains 10 rows and you constrain your query to return just the TOP 5 rows, the last 5 rows on this page will never be selected. This is a trade-off when using the TABLESAMPLE clause.

Another problem with TABLESAMPLE is that if you have a table with just one page then TABLESAMPLE will return either all rows or no rows at all. That probably isn't what you want!

TABLESAMPLE is good for obtaining an approximate number of rows from a large table, but poor at obtaining a single row at random from smaller tables.

The limitations of TABLESAMPLE are by design, and are well-described in the official documentation on MSDN. The documentation includes an alternative (as follows) for when you "really want a random sample of individual rows."

Here is the documented suggestion for obtaining a 1 percent sample of random rows from a table called SalesOrderDetail:

```
SELECT * FROM Sales.SalesOrderDetail
WHERE 0.01 >= CAST(CHECKSUM(NEWID(), SalesOrderID)
              & 0x7fffffff AS float)
/ CAST (0x7fffffff AS int)
```

This query is worth a closer look because it contains a few useful techniques. First, notice that the CHECKSUM function takes two arguments: the built-in function NEWID() and the value of SalesOrderID for each row. Basing a checksum on these values ensures that a unique *checksum* value will be generated for each row in the table.

The second thing to notice is how this query converts this unique value to a number between 0 and 1. The CHECKSUM function returns an INT in the range -2^{31} to 2^{31}. This INT is converted to a positive number by discarding the sign-bit (bitwise AND with 0x7fffffff) and then casting as a float. The final step of dividing by 0x7fffffff results in a number between 0 and 1. If this number is less than or equal to 0.01 (1%), then the row is included in the selected results. This query relies on a uniform distribution of random numbers.

If a single row (or a fixed number of rows) is required then this query can be greatly simplified as follows:

```
SELECT TOP 1 * FROM Users
ORDER BY NEWID()
```

This is the simplest method to select one row at random and it is the answer most interviewers will be looking for.

Testing—Not Just for Testers

There are many different kinds of testing and nearly all of them are annoying to the typical programmer. Programmers are driven to create things, build products, add features, and make things work. Testing is just the opposite. It's about finding weaknesses, exploiting edge cases, burrowing into a system, and making it break. It is a totally different mindset, which, to many people, is a good reason why programmers should not be allowed to test their own work.

"I don't understand—it worked on my machine"

—Almost every programmer at some point

But there is one kind of testing that is universally accepted as being suitable for programmers, and that is *unit testing*. Everyone agrees it would be a good idea if programmers did more of it, and some people think that programmers should write unit tests even before they write any functional code. Writing tests first is called *test-driven development* (*TDD*) and although it hasn't quite achieved the same degree of popular acceptance as plain old unit testing (POUT), TDD evangelists claim that it makes programmers more productive and improves code quality.

Some aspects of unit testing remain difficult—most notably, factoring out external dependencies (such as databases and networks) from unit tests without introducing an undesirable level of complexity. Adding unit tests to legacy code can be hindered by excessive coupling (where component A depends on B, C, D, E), which can make isolating a given function for proper unit testing difficult.

Tools and techniques are available that can tackle these difficulties. One of the most common techniques is to factor out concrete dependencies (that is, classes) into abstract dependencies (that is, interfaces), which makes substituting fake (or "mock") classes for the purpose of testing easy. Tools are available that allow a programmer to dynamically (that is, at runtime) break these dependencies and substitute fake classes and functionality via *mock objects*. Some of these tools are free, and some are very much not free.

Unit Tests

A *unit test* is a method for testing a unit of code to determine its fitness for use. This immediately raises the question of what constitutes a "unit," and thereby hangs a pointless debate. Some programmers believe a unit equates to a class, and others think a unit equates to a method or function. Still others think a unit is simply the smallest isolatable component of a program. Perhaps the most sophisticated opinion is that a unit is a single path of execution through a function or method (perhaps one of many such paths, depending on how much logic the function contains).

Pragmatic programmers define a unit as being "one thing" and then excuse themselves from the debate to get back to writing clean code and shipping software.

Whichever definition is used, all sane programmers agree that a unit test is not something that is done by hand. A unit test is an *automated* test that exercises an *isolated component* and confirms that the *outcome is according to expectations*.

Test-Driven Development

Many programmers are strongly in favor of writing tests before they write the actual code to be tested. These programmers reason that writing tests first has a number of benefits:

- It forces a programmer to answer the question, "What should this code do?" at a very detailed level. In other words, writing the tests first requires the programmer to think about concrete requirements before coding. This can reduce the time spent reworking code during later stages of development.

- It encourages the programmer to write the minimum amount of code necessary to pass the test, and then to stop. This keeps code-bloat to a minimum.

- It encourages the programmer to write code that is easy to test. Code that is easy to test is usually also modular and has minimal dependencies.

TDD is an increasingly popular school of thought and experience of TDD is prized by many interviewers.

Behavior-driven development

Behavior-driven development (*BDD*) is an evolution of TDD that produces the same outcome (coded unit tests) but which places more emphasis on specifying the *behavior* of "units" and introduces a domain-specific vocabulary to aid team communications and testing documentation. BDD activities are usually supported by a tool such as NBehave.

Red, green, refactor

Just like any decent school of thought, TDD has its own mantra. The TDD mantra is "Red, green, refactor." This mantra describes an ideal process of writing code and tests.

- **Red:** First, one or more tests are written that will be used to exercise the not-yet-written code. This test will fail and cause the testing framework to show a red test result.

- **Green:** The next stage is to write the minimum amount of code required to make the newly written test pass. The idea is that you give little consideration to writing elegant or extensible code at this stage, focusing on nothing more than making the tests pass. Passing tests are usually displayed in green in the UI of the testing framework.

- **Refactor:** The final stage is to take the code that passes the new test and to rewrite it so that it is maintainable and meets other important quality criteria. One of the key benefits of first having a test in place is that it increases the programmers' confidence that they have not inadvertently broken the correct behavior of their newly written code while refactoring it.

Writing Good Unit Tests

The idea of unit testing has been around for quite some time and although areas of debate persist, a few widely accepted good practices have risen to the surface.

Run quickly

Foremost among the good practices is that *a unit test should run quickly*. A single test that takes a whole second to run might seem harmless when it is first created, but when joined by 10,000 other tests each taking a second, then the test suite suddenly becomes impractical (10,000 seconds is nearly three hours) to run as often as needed. Anything that you do in a test suite that slows down test execution is probably not the right thing to do—for instance, a database round-trip is usually not part of a good unit test. It simply takes too long.

Be simple

A unit test should be simple. Unit tests should be easy to write and simple to read. Complex unit tests can easily end up bogging down development. You must avoid creating a burdensome suite of tests where programmers in your team avoid updating the tests simply because they are hard to understand. (Obviously the same applies to all code, not just tests, but the point is well applied here.)

A unit test should ideally test just one thing. This makes tracing the cause of a test failure easy to do. If a unit test covers more than one thing then finding out which thing failed the test takes more effort than it ought to. This is not a hard and fast rule; sometimes it can be expedient to test several things in a single unit test in order to minimize the repetition of setup/teardown routines.

Be self-evident

A unit test should be self-evident. In other words the point of a test should be plain as day. If you have to wrinkle your nose and squint before you can see what a unit test does then the test is probably too complex. All the usual rules of good coding practice apply to unit tests (with the possible exception of Don't Repeat Yourself—unit tests do tend to look similar). To help make a unit test self-evident choose good method and variable names, use whitespace to assist readers, and use code comments when some aspect of your test is unavoidably opaque.

Be helpful when failing

A unit test should be helpful when it fails, it should indicate exactly what went wrong, and when a test fails you should be pleased. You should be happy because it means that the test has noticed something has gone wrong and prevented you from noticing it later, say during an important customer demo or when your rocket reaches the stratosphere. A good unit test not only serves to catch your mistakes, but also pinpoints the source of a problem when it finds one. The output of a unit test should resemble the finest bug report you've ever seen. Good bug reports make me happy.

Be self-contained

A unit test should be self-contained. If a test has dependencies that are out of its control then it can fail at any time and you won't know why without spending time investigating. Suppose the test relies on an environment variable having a certain value. If another test is added to the test suite and it relies on that variable having a different value then one of these tests is bound to fail. This can devolve into a race-condition (or whack-a-mole if you prefer) where one test sets a value only to have it immediately set to a different value by another test running at the same time.

NOTE If your code is riddled with globally shared state variables then you have other more significant things to worry about than the stability of your unit tests.

Testing Slow Things

The ideal that a unit test must run quickly generates a surprising amount of controversy. The ideal of "must run quickly" seems to be interpreted by some programmers as if it means you shouldn't test slow things. These programmers think that if you have a routine that reaches out to the database, that communicates over a network, or that thrashes the hard disk for a while, then because the test might be slow you shouldn't test it.

That idea is plainly wrong. The only time you can ignore testing is if the correctness of your application doesn't matter.

In short, any worthwhile tests that do not run quickly should be segregated, kept apart from the suite of unit tests. They could be run in the background at periodic intervals, maybe once per day if they are really slow. They might be split into several sets of tests and run in parallel on different machines. They might serve as a useful suite of *regression tests* just prior to staging an application for user acceptance testing.

There are all kinds of things you can do with these slow tests, but you mustn't be tempted to mix them up with unit tests or toss them out just because they are slow.

Unit Testing Frameworks

It is perfectly possible, if a little masochistic, to write unit tests without using a unit testing framework. However, the advantages of a unit testing framework are many, and the disadvantages...actually, I can't think of any. If you write unit tests then you should use a framework.

One of the best known and widely used family of unit testing frameworks is *xUnit*. Most popular programming languages have a variant of xUnit:

- NUnit for .NET
- CppUnit for C++
- JUnit for Java

- Test::Class for Perl
- Test::Unit for Ruby
- PHPUnit for PHP
- Unittest (previous known as PyUnit) for Python
- DUnit for Delphi

If you write code using Visual Studio then you are probably aware of Microsoft's Visual Studio unit testing framework, known affectionately as "The Microsoft Visual Studio Unit Testing Framework." Support for this testing framework is built into the Visual Studio IDE and a command-line utility (MSTest.exe) can be used to run these tests. Many programmers understandably use "MS Test" as kind of shorthand for the Visual Studio framework though strictly speaking they are different things. The Microsoft framework is very similar to NUnit, the testing framework that predates it. Both of these frameworks use code attributes to indicate test classes (that is, the classes containing unit tests) and test methods (that is, the actual unit tests).

Here is an example of a Visual Studio test class containing one unit test. The attributes used to indicate a test class and a test method are highlighted.

```
[TestClass]
public class TestClass
{
    [TestMethod]
    public void MyTest()
    {
        Assert.IsTrue(true);
    }
}
```

The equivalent attributes in NUnit are `[TestFixture]` and `[Test]`:

```
[TestFixture]
public class TestClass
{
    [Test]
    public void MyTest()
    {
        Assert.IsTrue(true);
    }
}
```

Notice that this test contains exactly one line that calls the static `IsTrue` method of the `Assert` class. As written this test is useless; it doesn't test anything. A typical test compares an expected result to an actual result, something more like this:

```
[TestClass]
public class TestClass
{
```

```
[TestMethod]
public void MyTest()
{
    bool actualResult = Foo();

    Assert.IsTrue(actualResult);
}
}
```

Mock Objects

Sometimes an object is bound up with another object in such a way that makes testing it in isolation difficult. You might, for instance, have a method that performs a calculation using data retrieved from a database. For a unit test you ideally want to avoid retrieving actual data from a database because

- You want tight control over the data that is used for this test; for instance, you want to ensure that your test covers rare edge cases that might not exist in the database when the test is run. Alternatively, you want to avoid the overhead of ensuring that certain data exists in the database before running the unit test.

- You want to avoid the overhead of establishing a database connection and retrieving data from the database so that (in keeping with the attributes of a good unit test) the test will run quickly.

Consider the following method:

```
public decimal CalcFoo()
{
    var df = new DataFetcher();
    var data = df.GetData();

    var result = data.Take(100).Average();

    return result;
}
```

The `CalcFoo` method relies on the `GetData` method of the concrete `DataFetcher` class. If you replace the reference to `DataFetcher` with a reference to an `IDataFetcher` interface then you can easily substitute a fake (mock) class when you need to; that is, when you write a unit test. Here is the revised code that references an interface:

```
public decimal CalcFoo(IDataFetcher df)
{
    var data = df.GetData();
```

```
    var result = data.Take(100).Average();

    return result;
}
```

For the sake of completeness, here is the code for the IDataFetcher interface and the DataFetcher class:

```
interface IDataFetcher
{
    void Combobulate();
    List<decimal> GetData();
    bool IsFancy { get; set; }
}

public class DataFetcher : IDataFetcher
{

    public List<decimal> GetData()
    {
        var result = new List<Decimal>();

        #region Data-intensive code here

        // ...

        #endregion

        return result;
    }

    public bool IsFancy { get; set; }

    public void Combobulate()
    {
        #region data intensive combobulation
        // ...
        #endregion
    }
}
```

A mock object would typically implement this interface with a fixed return value for the GetData() method, as shown here:

```
public class FakeDataFetcher : IDataFetcher
{

    // Fake method, returns a fixed list of decimals
    public List<decimal> GetData()
    {
        return new List<decimal> {1,2,3};
```

```
    }

    // Don't need this property for my unit test
    public bool IsFancy { get; set; }

    public void Combobulate()
    {
        // Don't need this method for my unit test
        throw new NotImplementedException();
    }
}
```

Now you can write a unit test using this `FakeDataFetcher` with complete control over the data that will be fed to the `FancyCalc` method.

```
[TestMethod]
public void FancyCalcTest()
{
    var fakeDataFetcher = new FakeDataFetcher();

    var fc = new FancyCalc();
    var result = fc.CalcFoo(fakeDataFetcher);

    Assert.IsTrue(result == 2m);
}
```

In summary, you have isolated the `FancyCalc` method, breaking its dependency on `DataFetcher`, and now you can test it with specific data in each unit test you write. Note that this method has one significant drawback—you would need to create a slightly different version of `DataFetcher` for every variation of data you want to test. This drawback is one of the reasons why *mocking frameworks* were invented.

Mocking frameworks (Moq) remove the need to implement the entire interface for the purpose of overriding just one method (or just a few methods). If you were using Moq (to pick a mocking framework at random) then you would be able to specify an implementation for `GetData` without the need to also specify an implementation for `IsFancy` and `Combobulate`. This is clearly more of a help when interfaces are more extensive than shown in this simple example.

Incidentally, this technique of referencing interfaces instead of concrete classes is a form of *dependency injection*, where dependencies like `DataFetcher` can be easily switched out for alternative Implementations.

QUESTIONS

Now that you have some concepts on testing down, it's time to try your hand at answering some questions.

1. What should you test?

Consider the following code; do you think this qualifies as a unit test?

```
private static void TestRandomIntBetween()
{
    int expectedResult = 99;

    int actualResult = RandomIntBetween(98, 100);

    if (expectedResult == actualResult)
        Console.WriteLine("Test succeeded");
    else
        Console.WriteLine("Test failed");
}
```

2. What exactly should you test for?

Consider the following code; do you think this is an appropriate unit test?

```
private static void TestRandom()
{
    int unexpectedResult = 42;
    Random rand = new Random();

    int actualResult = rand.Next(1, 1000000);

    if (unexpectedResult != actualResult)
        Console.WriteLine("Test succeeded");
    else
        Console.WriteLine("Test failed");
}
```

3. TDD part 1

Write a unit test that calls a method named IsLeapYear, passing it an arbitrary date in the year 2013. The IsLeapYear method has a signature as follows:

```
public static bool IsLeapYear(DateTime date)
```

The year 2013 is not a leap year so your test should assert that this method returns false. You do not need to write the IsLeapYear method.

4. TDD part 2

Assume a fictitious scenario where someone else in your team has copied the following code from the Web:

```
public static bool IsLeapYear(DateTime date)
{
    return date.Year % 4 == 0;
}
```

Also assume that you spend another three or four seconds searching the Web and manage to find a reliable source that describes a leap year as "years that are divisible by 400 or years that are divisible by 4 but not by 100."

Now:

1. Write a test for the earlier `IsLeapYear` method that shows the method fails for the year 1900 (not a leap year).

2. Rewrite the `IsLeapYear` method according to the previously described algorithm.

3. Rerun your tests to show that your implementation of the previously describe algorithm is correct.

5. Unit and integration testing

What is the difference between unit and integration testing?

6. Additional benefits of unit testing

Apart from the obvious benefit of testing, what are some other reasons for writing unit tests?

7. Why use mock objects?

Describe some of the key reasons why a programmer might want to use mock objects when writing unit tests?

8. Limits of unit testing

Unit testing has many benefits; what are some of its limitations?

9. Thinking up good test values

Suppose you are given a function that returns the most common character contained in a string. For example, if the string is "aaabbc" then the function should return "a." If the string is empty or has more than one "most common" character, then the function should return `null`.

What test values should you use in unit testing to ensure that this function works correctly?

10. For code coverage, what percent should you aim for?

When a unit test runs a line of code it is counted toward an overall figure of code coverage. If 100 lines of code are in an application, and unit testing runs 75 of these lines then the code coverage is 75 percent.

What is the ideal number for code coverage as a percentage of all code in an application?

11. What tests the unit tests?

If programmers are so concerned about writing tests to ensure the correctness of their code, why don't they write unit tests that test other unit tests?

ANSWERS

1. **What should you test?**

   Consider the following code; do you think this qualifies as a unit test?

   ```
   private static void TestRandomIntBetween()
   {
       int expectedResult = 99;

       int actualResult = RandomIntBetween(98, 100);

       if (expectedResult == actualResult)
           Console.WriteLine("Test succeeded");
       else
           Console.WriteLine("Test failed");
   }
   ```

   This is not a trick question. This is a simple example of a unit test that confirms an expected result (99) is obtained when calling the RandomIntBetween method. It doesn't use a unit-testing framework, but that has no bearing on whether it qualifies as a valid unit test. This is a valid unit test, albeit a primitive one.

2. **What exactly should you test for?**

   Consider the following code; do you think this is an appropriate unit test?

   ```
   private static void TestRandom()
   {
       int unexpectedResult = 42;
       Random rand = new Random();

       int actualResult = rand.Next(1, 1000000);

       if (unexpectedResult != actualResult)
           Console.WriteLine("Test succeeded");
       else
           Console.WriteLine("Test failed");
   }
   ```

   This test obtains a random number between 1 and 1,000,000 and checks that the number is not equal to 42. It will "succeed" in 999,999 cases and "fail" in one case. You might reasonably guess that the programmer was thinking that a random number between 1 and 1 million would never return the number 42 (what are the chances?!) and consequently wrote a test of the Random class that relies on this faulty assumption.

   As a rule (and it is a firm rule, not just guidance) tests should not rely on chance outcomes in order to succeed or fail.

Another problem is shown here: It is inappropriate for a unit test to test the underlying framework. In this question the test is creating an instance of a .NET System.Random object and then confirming that it does, indeed, return a random number that is not equal to 42.

The application programmer does not benefit except for the dubious theoretical potential for detecting an error in the .NET Framework. This theoretical benefit is far outweighed by the cost of writing, debugging, and maintaining this test into the future. (Of course, if you *do* happen to find a bug in the .NET Framework, then I take it all back. You rock.)

Tests like this are written by programmers who are new to unit testing and who aren't sure what they ought to be testing. In a nutshell your tests should test the code you have written, not the code in the underlying framework.

3. **TDD part 1**

   Write a unit test that calls a method named IsLeapYear, *passing it an arbitrary date in the year 2013. The* IsLeapYear *method has a signature as follows:*

   ```
   public static bool IsLeapYear(DateTime date)
   ```

   The year 2013 is not a leap year so your test should assert that this method returns false. *You do not need to write the* IsLeapYear *method.*

   The code is as follows:

   ```
   using System;
   using Microsoft.VisualStudio.TestTools.UnitTesting;

   namespace UnitTests
   {
       [TestClass]
       public class TestClass
       {
           [TestMethod]
           public void IsLeapYear2013()
           {
               Assert.IsFalse(IsLeapYear(new DateTime(2013, 1, 1)));
           }

           public static bool IsLeapYear(DateTime date)
           {
               // code not yet written...

               return false;
           }

       }
   }
   ```

4. TDD part 2

Assume a fictitious scenario where someone else in your team has copied the following code from the Web:

```
public static bool IsLeapYear(DateTime date)
{
    return date.Year % 4 == 0;
}
```

Also assume that you spend another three or four seconds searching the Web and manage to find a reliable source that describes a leap year as "years that are divisible by 400 or years that are divisible by 4 but not by 100."

Now:

1. *Write a test for the* IsLeapYear *code that show it fails for the year 1900 (not a leap year).*

2. *Rewrite the* IsLeapYear *method according to the previously described algorithm.*

3. *Rerun your tests to show that your implementation of the previously described algorithm is correct.*

This question has three parts. Your answer to the first part should look something like this:

```
[TestMethod]
public void IsNotLeapYear1900()
{
    Assert.IsFalse(IsLeapYear(new DateTime(1900, 1, 1)));
}
```

Converting the given algorithm to code is simple. You must account for two clauses. The first is a test for "years that are divisible by 400":

```
(date.Year % 400 == 0)
```

The second clause covers "years that are divisible by 4, but not by 100":

```
(date.Year % 4 == 0 && date.Year % 100 != 0)
```

So now you can rewrite your IsLeapYear method as:

```
public static bool IsLeapYear(DateTime date)
{
    return (date.Year % 400 == 0)
        || (date.Year % 4 == 0 && date.Year % 100 != 0);
}
```

Finally, you can rerun the test and show that it now passes for the year 1900 (not a leap year). Figure 9-1 shows the output from running this test using MSTest.exe.

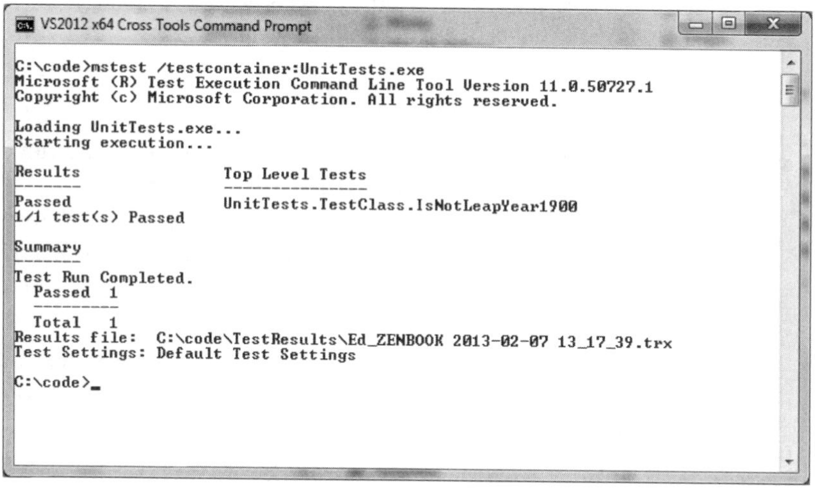

Figure 9-1: Test run with MSTest.exe

5. Unit and integration testing

What is the difference between unit and integration testing?

Sometimes the difference between unit and integration testing is subtle, and sometimes it isn't a useful distinction to make. However, some widely accepted general rules exist about what makes a good unit test, and if a unit test breaks these rules it is probably not a unit test in the strictest sense.

A unit test should

- Test a single unit
- Have few or no external dependencies except on the code being tested
- Not query a database or external resource
- Not touch the file system
- Not rely on environment or configuration variables
- Not rely on being run in a certain order
- Not rely on the outcome of any other test
- Run quickly
- Be consistent, producing the same result each time it is run

A test that does not follow these rules is probably an integration test. These can be very valuable tests but they should not be mixed in with unit tests.

6. **Additional benefits of unit testing**

   Apart from the obvious benefit of testing, what are some other reasons for writing unit tests?

   Some other reasons include the following:

   - Unit testing helps to find errors earlier in the software development life-cycle (SDLC) where they are cheaper to fix.
   - When a good suite of unit tests is in place the programmer who subsequently makes a code modification has reassurance (in the form of unit tests that pass) that his or her change has not broken the system in some way.
   - Unit testing encourages the programmer to consider a systematic enumeration of edge cases. These are re-runnable and can serve as a form of regression testing.
   - Unit tests provide concrete and runnable examples of how to use the application code, serving as a form of "live" technical documentation.

7. **Why use mock objects?**

   Describe some of the key reasons why a programmer might want to use mock objects when writing unit tests.

   Some key reasons include the following:

   - For isolation, meaning the test can focus on just one unit of the application. This is especially valuable when testing legacy code, or code that was written in a way that makes it difficult to test due to tight coupling of components
   - To ensure the test runs quickly, by eliminating dependencies on hardware, databases, networks, and other external factors
   - To control inputs to a function by faking an otherwise non-deterministic component
   - To enable testing before all dependencies are implemented

8. **Limits of unit testing**

   Unit testing has many benefits; what are some of its limitations?

   Most programmers and most interviewers are enthusiastic about unit testing, but some interviewers will also want to know whether you have had enough experience with unit testing to understand some of its limitations.

Here are some situations in which the benefits of unit testing might be outweighed by the cost:

- **Writing unit tests for trivial code (for example, automatic properties in .NET).** This is rarely worth the effort.
- **Testing code that contains no logic.** For example, if it is simply a thin shell that passes through to another API
- **If a test is significantly more difficult to write than the code it is intended to test.** In this situation, writing unit tests might not be worth it. This is probably an indication that the code being tested is in need of simplification, in which case once it is simplified, unit tests should still be written.
- **When you cannot possibly tell whether the return values from a unit of code are correct.**
- **When the code is exploratory.** When code is being written purely as a way to explore an idea, and (here's the catch) you can guarantee that the code will be thrown away, then writing unit tests is probably not worth it.

In addition to these scenarios some logical limitations exist:

- Unit testing by definition will not test the integration of components.
- Unit testing can prove that code does or does not contain a specific set of errors, but it cannot prove that the code contains no errors at all except in trivial cases.
- The amount of code that is required for testing may be far greater than the amount of code being tested. The effort required to write and maintain this code might not be worthwhile.
- Unit testing code might itself contain bugs, and this is especially true when a significant amount of unit test code has been written.
- If a suite of unit tests is not run frequently then the unit test code can easily get out of sync with the code it is supposed to test. When this happens the effort of bringing the unit test code back into sync might not be worthwhile

It is also worth looking quickly at a few *invalid* reasons for not writing unit tests. These are answers that you should avoid giving at an interview, for obvious reasons:

- "Unit testing takes too long." This is probably the most common objection to writing unit tests. It ignores the ever-present need to perform testing regardless of how the testing is performed, and it overlooks the longer term benefit of having a suite of automated tests rather than performing tests by hand or not at all.

- "Unit testing can't test every possible combination of inputs so it isn't worth doing." This is a logical fallacy, a form of false dilemma, because benefit can still be gained from writing unit tests even if they do not represent every possible combination of inputs. The choice is not a binary one.

- "Unit testing is a form of code bloat." This argument has some merit in the sense that a large amount of poorly organized code will be a strain on any team. This is, however, an argument to keep all code, including unit test code, well-organized and in a state that facilitates ongoing maintenance and support. It is not a valid reason to avoid writing unit tests.

9. **Thinking up good test values**

Suppose you are given a function that returns the most common character contained in a string. For example, if the string is "aaabbc" then the function should return "a." If the string is empty or if it has more than one "most common" character then the function should return null.

What test values should be used in unit testing to ensure that this function works correctly?

The answer to this question is a list of values that test the function for correct behavior not just in the normal case (that is, the string given example) but also for *edge cases*. An edge case is an unlikely or unusual input value that the programmer might have overlooked or ignored when writing the function. Some reasonable constraints can be assumed; for instance, you can assume that the supplied string is a valid string and not some other data type. On the other hand you cannot assume that the string is not a null value. Your list of test values should include at least one of each of the following types of string.

- The string given in the question: "aaabbc"
- A string with no "most common" character: "abc"
- An empty string: ""
- A null string
- A string containing numeric characters: "1112223"
- A string containing punctuation symbols: "!!!$$%"
- A string containing whitespace: "\t\t\t\n\n\r"

- A string containing accented characters: "éééááó"
- A string containing unicode characters: "»»»½½¾"
- A string containing string-quotation characters: " " " ' ' "
- A string containing non-printable/control characters: "ᴺᵁᴸ ᴺᵁᴸ ᴺᵁᴸ ˢᴼᴴ ˢᴼᴴ ˢᵀˣ"
- A very large string
- A string with a large quantity of each character
- A string with a large but equal quantity of each character

10. What percent of code coverage should you aim for?

When a unit test runs a line of code it is counted toward an overall figure of code coverage. If there are 100 lines of code in an application and unit testing runs 75 of these lines then the code coverage is 75 percent.

What is the ideal number for code-coverage as a percentage of all code in an application?

This is a bit of a trick question, because no consistent correlation exists between the percentage of code coverage and the quality of unit tests. For example, having 100 percent code coverage without testing anything except that the code runs without crashing is possible, and having a very low code coverage figure while still having very valuable unit tests is also quite possible.

Experience should inform your judgment about the right balance of unit test quantity, code coverage, and the quality of your unit tests. No rote calculation exists that you can perform to arrive at a correct figure for code coverage.

If your interviewer is persistent, it probably means he has a figure in mind. A common suggestion is 80 percent and if you feel compelled to pick a number then you might as well go with that. You should also mention the prospect of diminishing returns beyond a figure of around 80 percent, and also that many other factors will influence the choice of a code-coverage target. The goal of writing unit tests is to produce useful tests, not to achieve an arbitrary code coverage figure.

11. What tests the unit tests?

If programmers are so concerned about writing tests to ensure the correctness of their code, why don't they write unit tests that test other unit tests?

Two main reasons exist why programmers do not normally write tests for tests:

- Unit tests should be simple, meaning they should contain very little or no logic. This means they contain very little that is worth testing.
- Because unit tests are, by their nature, a comparison of results obtained from application code against expected results the unit tests are in effect validated by the application code. If results are not what a test expects, then it could be the application code that is wrong or it could equally well be the test that is wrong. Either way the test failure will need to be investigated and resolved, which means that unit tests and application code are effective tests of each other.

# CHAPTER 10

The Right Tools

Developers are today both blessed and cursed by an unprecedented number and variety of software development tools. If you need a text editor, dozens of superb editors are available that you can download for free. If you need to convert UNIX line-endings to Windows, you can choose from several hundred utilities (assuming you haven't written your own). Most programmers have a favorite utility for constructing and testing regular expressions, and every Windows programmer should be aware of the Sysinternals utilities. While you enjoy the convenience and power of modern integrated development environments such as Visual Studio and Eclipse, you should remain mindful of what sed, awk, and grep can do for you. If you aren't aware of utilities like these then you are missing a trick. Visual Studio is an extremely capable development tool, but beware that you aren't suffering from the *law of the instrument*.

I call it the law of the instrument, and it may be formulated as follows:
Give a small boy a hammer, and he will find that everything he encounters needs pounding.

—Abraham Kaplan

Exploring Visual Studio

If you write code using the Microsoft stack of technologies then Visual Studio needs no introduction. Many programmers have a love/hate relationship with Visual Studio, loving it for its power and convenience, hating it for its quirks and idiosyncrasies. To be perfectly fair, recent Visual Studio releases have seen the balance shifting away from quirks toward more power and convenience. If the new default color scheme and the ALL CAPS menu doesn't put you off then you will probably love the latest version. Test your knowledge of the Visual Studio IDE with the following questions.

QUESTIONS

1. **Visual Studio Build and Rebuild**

   In Visual Studio, what is the difference between the Build Solution and Rebuild Solution options (see Figure 10-1)? Why would you choose one over the other?

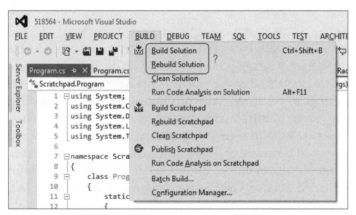

Figure 10-1: Build and Rebuild

2. **Finding hidden exceptions**

   Consider a scenario in which you suspect that a poorly coded `try/catch` block is hiding an important exception, something like the following code:

   ```
   try {
       RiskyOperation();
   }
   catch (Exception ex) {
       // TO DO - Ask Mark what to do here
   }
   ```

   The `catch` block will catch every kind of exception and silently swallow all of them. The program will continue as if the exception hadn't occurred. If this kind of poorly constructed (or incomplete) exception handling is rife throughout the application then setting a breakpoint inside each of the `catch` blocks in order to confirm the source of a problem will be impractical.

What else can you do with Visual Studio that might help you prove (or disprove) your theory about a hidden or "swallowed" exception?

3. **Targeting any CPU**

   Figure 10-2 shows (circled) that you can instruct Visual Studio to build a project to target a 32-bit platform (x86), a 64-bit platform (x64), or Any CPU.

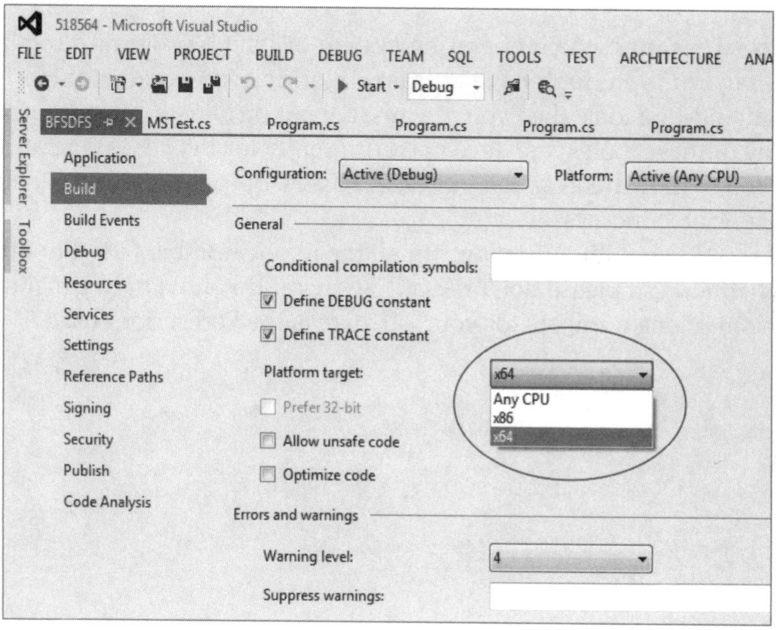

Figure 10-2: Build targets

With regard to these options:

- What does the Any CPU option actually mean with regard to the executable file that is produced?
- If you build an executable on a 32-bit machine with the Any CPU option, can you then copy the executable to a 64-bit machine and expect it to work without modification? What about vice versa?
- Suppose a vendor gives you a non-managed 64-bit DLL. What kind of problem might you encounter by using this DLL on a 32-bit machine when your executable is built for Any CPU?
- How can you tell what platform a .NET executable targets (that is, 32, 64, any) when all you have is the executable itself (that is, when you don't have the project settings file)?

4. **Understanding Visual Studio project configuration**

Consider a scenario in which you are working on a new product feature. You write and test your code using the default Debug configuration, but when your code is incorporated into the main team build—which uses the project's Release configuration—your code doesn't appear to work correctly. You are unable to reproduce the problem in Debug mode.

What should you look for in your code that might explain the different behavior when the application is built in Release configuration?

Exploiting Command-Line Tools

It doesn't matter which operating system or which programming languages you favor, if you don't have at least a working knowledge of the following command-line tools then you are missing out on a lot of fun and productivity. Many of these tools were developed originally for the UNIX operating system but today they are available for nearly every operating system, including all versions of Windows.

It should go without saying, but all the phone numbers used in this chapter are fictitious so please don't try calling them. If you want to generate a list of random phone numbers for yourself, here is the Perl script I used.

```perl
use strict; use warnings;

use Date::Calc qw( Add_Delta_DHMS );

my @start = (1980,1,1,0,0,0);

for ( my $i = 0; $i < 12500; $i++ )
{
    my $h = int( rand( 24 ) );
    my $m =  int( rand( 60 ) );

    my $p1 = int( rand( 1000 ) );
    my $p2 = int( rand( 10000 ) );

    my @date = Add_Delta_DHMS(@start,$i,0,$h,$m);

    printf("%4d-%02d-%02d %02d:%02d:%02d %03d-%04d\n", @date, $p1, $p2);
}
```

This script outputs 12,500 fake log entries, each with a random phone number. To create a file from it, you can redirect the output from this script as shown in

Figure 10-3. If you need to install Perl on a Windows PC then you can obtain it from `http://www.activestate.com/activeperl/downloads`.

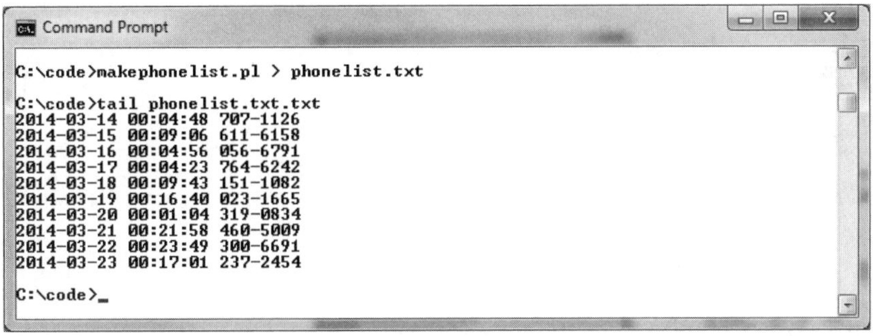

Figure 10-3: Generating a log file for testing

QUESTIONS

5. **Finding a needle in a haystack with grep**

   Given a text file containing a list of several million phone numbers, use grep to determine whether the specific number 555-1234 exists in this file.

   An excerpt from this file is shown in Figure 10-3. (Note: the tail utility is used to show the last part of this file, it is not necessary to use tail in your answer.)

6. **Finding more than one needle with grep**

   Given a text file containing a list of several million phone numbers (an excerpt from this file is shown in Figure 10-3), use grep to obtain a list of telephone numbers beginning with 555.

   For example, your grep command should find 555-1234, 555-0000, and so on, but it should not find 999-1234 or 000-0000.

7. **Sorting output with sort**

   In addition to reading from and writing to files, most tools work perfectly well with the *standard streams*: stdin (input), stdout (output), and stderr (errors). Write a command line that takes advantage of streaming to send output from grep to sort. Your commands should use grep to find phone numbers beginning with 555- and then use sort to sort this list into alphabetical order.

   The output you obtain should look like Figure 10-4.

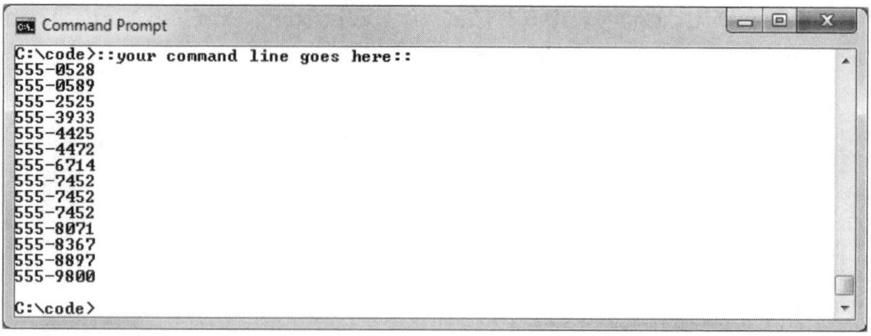

Figure 10-4: Sorted output

8. **Finding unique values with `uniq` and `sort`**

   The list of phone numbers shown in Figure 10-4 contains several duplicates. Modify or append to the command line used to produce this list so that it only shows one line per unique telephone number.

9. **Ignoring errors by redirecting `stderr`**

   Suppose you have a utility that, in the normal course of operation, generates so many error messages that it makes it difficult to see the messages that are not errors.

   Assuming that this utility sends its error messages to `stderr`, write a command line that uses redirection to filter out these error messages, leaving the command window (or the terminal window) free of errors.

   For the purpose of constructing a command line you can assume the utility is named `chatterbox`.

10. **Slicing text files with `awk`**

    Using the same file shown in Figure 10-3, write an `awk` command line that extracts a list of phone numbers from this file. Pipe this output to `sort` and then `uniq` to obtain a unique list of phone numbers.

    You can assume that the list shown in Figure 10-3 is representative of the entire file. That is, the format for every line of the file is strictly the same as shown in the sample.

11. **Anonymizing data with `sed`**

    Suppose that you have found some duplicate phone numbers in the file `phonelist.txt` and now you need to write a report to your boss about these numbers. You know that the report might be forwarded to others so, conscious of data protection, you want to somehow redact part of the number before including it in your report.

For example, instead of `555-7452` you want to include `xxx-7452`.

Write a command line using `sed` that will replace all area codes (that is, all three-digit numbers) with `xxx`. Make sure to avoid replacing numbers that are not area codes. In other words, ensure that your command does not result in `xxx-xxx2`.

Understanding PowerShell

PowerShell is primarily a tool for the administration of Windows systems via a command shell but its tight integration with the .NET framework and the ability to create scripts with its built-in scripting language make it a valuable tool for programmers as well as administrators. If you've never tried PowerShell (many programmers haven't) then take a look at what you're missing out on by reviewing the following questions.

QUESTIONS

12. **Experimenting with `String.Formats` in Powershell**

    Write a PowerShell command that will allow you to conveniently experiment with different date formats for use in a call to the .NET `String.Format` method.

    Here is an example of this kind of formatting in C#:

    ```
    String.Format("{0:d/M/yyyy HH:mm:ss}", date);
    ```

13. **Working with objects in PowerShell**

    Use PowerShell to update the `platform` element in the following XML from `LIVE` to `TEST`. Assume the XML file is named `release.xml`.

    Here is the original XML:

    ```
    <release>
      <platform>LIVE</platform>
    </release>
    ```

    Here is the XML your command should produce:

    ```
    <release>
      <platform>TEST</platform>
    </release>
    ```

Troubleshooting with Utilities from Sysinternals

Few things are more irritating to a Windows user than trying to perform some operation—perhaps compiling a solution in Visual Studio—and to be hit with a "file in use" error that won't go away. You might close all of your Explorer windows, restart Visual Studio, spin three times on your office chair, and still get the message. If this has happened to you then you are probably aware of how *Process Explorer* from Sysinternals can help. If you aren't aware then you should immediately download these utilities (http://technet.microsoft.com/en-US /sysinternals) and review the following questions.

QUESTIONS

14. **Find open file handles with Process Explorer**

    Describe how you can use Process Explorer to determine which processes have a file open (which is preventing you from deleting or renaming that file).

15. **Finding which processes update a registry key**

    Suppose that you have installed Visual Studio 2012 and you don't like the new uppercase menus. You search the Web and find a registry hack that restores the familiar Visual Studio lowercase menus. All is well until the following day when you see that menus have reverted to uppercase. You suspect that something on your machine is resetting the registry key but you have no idea what it might be.

    The registry value that determines the case of Visual Studio menus is stored at HKEY_CURRENT_USER\Software\Microsoft\VisualStudio\11.0 \General\SuppressUppercaseConversion.

    Describe how you might use Process Monitor to identify processes that update this registry value.

Managing Source Code

If you work with other programmers in a team then it's a reasonably safe bet that your team uses source control. If your team doesn't use source control then it's a reasonably safe bet that your team wishes it did use source control (and that the team finds it difficult or awkward to synchronize code changes between team members). Source control is a vital tool in any professional programming environment, arguably ranking just below an IDE (or a compiler plus a text editor) in importance and usefulness.

Review the questions in this section to test your knowledge of various source-control systems. All version control systems share common goals but each has its own unique approach to satisfying those goals.

Source control with Team Foundation Server

If you develop software for the Microsoft stack then sooner or later you will encounter Team Foundation Server (TFS). This tool offers much more than just source control. It also offers project tracking, automatic data collection and reporting, and support for automated builds via *Team Build*. It is sometimes said of TFS that if a team were using it purely for source control then the team would be better off using some other tool and avoiding all of the administrative overhead that comes with TFS. It pays to know some of the more advanced features of TFS so you can get more out of it than just revision control.

QUESTIONS

16. **Shelving changes in TFS**

    Describe *shelving* in TFS and how it can be useful to a programmer working in a team.

17. **Safeguarding the build with gated check-ins**

    Describe some of the key benefits of the TFS *gated check-in* feature and contrast *gated check-in* with *continuous integration*.

Source control with Subversion

Subversion was designed as a replacement for CVS (Concurrent Versioning System, a much older source control system that began its life as a collection of shell scripts). Subversion improves on CVS in a number of ways including:

- Atomic commits
- More efficient branching
- Tree-based commits (not just file-based)

QUESTIONS

18. **Understanding Subversion basics**

    Describe the basic Subversion commands required to perform the following actions:

    - Create a new, local repository
    - Import a folder into a new project in the newly created repository
    - Check out a project from a repository
    - Add a file to the project
    - Commit working copy changes to a repository

19. **Branching and tagging with Subversion**

    Describe the difference between a branch and a tag in Subversion.

20. **Reverting committed changes from Subversion**

    Assume that you have the following commit history in a Subversion branch:

    ```
    123 (250 new files, 137 changed files, 14 deleted files)
    122 (150 changed files)
    121 (renamed folder)
    120 (90 changed files)
    119 (115 changed files, 14 deleted files, 12 added files)
    118 (113 changed files)
    117 (10 changed files)
    ```

    Commit number 123 represents the latest version of this branch, and your working copy of this branch is up to date.

    What Subversion commands could you issue that would undo the changes made in commits 118 and 120 while retaining all the other changes?

Source control with git

A distinguishing feature of git is that it is a *distributed version control system (DVCS)*. No central git server acts as the master repository, which is different from other source control systems such as Subversion and TFS where a central server is an integral part of the system.

With git, instead of code changes being committed to a master repository and from there synchronized with each developer's working copy, git repositories are synchronized by exchanging sets of changes (*patches*) in a peer-to-peer arrangement. This has a number of significant benefits, including:

- Users can continue to commit changes even when disconnected from the network.
- Many git operations are faster because they don't involve a remote server.

- The impact of a corrupted or destroyed repository is minimal because every other developer in the team has a copy of the same repository.

One relatively minor but potentially confusing aspect of `git` for newcomers is how it uses SHA1 hashes instead of revision numbers to uniquely identify each commit. Figure 10-26 (shown later in the "Answers" section for this chapter) shows the log for a working copy; notice that (for example) the initial commit is identified as:

```
commit 0e1771a65e03e25de2be10706f5655bf798d62b8
```

This isn't as awkward as it might seem. Most `git` commands accept the first few characters of the hash so you don't need to type (or copy/paste) more characters than necessary to unambiguously identify the revision. For instance, the following `git` commands have the same effect:

```
git checkout 0e1771a65e03e25de2be10706f5655bf798d62b8

git checkout 0e17  # same as above provided no other revisions
                   # have the same first 4 characters '0e17'
```

This reliance on SHA1 hashes is a logical consequence of the distributed nature of `git`. It doesn't have a central server, which makes tracking and issuing sequential revision numbers impractical.

QUESTIONS

21. **Understanding git basics**

    Describe the basic `git` commands required to perform the following actions:

    - Create a new, local repository
    - Add files to the newly created repository
    - Commit working copy changes to a repository

22. **Finding a bad commit with** `git bisect`

    Explain how the `git bisect` command can help you track down the commit in which a bug was introduced.

ANSWERS

1. **Visual Studio Build and Rebuild**

    In Visual Studio, what is the difference between the Build Solution and Rebuild Solution options (see Figure 10-1)? Why would you choose one over the other?

    When you use the Build Solution option, Visual Studio builds only what it thinks necessary to bring the solution output up to date. If it thinks everything is up to date then Visual Studio essentially does nothing. This approach to building a solution or a project is called an *incremental build* and it is the default build behavior.

When you press F5 to start debugging a project, Visual Studio saves all the source files that have been updated and then performs a build, just as if you had saved the files yourself and then requested to Build Solution.

The Clean Solution option (shown but not circled in Figure 10-1) removes solution output files (not necessarily all of them) leaving the solution in a so-called clean state. This can be useful if, for instance, you want to copy the solution folder without copying all the large binary (for example, executable) files. It also means that the next build will need to recompile all the necessary source files in order to reconstruct these solution output files.

The Rebuild Solution option essentially performs a "clean" and then a "build," combining these two actions into one. This is useful when you suspect Visual Studio's tracking of changed files might be incorrect or out of sync.

2. Finding hidden exceptions

Consider a scenario in which you suspect that a poorly coded try/catch *block is hiding an important exception, something like the following code:*

```
try {
    RiskyOperation();
}
catch (Exception ex) {
    // TO DO - Ask Mark what to do here
}
```

The catch *block will catch every kind of exception and silently swallow all of them. The program will continue as if the exception hadn't occurred. If this kind of poorly constructed (or incomplete) exception handling is rife throughout the application then setting a breakpoint inside each of the catch blocks in order to confirm the source of a problem will be impractical.*

What else can you do with Visual Studio that might help you prove (or disprove) your theory about a hidden or "swallowed" exception?

When running an application Visual Studio will by default break into debug mode when it encounters an unhandled CLR exception. The problem with the code in this question is that it technically handles the exception, even though it does nothing useful with it.

You can ask Visual Studio to break into debug mode when an exception is thrown, regardless of whether it is caught or not. This can be used to test the theory that an exception is being hidden (that is, caught and not rethrown or otherwise handled in a useful way).

You can find the option for this behavior under DEBUG ➤ Exceptions as shown in Figures 10-5 and 10-6.

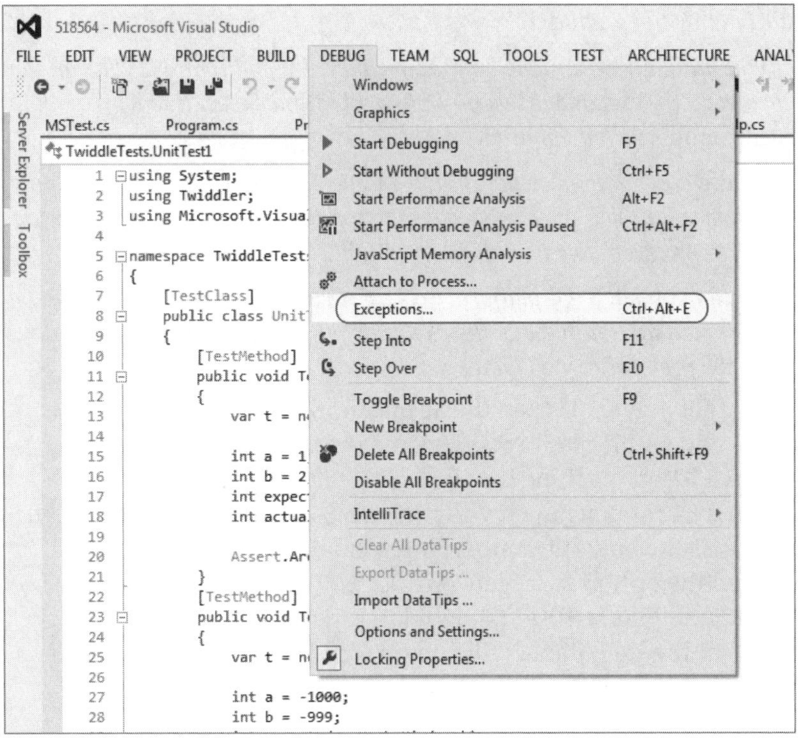

Figure 10-5: Navigating to the Exceptions dialog

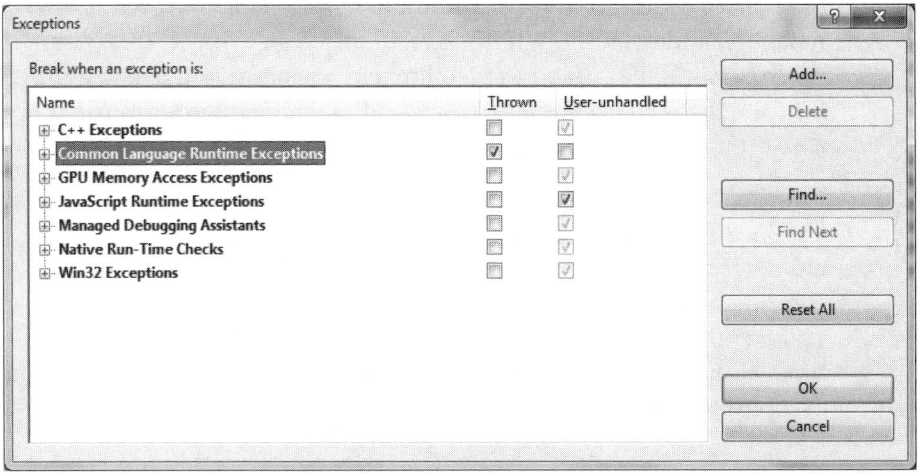

Figure 10-6: Break when CLR Exception is thrown

3. **Targeting any CPU**

   Figure 10-4 shows (circled) that you can instruct Visual Studio to build a project to target a 32-bit platform (x86), a 64-bit platform (x64), or Any CPU.

   With regard to these options;

   - *What does the Any CPU option actually mean with regard to the executable file that is produced?*

   - *If you build an executable on a 32-bit machine with Any CPU, can you then copy the executable to a 64-bit machine and expect it to work without modification? What about vice versa?*

   - *Suppose a vendor gives you a non-managed 64-bit DLL. What kind of problem might you encounter when using this DLL on a 32-bit machine when your executable is built for Any CPU?*

   - *How can you tell what platform a .NET executable targets (that is, 32, 64, Any) when all you have is the executable itself (that is, when you don't have the project settings file)?*

   If you target Any CPU then the application will be built to run on both 32- and 64-bit platforms. This means that if the application starts on a 32-bit machine it will run as a 32-bit process, and if it starts on a 64-bit machine it will run as a 64 bit process. Prior to .NET 4.5 this was the end of the story, but Visual Studio 2012 and .NET 4.5 added the option to target "Any CPU, Prefer 32-bit." You can see this option in Figure 10-11 (shown later in this section). This option means that the executable will run on a 64-bit machine as a 32-bit process, even when it could in theory run as a 64-bit process.

   Building a .NET executable on a 32-bit (or 64-bit) machine does not determine on which platforms the executable can then be run. It's all about the project settings (or the command-line options if you build with MSBuild). You can build a 64-bit executable on a 32-bit machine, and even though this executable won't run on that 32-bit machine it can be copied to 64-bit machines and it will run just fine. Building a 32-bit executable on a 64-bit machine in order to run it on a 32-bit machine works equally well.

   Prior to .NET 4.5 the Any CPU option was sometimes problematic. Unlike .NET assemblies, the target platforms for non-managed DLLs are determined when they are compiled, so a non-managed DLL compiled to run as 64-bit will only ever run on a 64-bit platform. If you try to use this DLL from a 32-bit .NET executable you get a run-time exception in the form of a `BadImageFormatException`. The same exception occurs if you try to load a 32-bit unmanaged DLL from a 64-bit .NET process. The same problem can occur with managed assemblies if they are set to target 32-bit only or 64-bit only. Note that the executable file determines whether an application is loaded and run as a 32-bit or 64-bit process, not the supporting assemblies and DLLs.

If you are given a .NET executable and you need to determine which platforms it will run on, you can use the .NET Framework tool, corflags.exe, as illustrated in Figures 10-7, 10-8, 10-9, and 10-10.

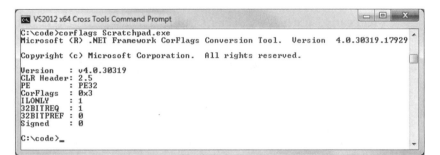

Figure 10-7: CorFlags output for x86

```
VS2012 x64 Cross Tools Command Prompt

C:\code>corflags Scratchpad.exe
Microsoft (R) .NET Framework CorFlags Conversion Tool.  Version  4.0.30319.17929

Copyright (c) Microsoft Corporation.  All rights reserved.

Version   : v4.0.30319
CLR Header: 2.5
PE        : PE32
CorFlags  : 0x3
ILONLY    : 1
32BITREQ  : 1
32BITPREF : 0
Signed    : 0

C:\code>
```

Figure 10-8: CorFlags output for x64

```
VS2012 x64 Cross Tools Command Prompt

C:\code>corflags Scratchpad.exe
Microsoft (R) .NET Framework CorFlags Conversion Tool.  Version  4.0.30319.17929

Copyright (c) Microsoft Corporation.  All rights reserved.

Version   : v4.0.30319
CLR Header: 2.5
PE        : PE32+
CorFlags  : 0x1
ILONLY    : 1
32BITREQ  : 0
32BITPREF : 0
Signed    : 0

C:\code>
```

Figure 10-9: CorFlags output for Any CPU

```
VS2012 x64 Cross Tools Command Prompt

C:\code>corflags Scratchpad.exe
Microsoft (R) .NET Framework CorFlags Conversion Tool.  Version  4.0.30319.17929

Copyright (c) Microsoft Corporation.  All rights reserved.

Version   : v4.0.30319
CLR Header: 2.5
PE        : PE32
CorFlags  : 0x1
ILONLY    : 1
32BITREQ  : 0
32BITPREF : 0
Signed    : 0

C:\code>
```

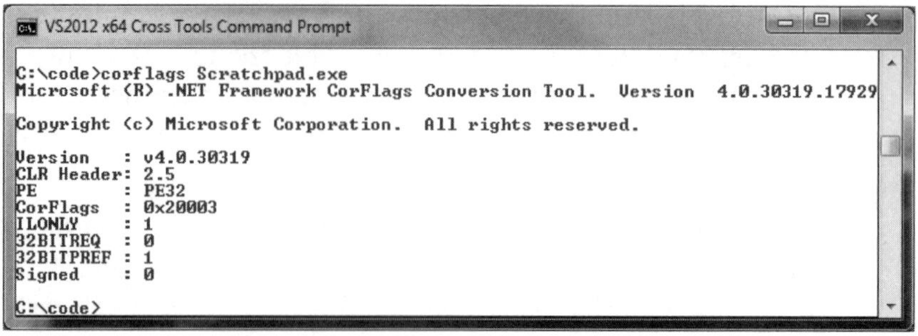

Figure 10-10: CorFlags output for Any CPU, 32-bit Preferred

You can also use the CorFlags utility to change the target platform of a .NET executable.

4. Understanding Visual Studio project configuration

Consider a scenario in which you are working on a new product feature. You write and test your code using the default Debug configuration, but when your code is incorporated into the main team build—which uses the project's Release configuration—your code doesn't appear to work correctly. You are unable to reproduce the problem in Debug mode.

What should you look for in your code that might explain the different behavior when the application is built in Release configuration?

When considering the difference between Debug and Release builds, most programmers think of the debugging information that is stored in PDB files. This is an important difference (it enables interactive debugging) but it does not explain how code can behave differently when built using a Release configuration.

If you look at the property page of a Visual Studio project and switch between Debug and Release configurations (see Figures 10-11 and 10-12) you will notice that (by default) Release mode turns off the "Define DEBUG constant" option.

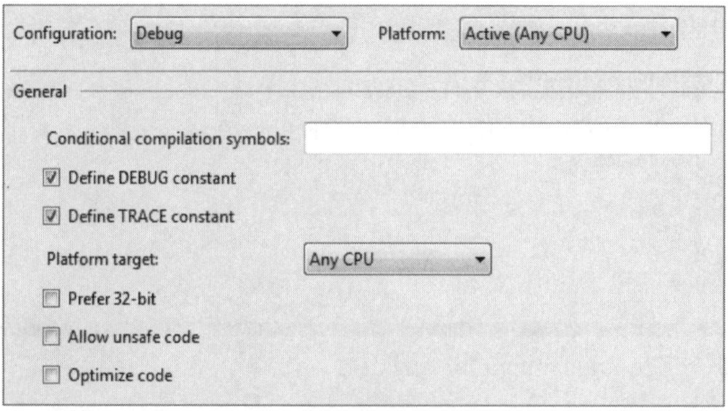

Figure 10-11: Debug mode constants

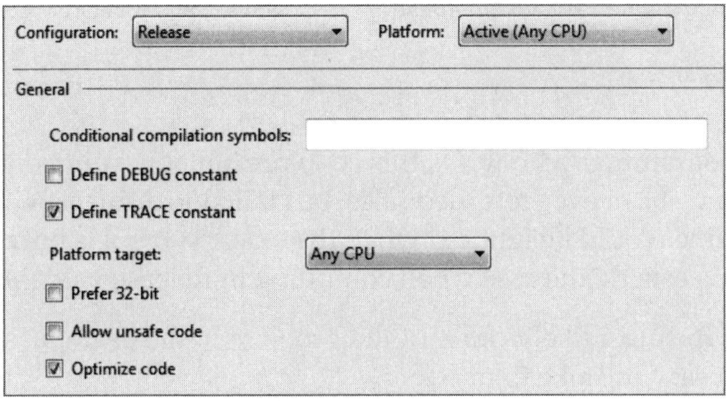

Figure 10-12: Release mode constants

When checked, this option is equivalent to writing:

```
#define DEBUG
```

When unchecked, this option is equivalent to writing:

```
#undef DEBUG
```

If you write code that is surrounded by an `#if DEBUG` directive then this code will be excluded when DEBUG is not defined.

```
static void Main(string[] args)
{
    Init();

    DoWork();

#if DEBUG
    CheckDatabase();   // Won't be included unless DEBUG is defined
#endif

    Finish();
}
```

Most programmers would not surround an important function like CheckDatabase with #if/#endif because it is obviously incorrect—the method should be called regardless of the DEBUG symbol.

More realistically, what can happen, particularly when the programmer is conscientiously writing defensive code, is that the programmer surrounds the call to CheckDatabase with an assertion like this:

```
static void Main(string[] args)
{
    Init();

    DoWork();
```

```
Debug.Assert(CheckDatabase()); // Note: MUST return true!

    Finish();
}
```

The programmer who wrote this code presumably wanted an alert if `CheckDatabase` ever returned false, but failed to appreciate that the entire line would be ignored when the DEBUG symbol is not defined, which is exactly the case when compiling in Release mode.

This is the most likely cause of the problem in the example scenario, and an easy mistake to make.

5. Finding a needle in a haystack with `grep`

Given a text file containing a list of several million phone numbers, use `grep` to determine whether the specific number 555-1234 exists in this file.

An excerpt from this file is shown in Figure 10-3 (shown earlier in this chapter).

This straightforward problem is easily solved with `grep`. Your interviewer might not mention `grep` explicitly, but when given this kind of problem ("find all of X in a large file") you should always consider using `grep` before you start writing your own utility from scratch.

To confirm that the number 555-1234 exists in the file you can use `grep` as follows:

```
grep 555-1234 phonelist.txt
```

If the number 555-1234 exists in the file then the matching line will be shown. If not, nothing will be shown.

6. Finding more than one needle with `grep`

Given a text file containing a list of several million phone numbers, use `grep` to obtain a list of telephone numbers beginning with 555.

For example, your `grep` command should find 555-1234, 555-0000, and so on, but it should not find 999-1234 or 000-0000.

An excerpt from this file is shown in Figure 10-3.

To answer this question you need to use `grep` with a regular expression. Your regular expression should look similar to this:

```
555-[0-9][0-9][0-9][0-9]
```

You could use a simpler pattern such as 555-, but it is usually a good idea to be more specific and avoid potential false matches. Now you can use this regular expression in the `grep` command as shown in Figure 10-13.

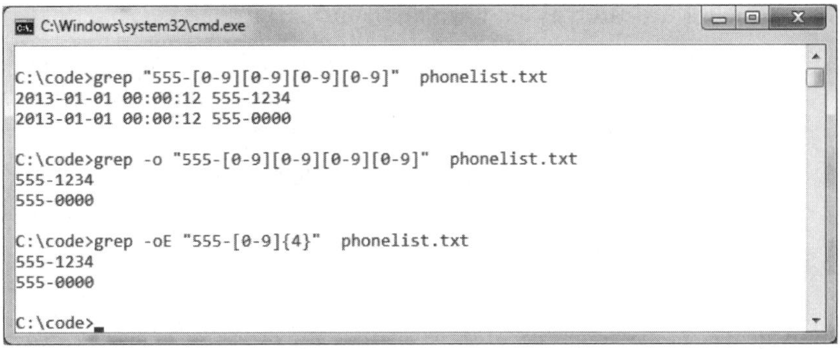

```
C:\Windows\system32\cmd.exe

C:\code>grep "555-[0-9][0-9][0-9][0-9]"  phonelist.txt
2013-01-01 00:00:12 555-1234
2013-01-01 00:00:12 555-0000

C:\code>grep -o "555-[0-9][0-9][0-9][0-9]"  phonelist.txt
555-1234
555-0000

C:\code>grep -oE "555-[0-9]{4}"  phonelist.txt
555-1234
555-0000

C:\code>_
```

Figure 10-13: Finding phone numbers

Note that if this question had asked for just the numbers (rather than the entire line) you could have used the -o option to output just the matching text. You could also make the regular expression a little more compact by using the -E option to take advantage of grep's support for the extended regular-expression syntax. Both of these options are shown in Figure 10-13.

7. **Sorting output with** sort

   In addition to reading from and writing to files, most tools work perfectly well with the standard streams: stdin *(input),* stdout *(output), and* stderr *(errors). Write a command line that accepts input from* stdin, *uses* grep *to find phone numbers beginning with* 555-, *and sorts the output from* grep *into alphabetical order with the* sort *utility.*

   If you've ever piped output from one utility to another then you can easily answer this question.

   Using the grep command from the previous question you can combine it with sort to produce the required output as shown in Figure 10-14.

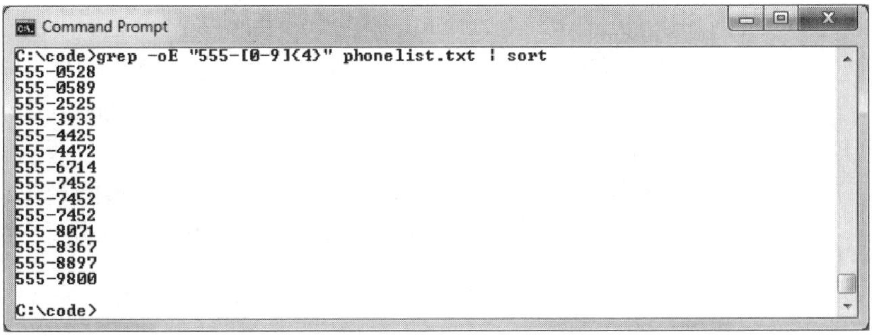

```
Command Prompt

C:\code>grep -oE "555-[0-9]{4}" phonelist.txt | sort
555-0528
555-0589
555-2525
555-3933
555-4425
555-4472
555-6714
555-7452
555-7452
555-7452
555-8071
555-8367
555-8897
555-9800
C:\code>
```

Figure 10-14: Sorting piped output

8. **Finding unique values with `uniq` and `sort`**

   The list of phone numbers shown in Figure 10-14 contains several duplicates. Modify or append to the command line used to produce this list so that it only shows one line per unique telephone number.

   This is another easy question provided you are familiar with piping output and the `sort` utility. Figure 10-15 shows one way of obtaining a sorted list of unique values.

   ```
   C:\Windows\system32\cmd.exe

   C:\code>grep -oE "555-[0-9]{4}"  phonelist.txt | sort | uniq
   555-0528
   555-0589
   555-2525
   555-3933
   555-4425
   555-4472
   555-6714
   555-7452
   555-8071
   555-8367
   555-8897
   555-9800

   C:\code>
   ```

   Figure 10-15: Sorted, unique numbers

   Many versions of `sort` have a built-in ability to return a unique list of values in addition to sorting so you could alternatively use a command line like this:

   ```
   grep -oE "555-[0-9]{4}"  phonelist.txt | sort -u
   ```

9. **Ignoring errors by redirecting `stderr`**

   Suppose you have a utility that, in the normal course of operation, generates so many error messages that it makes it difficult to see the messages that are not errors.

   Assuming that this utility sends its error messages to `stderr`, write a command line that uses redirection to filter out these error messages, leaving the command window (or the terminal window) free of errors.

   For the purpose of constructing a command line you can assume the utility is named `chatterbox`.

   The key to this question is to know that on both Windows and UNIX you can reference the three standard streams using their *file descriptors*. These are always 0 (stdin), 1 (stdout), and 2 (stderr). When combined with the redirect operator (the greater-than symbol: >), you can send error messages to a file or to a place where they will never been seen again (the null device).

In UNIX-based operating systems you can send the stderr stream to /dev/null as follows:

```
chatterbox 2> /dev/null
```

In Windows you can send it to the NUL device with:

```
chatterbox 2> NUL
```

Of course, if you don't want to ignore the errors and you also don't want them to pollute the console/terminal window, you could send the errors to a file:

```
chatterbox 2> errors
```

You could also send stdout and stderr to two different files:

```
chatterbox 1> output 2> errors
```

Conversely you can redirect stderr to stdout:

```
chatterbox 2>&1
```

10. Slicing text files with awk

Using the same file as shown in Figure 10-3, write an awk command line that extracts a list of phone numbers from this file. Pipe this output to sort and then uniq to obtain a unique list of phone numbers.

You can assume that the list shown in Figure 10-3 is representative of the entire file. That is, the format for every line of the file is strictly the same as shown in the sample.

The awk utility makes extracting columns from text files a trivial task. By default, it splits a line of text into parts using whitespace as a delimiter and assigns each part to the built-in awk variables, $1, $2, $3, and so on ($0 contains the entire line).

The command line to obtain a unique, sorted list of phone numbers from the file phonelist.txt is as follows:

```
awk '{print $3}' phonelist.txt | sort | uniq
```

This `awk` command prints the 3rd "column" in the file `phonelist.txt`. If you want to try this out for yourself, note two things:

- The GNU equivalent of `awk` is `gawk`, and `gawk` is commonly used as a drop-in replacement for `awk`. In other words, if you don't have `awk` on your machine, try `gawk`.

- If you run this command on Windows you might need to use double quotes (") instead of single quotes (') as shown earlier.

If you do a lot of text-processing then studying a few more sophisticated examples of `awk` in action will pay off; in particular, look at how `awk` handles associative arrays. For instance, here is an example that obtains a list of duplicated numbers in the file `phonelist.txt`.

```
awk '{ if(a[$3]) {print $3 } a[$3]=$3 }' phonelist.txt
```

This example works by building up an associative array for all phone numbers in the file. If the number has been previously seen by `awk` as it iterates through the file then it will print the number. It will not print numbers that occur exactly once because the expression `if(a[$3])` will never evaluate to `true` for those phone numbers.

11. Anonymizing data with `sed`

Suppose that you have found some duplicate phone numbers in the file `phonelist.txt` and now you need to write a report to your boss about these numbers. You know that the report might be forwarded to others so, conscious of data protection, you want to somehow redact part of the number before including it in your report.

For example, instead of 555-7452 you want to include xxx-7452.

Write a command line using `sed` that replaces all area codes (that is, all three-digit numbers) with xxx. Make sure to avoid replacing numbers that are not area codes. In other words, ensure that your command does not result in xxx-xxx2.

The `sed` utility (the name "sed" is short for "stream editor") is perfect for quick substitutions like the one required by this question. The only special knowledge you need is regular expressions; the rest is simple. Here is the `sed` command to make phone numbers anonymous:

```
sed 's/[0-9][0-9][0-9]-/xxx-/'
```

You can combine this with `awk` to obtain a list of duplicated numbers and then make them anonymous for publication:

```
awk '{ if(a[$3]) {print $3 } a[$3]=$3 }' phonelist.txt
    | sed 's/[0-9][0-9][0-9]-/xxx-/'
```

You can see the results of this command line in Figure 10-16. Note that this examples shows gawk and sed in a Windows command window, thus requiring the use of double quotes rather than single quotes.

```
C:\Windows\system32\cmd.exe
C:\code>gawk "{ if(a[$3]) {print $3 } a[$3]=$3 }" phonelist.txt | sed "s/[0-9][0
-9][0-9]-/xxx-/" | sort | uniq
xxx-4184
xxx-4791
xxx-7452
xxx-7805
xxx-9257

C:\code>
```

Figure 10-16: Making data anonymous with sed

12. Experimenting with string.Formats in PowerShell

Write a PowerShell command that allows you to conveniently experiment with different date formats for use in a call to the .NET string.Format method.

Here is an example of this kind of formatting in C#:

```
String.Format("{0:d/M/yyyy HH:mm:ss}", date);
```

Because PowerShell is tightly integrated with .NET, you are able to use .NET Framework classes directly at the command line. This can be a convenient way to try out a .NET feature without the overhead of writing and compiling an application to test with.

You can use the static method string.Format directly:

```
[string]::Format("{0:f}", (Get-Date) )
```

Note that this example uses the PowerShell *cmdlet* Get-Date to retrieve the current date and time to use as an argument in string.Format. You could also use the built-in format operator -f without directly invoking string.Format as follows:

```
"{0:f}" -f (Get-Date)
```

You could also use the -format option of the Get-Date cmdlet as follows:

```
Get-Date -format "f"
```

With any of these approaches you can now experiment with date formats without the overhead of writing and compiling a full .NET application.

More examples are shown in figure 10-17.

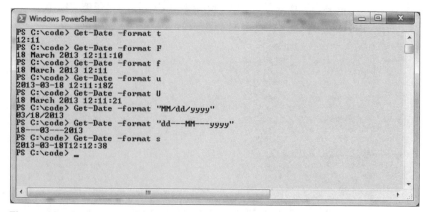

Figure 10-17: Convenient experimentation with date formats

13. Working with objects in PowerShell

Use PowerShell to update the `platform` *element in the following XML from* LIVE *to* TEST. *Assume the XML file is named* `release.xml`.

Here is the original XML:

```
<release>
  <platform>LIVE</platform>
</release>
```

Here is the XML your command should produce:
```
<release>
  <platform>TEST</platform>
</release>
```

PowerShell differs from traditional command shells in one significant way: It allows you to create and interact with .NET objects as actual objects and not just textual representations of objects. PowerShell documentation refers to this as the *object pipeline*. You have seen (in a previous section of this chapter) the power of combining command-line utilities by piping text; PowerShell takes this to another level by allowing you to pipe objects and object properties between commands. This means that if you load an XML document into a PowerShell variable you can manipulate the elements of that document directly; you don't need to hack away with awk or grep.

Figure 10-18 shows how to do this with just a few PowerShell commands.

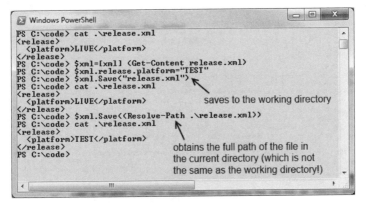

Figure 10-18: Updating XML with PowerShell

Note that Figure 10-18 also illustrates one of PowerShell's quirks. When you start a PowerShell command window and "change directory" with the cd command to a folder, you are not actually changing the *working directory* of that window. Applications that you start and .NET objects that you instantiate have a working directory that is different from the current *location* shown in the PowerShell prompt. PowerShell uses the more general word "location" (rather than "directory") because you can set the location to a place that is not part of the file system. For instance, you can navigate to a location in the Windows registry:

```
Set-Location HKCU:\Software\Microsoft\Windows
```

In Figure 10-18 you can see that I saved a file as .\release.xml. This file was actually saved in my working directory rather than the current location c:\code. It is for this reason that I then used the cmdlet Resolve-Path, which returns the full path of the specified file, enabling me to save my updated XML in the right place.

You can use the static method Environment.CurrentDirectory to see your current working directory, as illustrated in Figure 10-19.

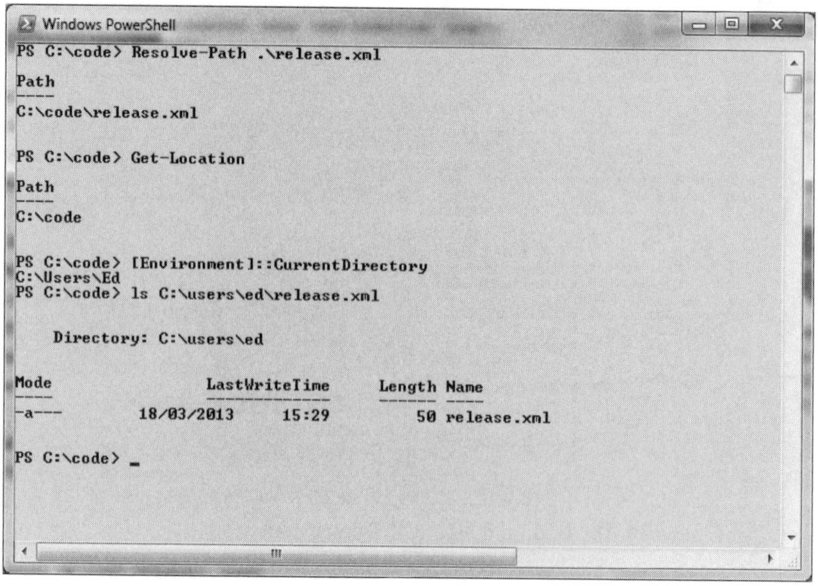

Figure 10-19: PowerShell's working folder is not obvious

14. Find open file handles with Process Explorer

Describe how you can use Process Explorer to determine which processes have a file open (which is preventing you from deleting or renaming that file).

Process Explorer is probably the most well-known of the utilities from Sysinternals. This utility lives up to its name and shows you a great deal of information about running processes, including open file handles. You can search for a file handle (or DLL) from the Find menu or by pressing Ctrl+F and typing in the name of the file in question. See Figure 10-20 for an example.

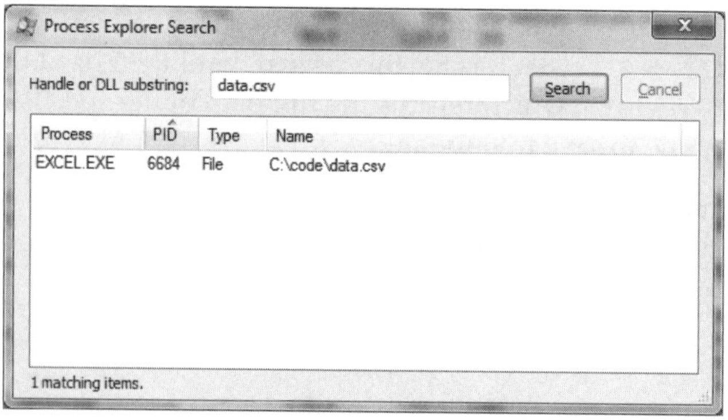

Figure 10-20: Finding which process has a file open

15. Finding which Processes Update a registry key

Suppose that you have installed Visual Studio 2012 and you don't like the new all-uppercase menus. You search the Web and find a registry hack that restores the familiar Visual Studio lowercase menus. All is well until the following day when you see that menus have reverted to uppercase. You suspect that something on your machine is resetting the registry key but you have no idea what it might be.

The registry value that determines the case of Visual Studio menus is stored at `HKEY_CURRENT_USER\Software\Microsoft\VisualStudio\11.0\General\SuppressUppercaseConversion.`

Describe how you might use Process Monitor to identify processes that update this registry value.

Process Monitor lets you view Windows system activity in real time. It also lets you filter these activities in a number of ways, including filtering by path. This is one way that you might track down which processes are changing a given registry value. Figure 10-21 shows how you can set a filter in Process Monitor and Figure 10-22 shows the resulting list of processes that have updated the `SuppressUppercaseConversion` registry key.

Note that the same approach could be used to identify processes that update files in a folder.

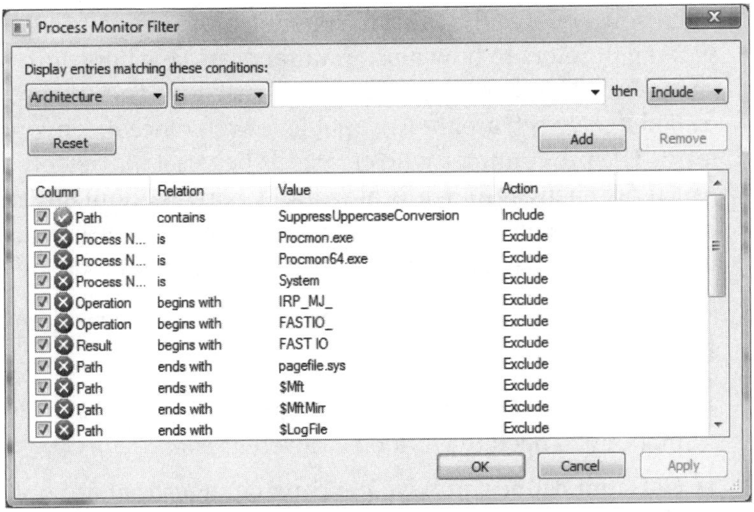

Figure 10-21: Filtering by path in procmon

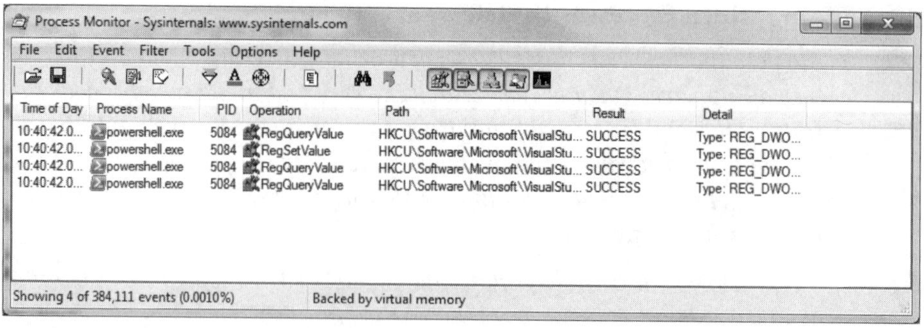

Figure 10-22: Processes found by procmon

If you want to try this out for yourself (or if you are just curious about how to toggle menu case in Visual Studio 2012), here is a PowerShell command line that updates the relevant registry key. Set this value to 1 to disable the uppercase menus, or set it to 0 to enable them.

```
Set-ItemProperty -Path
HKCU:\Software\Microsoft\VisualStudio\11.0\General
-Name SuppressUppercaseConversion -Type DWord -Value 1
```

16. **Shelving changes in TFS**

Describe shelving in TFS and how it can be useful to a programmer working in a team.

Microsoft TFS was the first source-control system to use the term *shelving*. It refers to how a programmer can save her source code changes in TFS without performing a check-in. These saved changes (called a *shelveset*) are then available for reference by anyone in the team. The programmer who creates a shelveset may safely undo or overwrite changes in her local working copy without any risk of losing them. Shelvesets are not versioned; in other words, you cannot update a shelveset and retain previous versions of that shelveset.

Microsoft's documentation lists six primary reasons for creating a shelveset:

- **Interruption:** You have pending changes that are not ready for check in, but you need to work on a different task.

- **Collaboration:** You have pending changes that are not ready for check in but you need to share them with another team member.

- **Code Review:** You want another team member to perform a code review of your pending changes.

- **Private Build:** Before you check in your changes, you can use your automated build system to build and test your code.

- **Backup:** You have work in progress that you cannot finish now so you want a backup copy that is stored on your server and available to other team members who might need to access it.

- **Handoff:** You have work in progress that you want to hand off to another team member.

Source: `http://msdn.microsoft.com/en-us/library/ms181403(v=vs.110).aspx`

My experience of using TFS in a large team has been that the top two items in this list (interruption and collaboration) are the most common reasons for creating a shelveset, but your experience might be different.

17. **Safeguarding the build with gated check-ins**

Describe some of the key benefits of the TFS gated check-in feature and contrast gated check-in with continuous integration.

Continuous integration (CI) is popular with development teams. The basic idea is that each time a developer performs a check-in (or on a schedule) a build system gets those changes and attempts to perform a build. If the build fails then this failure is flagged to other team members who then know that the latest version of the source code has a problem (and often who caused the problem).

One of the drawbacks of CI is that by the time the team becomes aware of a problem in the build the faulty source code changes are already committed to the source repository. If a developer isn't aware of the failed build or gets the latest source code without waiting for a CI build to complete then she might suffer problems that could have been avoided.

Gated check-in is a way of mitigating this risk. When gated check-in is set up for a TFS installation each check-in is tested by TFS to ensure that it builds prior to being accepted. TFS creates a shelveset for these changes and if the build fails then the shelveset is not checked-in. This provides much of the benefit of continuous integration but without the risk of "breaking the build."

18. **Understanding Subversion basics**

    Describe the basic Subversion commands required to perform the following actions:

    - *Create a new, local repository*
    - *Import a folder into a new project in the newly created repository*
    - *Check out a project from a repository*
    - *Add a file to the project*
    - *Commit working copy changes to a repository*

    Create a new, local repository:

    ```
    svnadmin create svnrepo
    ```

    Import a folder into the new repository:

    ```
    svn import xmlfiles file:///c:/code/svnrepo/xmlfiles -m
        "Initial import"
    ```

    Check out a project from a repository:

    ```
    svn checkout file:///c:/code/svnrepo/xmlfiles xmlwork
    ```

    Add a file to the project:

    ```
    svn add xmlwork\newfile.xml
    ```

    Commit working copy changes to a repository:

    ```
    svn commit -m "Added newfile.xml, updated release.xml" xmlwork
    ```

    Figure 10-23 shows these commands in action along with the Subversion responses to each command.

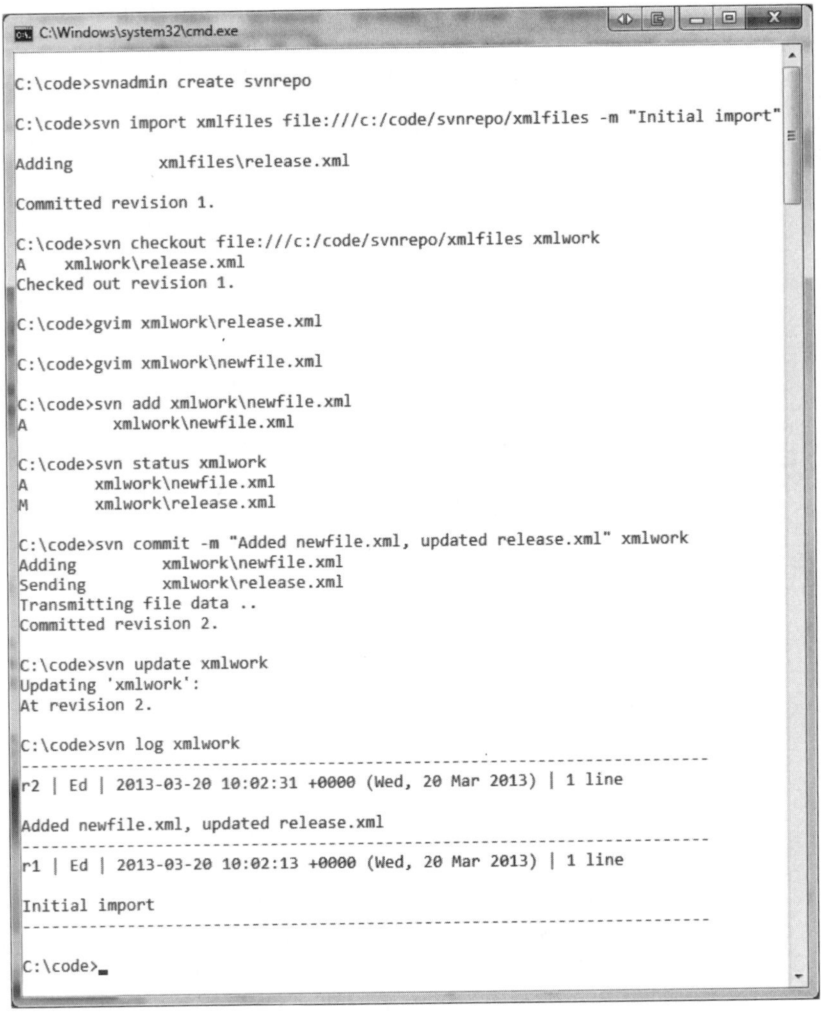

```
C:\Windows\system32\cmd.exe

C:\code>svnadmin create svnrepo

C:\code>svn import xmlfiles file:///c:/code/svnrepo/xmlfiles -m "Initial import"

Adding          xmlfiles\release.xml

Committed revision 1.

C:\code>svn checkout file:///c:/code/svnrepo/xmlfiles xmlwork
A     xmlwork\release.xml
Checked out revision 1.

C:\code>gvim xmlwork\release.xml

C:\code>gvim xmlwork\newfile.xml

C:\code>svn add xmlwork\newfile.xml
A          xmlwork\newfile.xml

C:\code>svn status xmlwork
A          xmlwork\newfile.xml
M          xmlwork\release.xml

C:\code>svn commit -m "Added newfile.xml, updated release.xml" xmlwork
Adding          xmlwork\newfile.xml
Sending         xmlwork\release.xml
Transmitting file data ..
Committed revision 2.

C:\code>svn update xmlwork
Updating 'xmlwork':
At revision 2.

C:\code>svn log xmlwork
------------------------------------------------------------------------
r2 | Ed | 2013-03-20 10:02:31 +0000 (Wed, 20 Mar 2013) | 1 line

Added newfile.xml, updated release.xml
------------------------------------------------------------------------
r1 | Ed | 2013-03-20 10:02:13 +0000 (Wed, 20 Mar 2013) | 1 line

Initial import
------------------------------------------------------------------------
C:\code>_
```

Figure 10-23: Understanding Subversion basics

19. Branching and tagging with Subversion

Describe the difference between a branch and a tag in subversion.

This is almost a trick question because Subversion handles branches and tags in exactly the same way. Both are created by issuing a svn copy command.

While Subversion does not make any technical distinction between a branch and a tag, there is an important *logical* distinction, one that is common to most source control systems, including Subversion.

To illustrate the logical difference between a branch and a tag in Subversion, consider the following typical scenario.

A development team is working on a (fictitious) product called Mega and come to a point where they decide it is ready for its first release. They package up the Mega 1.0 application and install it on a server for use by MegaCorp customers.

MegaCorp's customers love the Mega product, but after a week or so they have reported a few significant bugs. Meanwhile the team has continued work on the next release of Mega (Mega 1.1) and has made many significant changes to the source code.

Alongside the ongoing development work on Mega 1.1 another team has been formed to rewrite Mega as a jQuery plugin.

Mega now has three active and concurrent streams of work:

- Mega 1.0 bug fixes
- Mega 1.1 ongoing development
- Mega jQuery rewrite "jMega"

Obviously MegaCorp does not want to release all of this work (some of it unfinished) to the live server at the same time as it releases bug fixes. MegaCorp needs a strategy for managing the concurrent streams of work while allowing all of them to proceed unconstrained by the ongoing work of other teams. One possible strategy that relies on branches, tags, and the concept of a *trunk* is as follows.

- The *trunk* is where Mega 1.0 was first produced and where the next version of Mega will come from. This is where developers working on Mega 1.1 will commit their source code changes.
- At the point when Mega 1.0 was released, a *tag* was created from the trunk. This is where the team will make urgent bug fixes; that is, fixes that can't wait until Mega 1.1 is released. All the bug fixes that go into this tag will also go into the trunk so that they are included in the next release of Mega.

▪ When the jMega team starts work it will take a *branch* of the Mega source code. This branch is where it will commit its source code changes. The jMega team might decide to adopt changes from the trunk (for example, bug fixes and new features) although because jMega is a complete rewrite, some of these will lose relevance.

To summarize, a branch and a tag in Subversion are technically the exact same thing; however, a branch and tag might be treated differently by the programmers who create and use them. No fixed rules exist about how to manage branches and tags, but branches are often used for long-running or divergent items of work whereas tags are often used as a snapshot of a branch at a certain point of time.

20. Reverting committed changes from Subversion

Assume that you have the following commit history in a Subversion branch:

```
123 (250 new files, 137 changed files, 14 deleted files)
122 (150 changed files)
121 (renamed folder)
120 (90 changed files)
119 (115 changed files, 14 deleted files, 12 added files)
118 (113 changed files)
117 (10 changed files)
```

Commit number 123 represents the latest version of this branch, and your working copy of this branch is up to date.

What Subversion commands could you issue that would undo the changes made in commits 118 and 120 while retaining all the other changes?

Subversion excels in situations like this. Because every change to a trunk (or branch or tag) is recorded against the tree of files (rather than against each individual file) then undoing changes, even when they include file deletions, additions, and file renaming, is not difficult.

Assuming that you have an up-to-date working copy of this branch then the commands that will undo commits 118 and 120 are as follows:

```
svn merge -c -120 .
svn merge -c -118 .
```

Notice that the revision numbers that are to be undone are specified with a leading minus; that is, -120 rather than 120. This undoes these revisions in your working copy. After you are satisfied with the state of your working copy then you can commit it to the branch.

```
svn commit
```

21. **Understanding git basics**

   Describe the basic git commands required to perform the following actions:

   ■ *Create a new, local repository*

   ■ *Add files to the newly created repository*

   ■ *Commit working copy changes to a repository*

   A git repository is a collection of files inside a .git folder that is created when you run the command git init, as shown in Figure 10-24.

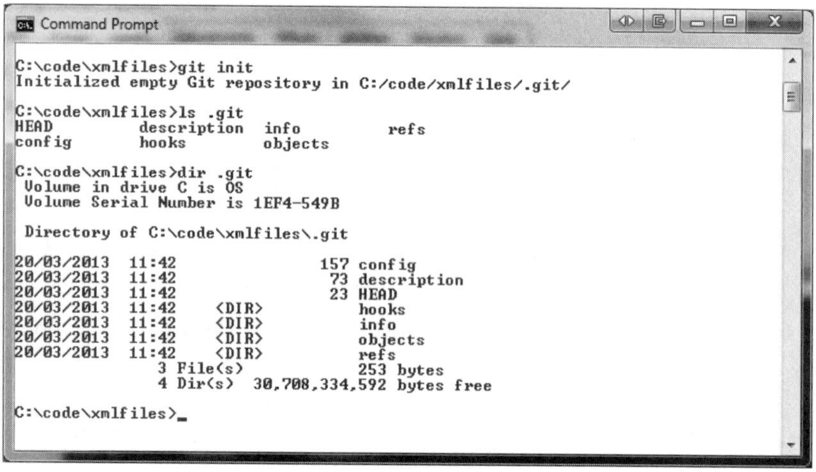

Figure 10-24: Creating a new git repository

Importing ("adding") files and folders to this new git repository is equally simple. Here is the command to add everything in the current folder into the repository that was set up inside this folder (in Figure 10-24):

```
git add .
```

After you have edited a file and added a file you can commit these changes to the repository with the following commands:

```
git add .    # Adds the new files to staging
```

```
git commit -a -m "Edited release.xml, added newfile.xml"
```

The -a option tells `git commit` to automatically stage files that have been modified and deleted. The -m option lets you specify a commit message. Prior to this commit you also needed to add new files with `git add`.

Figure 10-25 shows these commands in action.

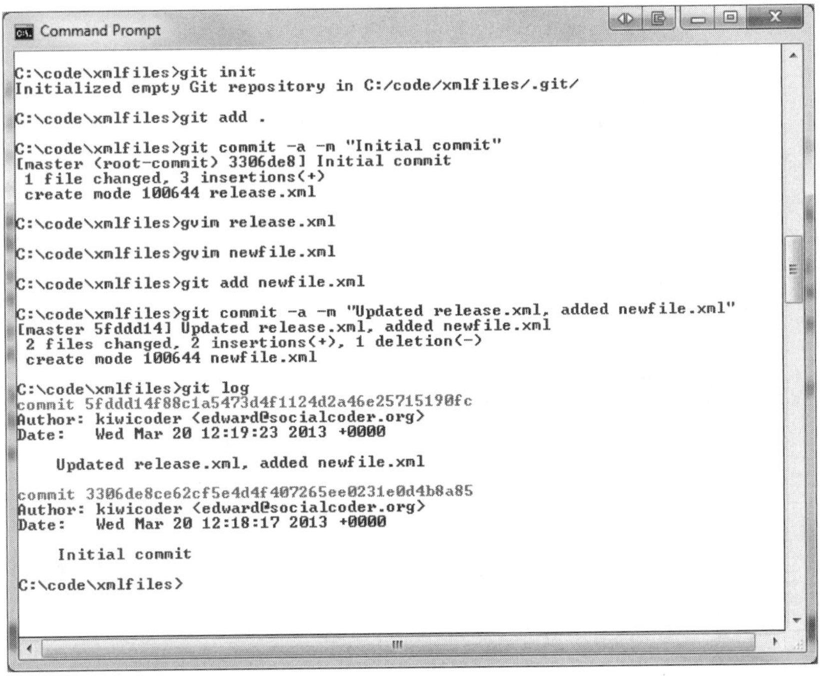

Figure 10-25: git in action

22. Finding a bad commit with `git bisect`

Explain how the `git bisect` command can help you track down the commit in which a bug was introduced.

Quite often a bug is introduced to a body of source code without anyone noticing. A bug might go undetected for months or longer, and when finally it is detected tracing its origin can be very difficult.

The `git bisect` command essentially performs an interactive binary search through the history of a repository to quickly home in on a bad commit. It works by starting with a known "bad" point (that is, a commit in which the bug is present) and a known "good" point (that is, a prior commit in which the bug is not present) and bisecting these two points until the origin of the bug is found. At each step it is up to you to tell git whether the commit is good or bad.

To illustrate `git bisect` in practice, consider the short history of a working copy folder as shown in Figure 10-26. Somewhere in this history there is a bad commit.

```
C:\Windows\system32\cmd.exe                                    _ □ X

C:\code\git>git log
commit 64a9ed87eb4f861e3c8c6672afaf5279c429125e
Author: kiwicoder <edward@socialcoder.org>
Date:   Tue Mar 19 23:13:31 2013 +0000

    World is a proper noun

commit 3a56ad601f8a7918886a6049f5e097158738f6f3
Author: kiwicoder <edward@socialcoder.org>
Date:   Tue Mar 19 23:13:17 2013 +0000

    I checked the spec, it should be HELLO

commit 0d1020ee731199aa2e09f1b36c0685e7b5c3a576
Author: kiwicoder <edward@socialcoder.org>
Date:   Tue Mar 19 23:12:59 2013 +0000

    Maybe the world isn't so cruel after all

commit df69f5501df314238203dd270d20c26ba8084174
Author: kiwicoder <edward@socialcoder.org>
Date:   Tue Mar 19 23:12:40 2013 +0000

    Emphasis added

commit 310bc973fbd542648e87bef80d2e8ff10f396e51
Author: kiwicoder <edward@socialcoder.org>
Date:   Tue Mar 19 23:09:23 2013 +0000

    The world can be a cruel place

commit 64c7c19dce28d1c7e37aed5fdba30ad86c6ebf19
Author: kiwicoder <edward@socialcoder.org>
Date:   Tue Mar 19 23:08:43 2013 +0000

    Hello should be goodbye!

commit 0e1771a65e03e25de2be10706f5655bf798d62b8
Author: kiwicoder <edward@socialcoder.org>
Date:   Tue Mar 19 23:08:26 2013 +0000

    Initial commit

C:\code\git>
```

Figure 10-26: A short history of index.html

The following transcript shows the series of commands that leads to the identification of the bad commit. First, notice that the HEAD revision of index.html contains a mismatched closing `</div>` tag:

```
C:\code\git>cat index.html

<!DOCTYPE html>
<html>
```

```
    <body>
        <span style="font-size:x-large;">Hello</div>, World!
    </body>
</html>
```

You want to find the revision that introduced these mismatched tags. You begin by telling git that you are on the hunt:

```
C:\code\git>git bisect start
```

Next, you tell git to note a known "good" version (this commit ID is from the log shown in Figure 10-24):

```
C:\code\git>git bisect good 0e177
```

You also tell git that the latest version is bad:

```
C:\code\git>git bisect bad HEAD
```

```
Bisecting: 3 revisions left to test after this (roughly 2 steps)
[df69f5501df314238203dd270d20c26ba8084174] Emphasis added
```

Git responds by choosing a commit halfway between the two points and checking this version out (so that the working copy contains this version):

```
C:\code\git>cat index.html
```

```
<!DOCTYPE html>
<html>
    <body>
        <span style="font-size:x-large;">Goodbye</div>, cruel world!
    </body>
</html>
```

You can see that this version contains the tag mismatch, so now you tell git that it is a "bad" commit.

```
C:\code\git>git bisect bad
Bisecting: 0 revisions left to test after this (roughly 1 step)
[310bc973fbd542648e87bef80d2e8ff10f396e51] The world can be cruel
```

```
C:\code\git>
C:\code\git>cat index.html
```

```
<!DOCTYPE html>
<html>
    <body>
        Goodbye, cruel world!
    </body>
</html>
```

You can see that this version doesn't have these mismatched tags and so you deem it "good" and tell git:

```
C:\code\git>git bisect good

df69f5501df314238203dd270d20c26ba8084174 is the first bad commit
commit df69f5501df314238203dd270d20c26ba8084174
Author: kiwicoder <edward@socialcoder.org>
Date:    Tue Mar 19 23:12:40 2013 +0000

    Emphasis added

:100644 100644 ea10847270df53ca03d62123b5c6347920aec354
d17d29200de22f27d3228950
9e1eeff3cee35a9d M      index.html
```

Git now responds by telling you the commit in which these mismatched tags were added (revision df69f5...) and now its work is done! You can go have a word with the author of this commit and make an appropriate note in the bug tracker.

To tell git that you are finished bisecting you issue a `git bisect reset` command. git will restore the working copy back to the state it was in before you started bisecting.

```
C:\code\git>git bisect reset

Previous HEAD position was 310bc97... The world can be a cruel place
Switched to branch 'master'
```

Notorious Interview Questions

This chapter contains a number of questions that, in all honesty, you might never be asked at an interview. These interview questions have gained fame or notoriety on the Internet, and are what most people think of when someone mentions an interview at Google, Microsoft, or some other high-tech company. These questions might have been asked once or twice at real interviews sometime in the past but today they are rare, even at Google.

This style of interviewing is falling out of favor because interviewers today look for skills that are more directly relevant to the job of programming—for instance, the ability to write good-quality code.

Nonetheless, these questions are still notable partly because if you happen to be asked one of these and you don't react well, they can transform a smooth interview into a horror show. You should be aware of them, just in case.

Estimating on the Spot

No book about programmer interviews is complete until it answers the question of how many golf balls you can fit into a school bus.

That probably sounds like I'm being funny but actually there is some (just a little) method in the apparent madness. An interviewer who asks you an apparently random question like this has an ulterior motive: He wants to see how you approach a problem that you've probably never thought about prior to the interview. Unless you arrive at an obviously incorrect answer such as $\sqrt{-1}$ or "infinity," he won't care what number your calculation produces. Understanding the ulterior motive turns a "crazy" question into an opportunity to

- Demonstrate creativity and logic
- Demonstrate good communication (with the interviewer) while thinking about the problem
- Show awareness of key assumptions and how they affect the answer
- Show you can handle the unexpected

Besides all that, now that the question of how many golf balls has been asked, aren't you a little bit curious to know the answer?

After you've practiced a few of these questions then you should be prepared for whatever wacky estimation problems an interviewer might dream up the night before the interview.

QUESTIONS

1. **Filling a school bus with golf balls**

   How many golf balls will it take to fill a school bus?

2. **Moving Mount Fuji**

   How would you move Mount Fuji?

Solving Puzzles and Brain-Teasers

The biggest problem for an interviewer who poses a brain-teaser during an interview is that the candidate might have heard it before and therefore have an unfair advantage. Some brain teasers can be worked out by logical deduction but most brain teasers require you to have a flash of inspiration or insight before you can solve them.

If you suspect that your interviewer is going to ask you to solve brain teasers then you should practice before the interview. Many books and online resources are available for this kind of practice so you won't have any trouble finding extra study materials if you feel the need.

QUESTIONS

3. **What color is the bear?**

   A bear walks 1 mile south, turns, and walks 1 mile east, turns again and walks 1 mile north, finishing at the same place it started.

   What color is the bear?

4. Why does a mirror switch left and right but not up and down?

Suppose you comb your hair with a part on the left side of your head. When you look in a mirror you will observe that the part is now on the right side of the head looking back at you. You will also observe that your head is still at the top and your feet are still at the bottom. If you lie down horizontally on your side and look into a mirror you will observe that the mirror image of your hair parting is still switched left to right.

Why does a mirror reverse left and right but not up and down?

5. How would five pirates share 100 gold coins?

A pirate king and his band of four pirates plunder a ship and find 100 gold coins. According to pirate law each pirate has the right to propose how to divide the coins. After a proposal is tabled the pirates take a vote. If fewer than half agree, the proposer is killed and the next highest ranked pirate will make a proposal. Naturally, the Pirate King is the first to make a proposal.

For reference, Figure 11-1 shows the pirates in order of rank.

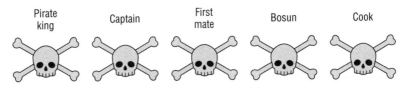

Figure 11-1: Pirates in rank order

How should the pirate king allocate the 100 coins to maximize his profit and remain alive?

6. Calculating the angle between clock hands

An analog clock on the wall indicates the time is 6:30 p.m. (see Figure 11-2). What is the angle between the hour and the minute hands? (There are two angles—you want the smaller one.)

Figure 11-2: Clock at 6:30 p.m.

7. Finding the heaviest ball

Suppose you are given eight balls of the same size. These balls are all the same weight except for one, which is a little heavier.

You are given a balance (a weighing machine that tells you which of two weights is heaviest) and asked to find the heaviest ball with just two weighings.

Assuming this task is possible, how can you do it?

Solving Probability Problems

What are the chances that your interviewer will ask you to solve a probability problem? Well, that depends. Companies that produce CRUD applications (applications that Create, Read, Update, and Delete records) are less likely to ask probability questions than companies that work in the financial markets. If your interviewer has a background in statistics then the chances are much higher (rumor has it the average statistician is just plain *mean*).

QUESTIONS

8. Monty Hall

You've probably heard this one. It is arguably the most contentious problem of probability ever to reach the mainstream media. The basic question is as follows:

You are a contestant on a game show hosted by Monty Hall. You are shown three doors (labeled A, B, and C) and asked to choose one of them. Two of these doors conceal worthless prizes but behind one is a fantastic prize. The prizes are placed at random, but Monty knows their placement.

Suppose you choose door A. Without opening door A Monty opens one of the other two doors to reveal a worthless prize. Monty then offers you the choice of staying with door A or switching to the other, unopened door.

The question is, should you switch or should you stay with door A?

First, decide whether you should stay with door A or switch to the other unopened door. Next, write a program that simulates this game being played 1 million times and use your program to confirm your answer.

9. The birthday problem

At the offices in which I work it always seems to be someone's birthday. I am certainly not complaining (and I particularly enjoy sponge cake) but it does remind me of *the birthday problem*, sometimes called the *birthday paradox* because the answer runs counter to most people's intuition.

As a starting point you will agree that when an office contains more than 365 people it is certain that two of these people share a birthday. (Leap years would require more than 366 people.)

In an office of just 23 people, what are the chances that two of them share a birthday? For the purposes of this question you can assume that birthdays are randomly distributed throughout the year.

Coping with Concurrency

This section poses questions that are notorious for all the right reasons. Despite the slightly humorous images painted by these questions, each one is representative of a significant computing problem.

QUESTIONS

10. The Dining Philosophers

Five hungry philosophers sit around a table. Between each philosopher is a single fork, and in the middle of the table is a large bowl of spaghetti. This unlikely scene is pictured in Figure 11-3.

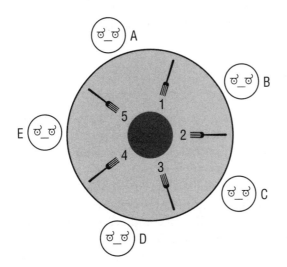

Figure 11-3: Dining philosophers

When the meal commences each philosopher will attempt to pick up two forks, one from his left and one from his right. If a philosopher cannot obtain both forks he will sit and think.

Each philosopher must alternate between eating and thinking, but will eat only when in possession of both left and right forks. A philosopher who has both forks will eat for a while and then put both forks down in order to think.

To make this mealtime more interesting the philosophers are forbidden from communicating with each another. A waiter will ensure that the bowl of spaghetti is never empty.

Suggest a way of coordinating eating and thinking that will ensure all philosophers are fed, none of them starve, and the meal will continue indefinitely with all philosophers alternating between eating and thinking.

11. **The Sleeping Barber Problem**

A barber has a chair in which he cuts hair and a waiting room in which his customers sit and wait.

When a customer arrives he will look to see what the barber is doing. If a customer finds the barber asleep he will wake the barber and sit in the chair for a haircut. If the barber is cutting hair the customer will go to the waiting room and take a seat. If no seats are available, the customer will leave.

When the barber finishes cutting a customer's hair he will escort the customer out of the shop and then check the waiting room for customers. If no customers are in the waiting room, the barber will sit in his chair and go to sleep.

Describe a method for running the barber's shop that ensures customers are never left waiting while the barber sleeps.

Doing Tricks with Bits

When you interview for a job that involves programming at a low-level you must be prepared for the interviewer to test your knowledge of bitwise operations. In addition to the standard operations (AND, OR, XOR, and so on), you should be familiar with the "clever" questions an interviewer might ask. Although, in general, it is true and generally accepted that you should avoid being overly clever (and consequently producing unmaintainable code) it is also true that some "clever" bitwise operations are idiomatic and even occasionally representative of good style when programming at a low-level.

Nonetheless, it is also true that compilers have advanced to the point where twiddling bits is rarely necessary. A good compiler (or run-time engine) can rearrange your higher-level code into compact and efficient lower-level instructions without much work on your part. Moreover, sometimes the case is that by mixing high- and low-level code for the sake of optimization you thwart the optimization efforts of the compiler.

All things considered, writing code as clearly as possible, following good design principles, and then allowing the compiler to take care of the translation into efficient native code is usually best.

If you ever feel the need to hand-optimize a section of code be sure to establish a performance/timing benchmark first. Without a benchmark you have no objective way of telling whether your changes have improved the code or made it worse.

QUESTIONS

12. Find the smaller of two integers without branching

Write code that uses bitwise operations to find the smaller of two integers. You may not use conditional branching (for example, if statements) or framework methods such as Math.Min(a,b).

13. Find the larger of two integers without branching

Write code that uses bitwise operations to find the larger of two integers. You may not use conditional branching (for example, if statements) or framework methods like Math.Max(a,b).

14. Determine whether an integer is a power of 2

Use bitwise operators to determine whether an integer is a power of 2.

15. Counting set bits

Write code to find the number of set bits in an integer. For example:

- The number 1 is binary 0001 so it has 1 set bit.
- The number 15 is binary 1111 so it has 4 set bits.
- The number 63 is binary 111111 so it has 6 set bits.
- The number 64 is binary 1000000 so it has 1 set bit.

Devising Recursive Algorithms

Problems that are based on games such as chess and cards are very popular with interviewers. They are popular because the solution to many of them involves a recursive algorithm, which is a legitimate topic at a programming interview. Recursion is the official connection, but it doesn't hurt that most people also like to play games.

QUESTIONS

16. Eight queens

Given a standard 8 × 8 chess board and eight queens, devise an algorithm to place the queens on the board so that none of the queens are attacked by another queen. In other words, each queen must not share a rank (row), file (column), or diagonal with any other queen. Figure 11-4 shows one possible correct placement whereas Figure 11-5 shows one incorrect placement.

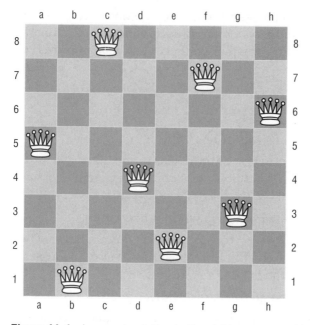

Figure 11-4: A correct solution to the eight-queens problem

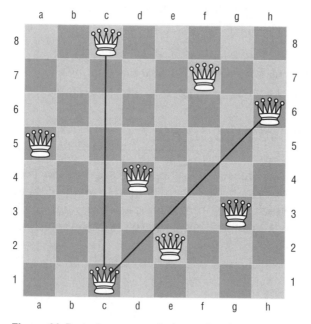

Figure 11-5: An incorrect solution to the eight-queens problem

17. Tower of Hanoi

The Tower of Hanoi is a well-known puzzle. It consists of three rods and a number of different-size disks that fit onto these rods.

The challenge is to move the disks from their start position as shown in Figure 11-6 to their end position as shown in Figure 11-7.

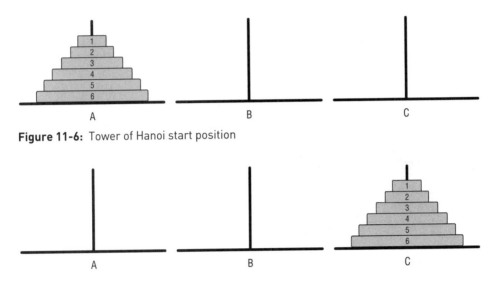

Figure 11-6: Tower of Hanoi start position

Figure 11-7: Tower of Hanoi end position

The rules of this puzzle are

- Each move consists of taking the topmost disk from a rod and placing it onto another rod.
- A disk may be placed on top of bigger disk but not on top of a smaller disk.

Devise an algorithm that produces instructions for solving the Tower of Hanoi for an arbitrary number of disks.

Understanding Logic Gates

In a very real sense, logic gates are one of the most fundamental building blocks of modern computing. The humble logic gate, an invention that seems obvious in hindsight, is the enabling mechanism by which computers perform Boolean logic.

As a programmer, your needing to work with logic gates on a daily basis is unlikely, so these questions fall into the realm of "notorious" interview questions, on a par with brain-teasers. This is a shame because an understanding of electronic logic gates is profoundly rewarding.

Figure 11-8 shows the symbols used for the most common logic gates.

Every logic gate takes input signals and produces at least one output signal. These inputs and outputs are usually summarized in *truth tables*. Tables 11-1 through 11-6 are the truth tables for the logic gates shown in Figure 11-8.

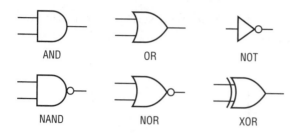

Figure 11-8: Gate symbols

Table 11-1: AND Truth Table

A	B	OUTPUT
0	0	0
1	0	0
0	1	0
1	1	1

Table 11-2: OR Truth Table

A	B	OUTPUT
0	0	0
1	0	1
0	1	1
1	1	1

A NOT gate is simply an inversion of a single input:

Table 11-3: NOT Truth Table

A	OUTPUT
0	1
1	0

The NOT gate can be combined with other gates to invert the gate's output. When a NOT gate is combined with an AND gate it is called a NAND (Not-AND) gate. Similarly, a NOT gate combined with an OR gate is a NOR gate.

Table 11-4: NAND Truth Table

A	B	OUTPUT
0	0	1
1	0	1
0	1	1
1	1	0

Table 11-5: NOR Truth Table

A	B	OUTPUT
0	0	1
1	0	0
0	1	0
1	1	0

An XOR ("eXclusive OR") logic gate is like an OR gate except that if both input values are 1 it produces an output of 0. The rule for an XOR gate is "one or the other but not both."

Table 11-6: XOR Truth Table

A	B	OUTPUT
0	0	0
1	0	1
0	1	1
1	1	0

QUESTIONS

18. **Draw a switch representation of an OR gate**

    Every logic gate can be drawn as a circuit diagram consisting of a power source, switches, and an output.

Figure 11-9 shows a diagram that represents an AND logic gate. When switches A and B are both closed, a circuit is completed and the light bulb (the output) is illuminated.

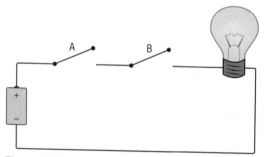

Figure 11-9: Circuit representing an AND gate

Draw a similar diagram that represents an OR logic gate.

19. **Construct an XOR gate**

    Construct an XOR logic gate from other types of logic gate.

20. **Construct a half-adder**

    A half-adder is a construction of gates used for adding two single bits. A half-adder produces two outputs: a sum value and a carry value. It is called a half-adder (rather than "full adder" or just "adder") because it adds bits without any consideration of a possible carry-bit from a previous addition. The two outputs (sum and carry) from a half-adder are given in Table 11-7.

    Table 11-7: Half-adder Inputs and Outputs

A	B	SUM	CARRY
0	0	0	0
0	1	1	0
1	0	1	0
1	1	0	1

    Construct a half-adder using logic gates. Your half-adder should allow for two inputs (A and B) and it should produce two outputs (sum and carry).

Writing Code to...Prove You Can Code

As an interviewer, there is little I find more surprising than a candidate programmer who cannot produce code for anything but the most trivial of programming problems. One thing that is slightly more surprising is the candidate programmer who cannot produce any code whatsoever.

The questions in this section are typical examples of problems that an interviewer might use to weed out these most obviously unqualified candidates.

None of these are trick questions and you should attempt to solve them in the most straightforward manner possible. In each case the obvious solution is probably the right solution. None of these questions should take you more than a few minutes to write and test.

QUESTIONS

21. Implement Fizz Buzz

The game called Fizz Buzz was originally invented as a teaching aid. The idea behind Fizz Buzz is that, by playing the game, children gain experience performing mental arithmetic. The rules of this game are as follow:

The players sit in a circle. One child is chosen to start the game and says "one" out loud. The next child (clockwise) says "two" and so on. Each child takes a turn saying the next number in sequence unless the number they are to say is a multiple of three or a multiple of five. If the number is a multiple of three the child says "fizz." If the number is a multiple of five the child says "buzz." If the number is a multiple of three *and* five then the child says "fizz buzz." Any child who hesitates or says the wrong thing is "out," and the game proceeds until one child remains. The last child to go "out" is deemed the winner and presumably is beaten up after class.

This game translates nicely to a simple programming challenge:

Write a program to print the numbers 1 to 100, replacing multiples of three with "Fizz," multiples of five with "Buzz," and multiples of both three and five with "Fizz Buzz."

22. Transform an array of items into a dictionary

Write code that will transform an array of integers into a dictionary with each key being the integers found in the array and each value being the number of occurrences of each integer.

For example, given the array

```
int[] array = {1,2,2,3,3,3,4,4,4,4,4};
```

your program should produce a dictionary of integers as follows:

```
dictionary[1]→1
dictionary[2]→2
dictionary[3]→3
dictionary[4]→5
```

23. **Find the remainder**

Write a function or method that accepts two arguments, both integers, and returns the remainder (an integer) left over after dividing the larger argument by the smaller. For example, if the values 13 and 4 are passed to the function it should return 1:

$13 \div 4 = 3$, *remainder* 1

If the values 142 and 1000 are passed to this function it should return 6:

$1000 \div 142 = 7$, *remainder* 6

ANSWERS

1. **Filling a school bus with golf balls**

   How many golf balls will it take to fill a school bus?

   Remember that an interviewer will be more interested in your approach than in the accuracy of your answer. You should approach all estimation questions in the same way:

   ▪ Clarify the question.

   ▪ Propose a method for estimating.

   ▪ Identify all relevant assumptions.

   ▪ Make the calculation.

   ▪ Reflect on your answer.

   To *clarify* the question you could ask:

   ▪ Why is the bus being loaded: Is this just a hypothetical question?

   ▪ Does the bus need to move after it has been loaded with golf balls?

   ▪ Can you tell me the size of a typical school bus and a standard golf ball or should I estimate?

   ▪ Can I assume the bus is not a double-decker?

After you have clarified the question you can start to think about how to calculate an estimate. At the same time you should be thinking about any assumptions you might need to make.

You could make the following *assumptions*:

- The golf balls and the bus are not modified in any relevant way (for instance, you assume the bus has no special golf ball compartment or trailer).

- You are not concerned with moving the golf balls after loading them into the bus, so you don't need to reserve any space for a driver or install a retaining wall to prevent the balls spilling into the driver's console.

- All the golf balls are spherical and equally sized.

- The golf balls will not be compressed or deformed.

- No students will be harmed during this exercise.

As a starting point for calculating an answer you might propose that the number of golf balls (G) you can fit into a school bus is equal to the volume of its interior space (V) divided by the volume of a single golf ball (g):

$$G = \frac{V}{g}$$

The act of writing down this formula might lead you to further considerations; for example:

- Golf balls have a spherical shape (ignoring dimples) so when they are packed together they will occupy a space that contains both golf balls and air. You should therefore factor in an allowance for space occupied by air (a).

- You can also assume that the interior of a school bus is going to contain seats and other things so you need to factor in the volume of these things (v) when calculating the space available for golf balls.

Modifying the original proposal you now have:

$$G = \frac{V - v}{g} \times a$$

You have also identified two new assumptions:

- The bus seats and other things will remain in the bus when it is loaded with golf balls. You might guess that the sum total of this occupied space is 10 percent of the total interior space:

  $v = 0.1 \times V$

- The golf balls cannot be packed into the bus without leaving gaps between the balls. You might guess that the sum total of these gaps will be about a quarter of the total occupied space, implying a "packing efficiency" due to gaps containing air of:

  $a = 0.75$

Unless you happen to know the volume of a golf ball you need to guess what this might be. If you assume a golf ball has a diameter of about 4 cm then the volume of one ball is approximately 33.5 cm^3:

$$g = \frac{4}{3} \pi r^3 = \frac{4}{3} \times 3.14 \times 2^3 \cong 33.5$$

(If you don't remember how to calculate the volume of a sphere then you would need to guess this number outright and list it as an assumption!)

You also need to estimate the interior space of a school bus. You know an adult male can stand inside a bus so let's assume it is 6 feet (1.8 m) high. There are usually four seats plus an aisle so you could guess a width of 10 feet (3 m). You could estimate the length of a school bus by comparing it to the length of your car (assuming you know the length of your car). Let's assume the bus is 40 feet (about 12 meters) long. With these assumptions you would calculate an interior volume of approximately 65 cubic meters:

$$V = 1.8 \times 3 \times 12 \cong 65 \ m^3$$

With all these values in hand you can now perform the calculation of how many golf balls it takes to fill a school bus:

$$G = \frac{65 - (0.1 \times 65)}{0.0000335} \times 0.75 \cong 1{,}300{,}000$$

In other words, according to the proposed formula and with the listed assumptions it would take 1.3 million golf balls to fill a school bus.

You aren't quite finished; you need to *reflect* on this answer. This means you need to ask yourself (out loud, for the interviewer's benefit) a few important questions:

- Is this number surprising? Can you double-check the result by comparing it to something else?
- What happens if you vary your assumptions? For instance, you might have overestimated the size of a school bus. If you assume dimensions of $1.8 \text{ m} \times 2 \text{ m} \times 8 \text{ m}$ then you need far fewer golf balls (about 740,000).
- Have you overlooked any practical considerations?

I have intentionally overworked the answer to this problem, and it is unlikely you will have the luxury of going into this much detail at the interview. This example is to give you a feeling for the kind of approach you should take: analytical and methodical. After your interviewer sees that you are taking a sensible approach, she might specify certain assumptions to make the calculation easier or perhaps even move on to the next question.

Also, keep in mind that you don't want to paint yourself into a corner by coming up with a calculation you can't easily perform in your head or on a whiteboard. If you don't have access to a calculator then you should avoid using more than one decimal place, even for the value of π.

Don't forget to involve your interviewer at every step so that she can see how you approach the problem. If speaking your thoughts out loud makes you feel uncomfortable then practice it a few times in front of friends or family. Remember that the quality of your thinking counts for little unless you share your thoughts with the interviewer.

2. Moving Mount Fuji

How would you move Mount Fuji?

Partly because of the notoriety of this question you are very unlikely to ever face it during an interview. In any case, this problem is another example of estimating that is similar in nature to the problem of filling a school bus with golf balls. You should approach it the same way: Ask for clarification, propose a method, state your assumptions, perform a calculation, and then reflect on the answer.

For instance, to clarify the question you should ask whether the mountain must be moved in its entirety or whether shifting its footprint (say) one foot to the east would be sufficient. After you understand the problem then you can move on to consider a solution. If the problem involves moving all of the earth inside Mount Fuji, then the problem boils down to estimating dimensions and calculating volumes.

Here is an example of how you would estimate the number of earth-moving trucks needed to move Mount Fuji:

Fuji is roughly cone-shaped so you can calculate its volume by guessing (or looking up) its height and base diameter and then using the formula:

$$v = \frac{1}{3} \pi r^2 h$$

If you can't remember the formula (and unless you've studied cones recently you probably won't) then you can make an assumption and approximate. You could, for instance, assume that the volume of Mount Fuji is roughly equal to one-third of a comparable cuboid (a cube with unequal sides), which greatly simplifies the calculation albeit with a larger margin of error.

You would then estimate the volume of an earth-moving truck and then calculate how many trucks you would need to shift all that earth. Here is an example calculation:

The height of Mount Fuji is estimated to be 4,000 m.

The diameter of Mount Fuji is estimated to be 15,000 m.

Therefore, the volume of earth in Mount Fuji is

$v = \frac{1}{3} \pi \times 7500^2 \times 4000 \cong 230{,}000{,}000{,}000$ cubic meters.

If a large earth-moving truck can carry (say) 40 cubic meters then about

$\dfrac{230000000000}{40} = 5{,}750{,}000{,}000$ truckloads must be moved.

That's a lot of dirt.

After you have arrived at a number then you can have some fun with further analysis of the problem. You could consider some of the logistics around organizing thousands of workers, fueling and scheduling the trucks, and so on. You could mention the environmental impact and how the Japanese might feel about a relocation of their mountain.

If you use your imagination you might also manage to lead the conversation back to the topic of programming.

3. **What color is the bear?**

   A bear walks one mile south, turns and walks one mile east, turns again and walks one mile north, finishing at the same place it started.

   What color is the bear?

   Without much thought you can probably guess that the bear is most likely white. The Arctic is the only place that is home to bears all of the same color (white); anywhere else and the bear could be black, brown, yellow, red, and so on. No bears are at the South Pole.

   White is the correct answer but the answer written on the interviewer's quiz sheet is probably more like the following:

   There are two places on Earth from where you can perform such a walk: at the North Pole and near the South Pole. If you start at any other place, you will not return to your starting point without travelling extra distance or changing direction. Because no bears live at the South Pole the answer must be the North Pole. The only bears at the North Pole are polar bears and so the answer must be white.

   To illustrate, look at the colored section of the sphere in Figure 11-10. The polar bear will have taken a similar path starting at the North Pole of this sphere. If you look at other three-sided paths in the northern hemisphere that following lines of longitude and latitude you can see that none of them lead back to their starting point.

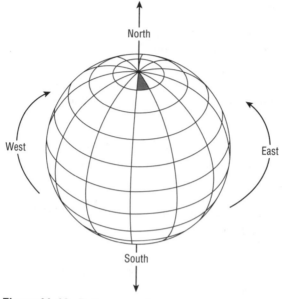

North

West

East

South

Figure 11-10: Paths on a sphere

4. **Why does a mirror reverse left and right but not up and down?**

Suppose you comb your hair with a part on the left side of your head. When you look in a mirror you can observe that the part is now on the right side of the head looking back at you. You also observe that your head is still at the top and your feet are still at the bottom. If you lie down horizontally on your side and look into a mirror you observe that the mirror image of your hair parting is still switched left to right.

Why does a mirror reverse left and right but not up and down?

The answer lies in how you perceive your mirror image. You should realize that your hand on the east side of the mirror remains on the east side, and ditto for your hand on the west side. You might realize that the reflected image is not reversed left to right but rather it is reversed front to back. The transformation of the image in the mirror is as if your nose had been pulled through your skull and out the back of your head.

To put it plainly, a mirror does not switch left and right. You incorrectly perceive a switch because of how you interpret the image you see in the mirror. When you look at your mirror image you interpret what you see as if you have walked around behind the mirror and are looking out at yourself. You expect your hair to be parted on the left side of the head in the mirror (the right-hand side from the viewer's perspective) but in fact your hair parting *is* on the left side of the image. You incorrectly interpret this as being the right-hand side of the head of the person in the mirror.

For bonus points during the interview be sure to gesticulate when describing east and west and left and right. Use your hand to indicate the direction of the reversal in the mirror (that is, front to back) and don't be too graphic when describing a nose that has been pulled through a skull.

5. **How would five pirates share 100 gold coins?**

   How should the pirate king allocate the 100 coins to maximize his profit and remain alive?

   The key to solving this problem is to first look at the problem as if there were just two pirates. With just two pirates (bosun and cook) the outcome is obvious—the bosun keeps 100 coins because he can't be outvoted. With just two pirates the cook gets nothing. See Figure 11-11.

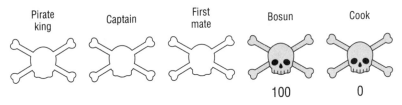

Figure 11-11: Dividing 100 coins between two pirates

Now suppose there were three pirates. The first mate must ensure he is not outvoted so he offers the cook one gold coin. The cook will accept this proposal because his alternative (if he votes against the proposal) is zero coins. The bosun cannot outvote the other two pirates and so the first mate gets to keep 99 coins. See Figure 11-12.

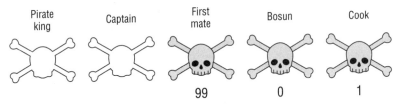

Figure 11-12: Dividing 100 coins between three pirates

Now suppose there were four pirates. The captain should give the bosun one gold coin because he knows that the bosun's alternative is zero coins. This is enough to ensure he will not be outvoted and so the captain gets to keep 99 coins. The bosun gets one coin and the first mate and the cook get nothing. See Figure 11-13.

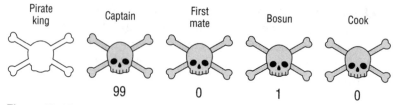

Figure 11-13: Dividing 100 coins between four pirates

If the pirate king was paying attention he will by now have realized he can keep 98 coins. He should give one coin to the cook and one coin to the first mate. They will accept because their alternative is zero coins. The captain and the bosun get nothing (see Figure 11-14).

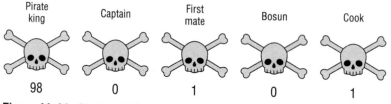

Figure 11-14: Dividing 100 coins between five pirates

6. Calculating the angle between clock hands

An analog clock on the wall indicates the time is 6:30 p.m. What is the angle between the hour and the minute hands? (There are two angles; you want the smaller one.)

The key to solving this problem is to convert the position of each hand to an angle and to then subtract one from the other to obtain the difference.

There are 360 degrees in one full rotation of each hand, and there are 60 minutes in an hour. You can therefore calculate that each minute represents a turn of 6 degrees:

$$\frac{360°}{60} = 6°$$

Converting the position of the minute hand to degrees is therefore straightforward. The calculation is:

$6° \times minutes$

For example, when the minute hand points to 12 (0 minutes past the hour) the calculation is:

$6° \times 0 = 0°$

When the minute hand points to 30 (half past the hour) the calculation is:

$6° \times 30 = 180°$

Converting the position of the hour hand to degrees is just a little more involved. It takes 12 hours (720 minutes) for the hour hand to turn 360 degrees. This means that the hour hand turns 0.5 degrees per minute:

$$\frac{360°}{720} = 0.5°$$

In other words each minute indicated by the hour hand represents a turn of 0.5 degrees.

To convert the position of the hour hand to degrees you, therefore, need to resolve its position to a number of minutes and then multiply by 0.5.

Returning to the original question, here is how you determine the angle between the clock hands at 6:30 p.m.

First, you must convert the hour to a number of minutes. An hour has 60 minutes so for 6:30 p.m. you have:

$6 \times 60 + 30 = 390$

Now you can convert 390 minutes to degrees:

$390 \times 0.5° = 195°$

Now that you have calculated an angle for both hands of the clock you can find the difference very simply:

$195° - 180° = 15°$

The answer is that the angle between the clock hands at 6:30 p.m. is 15°.

This approach works for any time of the day. Here are some more examples:

Example 1: When the time is 3:15 a.m. the hour hand has an angle of

$(3 \times 60 + 15) \times 0.5° = 97.5°$

The minute hand has an angle of

$15 \times 6° = 90°$

Therefore, the angle between the clock hands is 7.5 degrees.

Example 2: When the time is 9:50 p.m. the hour hand has an angle of

$(9 \times 60 + 50) \times 0.5° = 295°$

The minute hand has an angle of

$50 \times 6° = 300°$

Therefore, the angle between the clock hands is 5 degrees.

Example 3: When the time is 12:20 a.m. the hour hand has an angle of

$(0 \times 60 + 20) \times 0.5° = 10°$

The minute hand has an angle of

$20 \times 6° = 120°$

Therefore, the angle between the clock hands is 110 degrees.

7. Finding the heaviest ball

Suppose you are given eight balls of the same size. These balls are all the same weight except for one, which is a little heavier.

You are given a balance (a weighing machine that tells you which of two weights is heaviest) and asked to find the heaviest ball with just two weighings.

Assuming this is possible, how can you do it?

To crack this problem you need to realize that if you were given just three balls then you could find the heaviest in a single weighing: If two of the three balls are weighed and found to be equal then the third (unweighed) ball must be the heaviest. If they are unequal then the scale will indicate the heaviest.

From here it isn't much of a stretch to see how you can find the heaviest of eight balls with just two weighings.

To find the heaviest ball, you must divide the eight balls into three groups (one of these having just two balls). You then compare the weight of the two three-ball groups.

If both three-ball groups have the same weight then you know that the heaviest ball is one of the balls in the remaining two-ball group and you just need one more weighing to determine which ball it is.

If the three-ball groups have unequal weight then you now know that the heaviest ball is in the heavier of these two groups.

Choose any two balls from the heaviest group and compare their weights. If they are equal then you know that the remaining ball from that group (the one you didn't weigh) is the heaviest. If they are not equal then the balance will indicate which is heaviest. See Figure 11-15 for an illustration of this process.

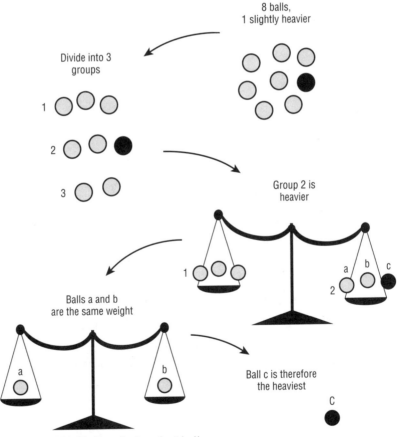

Figure 11-15: Finding the heaviest ball

As a side note this approach works for any number of balls and will find the heaviest ball, in a set of N balls in a maximum of $[\log_3 N]$ weighings.

8. Monty Hall

You are a contestant on a game show hosted by Monty Hall. You are shown three doors (labeled A, B, and C) and asked to choose one of them. Two of these doors conceal worthless prizes but behind one is a fantastic prize. The prizes are placed at random, but Monty knows their placement.

Suppose you choose door A. Without opening door A Monty opens one of the other two doors to reveal a worthless prize. Monty then offers you the choice of staying with door A or switching to the other, unopened door.

The question is, should you switch or should you stay with door A?

First, decide whether you should stay with door A or switch to the other unopened door. Next, write a program that simulates this game being played one million times and use your program to confirm your answer.

Intuition might tell you that it makes no difference whether you stay with door A or switch to the other, unopened door. It seems that because one of the doors has been removed from the problem it seems that you now have a 50-50 chance regardless of whether you stay or switch.

On the other hand, your *experience* with brain-teasers probably tells you that this is the wrong answer.

The controversial but correct answer is that you should *always switch*.

Here's why. Consider the table in Figure 11-16. This table shows the three possible arrangements of prizes together with the outcome depending on whether you stay with door A or switch to another door. Remember that after you choose door A, Monty will open one of the other doors that he knows does not conceal a prize. In doing this, Monty is giving you important information.

You can see that in the three possible scenarios the "switch" column has two favorable outcomes whereas the "stay" column has just one.

In other words if you switch your chance of winning increases to 66 percent whereas if you stay with the door you first chose your chance is just 33 percent.

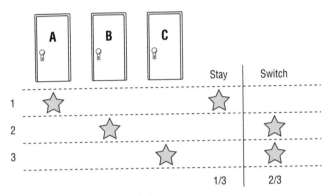

Figure 11-16: Stay or switch

Here is a C# program that simulates the Monty Hall problem with 1,000,000 attempts at "switching" and another 1,000,000 attempts at "staying." Figure 11-17 shows the output from running this program.

```csharp
using System;
using System.Collections;
using System.Collections.Generic;

namespace MontyHall
{
    class Program
    {

        const int ATTEMPTS = 1000000;
        static Random random = new Random();

        static void Main()
        {

            Console.WriteLine("\"Contestant always switches\"wins:"
                              + "{0} / {1}",
                Play(ContestantSwitches: true ), ATTEMPTS);

            Console.WriteLine("\"Contestant always stays\"wins: "
                              + " {0} / {1}",
                Play(ContestantSwitches: false), ATTEMPTS);

            Console.ReadKey();
        }
```

```
static int Play(bool ContestantSwitches)
{
    int wins = 0;
    var doors = new bool[3];
    for (int i = 0; i < ATTEMPTS; i++)
    {
        // Reset the doors
        int winningDoor = random.Next(3);
        for (int j = 0; j < 3; j++)
            doors[j] = winningDoor == j;

        // Contestant chooses a door
        int chosen = random.Next(3);

        // Monty shows a losing door
        int montyDoor = 0;
        do
        {
            montyDoor = random.Next(3);
        } while (montyDoor == chosen || doors[montyDoor]);

        // Which door remains?
        int remainingDoor = 0;
        while (remainingDoor == chosen ||
                remainingDoor == montyDoor)
            remainingDoor += 1;

        // Contestant switches or stays
        if (ContestantSwitches)
            chosen = remainingDoor;

        // Did the contestant win?
        wins += (chosen == winningDoor) ? 1 : 0;

    }
    return wins;
}
}
```

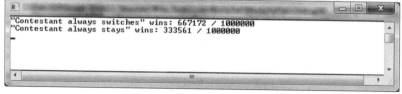

Figure 11-17: Monty Hall simulation

9. The birthday problem

In an office of just 23 people, what are the chances that two of them share a birthday? For the purposes of this question you can assume that birthdays are randomly distributed throughout the year.

Note that the question is not asking for the probability that two people share the same *specific* birthday. The question asks about the likelihood of two people sharing *any* birthday.

Note also that if the probability of an event occurring is P then the probability of it *not* occurring (the converse probability) is $1 - P$. This is useful because it means you can calculate a probability in two ways: You can calculate it directly or you can calculate the converse probability.

To calculate the chance of two people out of 23 sharing a birthday, calculating the converse is easier. In other words calculating the probability that each of the 23 people have a different birthday is easier.

Starting with the simplest case, if you have two people in a group then the chance of them *not* sharing a birthday is:

$$\frac{364}{365} = 99.73\%$$

You arrive at this fraction by noting that the first person "claims" one of the 365 days in the year leaving 364 days "available" for the second person. The chance of that person having a birthday on one of the 364 "available" days is $\frac{364}{365}$.

If you have three people the chance is

$$\frac{364}{365} \times \frac{343}{365} = 99.18\%$$

If you have four people the chance is

$$\frac{364}{365} \times \frac{343}{365} \times \frac{362}{365} = 98.36\%$$

And so on, until you reach a calculation for 23 people:

$$\frac{364}{365} \times \frac{343}{365} \times \frac{362}{365} \times \dots \times \frac{343}{365} = 49.27\%$$

Now that you have calculated the chance of 23 people *not* sharing a birthday you can easily obtain the chance that at least two *will* share a birthday:

$$1 - 0.4927 = 0.5073 = 50.73\%$$

And so you come to the somewhat surprising conclusion that if you have 23 people in an office, there is a better than 50 percent chance that two of them will share a birthday.

10. The Dining Philosophers

Suggest a way of coordinating eating and thinking that ensures all philosophers are fed, none of them starve, and the meal will continue indefinitely with all philosophers alternating between eating and thinking.

This is a problem of concurrency. It illustrates how a naïve approach to managing concurrent access to resources can lead to deadlocks or, even worse, to the starvation of a philosopher. This problem was originally formulated by Edsger Dijkstra (a Dutch computer scientist) but it was Tony Hoare (a British computer scientist) who reformulated the question to involve an endless supply of spaghetti.

Without a suitable approach the possibility exists that a philosopher in this scenario will starve. Consider the following naïve approach:

- Each philosopher will attempt to pick up a fork on their left when it becomes available.

- After a philosopher has a fork from his left he will attempt to pick up a fork from his right.

- A philosopher with two forks will eat for a while and then put down his right fork followed by his left fork.

- A philosopher will spend some time thinking after he finishes eating, and will then attempt to resume eating.

Without thinking too hard about this approach you should be able to see that the philosophers have a problem. If each philosopher simultaneously picks up a fork on their left there will then be no forks remaining on the table. All the philosophers will therefore be waiting for a right fork to become available and this will never happen. The philosophers will starve. In computing terms (if you replace philosophers with processes, and forks with resources such as database records) this is a *deadlock* scenario.

The solution to this problem is perhaps surprisingly simple. Each fork is assigned a number, 1–5, and each philosopher must pick up an adjacent fork with the *lowest number* before attempting to pick up another fork. If the lower-numbered fork is not available then the philosopher must wait for it.

With this simple constraint you avoid the possibility of a deadlock. Suppose the philosophers commence dining and all attempt to pick up the nearest fork. All the forks will be picked up except the highest-numbered fork (fork 5 in Figure 11-3). Fork 5 will be picked up by either philosopher A or philosopher E and one of them will wait while the other eats. When fork 5 is returned to the table the waiting philosopher will be able to eat. Around the table eating and thinking will continue indefinitely.

11. The Sleeping Barber Problem

Describe a method for running the barber's shop that ensures customers are never left waiting while the barber sleeps.

To understand and solve this problem you must first have an appreciation of how problems can arise if the running of the barber's shop is not coordinated in some way.

Consider what will happen if the waiting room is empty and a new customer arrives the moment before the barber finishes cutting a customer's hair. The new customer will see that the barber is busy so he will proceed to the waiting room. At almost the same time the barber will escort his customer out of the shop, find his waiting room empty (because the new customer has not yet taken a seat) and will go to sleep in his chair. The new customer will arrive in the waiting room, take a seat and wait while the barber sleeps. This is exactly the outcome you want to avoid.

This is obviously an artificial scenario, but if you think of the barber and his customers as independent processes running on a computer then you will see the relevance of the question. Without some kind of coordination these processes will potentially all "go to sleep" instead of interacting in some fashion. It all depends on the timing of these processes.

To fix this problem and to ensure you don't rely on luck for the smooth operation of the barber's shop, you must ensure that the barber and his customers don't take potentially conflicting actions at the same time is necessary. For example:

▪ You must prevent two or more customers simultaneously checking the barber's status.

▪ You must prevent customers from checking the barber's status just as the barber is finishing with a customer.

▪ You must prevent the barber checking for waiting customers when a customer is moving to sit in the waiting room.

The simplest way to avoid these conflicts is to introduce some kind of flag that can be held by only one person at a time, and to require the barber and his customers to obtain this flag before they check each other's state and before they change state, releasing it when they finish checking or changing state.

In programming terms this flag is known as a *lock* or a *mutex*.

12. Find the smaller of two integers without branching

Write code that uses bitwise operations to find the smaller of two integers. You may not use branching (`if-else` and so on) or framework methods such as `Math.Min(a,b)`.

If this question permitted branching then the simplest answer would be:

```
int min = a < b ? a : b;
```

If framework methods were permitted you could write:

```
int min = Math.Min(a,b);
```

The question forbids either of these methods so you need to be more creative.

First, you should note that a signed integer uses the high-order bit to indicate a negative number. If you look at the binary representations of 1 and -1 (see Figure 11-18) you can see the difference.

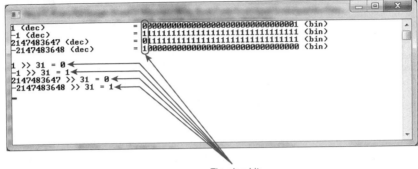

The sign-bit

Figure 11-18: Examining the sign-bit

Use the following code if you want to try this yourself:

```
int a = 1;
int b = -1;
int x = int.MaxValue;
int y = int.MinValue;

int width = sizeof(int) * 8;

Console.WriteLine("{0} (dec)\t\t\t = {1} (bin)", a,
    Convert.ToString(a,2).PadLeft(width, '0'));

Console.WriteLine("{0} (dec)\t\t = {1} (bin)", b,
    Convert.ToString(b,2).PadLeft(width, '0'));

Console.WriteLine("{0} (dec)\t = {1} (bin)", x,
    Convert.ToString(x,2).PadLeft(width, '0'));

Console.WriteLine("{0} (dec)\t = {1} (bin)", y,
    Convert.ToString(y,2).PadLeft(width, '0'));

Console.WriteLine("{0} >> {1} = {2}", a, (width - 1),
    a >> (width - 1));

Console.WriteLine("{0} >> {1} = {2}", b, (width - 1),
    ((uint)b) >> (width - 1));

Console.WriteLine("{0} >> {1} = {2}", x, (width - 1),
    x >> (width - 1));

Console.WriteLine("{0} >> {1} = {2}", y, (width - 1),
```

```
((uint)y) >> (width - 1));

Console.ReadLine();
```

NOTE The >> operator in C# performs **arithmetic** shifts on signed integers. An arithmetic right shift retains the sign-bit. To force C# to shift the sign-bit you must cast `int` to `uint` (unsigned integer).

The interesting aspect of performing an arithmetic right shift is that the sign-bit is retained, so right-shifting a positive number by 31 results in 0 but right-shifting a negative number by 31 results in −1 (or 1 if you force a bitwise shift), assuming here that the width of an `int` is 32 bits.

Now, if you take the result of a 31-bit arithmetic right shift (which will be either 0 or −1) you can use it in combination with your variable a and b to determine the minimum.

Here is one possible solution to the original problem:

```
public int BitwiseMin(int a, int b)
{
    a -= b;

    a &= a >> (sizeof(int) * 8 - 1);

    return a + b;
}
```

This solution works unless $a - b$ is less than `int.MinValue`, in which case it underflows. To prevent an underflow you can work with `long` values as follows:

```
 public int BitwiseMin(int a, int b)
{
    long a_ = a; long b_ = b;

    a_ -= b_;

    a_ &= a_ >> (sizeof(long) *8 - 1);

    return (int)(a_ + b_);
}
```

13. **Find the larger of two integers without branching**

Write code that uses bitwise operations to find the larger of two integers. You may not use branching (if-else and so on) or framework methods such as Math.Max(a,b).

The problem is similar to finding the minimum of two integers without branching.

```
public int BitwiseMax(int a, int b)
{
    long a_ = a; long b_ = b;

    a_ -= b_;

    a_ &= (~a_) >> (sizeof(long)*8-1);

    return (int)(a_ + b_);
}
```

14. Determine whether an integer is a power of 2

Use bitwise operators to determine whether an integer is a power of 2.

The key to this question is to appreciate two facts:

- Any power of 2 in binary starts with a 1 and thereafter is all zeros; for example, 10, 100, 1000, 10000, and so on.
- When you subtract 1 from any power of 2 the binary number is all ones; for example, 1, 11, 111, 1111, and so on.

Consider the following examples:

Example 1: Is 8 a power of 2?

8 (dec) = 1000 (bin)

8–1 = 7 = 0111 (bin)

1000 & 0111 = 0000

Therefore, 8 is a power of 2.

Example 2: Is 16 a power of 2?

16 (dec) = 10000 (bin)

16–1 = 15 = 01111 (bin)

10000 & 01111 = 00000

Therefore, 16 is a power of 2.

Example 3: Is 15 a power of 2?

15 (dec) = 1111 (bin)

15–1 = 14 = 1110 (bin)

1111 & 1110 = 1110

Therefore, 15 is not a power of 2.

In the general case the coded test for "power of 2" should look like this:

```
bool isPowerOf2 = (v & (v - 1)) == 0;
```

You also need to allow for the number 0, which is a special case:

```
bool isPowerOf2 = ((v != 0) && (v & (v - 1)) == 0);
```

15. **Counting set bits**

Write code to find the number of set bits in an integer. For example:

- *The number 1 is binary 0001 so it has 1 set bit.*
- *The number 15 is binary 1111 so it has 4 set bits.*
- *The number 63 is binary 111111 so it has 6 set bits.*
- *The number 64 is binary 1000000 so it has 1 set bit.*

The simplest approach is to iterate over the bits in an integer and test each one.

```
public uint NumberOfSetBits(uint n)
{
    uint setbits;

    for (setbits = 0; n>0; n >>= 1)
    {
        setbits += n & 1;
    }

    return setbits;
}
```

A more efficient approach is to iterate once per set bit:

```
public uint NumberOfSetBits(uint n)
{
    uint setbits;

    for (setbits = 0; n > 0; setbits++)
    {
        n &= n - 1;
    }

    return setbits;
}
```

16. **Eight queens**

Given a standard 8 × 8 chess board and eight queens, devise an algorithm to place the queens on the board so that none of the queens are attacked by another queen. In other words each queen must not share a rank (row) or file (column) or diagonal with any other queen.

You can place the first queen anywhere. Let's assume you place it on *a1*. Now the second queen is restricted in where it can be placed because file *a* and rank *1* and the diagonal *a1-h8* are "taken" by the first queen. See Figure 11-19.

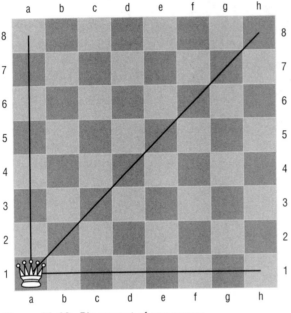

Figure 11-19: Placement of one queen

If you want to place a queen on the *b* file you cannot place it on *b1* or *b2*. Let's assume you place it on the *b3* square. Now the placement of a queen on the *c* file is similarly restricted. See Figure 11-20.

This problem is very well-suited to a recursive algorithm because in order to place the *Nth* queen you need to know where the previous queens were placed. The possibility exists that when you attempt to place a queen on a file there is no good square remaining for it on that file. In this case, you need to back up and adjust the placement of the previously placed queen. If that still leaves no good square then you must backtrack further, and so on until you have placed all the previous queens in such a way that allows the *Nth* queen to find a safe home.

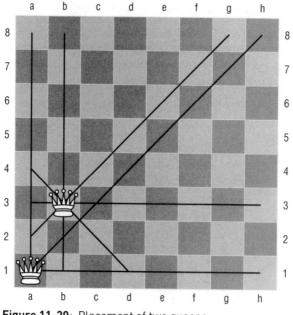

Figure 11-20: Placement of two queens

Here is a minimalist C# program that finds all possible placements
of *N* queens:

```
using System;
using System.Collections.Generic;
using System.Diagnostics;

namespace EightQueens
{
    public class Queens
    {
        const int N = 8;
        static int[] queenSquares = new int[N];
        static List<int[]> solutions = new List<int[]>();

        public static void Main(String[] args)
        {
            placeQueen(file: 0);

            int count = 1;
            foreach (int[] solution in solutions)
            {
                Console.WriteLine(string.Format("Solution {0}:",
                            count++));
                printBoard(solution);
                Console.WriteLine();
            }
```

```
        Console.ReadKey();
}

static bool isNotAttacked(int file, int rank)
{
    /* returns true if the placement of a Q
     * is not attached by any previously placed Q */

    // for all previously placed queens...
    for (int i = 1; i <= file; i++)
    {
        int queenrank = queenSquares[file - i];

        // same rank?
        if (queenrank == rank)
            return false;

        // same diagonal?
        if (queenrank == rank - i || queenrank == rank + i)
            return false;
    }
    return true;
}

static void placeQueen(int file)
{

    /* place a Q on a file so that
     * it is not attacked by any other Q */

    // Reached N queens?
    if (file == N)
    {
        solutions.Add((int[])queenSquares.Clone());
    }
    else
    {
        for (int rank = 0; rank < N; rank++)
        {
            if (isNotAttacked(file, rank))
            {
                queenSquares[file] = rank;
                placeQueen(file + 1);
            }
        }
    }
}

static void printBoard(int[] queenSquares) {
    for (int file = 0; file < queenSquares.Length; file++)
```

```
        {
            for (int rank = 0;
                rank < queenSquares.Length;
                rank++)
            {
                if (queenSquares[file] == rank)
                    Console.Write("Q ");
                else
                    Console.Write(". ");
            }
            Console.WriteLine();
        }
        Console.WriteLine();
    }
}
}
```

Notice that this program stores the placement of queens in an array of integers (queenSquares). Each element of queenSquares indicates the placement of a queen.

The index *N* indicates the *Nth* queen is on the *Nth* file (column).

The value of element *N* indicates the placement rank (row).

For example, the array [1,3,0,2] indicates four queens placed at board coordinates (0,1), (1,3), (2,0), (3,2).

This program includes a method printBoard that prints a visualization of each set of queen placements. See Figure 11-21 for an example.

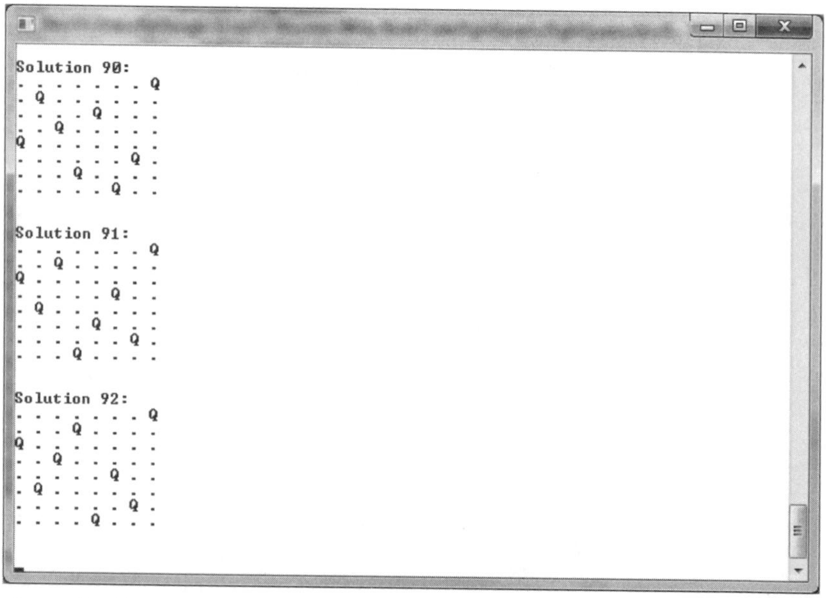

Figure 11-21: Visualizing the placement of eight queens

17. Tower of Hanoi

Devise an algorithm that produces instructions for solving the Tower of Hanoi for an arbitrary number of disks.

This problem is another good example of how recursion can build on an easily solved base case to solve a harder problem.

If you have just one disk (the base case) you solve the problem by moving disk 1 from *A* directly to *C*.

Move disk 1 from $A \rightarrow C$.

For two disks you need to use tower *B* as an intermediate resting place:

Move disk 1 from $A \rightarrow B$.

Move disk 2 from $A \rightarrow C$.

Move disk 1 from $B \rightarrow C$.

In general, to move three disks from *A* to *C* you first need to move two disks from *A* to *B* before you can move the third disk. After you have moved the third disk then you can move the two disks from *B* to *C*

You can generalize from these simple cases that to move *n* disks from *A* to *C* you first need to move $n - 1$ disks from *A* to *B*, then move disk *n*, and finally move $n - 1$ disks from *B* to *C*.

In pseudo-code you, therefore, derive a recursive function to move *n* disks as follows:

```
function hanoi(int n, Tower from, Tower to, Tower intermediate) {

    if (n == 0) { return }

    hanoi(n-1, from, intermediate, to)

    move(n, from, to)

    hanoi(n-1, intermediate, to, from)

}
```

Here is a complete C# program that produces instructions for moving five disks from A to C:

```
using System;
using System.Collections.Generic;
using System.Text;

namespace Hanoi
```

```
{
    class Tower : Stack<int>
    {
        public string Name { get; set; }
        public Tower(string name)
        {
            Name = name;
        }
    }

    class Program
    {
        static Tower A = new Tower("Tower A");
        static Tower B = new Tower("Tower B");
        static Tower C = new Tower("Tower C");

        static void Main(string[] args)
        {

            int numberOfDisks = 5;

            for (int i = numberOfDisks; i > 0; i--)
                A.Push(i);

            visualizeTowers();

            hanoi(numberOfDisks, from: A, to: C, intermediate: B);

            Console.ReadKey();
        }

        static void hanoi(int x,
                          Tower from,
                          Tower to,
                          Tower intermediate)
        {
            if (x == 0) return;

            hanoi(x - 1, from, intermediate, to);

            move(x, from, to);

            hanoi(x - 1, intermediate, to, from);


        }

        static void move(int n, Tower from, Tower to)
        {
```

```
    Console.WriteLine(
            string.Format("Move disk {0} from {1} to {2}",
        n, from.Name, to.Name));

    int x = from.Pop();
    to.Push(x);

    visualizeTowers();
}

static void visualizeTowers()
{
    foreach (Tower t in new List<Tower> { A, B, C })
    {
        Console.WriteLine(t.Name + ":");
        foreach (int i in t.ToArray())
        {
            for (int j = 1; j <= i; j++)
                Console.Write('-');
            Console.WriteLine();
        }
    }
}
        }
    }
}
```

18. Draw a switch representation of an OR gate

Draw a diagram that represents an OR logic gate.

The circuit shown back in Figure 11-9 illuminates the bulb when both switches are in the ON position. This represents an AND gate.

To represent an OR gate you need to show a circuit that illuminates the bulb when either switch A or switch B (or both) is set to ON. A circuit that meets this requirement is shown in Figure 11-22.

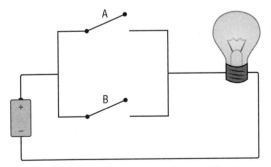

Figure 11-22: Circuit representing an OR gate

19. Construct an XOR gate

Construct an XOR logic gate from other types of logic gate.

This question requires you to produce a combination of logic gates that produce the same result as an XOR gate. In other words, you need to connect a series of gates in such a way that the output signal is according to the truth table for an XOR gate (see Table 11-8).

Table 11-8: XOR Truth Table

A	B	OUTPUT
0	0	0
1	0	1
0	1	1
1	1	0

You might already be aware of two logic gates—the NOR and NAND gates—that are sometimes referred to as *universal gates*. Using either of these gates to produce the same result as any other logic gate is possible. For example, Figure 11-23 shows a combination of NOR gates that produces the same output as an AND gate.

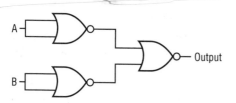

Figure 11-23: NOR gates combine to make an AND gate.

Figure 11-24 shows an XOR gate composed of NAND gates.

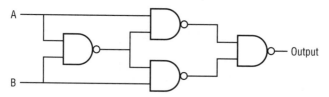

Figure 11-24: NAND gates combine to make an XOR gate.

Other constructions are possible. Figure 11-25 shows an XOR gate composed of one OR gate, one AND gate, and a NAND gate.

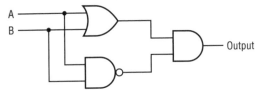

Figure 11-25: Alternative to XOR

20. Construct a half-adder

Construct a half-adder using logic gates. Your half-adder should allow for two inputs (A and B) and it should produce two outputs (sum and carry).

If you look carefully at the sum column of a half-adder (see Table 11-7) you will see it matches perfectly with an XOR gate. You can therefore use an XOR gate to compute the sum value of a half-adder.

Conveniently, values in the carry column match perfectly with an AND gate. You can therefore use an AND gate to compute the carry value in a half-adder.

Figure 11-26 shows how you combine these two gates to create a half-adder.

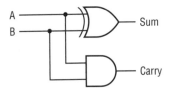

Figure 11-26: A half-adder

21. Implement Fizz Buzz

Write a program to print the numbers 1 to 100, replacing multiples of three with "Fizz," multiples of five with "Buzz," and multiples of both three and five with "Fizz Buzz."

Many possible solutions exist for this simple problem.

Here is a straightforward solution in C#:

```
static void FizzBuzz()
{
    for (int i = 1; i <= 100; i++)
```

```
    {
        if (i % 3 == 0 && i % 5 == 0)
            Console.WriteLine("Fizz Buzz");
        else if (i % 5 == 0)
            Console.WriteLine("Buzz");
        else if (i % 3 == 0)
            Console.Write("Fizz");
        else
            Console.Write(i);
    }
}
```

Here is a terse version in Perl:

```
print $_ %3 ? $_ %5 ? $_ : 'Buzz' : $_ %5 ? 'Fizz'
    : 'Fizz Buzz', "\n" for 1..100;
```

Here is a functional version in F#:

```
[<EntryPoint>]
[1..100]
|> Seq.map (function
    | x when x % 5 = 0 && x % 3 = 0 -> "Fizz Buzz"
    | x when x % 3 = 0 -> "Fizz"
    | x when x % 5 = 0 -> "Buzz"
    | x -> string x)
|> Seq.iter (printfn "%s")
```

22. Transform an array of items into a dictionary

Write code that transforms an array of integers into a dictionary with each key being the integers found in the array and each value being the number of occurrences of each integer.

For example, given the array

```
int[] array = {1,2,2,3,3,3,4,4,4,4,4};
```

your program should produce a dictionary of integers as follows:

```
dictionary[1]→1
dictionary[2]→2
dictionary[3]→3
dictionary[4]→5
```

In C#:

```
static void MakeDictionaryFromArray()
{
```

```
int[] array = { 1, 2, 2, 3, 3, 3, 4, 4, 4, 4, 4 };

var dictionary = new Dictionary<int, int>();

foreach (int i in array)
    if (dictionary.ContainsKey(i))
        dictionary[i] += 1;
    else
        dictionary.Add(i, 1);

}
```

In Perl:

```
$dictionary{$_} += 1 for (1,2,2,3,3,3,4,4,4,4,4);
```

23. Find the remainder

Write a function or method that accepts two arguments, both integers, and returns the remainder (an integer) left over after dividing the larger argument by the smaller. For example, if passed 13 and 4 this function should return 1:

$13 \div 4 = 3$, remainder 1

If passed 142 and 1000 this function should return 6:

$1000 \div 142 = 7$, remainder 6

The only potential "gotcha" with this question is a divide-by zero error, which you should either handle explicitly or leave as a possible unhandled exception. Otherwise, this is nearly as simple as programming gets.

Here is a C# solution:

```
static int FindRemainder(int x, int y)
{
    int larger;
    int smaller;

    if (x > y)
    {
        larger = x; smaller = y;
    }
    else
    {
        larger = y; smaller = x;
    }
```

```
if (smaller == 0)
{
    // Ask your interviewer how you should handle this
    throw new NotImplementedException();
}

return larger % smaller;
}
```

# CHAPTER 12

Programming Wisdom

When I interview experienced programmers I always expect to enjoy the experience. Regardless of our personal backgrounds, I know that we will have some important things in common. In all likelihood we will both have:

- Struggled with elusive bugs
- Been asked to write code from unclear requirements
- Been asked for estimates without any tangible requirements
- Faced unrealistic deadlines
- Had many "ah-hah!" moments
- Feelings of nostalgia over old, superseded tools
- Feelings of great satisfaction from coding it, and...*it works*

I could fill an entire book with a list of experiences shared by programmers around the world, regardless of where they come from or what software they write. The questions in this chapter are all about exploring this common ground. These questions are different from other questions in this book because the answers to most of them are subjective. Almost certainly you will find an answer (or maybe even the wording of a question) in this chapter with which you strongly disagree. Well, that's fine, and I look forward to debating the point with you online or perhaps even in person.

QUESTIONS

The worst answer you can give to any of these questions is a dismissive shrug. If an interviewer asks for your opinion, be sure that you give it, even if your opinion is that it (whatever it is) doesn't matter. Be ready to defend your point of view as if you were debating with a fellow programmer, perhaps as if you were debating with someone in your development team. In this way, both you and the interviewer get to see what it will be like working with each other. There's no point submissively deferring to everything the interviewer says unless that is the kind of working relationship you're happy to have. I hope it isn't.

1. **Why use source control?**

   What arguments would you make to convince a non-technical manager that your development team should adopt source code revision control?

2. **What popular programming wisdom do you disagree with?**

   You might have heard the story of the little girl who asks her mother why she cuts the legs and wings off the turkey before putting it in the oven. The girl's mother says that she learned how to cook a turkey from the girls' grandmother. The girl's grandmother explains that she was taught by her own mother, and so on, until the girl discovers that her great-great-great grandmother cut the legs and wings off the turkey because, otherwise, it would not fit into the very small oven she owned 100 years ago.

   A lot of programming wisdom is like this. There might once have been a good reason to do a certain thing but it was long ago. Whenever you receive some wisdom you should pause to consider whether the reasoning behind this wisdom as valid today as it was back then.

   As an experienced programmer, what are some examples of *received wisdom* that you don't agree with?

3. **Why are software projects always late?**

   If one thing is true of software projects it is that they are usually late and over budget. Why is this the case?

4. **Why can't you keep adding programmers?**

   Why can't you keep adding programmers to a software project to bring it in on time?

5. **How do you ensure that your estimates are sound?**

   As a programmer responsible for giving estimates that are as accurate as possible, how do you ensure that your estimates are sound?

6. **Why is code clarity important?**

   Everyone agrees that code clarity is important, but not everyone agrees what it means exactly. Give a definition of "code clarity" and explain why it is important.

7. **What are your red flags during code review?**

   When you review another programmer's code, what are the things you look for that might indicate a deeper problem? In other words, what are your red flags when reviewing code?

8. **Describe some things you always do when troubleshooting**

   Some programmers seem to have a knack for troubleshooting. When a customer reports a problem that can't be reproduced in the testing environment, these savant programmers will start twitching and blinking, and before you know it they have guessed the problem and are halfway done coding a solution.

   The rest of us, unfortunately, need to work a bit harder.

   What are some things that you always do (or try to do) when diagnosing a problem?

9. **How do you go about getting familiar with a large code project?**

   Every time you change jobs a good chance exists that you will need to quickly become familiar with a large new code base.

   How do you do that?

10. **Describe your understanding of *cargo-cult* programming**

    The phrase cargo-cult programming (or cargo-cult software engineering) is sometimes used to describe an undesirable approach to programming.

    Describe what the term means and why this approach is undesirable.

11. **Describe some potential downsides of code comments**

    When students are taught programming at school, one of the first lessons they learn is that they should make sure to include appropriate code comments.

    This is probably good advice, but what are some of the potential downsides of code comments?

12. **When is it acceptable to produce lower-quality code?**

    Everyone agrees that programmers should strive to write good-quality code. Everyone might not agree on what this means, exactly, but in general all of us prefer to write good code rather than bad code.

Can you think of a valid, ethical reason why you would be motivated to write substandard code?

13. How can large code projects be kept under control?

Large software products always seem to contain a lot of regrettable code, and this is especially true for successful products that are maintained over many years. Almost everyone who has worked on a large code base will have issues with it in some way or another. It might be that it has too many or too few layers of indirection, or that inconsistencies are throughout the code base, or any number of other problems.

As a programmer working on a large code project, how do you keep these kinds of problems under control?

14. How do you add features to unfamiliar code?

Describe how you would go about adding new features to a large, unfamiliar code project.

15. What exactly is wrong with so-called clever code?

Now and then every programmer will write a bit of code and feel justifiably proud of their achievement. This is part of the fun in programming. Sometimes, unfortunately, the pursuit of this happy feeling will lead programmers astray and cause us to write code that is, frankly, *too clever*.

What does it mean by code being "too clever," and what exactly is wrong with clever code?

16. How do you improve your programming ability?

Suppose you want to improve your coding ability, how would you go about it?

17. Describe a coding project of which you're proud

Interviewers often ask about projects that made you proud. Talking about work-related projects is customary but most interviewers will let you talk about any programming project you've worked on, at work, at school, or even at home. The interviewer's aim is to give you a platform to display your enthusiasm for programming.

18. Explain programming in non-technical terms

Suppose you are at a family event and your grandmother asks you to explain what it is that you do as a "programmer." What do you tell her?

19. Explain the significance of *coupling* and *cohesion*

You often hear these terms in debates about the implementation of an application. What is the programming-related meaning of the words *coupling* and *cohesion*, and why are they significant?

20. **What is the real problem with global variables?**

   A global variable is a variable that is available throughout an entire application, regardless of where it is referenced.

   That sounds quite handy, so what is the real problem with global variables?

21. **Explain the term *technical debt* in terms a non-technical manager will understand**

   Most programmers love the term *technical debt* because it is an apt metaphor for a problem they face every day. Unfortunately, the significance of the term appears to not be quite as apparent to as many non-technical managers.

   Explain the meaning and significance of technical debt in terms that a non-technical manager will understand.

22. **Explain the term *refactoring* in terms that a non-technical manager will understand**

   The term *refactoring* is commonly used by many programmers and is generally understood to mean something positive. Explain in non-technical terms what the term means.

23. **What is the significance of a *leaky abstraction*?**

   In 2002, Joel Spolsky wrote a blog post entitled *The Law of Leaky Abstractions*:

   ```
   http://www.joelonsoftware.com/articles/LeakyAbstractions.html
   ```

   The term *leaky abstraction* has now entered the mainstream of programmer jargon.

   Explain the meaning and significance of this term.

24. **What is *continuous integration* and how is it helpful?**

   The concept of *continuous integration* has progressed to the point where you can buy specialized tools to support the practice.

   What does the term *continuous integration* mean, and how is it helpful?

25. **What is your favorite software development methodology?**

   I once worked with a very plain-speaking programmer who snorted loudly when I asked a candidate this question at an interview. He explained afterwards that he thought the question was trendy and meaningless, and that the word *methodology* was a pretentious substitute for the word *method*. He was probably right, so here is the same question asked in a more plain-speaking way:

   In your experience, what methods most improve the effectiveness of a software development team?

26. How do I tell the product owner that his requirements are ridiculous?

Programmers are usually not backward in regard to assessing the merits of a requirement that appears to be unrealistic or impossible.

How would you explain to a product owner that you cannot implement his requirements?

27. What advice do you have for new programmers?

Suppose you were given the responsibility of mentoring a new and inexperienced programmer. What key bits of advice would you want to ensure this programmer understands as she embarks on her programming career?

28. Do coding standards influence code quality?

Do you think raising the quality of code by enforcing coding standards is possible?

29. Which coding standards are the most important?

Every software development team seems to have a set of coding standards. Describe some coding standards that you think are important for a team striving to produce good-quality code.

30. Why is the number of lines of code produced by a programmer a poor measurement of programmer productivity?

Every now and then it will occur to a non-technical manager that measuring the cost-effectiveness of a software development team ought to be possible. This manager might do some reading about the practice of programming and it will occur to him that because programmers write code, just like authors write books and lawyers write contracts, then deriving some useful information by counting the number of lines of code produced by a programmer over time should be possible.

Why is *lines of code* (*LoC*) a poor measurement of programmer productivity?

31. Is the goto statement really that harmful?

Most programmers have been instilled with a strong sense of certainty that the `goto` statement is a source of untold misery and that it must be avoided at all costs.

Explain why the `goto` statement is considered harmful.

32. Should software managers have technical backgrounds?

Should software development managers have technical backgrounds? To ask this another way, can a software development manager without a technical background be effective? (Notice that no stipulation exists that this technical background is necessarily programming experience.)

33. **Should application architects know how to write code?**

Similar to the question about technical and non-technical managers, another question I often hear is whether application architects should be capable of writing code. What is your opinion?

34. **What is your desert-island** *best practice*?

If you could choose one so-called "best practice" that everyone in your team (or, if you prefer, the world) would instantly start following, what would it be?

ANSWERS

1. **Why use source control?**

What arguments would you make to convince a non-technical manager that your development team should adopt source code revision control?

From experience I have found that non-technical managers respond best to analogies to which they can relate. Most managers will use word-processing software, and everyone who uses word-processing software to write documents will eventually make a mistake they want to fix. Fortunately, every word processor has an *undo* function so that accidents, even big ones, can be undone at the click of a button. No one would seriously think of a word-processor's *undo* function as a "nice to have" feature.

Revision control is the software developer's *undo* function. If you make a mistake it can be undone without any fuss.

But revision control is more than that.

You can go right back to a change that was made days or weeks or years ago and undo that change. You can go right back to the time the document was created. You can undo a change made weeks or years ago while retaining all the changes that were made since then. It's a very, very powerful undo feature.

But it's even more than that.

Suppose you need to produce two similar documents: one for public viewing and another for internal circulation. In a word processor you would write the first document, or part of it, then make a copy, then make changes in one or both documents. From the moment that you take a copy of the original document you need to consider whether a change to one document should be made to the other document as well. Every change has to be copied by hand from one document to another. If you have created more than one copy of the original document then you need to copy your change into each of these documents. Keeping documents in sync can be an error-prone and frustrating exercise.

Revision control solves this problem for the programmer. It tracks changes so it knows what needs to be copied between documents. It can show the programmer each of the differences between two documents and the programmer can pick and choose which changes should be copied and which should not. This feature of revision control software is called *merging*.

But revision control is even more than that.

Suppose that you have a large collection of documents and a number of projects in progress, each with a team of writers. There will be many changes that need to somehow be synchronized and a good chance exists that many of these changes will be in conflict. One team might have deleted a paragraph whereas another team has fixed some grammatical errors and added a new sentence to that paragraph. A third team might have replaced the paragraph with completely new wording whereas a fourth team might have moved it to the end of the document and converted it to a footnote. Resolving these changes by hand, well, it isn't something I would want to attempt, not for anything important.

Revision control solves that problem, too. It shows you *who* changed *what*, and *when* they changed it, and whether the programmers have been diligent with their changes. It even shows *why* they changed it. Revision control handles changes from multiple teams. It coordinates the distribution of those changes, all the while tracking every change that has ever been made.

Every software developer benefits from using revision control. It is one of the essential tools of software development, on par with a compiler and a text editor. If a business values its source code then it will use revision control. No valid reason exists to not use source code revision control.

2. **What popular programming wisdom do you disagree with?**

    You might have heard the story of the little girl who asks her mother why she cuts the legs and wings off the turkey before putting it in the oven. The girl's mother says that she learned how to cook a turkey from the girls' grandmother. The girl's grandmother explains that she was taught by her own mother, and so on, until the girl discovers that her great-great-great grandmother cut the legs and wings off the turkey because, otherwise, it would not fit into the very small oven she owned 100 years ago.

A lot of programming wisdom is like this. There might once have been a good reason to do a certain thing, but it was long ago. Whenever you receive some wisdom you should pause to consider whether the reasoning behind this wisdom as valid today as it was back then.

As an experienced programmer, what are some examples of received wisdom that you don't agree with?

For a profession that has its origins in mathematics and science, a surprising amount of superstition masquerades as wisdom. The new programmer suffers the most because every experienced programmer has strong views on the *right way* to program, things that should *never* be done, and things that should *always* be done. Experienced programmers are always happy to share their wisdom with anyone who will listen, and quite often this wisdom is enshrined as a set of commandments entitled *coding standards.*

You will, over time, form your own opinion of what is good and what is bad, and that is just as it should be—any worthwhile programming experience will leave its mark on you. Your experience will inform your decisions, and sometimes your experiences will give you a gut feeling about why you should code one way or another, even if you can't articulate exactly why you chose to code the way you did.

But don't fall for the trap of thinking that your experiences are universal. Avoid thinking that your way is *the best* or the *only right way.* Retain some humility in your outlook, and continue to learn from new experiences even when they challenge your established habits and practices.

Here are some examples of received wisdom. Think about how your experience aligns with each of these. Think about the arguments on both sides (although usually more than two sides exist in any programming debate), and think about how you would react in an interview when asked the question "What programming wisdom do you disagree with?"

- Code comments are essential and should be used liberally throughout all of your code.
- You should never reinvent the wheel.
- Modern programming should be a matter of finding the right combination of *design patterns.*
- Global variables are always bad.
- Goto statements should be banned.

- In-line SQL must be avoided at all costs.
- Methods must not consist of more than n lines of code.
- Functional programming is superior to object-oriented programming.
- Relational database technology has been superseded by XML and NoSQL technologies.
- Code quality is always the most important thing.
- Writing good software is an art.
- Writing good software is a science.
- You can't manage what you can't measure.
- Software quality is a function of a good methodology.
- Premature optimization is the root of all evil.

3. **Why are software projects always late?**

   If one thing is true of software projects it is that they are usually late and over budget. Why is this the case?

   For many experienced programmers the hardest part of answering this question at the interview will be giving a balanced answer while avoiding a tirade. Many reasons exist as to why software projects are late, and while some might be the fault of the programmer, many more are not.

   Here are a few reasons to get you started. No doubt you will have a long list of your own.

   Let's start with something the software industry has known since 1975 when Fred Brooks published *The Mythical Man Month*: If a project is in trouble, throwing money and people at it will almost always make things worse. Or in Brooks' words:

   "...adding manpower to a late software project makes it later"

   Software projects are complex, and new arrivals will take time to get up to speed. New arrivals will temporarily reduce the productivity of those who were already working on the project while they support the newcomers. As the number of people working on a project increases, so does the communication overhead. Every new person adds not one but many new channels of communication.

   Another common reason for projects running late is that requirements keep changing. Building a house would be impossible if the plans kept changing throughout the build, and this is more or less true in software development.

The metaphor of building a house is (ironically) itself a reason why some projects run late. Software projects are estimated as if they were the same as building a brick wall. If you can estimate the number of bricks required and if you know the rate at which they can be placed then you can calculate with reasonable confidence how long it will take to construct a brick wall. Therefore, the reasoning goes, you can estimate with confidence how long it will take to construct this software. After all, you can count the number of features and screens and reports. You can estimate how long each will take to build based on how long it took to do something similar. You add up those estimates and add a bit of contingency—easy!

Software is a bit like construction, so the metaphor works to some extent, but it is different enough that the metaphor breaks down completely in the face of routine events. Consider how difficult estimating the time would be to build a brick wall if during the build:

- You discover a problem with the bricks that makes them crumble if placed in stacks of 17 or 42 (there might be other problematic stack sizes, you don't know).

- The brick manufacturer releases a critical brick fix, which means you have to tear down the partly completed wall and start again.

- You realize halfway through construction that the bricks are not compatible with the mortar you've been using, even though both the bricks and the mortar are *supposed* to be industry standard and therefore compatible.

- The build architect insists that you must *queue* the bricks rather than *stack* them. It takes you a week to figure out what this means.

- Your client insists part way through the build that every alternate brick should be placed vertically rather than horizontally. They assumed you knew about this requirement so they didn't make it clear at the outset.

- A tester tests your brick wall with blasts of dynamite and consequently raises several high-priority defects. It takes a week to resolve a debate about the validity of testing with explosives and another two weeks to rebuild the wall.

Another reason projects run late or get cancelled is *poor risk management*. Every project management approach has a theoretical answer to the question of dealing with project risk, and yet almost every project fails because an obvious risk was ignored or dismissed. How many times have you contributed to a risk log of some kind, only to see the risk log filed in a drawer (or the electronic equivalent) and never mentioned again, let alone acted on? Risk management is an active, ongoing process, and just like complex software projects there is no silver bullet.

I've discussed a few reasons why software projects are late. You should add your own experiences to this list. Here are few more ideas you can use to stimulate your thinking on this topic:

- Excessive optimism
- Unrealistic expectations
- Poor communication
- An absent project sponsor
- A micro-managing project sponsor
- Low team morale
- Team inexperience
- Technology immaturity (that is, "version 1.0")
- Unrecognized political/social antics
- Incompetence
- Scope creep (similar to changing requirements)
- Lack of stakeholder involvement
- Poor planning/no planning

4. **Why can't you keep adding programmers?**

   Why can't you keep adding programmers to a software project to bring it in on time?

   This question is often asked as a follow-up to the question of why software projects are always late.

   A good way to answer this specific question is to highlight the nature of software development. Software project schedules are not driven by the number of people who are assigned to it.

I need this baby in a month—send me nine women!

   —Ed Guiness, writing on StackOverflow.com

Many other analogies exist:

- You cannot take a photo any faster by assigning more photographers.
- You cannot deliver a speech any quicker by adding more speakers.
- After a construction site is filled with workers, you cannot add any more and hope to increase productivity; they will trip over each other and progress will slow down.

5. **How do you ensure that your estimates are sound?**

   As a programmer responsible for giving estimates that are as accurate as possible, how do you ensure that your estimates are sound?

   Estimating the duration of a project is perhaps one of the hardest aspects of software development to get right. It is also fraught with peril. A project might be cancelled or never started because of a bad estimate, and most of the misery experienced in software projects is due to unrealistic optimism crushing developers up against an immovable deadline.

   So how should a programmer produce an estimate that is better than pure guesswork?

   Well, at the very start of a project, before requirements have been agreed upon, a programmer's guess is about as good as it gets. That is not to say that a number should be chosen at random but that, until there is something to analyze, no real way exists for predicting what the project will involve, and therefore no way exists to predict what work will be required and how long that work might take.

   Unfortunately, many programmers, particularly those at larger companies, will at some point find that they are assigned to a project where the overall project estimate was plucked out of the air by an optimistic salesperson even before the development team was formed. Expectations might have been set at the highest level of the business long before the first requirement was written down and certainly long before the first line of code has been written.

   After the scope of a project has been agreed upon (if such a thing is possible—it depends on the project) it is only then that an estimate has a chance of being in the right ballpark.

   It is self-evident that an estimate can be improved as a project progresses, based on the experience of the project team as they work on the project. The only point at which an estimate is guaranteed to be 100 percent accurate is when the project has finished. You could, therefore, take the approach that an estimate provided at the start of a project has a degree of uncertainty that is probably as large as it will ever be. This uncertainty, in theory if not in practice, will reduce as the project progresses toward a final outcome. Steve McConnell writing in *Software Estimation: Demystifying the Black Art* calls this the *Cone of Uncertainty*. McConnell writes:

   An important—and difficult—concept is that the Cone of Uncertainty represents the best-case accuracy that is possible to have in software estimates at different points in a project. The Cone represents the error in estimates created by skilled estimators. It's easily possible to do worse. It isn't possible to be more accurate; it's only possible to be more lucky.

My own experience has been that the best, most accurate estimates come from a diligent effort to identify the tasks of a project and then to break those tasks down into small chunks of work. The estimates for these small chunks of work are then added up and adjusted by a risk factor that should tend toward pessimistic, especially for those things that are largely unknown or risky. These estimates should be (but rarely are) updated periodically throughout the project.

This is a gross oversimplification, but hopefully you get the idea that you should try to base your estimate on things you know will need to be done rather than any "gut feel." Programmers, architects, and even project managers are notoriously optimistic about their team's ability to write code quickly.

Hofstadter's Law: It always takes longer than you expect, even when you take into account Hofstadter's Law.

—Douglas Hofstadter

One of the worst outcomes for a programmer who gives an estimate early in a project is when that estimate is taken as a promise. Software companies that make a living by quoting for projects will always factor in a large (larger than you might expect) padding factor to account for the unknown variables of a project. If too many unknown factors exist then most software companies will charge by time and materials, rather than risk losing money on an upfront quote that turns out to be horribly wrong. As programmers working in a team, you should take a similar approach. You should give estimates only when you have a reasonable understanding of what a project involves. If you don't have that understanding then you should postpone estimation until you get it. As professionals, to do anything else is to do a disservice to your customer, even if your customer is also your employer. Nobody benefits from a wildly inaccurate estimate, and a lot can be at stake.

If too much risk exists in a project (something you have to judge) then you should not give an estimate. In most cases this is easier said than done, but think of it this way: If you give an estimate that is out by a factor of 1000 percent then what is the likely outcome?

Here are some of the things you should consider every time you produce an estimate. A lot of these things are related to risk.

- Has the team worked together before?
- Is the team going to sit together? (Will all team members be in the same time zone?)
- What tools will the team use?

- Is an experienced technical leader full time on the project?
- Is an experienced project leader full time on the project?
- How new are the technologies involved?
- Has the team any prior experience of a similar project?
- How many features are required? What are they exactly?
- What level of integration with third-party systems is required?
- What constraints must be met, technical or otherwise?
- What project management approach will be used (for example, SCRUM)?
- How much of a dependency does this project have on third parties or systems outside of the team's control?
- What kind of environment will the team work in, for example how often will the team be interrupted with non-project work?
- Don't forget to allow for holidays and other foreseeable absences.

NOTE   If you haven't already read it, please do yourself a big favor and read Steve McConnell's book on this subject. It could save your career. His book is *Software Estimation: Demystifying the Black Art*, Microsoft Press, 2006 (ISBN: 978-0-7356-0535-0).

6. Why is code clarity important?

Everyone agrees that code clarity is important, but not everyone agrees what it means exactly. Give a definition of "code clarity" and explain why it is important.

If you think about the life cycle of a successful software product, you will quickly appreciate that much, much more time is spent maintaining and upgrading it than is spent writing the first version. If your code is hard to understand then you are creating more work for yourself or for the unfortunate programmer who inherits your code. This time and effort invariably has a real business cost attached to it, and this is certainly not just a theoretical cost.

A good way to answer this question, therefore, is to think of it from the maintenance programmer's point of view. If the maintenance programmer would find an item of code difficult to understand, and therefore difficult to work with, then the code probably isn't clear enough. Clear code, therefore, is any code that is readily understood by a competent maintenance programmer.

During an interview it will usually help to give an example of unclear code and show how this code could be made clearer.

Here's an example of unclear code presented back in Chapter 6:

```
for ( int i=0 ; i < MyControl.TabPages.Count ; i++ )
{
   MyControl.TabPages.Remove (MyControl.TabPages[i] );
   i--;
}
```

This isn't a lot of code to look at, but even a casual glance should tell you that something funny is going on. The most obvious problem is that the loop index is modified inside the loop. Experience should tell you that this is unusual, even before you consider what the loop is trying to achieve.

You can refer to Chapter 6 for a closer look at this strange loop, but the clear version of this code is simply:

```
MyControl.TabPages.Clear();
```

7. What are your red flags during code review?

When you review another programmer's code, what are the things you look for that might indicate a deeper problem? In other words, what are your red flags when reviewing code?

Every programmer has his own list of pet peeves. For many it is code formatting, perhaps the use of tabs instead of spaces. Others grind their teeth over easily fixed annoyances like the misalignment of a brace.

These things are annoying, but code formatting is easily fixed. Here are some things that can indicate deeper problems:

- *Empty* `catch` *blocks* often indicate missing logic (the programmer knows an error might occur and chose to do nothing about it).
- *Meaningless names* sometimes indicate a lack of clarity around the purpose of a variable or method. These variables and methods often end up as dumping grounds for unrelated bits of functionality. If you see a name like `mydata` or `workmethod` then you've probably found code without a clear purpose.
- *Obviously duplicated blocks of code* are errors waiting to happen. When one of these blocks is modified, what happens to the other duplicated block?
- *Terse, impenetrable code* is always going to be hard to maintain.
- *Methods or functions that are hundreds of lines long* are usually a violation of the Single Responsibility Principle (discussed in Chapter 6), which is clearly a problem for maintenance.
- *Code comments that tell you nothing useful* are a waste of space. The code will always tell you *how* something is done; code comments should tell you *why*.

- *Unexplained magic numbers* are a major impediment to understanding code. For example, if a limit is $200 then at the very least you should create a `const` called something like OVERDRAFT_LIMIT. You should never use the bare number without an explanation, nor should you let a bare number appear in more than one place.

- *Every compiler warning* is a potential bug in your code. You should fix those before they bite.

- *Code that serves no obvious purpose* often indicates a lack of clarity in the design of the software.

- *Anything that is inconsistent* with the rest of the code in the project is probably a mistake of some kind.

- *Long series of* `if-then-else` *statements or* `switch` *statements* can often be expressed more clearly as a dictionary of lookup values.

- *Untestable code* often results from a lack of structure and can indicate a violation of the SOLID principles.

8. Describe some things you always do when troubleshooting

Some programmers seem to have a knack for troubleshooting. When a customer reports a problem that can't be reproduced in the testing environment, these savant programmers will start twitching and blinking, and before you know it they have guessed the problem and are halfway done coding a solution.

The rest of us, unfortunately, need to work a bit harder.

What are some things that you always do (or try to do) when diagnosing a problem?

The first thing to do is try to get a *clear understanding of the problem*. All too often a bug report is vague or ambiguous. This is a common problem because most users are not trained in how to give good bug reports (nor should they necessarily be trained), and so they will make a bug report that reads like a medical complaint.

"I was trying to print the annual report, and when I click on the print button the screen shows red blotches and then nothing happens."

If you're lucky the bug report will come from a professional tester or another programmer, and clarity won't be an issue.

After you understand the problem the next thing to try to do is *reproduce the problem*. Sometimes the problem can't be reproduced in the test or development environments and so you need to—very carefully, cognizant of possible bad outcomes—try to reproduce the problem in the production environment.

Reproducing the problem is often a major obstacle. It can be very difficult to do because sometimes the cause of a problem is something that you least expect. Sometimes the cause of a problem is two or more events coinciding. When you're trying to reproduce a problem, keeping alert, observing carefully, and keeping an open mind are vital. At this stage, you are trying to develop testable theories about why and how a problem occurs.

After the problem is reproducible (and sometimes you have to accept that a problem will occur infrequently) the next step is to *isolate the source of the problem*. This means trying to identify which parts of the system and which lines of code are involved. This, too, can be very difficult, especially when a problem is caused by the design of a system rather than any specific line of code.

To isolate a problem caused by poor coding, reverting to a known good state and working forward until the problem reappears can be helpful. After you know the point at which a problem appears, isolating the code that is potentially causing the problem is much easier.

Sometimes a problem is caused by a new kind of data, something the system has not previously handled. This can uncover latent bugs in code even when the code has not been changed. In large databases it can be very difficult to find the "new type" of data because most often you won't know what exactly you are looking for. Good logging can help; in fact, in all cases having a good logging system in place is helpful.

A good logging system is one that you can switch on when you need it and one where you can adjust the level of detail recorded in the log. A good logging system is one where you can look at the timing of events and where you have enough detail about each event that you can simulate (or even better, replay) the event in your development or test environment.

After you have identified the source of a problem you need to *come up with a credible fix*. This is sometimes the most dangerous part of troubleshooting, especially when a programmer is under pressure to get something fixed as soon as possible. The danger lies in making a mistake while rushing to fix the problem. If anything, this is the time when the programmer needs to slow down, consider the implications of the fix, have the fix reviewed by another programmer or tester, and then test the fix before releasing it to the live system. The last thing you want to do is make the problem worse or introduce another kind of problem that is worse than the original.

Here are some more ideas for effective troubleshooting. This is not a comprehensive list, and you should be able to think of more things that have worked for you in the past.

- When a problem starts occurring you should ask, "What has changed?"

- Keep in mind that events that occur close in time are not necessarily related. As they say, correlation does not imply causation.

- Check most-likely causes before investigating less-likely causes.

- Keep in mind that some bugs are caused by more than one problem.

- Some bugs are caused by the precise timing of events.

- Sometimes you won't be able to use sophisticated debugging tools, so don't forget about the humble `print` statement as a debugging tool.

- Sometimes the problem will be outside your domain of expertise. If you need help to develop or test theories about a problem, you should not hesitate to involve other domain experts; for example, network or database administrators.

9. How do you go about getting familiar with a large code project?

Every time you change jobs a good chance exists that you will need to quickly become familiar with a large new code base.

How do you do that?

There is no single best way for a programmer to quickly become familiar with a large new code project. Here are some things that have worked for me, but your experience might be quite different:

- One good way to learn a new code base is to have another programmer, someone who is familiar with it, give you a tour.

- Every program has an entry point. Start a debugging session and see how the program sets itself up, which configuration files it reads, what database connections it establishes, which queries it runs, and so on. For most languages the entry point to an application is the `main` function. For static websites the default page is often `default.htm` or `index.htm` but it depends on how the site is configured. For ASP.NET applications usually some start-up code is in `global.asax`.

- Start working with the code base by trying to implement a small feature, perhaps a simple bug fix.

- Keep notes about what you find. My experience has been that I rarely refer back to these notes, but the act of writing down important things helps me remember them.

- Pay particular attention to anything you don't immediately understand. It could be that the code base relies on a particular convention or an idiomatic style of coding. These "strange" things are often very significant for an application.

- Don't forget that non-technical staff can also have good insight into how a system works.

- A modern IDE (and even some text editors) will help you navigate a code base; for example, making it easy to jump back and forth between class and method definitions.

- Treat any program documentation with suspicion. Look at when it was last updated.

- Unit tests (assuming they pass) can be very helpful in understanding how functions are supposed to work, the arguments they accept, and what kind of setup is needed to make things work.

- Bug-tracking software can give you an indication of typical problems found in the code base. This can give you some clues about its weaknesses and perhaps also its strengths.

- If the application persists data and if the data has been modelled properly you might find important clues about the key entities of the system in the persistence later or the database itself. Foreign-key relationships can give you significant information about how data is structured (for example, "a purchase order is associated with either zero invoices or one invoice"). If the application uses an ORM then you should be able quickly find the key entities, and how they are used throughout the application.

- Finally, don't think that you need to understand every little detail in order to work successfully with a new code base. You will need to treat some things as "black boxes," accepting that they perform a function without necessarily understanding how they work. This will help keep you focused on the big picture.

10. **Describe your understanding of *cargo-cult* programming**

   The phrase cargo-cult programming (*or* cargo-cult software engineering) *is sometimes used to describe an undesirable approach to programming.*

   Describe what the term means and why this approach is undesirable.

   Cargo cult refers to a number of South Pacific religions that appeared soon after World War II. The followers of these religions built mock-ups of airplanes and landing strips in the belief that by doing so they would summon the airplanes that had previously brought them cargo during the war.

   The term *cargo-cult programming* is a reference to these religious practices, where a programmer ritualistically includes code that serves no real purpose. I have seen many examples of this, including:

- Using the Hungarian naming convention without knowing what each prefix actually means
- Using the DISTINCT keyword indiscriminately in SELECT statements
- Writing a useless code comment above every line of code
- Splitting a function into two for no reason except "to make it smaller"

This approach is undesirable for many reasons but mostly because it prevents the cargo-cult programmer from gaining a proper understanding of his code. The cargo-cult programmer who runs into trouble will be concerned with the *appearance* of his code rather than the *functioning* of his code. This is a serious problem because the cargo-cult programmer will then be stuck, relying on good luck to resolve the problem, and without the confidence that a problem is ever truly resolved.

The cargo cult approach to programming is similar to what Andrew Hunt and David Thomas (writing in *The Pragmatic Programmer*) refer to as *Programming by Coincidence*:

Fred doesn't know why the code is failing because *he didn't know why it worked in the first place*. It seemed to work, given the limited "testing" that Fred did, but that was just a coincidence.

Steve McConnell also calls out this style of programming in *Code Complete, Second Edition*:

Inefficient programmers tend to experiment randomly until they find a combination that seems to work.

---

11. Describe some potential downsides of code comments

When students are taught programming at school one of the first lessons they learn is that they should make sure to include appropriate code comments.

This is probably good advice, but what are some of the potential downsides of code comments?

Programmers spend a lot of their time maintaining code written by others. Code comments that are poorly written, incorrect, outdated, or misleading must rank as one of the top annoyances. After many bad experiences I no longer study code comments, and if there is one kind of comment I routinely ignore is it the kind you often see at the top of large source files in legacy code:

```
/*************************************************************
 *** FILE: Program.cs                                    ***
 *** DATE CREATED: Jan 13, 1968                          ***
 *** DATE LAST MODIFIED: Mar 31, 2001                    ***
 *** MODIFIED BY: Nigel                                  ***
 *** PURPOSE: Facilitate the velocitous                  ***
 ***          extramuralisation of the pendigestatory ***
 ***          interledicule                              ***
 *** MODIFIED BY: Nigel                                  ***
 *** MODIFIED DATE: 1968-01-14                           ***
 *** MODIFIED REASON: Bug fix                            ***
 *** MODIFIED BY: Sandeep                                ***
 *** MODIFIED DATE: 1999-12-30                           ***
 *** MODIFIED REASON: Y2k bug fix                        ***
 *************************************************************/
```

I think eventually most programmers learn to ignore these comments, treating them as baggage to be towed around for the sake of appearances and eventually deleting them.

Another potential problem with comments is when they tell you nothing that isn't already obvious from the code.

```
static void MakeDictionaryFromArray()
{
    /* This method is commented poorly to make a point.
       Don't imitate this style of commenting */

    // Declare an array of integers
    int[] array = { 1, 2, 2, 3, 3, 3, 4, 4, 4, 4, 4 };

    // Declare a dictionary
    var dictionary = new Dictionary<int, int>();

    // For each integer in the array
    foreach (int i in array)

        // If the dictionary contains an integer...
        if (dictionary.ContainsKey(i))

            // Increment the dictionary value
            dictionary[i] += 1;
        else

            // Add this integer to the dictionary
            dictionary.Add(i, 1);
}
```

Another kind of problem is when code comments are outright lies:

```
static void MakeDictionaryFromArray()
{
    /* This method resets a user password */

    // Establish a database connection
    int[] array = { 1, 2, 2, 3, 3, 3, 4, 4, 4, 4, 4 };

    // Ensure we have an open connection
    var dictionary = new Dictionary<int, int>();

    // Reset the password
    foreach (int i in array)
        if (dictionary.ContainsKey(i))
            dictionary[i] += 1;
        else
            dictionary.Add(i, 1);

}
```

Lies of the kind shown here are introduced when a programmer copies a function, modifies the code, and forgets to update the code comments. It can be very confusing, especially when the code comments are *almost* correct.

Inappropriate code comments are a form of code duplication and cause many of the same problems. Misleading and incorrect comments are worse than no comments at all.

12. When is it acceptable to produce lower-quality code?

Everyone agrees that programmers should strive to write good-quality code. Everyone might not agree on what this means, exactly, but in general all of us prefer to write good code rather than bad code.

Can you think of a valid, ethical reason why you would be motivated to write substandard code?

This is a question to which the answers are, I'm sorry to say, almost all controversial. In some ways an interviewer who asks this question is being unfair; it is a question with few satisfactory answers and many possible bad answers, all of them subjective.

On the one extreme are programmers who seem willing to spill blood over the suggestion they should ever compromise their ideals of software quality.

On the other extreme are programmers who intentionally produce poor-quality code, believing that "good" means "fast and cheap" no matter what chaos ensues in their code base.

There are also programmers who will do whatever their boss tells them to do, even if their boss has zero knowledge of software development and zero appreciation of how *technical debt* can cripple a business.

And don't forget the new programmers who are still forming their opinions about what good-quality code actually means. These programmers might not even be aware that a certain practice (for example, code duplication) is considered harmful by more skilled programmers.

The only sensible way to answer this question is to reframe it in a way that is more specific and, therefore, less likely to generate an argument; for example, "Can you think of a realistic situation in which you would knowingly compromise one of the SOLID principles?"

Notice that I've defined "substandard code" as being code that somehow compromises the SOLID principles. At the interview you would want to ask your interviewer if she can give you an example of what she means by "substandard."

Let's pick on the principle of interface segregation (the "I" in SOLID) and make up an example of when you might willingly ignore this principle.

Immediately, one case comes to mind where I would be okay with not segregating my interfaces. If I were writing a disposable prototype system for the purpose of exploring requirements with a customer, then I might compromise interface segregation in order to get something up and running as fast as possible.

That said, I would stipulate several caveats:

- I would have to know that this prototype was not going to become version 1.0 of the real thing. I would need to assure myself that this prototype would be destroyed after it had served its purpose.

- I would also need to be unsure about the design of my interfaces. If I knew in advance, for example, that I needed an `IFlippy` interface and an `IFlappy` interface then I would not compromise the "I" in SOLID by mushing these two together. On the other hand, if the point of the exercise was to find out what my interfaces should be, and the prototype was going to help me do that, then I would have no problem with commingled interfaces.

To summarize, the best way to answer a loaded question like this is to reframe the question in a way that is specific and has less potential for violent disagreement. If possible you should encourage your interviewer to be more specific, and this will help you find an answer.

13. How can large code projects be kept under control?

Large software products always seem to contain a lot of regrettable code, and this is especially true for successful products that are maintained over many years. Almost everyone who has worked on a large code base will have issues with it in some way or another. It might be that it has too many or too few layers of indirection, that inconsistencies are throughout the code base, or any number of other problems.

As a programmer working on a large code project, how do you keep these kinds of problems under control?

This is one of those questions that if there were a simple answer the question would never need to be asked. If you could buy a tool or use a method that was guaranteed to keep a large code project under control then everyone would buy the tool and use the same method and the problem would disappear.

However, the reality is that large code projects almost inevitably slide into decrepitude. It's a function of their complexity, and there is little that one programmer can do about it except keep his own code as clean and consistent as possible.

Using tools to enforce things such as coding standards, naming conventions, and other stylistic aspects of code is sometimes helpful. To the extent that these tools work as advertised they are fine; it does pay to keep an eye on (for instance) cyclomatic complexity and (as another example) to ensure that all public methods are accompanied by code comments.

The trouble is that although measuring that (for example) a code comment exists is easy, measuring (automatically) that the code comments are actually helpful is quite difficult. I doubt very much whether any commercially available "code quality" tool will catch misleading code comments, identify poorly-named variables, or code that works but is needlessly complicated or difficult to read.

Ultimately, it is up to each individual programmer to actively resist the decline of a large code project. Passive resistance doesn't work.

14. How do you add features to unfamiliar code?

Describe how you would go about adding new features to a large, unfamiliar code project.

The biggest risk when working with a large, unfamiliar code project is the risk of breaking existing functionality. This problem is made worse when the code base has been allowed to deteriorate over the years. Let me give you an example of a deteriorated code base. I once worked on a large project that compiled with more than 30,000 compiler warnings. This project was full of duplicated functionality, quirky and inconsistent coding styles, circular project references (so you had to build it in two attempts), and many other tragi-comic problems that would have been funnier if it wasn't my responsibility to get new features working as quickly and error-free as possible.

A complete rewrite of a deteriorated, large code project is usually out of the question. Apart from anything else, when you consider how many hundreds of programmer-years have probably been sunk into that system you realize that throwing it away and starting again, despite the growing costs of maintaining it, is financially infeasible.

The idea of adding new features as a standalone application, perhaps integrated at the database layer but not sharing user-interface components, is usually shot down by users who won't like the idea of switching between different user interfaces in a supposedly integrated system. If you can successfully argue for this approach then perhaps this is the safest and most convenient way (for the programmer) to implement new functionality.

Assuming you have no choice but to add functionality directly into the existing code base then here are some tips on how you do it and survive the experience:

- Seek to understand the small components that are used throughout the project.
- Document (preferably in the code itself) how these components work and how to use them.
- If you don't have unit tests for these components then you should consider writing some.
- Start small and build up your understanding before tackling larger features.
- Respect any existing conventions that have been consistently applied throughout the code. A poor coding convention consistently applied is better than the inconsistent application of a superior convention.
- Resist the temptation to work on code that is unrelated to the new features you're supposed to be adding. No user will thank you for breaking an unrelated part of the system in the name of an improvement they can't see for themselves. Make a note for yourself and stay focused on the work you're supposed to be doing.

You should also read *Working Effectively with Legacy Code* by Michael Feathers. This is the go-to reference for, uh, working effectively with legacy code. There should be more books like this.

15. **What exactly is wrong with so-called clever code?**

Now and then every programmer will write a bit of code and feel justifiably proud of their achievement. This is part of the fun in programming. Sometimes, unfortunately, the pursuit of this happy feeling will lead programmers astray and cause us to write code that is, frankly, too clever.

What does it mean by code being "too clever," and what exactly is wrong with clever code?

I should be clear that I am certainly not against cleverness per se, no; I like clever, I admire clever, I aspire to be clever. I enjoy writing and deciphering clever code as much as the next programmer. But I don't enjoy clever code quite as much when I'm in a hurry, or when I need to stay focused on an important job, or when I need to fix a critical bug, or when I'm refactoring, or adding a new feature, or…in fact, thinking on it, I almost always prefer to work with plain code.

What do I mean by clever code? Good question! Here's my stab at a definition:

Clever code (or more precisely, code that is *too clever*) is any code that unjustifiably slows down a competent maintenance programmer.

It is interesting that this definition could be applied to bad code as much as it applies to too-clever code. Do I really put them in the same category? In so far as they should be avoided, yes I do.

Notice also that I stipulate a *competent* maintenance programmer, and by this I mean a programmer who is familiar with the language and the framework of the application, and someone who is also familiar with the quirks and idioms that apply in this domain. Chapter 8 covers this subject in more detail. An *incompetent* maintenance programmer has bigger problems to worry about than dealing with clever code.

16. **How do you improve your programming ability?**

Supposing you wanted to improve your coding ability, how would you go about it?

Many people, including many programmers, think that the only way to improve a skill is to practice it. Practice makes perfect, they might say. Oh, and perhaps a bit of reading.

Practice, however, is useless if you are practicing bad habits. Practice is also useless if you don't understand what "improvement" looks like. For these reasons combining practice with the expert advice of a teacher or a mentor is always best. This doesn't always have to be in person; for example, you can get excellent advice from reading books and watching tutorials. One big advantage of a teacher (in person) is that she will be able to spot things that you won't necessarily see for yourself.

It is also true that unless you are challenged in some way, you will rarely improve beyond a certain level. To be sufficiently challenged you must accept the possibility of failing at something. Unless you risk failure, and occasionally fail, you are unlikely to improve a skill.

Programmers can also learn a lot from reading code written by others, and, in particular, looking closely at anything they don't understand.

Training courses can be useful, provided that you don't sit silently while an instructor reads from their presentation slides. Learning needs to be interactive; otherwise, the best you can hope for is to memorize some new facts. You don't get experience, the really valuable stuff, without trying it for yourself and learning from your mistakes.

17. Describe a coding project of which you're proud

Interviewers often ask about projects that made you proud. Talking about work-related projects is customary but most interviewers will let you talk about any programming project you've worked on, at work, at school, or even at home. The interviewer's aim is to give you a platform to display your enthusiasm for programming.

This is your opportunity to talk about what you enjoy, and what kind of circumstances or interests led to you doing a good job. You can also talk about a major learning experience, or how you survived a mission-impossible scenario. This is a platform on which you can and should have some fun.

If you are lucky enough to have had some time to spend on a pet software project then you should relish this question. I had some spare time, once, and I used it write several chess-playing engines. This is what I would talk about if given the chance at an interview. I would talk about my experimentation with the *Minimax* algorithm, and I would talk about how difficult it was to debug some of the bad moves my engine would play. I would talk about my first attempt (in Visual Basic no less!) at a chess-playing engine that was able to compute roughly 200 moves ("plies") per second, and I would contrast this with the version I wrote later in Delphi that was about 100 times faster. I would talk about options for board representation and the various tricks I learned for generating moves with *bitboards*. I would talk about what I learned from studying the source code of the crafty chess engine. I would have a wonderful time reminiscing for as long as the interviewer would let me talk.

If you have never had this opportunity (and the reality is that some of us are swept along by circumstances that give us little or no spare time to play), then you will have to talk about an experience at work or school.

If this question scares you a little, just think about what you really enjoyed in a project. Don't worry if you enjoyed working on the graphic design of an application more than the programming, or if you enjoyed the database administration side of a project more than writing SQL. You are trying to show that you are excited by something, that your work has meaning to you, and that you find satisfaction in it.

If you are really stuck then I suggest you talk about a major learning experience that you've had. You could, for example, talk about a bug that you solved or helped to solve. What was hard about it? What did you overcome? What was the end result? What would you do differently?

And if you ever have the chance, I recommend trying to write a chess-playing engine. That way we will have lots to talk about at the interview.

18. Explain programming in non-technical terms

Suppose you are at a family event and your grandmother asks you to explain what it is that you do as a "programmer." What do you tell her?

If an interviewer has "good communication ability" on her list of "important qualities" then she might ask you a question like this.

Your answer should avoid using technical terms unless you can explain them simply. If you've never tried to explain programming in simple terms you can easily become tongue-tied as you realize halfway through a sentence about compilers that you haven't explained how machines are capable of following instructions, or how electricity can be manipulated to represent numbers, and in this tongue-tied state you might realize you haven't even thought to explain binary or logic gates.

Forget all that. What you need is a good analogy.

"Grandma, programming is like writing a knitting pattern. It's a list of instructions written so that someone can follow those instructions later to make a nice scarf or a pair of mittens."

Of course, most grandmothers will at this point give you a stare that means you've taken the grandmotherly stereotype a bit far. Not all grandmas knit.

Still, this knitting analogy does convey the essential qualities of programming. As a programmer you are writing a list of instructions for later interpretation. The instructions will be taken literally so you can't assume that an unexpected turn of events will be handled gracefully. You need to consider what the knitter should do if the ball of wool runs out, or if the knitter has wooden needles instead of standard plastic knitting equipment. If you don't think of these possibilities and write instructions to handle them then your pattern (your program) might fail to produce the scarf or mittens for which it was written.

19. **Explain the significance of *coupling* and *cohesion*.**

You often hear these terms in debates about the implementation of an application. What is the programming-related meaning of the words coupling *and* cohesion, *and why are they significant?*

If you have just one class in your application and everything you write goes into that class then you probably have low *cohesion*. On the other hand, if you have classes that follow the single responsibility principle (the "S" in SOLID) then you probably have higher cohesion. Cohesion is a measure of how well the parts of a module (or the members of a class) fit together. It's just like that game on *Sesame Street*, the one where they sing *one of these things is not like the other*. If you have lots of things that are not like the other then you probably have low cohesion.

The main problem with low cohesion is that it works against the central aims of writing modular, reusable code. It makes reusing a module harder because you get all the unwanted baggage that comes with it. With low cohesion you also find that changes become more complex, requiring tweaks in more places.

Coupling refers to the degree of interdependence between classes. If you make changes to code in a highly coupled application you are more likely to cause unintended side-effects.

The main problem with highly coupled code is obvious. You don't want to be needlessly worried about unintended consequences when you change a line of code.

Low cohesion and high coupling often go hand in hand, and both indicate a lack of planning (or upkeep) in designing and implementing an application.

20. **What is the real problem with *global variables*?**

A global variable *is a variable that is available throughout an entire application, regardless of where it is referenced.*

That sounds quite handy, so what is the real problem with global variables?

In very small programs, say less than 100 lines of code, a global variable isn't such a big deal. The programmer can probably keep all these variables in her head while she writes code, and being able to reference the variable at any point and at any place in the program is probably quite useful.

After a program grows beyond a certain size (as most useful programs invariably do) then the problems of global variables become more obvious. Here are a few of the worst problems:

- A global variable relies on the programmer remembering to set it as needed. They are implicitly present everywhere, so forgetting about them is easy.

- If a program has more than one thread then these threads can come into conflict when both attempt to set and/or get the value of this variable around the same time.

- Global variables make understanding code harder, because their existence must be either remembered or deduced and tracked down.

- Global variables never fall out of scope, so they stick around and consume memory for as long as an application is running.

21. **Explain the term** *technical debt* **in terms a non-technical manager will understand**

Most programmers love the term technical debt *because it is an apt metaphor for a problem they face every day. Unfortunately, the significance of the term appears to not be quite as apparent to as many non-technical managers.*

Explain the meaning and significance of technical debt in terms a non-technical manager will understand.

The fact that many non-technical managers do not readily see the significance of the term *technical debt* is somewhat ironic, because the term was coined by Ward Cunningham in order to explain the problem to his boss, a non-technical manager. You can find transcript of Ward explaining this concept at http://c2.com/cgi/wiki?WardExplainsDebtMetaphor.

In financial terms, debt is accumulated when you borrow money, often for the purpose of meeting a short-term goal. The borrowed money helps you meet that goal but it must then be repaid, usually with interest.

Ward's "debt" was the increasing mismatch between the code his team had written and the "proper way to think about [their] financial objects." Presumably at the time Ward coined this term he was trying to convince his boss that the team should spend time repaying the debt; that is, realigning their code to match their improved understanding, instead of continuing to add new features on top of the misaligned code.

Importantly, this is not a condemnation of the debt per se, but a reason to consider repaying the debt before accumulating more debt.

These days most programmers mean something a little different to what Ward meant when he first used the metaphor. When the term is used today it often refers to poorly-written code rather than code that is misaligned with a proper understanding of the domain.

In Ward's words:

A lot of bloggers at least have explained the debt metaphor and confused it, I think, with the idea that you could write code poorly with the intention of doing a good job later and thinking that that was the primary source of debt. I'm never in favor of writing code poorly, but I am in favor of writing code to reflect your current understanding of a problem even if that understanding is partial.

If the debt metaphor doesn't work with your non-technical manager you might consider an alternative. Perhaps your manager will find the metaphor of *dirty dishes* more persuasive.

Suppose every time you ate a meal you left the dishes in the sink. Eventually your sink will be filled with dirty dishes and you will have no clean dishes left in the house. Now every time you want to eat you first have to clean a dish. The accumulated dirty dishes slow you down, and they probably smell bad.

Rushing to write code, and presumably taking a few dirty shortcuts (like copying and pasting code, tweaking it to suit the new feature, and then releasing it in that state) is like avoiding doing the dishes after a meal. If you keep doing it then finding a clean dish to eat with becomes more difficult. Eventually, you have no choice but to buy more dishes, clean the dirty dishes, or go out to eat. I could compare "eating out" to the practice of outsourcing, but perhaps that would be stretching the metaphor a bit far.

22. **Explain the term *refactoring* in terms that a non-technical manager will understand**

The term refactoring *is commonly used by many programmers and is generally understood to mean something positive. Explain in non-technical terms what the term means.*

In the course of writing a program a programmer will routinely make many, many decisions about the detailed design of a program. In an ideal world, many of these decisions will have been considered long before the programmer started writing code but the reality is that writing code often reveals gaps in the analysis of a problem or in the design of a feature. These gaps are most often relatively minor; for example, choosing data types for a function, and the programmer will rely on judgement and experience to make good decisions. If the programmer were to pause for discussion at every decision point then progress would be painfully slow.

Programmers usually make the right decisions as they write code, but not always. Suppose a programmer decides to use a string data type to hold a date value, perhaps thinking that values like "tomorrow" and "five weeks from now" should be allowable in addition to proper dates such as "2001-01-01" and "2029-04-07."

The programmer who makes a decision like this might come to regret it, perhaps finding that a lot of time and effort is now being spent explaining why "tomorrow" never comes. The programmer might now want to *refactor* the code so that all date values entered into the system conform to a pattern of "YYYY-MM-DD." This is not a bug-fix per se, because the decision to permit unusual date values was deliberate, and the program is running according to the programmer's design.

The example of a poorly chosen data type is one where the end user will see evidence of the problem and will, therefore, readily agree that something needs fixing. Persuading a product owner that something needs fixing isn't hard to do when it is readily apparent that something is broken.

Programmers know that many things make the upkeep of a program more difficult than it should be, but that the end user will never see any of these things directly. If you find duplicated code you know that this can cause many kinds of problems but justifying the required time to fix it can be difficult when the end user sees no difference at all in the fixed product.

Refactoring is the process of fixing these internal problems without changing the external behavior of an application.

When trying to persuade a product owner that time should be spent fixing these internal problems, Andrew Hunt and David Thomas, writing *The Pragmatic Programmer* suggest that you use a medical analogy:

...think of the code that needs refactoring as a "growth." Removing it requires invasive surgery. You can go in now, and take it out while it is still small. Or, you could wait while it grows and spreads—but removing it then will be both more expensive and more dangerous. Wait even longer, and you may lose the patient entirely.

---

23. **What is the significance of a *leaky abstraction*?**

    In 2002 Joel Spolsky wrote a blog post entitled The Law of Leaky Abstractions:

    `http://www.joelonsoftware.com/articles/LeakyAbstractions.html`

    The term leaky abstraction *has now entered the mainstream of programmer jargon.*

    Explain the meaning and significance of this term.

    If you look past the façade of a high-level programming language such as C or Java to the native machine code generated by a compiler (or a runtime platform) you can see that the high-level language is an *abstraction*. The high-level programming language enables programmers to write instructions for a computer with less effort than if they were using a low-level language. The programmer using a high-level language is less concerned with implementation details, and clearly this is very convenient.

    Programmers are accustomed to taking advantage of all kinds of abstractions, each providing a convenient façade of simplicity. You are so comfortable with abstractions, including their occasional imperfections, that you sometimes forget that non-programmers depend on these abstractions even more heavily than you do. When an abstraction fails to hide the underlying complexity it can be paralyzing for the end user. An abstraction that exposes the complexity is sometimes said to have *leaked*.

    This has important implications for how you design applications. Suppose you write an application that communicates with a remote server to retrieve, say, market data. You know that the component you use for communication with the server is reasonably reliable, but you also know that it depends on communication over a network and is therefore vulnerable to network outages. When writing code to deal with an error returned by this component you have a choice. You can expose the underlying error message to the end user, or you can dress it up in some way, or you might decide to temporarily hide the problem and reveal it later only after you have tried and failed a number of times.

    In effect, you must decide how to handle the stuff that leaks out of the abstraction, and you should try to ensure that your own layer of abstraction remains consistent from the perspective of the end user—anything less sets up your users for some serious disappointment.

24. **What is *continuous integration* and how is it helpful?**

    The concept of continuous integration *has progressed to the point where you can buy specialized tools to support the practice.*

What does the term continuous integration *mean, and how is it helpful?*

In the (heavily stereotyped) bad old days of programming, individual programmers would work in isolation for periods of time before sharing their efforts (the code they produced) with the rest of the team. This would often result in serious delays and awkward problems caused by a mismatch of expectations and incompatibility between the code submissions of these developers.

Consequently, integrating these individual contributions as often as practically possible is now generally accepted as good practice. Developers following the practice of continuous integration are therefore encouraged to share their work-in-progress, and to accept the work-in-progress of other developers, thus minimizing the potential divergence of ideas and coded implementations within the team.

One of the immediate problems faced by teams practicing continuous integration is that they are often derailed by a submission of faulty code. If one developer "breaks the build" then all developers who have accepted this code into their working copy will have to either work on the problem or wait until another developer fixes it.

The problem of sharing faulty code is addressed by software that performs frequent *automated builds*. These builds are performed either periodically or whenever a developer commits code to the shared code repository. If the build fails, then developers in the team are notified that the most recent code submission is faulty and should be avoided.

When the automated build system informs the developers that the code has been fixed then they are again free to integrate the latest changes from other developers in the team.

The concept of *build failure* originally meant simply that the code would not compile, but today it means much more:

- *Unit tests* are run as part of a build, and if any of these tests fail then the build itself is considered to have failed.

- *Coding conventions* are checked by automated tools during the build, and if code is found to not follow these conventions then the build fails.

- *Code metrics* are checked by automated tools, and if these metrics are not within acceptable levels then the build fails.

- *Documentation* can be generated directly from the code, and if it cannot (for example, a public method is not commented) then the build fails.

25. **What is your favorite software development methodology?**

   I once worked with a very plain-speaking programmer who snorted loudly when I asked a candidate this question at an interview. He explained afterwards that he thought the question was trendy and meaningless, and that the word methodology *was a pretentious substitute for the word* method. *He was probably right, so here is the same question asked in a more plain-speaking way:*

   In your experience, what methods most improve the effectiveness of a software development team?

   Despite my attempt at plain-speaking, this is still a loaded question. Every unqualified answer to this question is bound to be wrong, more or less. A good answer depends on:

   - The people in the team and their experience and skills
   - The work the team is doing
   - The definition of *effective*

   As with most vague questions, and certainly with loaded questions, the best way to provide a sound answer is to define a limited context and answer within the bounds of that context. It is unfair but an interviewer who asks a vague, hand-wavy kind of question will probably also be disapproving of a vague, hand-wavy answer.

   Suppose the team was producing a lot of code that later failed in testing. You could define *effective* in that context as "failing fewer tests." Now, the question is much easier to answer. You can probably think of lots of good techniques for failing fewer tests. Here are three to get you started:

   - Have testers write tests at the same time that developers are building the system, and have both developers and testers base their work off a common, shared specification. Developers should review these tests to help the team gain a common understanding of the specification.
   - The development team, if it isn't already, should be structuring their code so that it is easy to test. This generally means following good practices such as the SOLID principles, in particular the principles of *Single Responsibility* and *Interface Segregation*.
   - Unit testing should be commonplace, and unit tests should be run as part of a continuous integration (CI) build.

   Suppose the team was struggling to get requirements correct. You can probably think of lots of things that might help; here is another short list to stimulate your own ideas:

- Requirements come from customers and the product owner. Be sure that the team is talking to the right people.

- Communication is generally best when a short feedback loop exists, or to phrase it in the negative: One-way communication is the least effective form of communication. Communication between the development team and the product owner should be interactive, frequent, and on-going.

- Detailed specification documents can be useful, but focusing on communicating the *why* rather than the *how* can be more useful.

- Anything that is written down needs to be written well.

26. How do I tell the product owner that his requirements are ridiculous?

Programmers are usually not backward in regard to assessing the merits of a requirement that appears to be unrealistic or impossible.

How would you explain to a product owner that you cannot implement his requirements?

An interviewer who asks you this will have several possible motivations for asking:

- He wants to understand how you might handle situations of conflict.

- He wants to see how you react to difficult or seemingly impossible requirements.

- He knows that you will be working with a difficult product owner.

When dealing with a difficult requirement the key thing to remember is that you are the programming expert, and in all likelihood the product owner is relying on you to help him find a good balance between what he would like and what can realistically be achieved. You can't, for example, take a newly formed and inexperienced team and in six months have it produce a search box that works "just like Google." What you can do is strive to understand the vision of the product owner and to define a realistic implementation of that vision, working with the product owner (not against him) to agree an implementation that is appropriate for your situation.

Let's take this example and break it down. "A search box just like Google" (or Bing, or Yahoo!) could mean a lot of different things:

- Faster than anything comparable
- Comprehensive

- Visually minimalistic
- Authoritative
- Scalable
- A platform for advertising
- Applying heuristics to find good results
- Ranking results with a secret algorithm

If you list out the possibilities like this and discuss them with the product owner then the job becomes a bit easier, maybe. Unfortunately, sometimes you will get a "yes, please" to all of them rather than a sensible rationalization of priorities.

Here are some generally applicable tips for exploring a seemingly impossible requirement:

- Stick to the facts. If your team (or you) have no idea how you would implement a requirement then say so. If the technology isn't capable of meeting a requirement then explain why this is the case.

- Estimate the probable development time for the requirement. Sometimes a cost-based argument is enough to lower the intensity of a debate and bring it back to reality. You might need to spend some time obtaining a credible estimate.

- Explore the expected value of the requirement. Is it to protect or generate revenue? Is it expected to provide a competitive advantage? Is it a unique or ground-breaking feature? When you look closely at a requirement you will often see that the underlying expectation is more easily satisfied with an alternative.

- You can often get to the underlying assumptions or expectations by politely and respectfully persisting with the question, "Why?"

27. What advice do you have for new programmers?

Suppose you were given the responsibility of mentoring a new and inexperienced programmer. What key bits of advice would you want to ensure this programmer understands as she embarks on her programming career?

Everyone is going to have his own ideas about this based on their own unique experiences. Here are some of mine:

- Writing code is an act of communication. Obviously you are instructing a machine but perhaps more important is the communication between you and the maintenance programmer who reads your code at a later time. That maintenance programmer might be you, or it might be a person from another culture altogether.

- Writing as clearly as you can should always be a priority. This applies to everything you write, not just code.

- Get involved in a programming communities both online and (if you can) also in the real world. You will learn a lot and make new friends. There is no downside.

- Study code you don't understand; it's a great way to learn new tricks.

- A lot of the fun in programming is learning new things. Keep a list of things you want to learn about in more detail and return to this list whenever you have spare time or when you get bored.

- Learn complimentary skills; in particular work on your writing, speaking, and presentation skills. You will never regret improving these.

- One of the most important but most overlooked measurements of code quality is customer satisfaction.

28. Do coding standards influence code quality?

Do you think raising the quality of code by enforcing coding standards is possible?

More often than not if you ask developers what things influence the quality of code their first answer will be "the quality of the developer," by which they mean the skill and experience and judgement of that developer.

If you press developers hard enough they will, eventually, admit that coding standards have a part to play.

The trouble with coding standards is that they are perceived as suppressing individual creativity and freedom of expression. That might be true to some extent but a key benefit of adherence to standards is improved *consistency* and therefore improved *readability* of code. Readability is a key factor in the ease with which code can be maintained. Code that is hard to read is always harder to maintain.

The alternative (that is, no standards) is that the developer will need additional time adjust to the individual styles of each developer as they move through a code base.

29. Which coding standards are the most important?

Every software development team seems to have a set of coding standards. Describe some coding standards that you think are important for a team striving to produce good-quality code.

This question presupposes that coding standards do influence code quality, and you can assume that by "code quality" the interviewer means consistency and readability. A team without coding standards might follow whatever seems fashionable at the time, and their code base will potentially suffer from individual idiomatic coding styles that harm readability.

After a team has agreed to follow a set of standards, here are some key standards that should probably appear at the top of its list. Notice that this list does not define what these standards should be. This is a list of standards that are important enough that the team should think about and agree to upfront.

- Encouraged idioms
- Discouraged idioms
- Naming conventions (yes, really, names are important!)
- Code-comment style guidelines
- Exception-handling style
- Use of assertions

30. **Why is the number of lines of code produced by a programmer a poor measurement of programmer productivity?**

    Every now and then it will occur to a non-technical manager that measuring the cost-effectiveness of a software development team ought to be possible. This manager might do some reading about the practice of programming and it will occur to him that because programmers write code, just like authors write books and lawyers write contracts, then deriving some useful information by counting the number of lines of code produced by a programmer over time should be possible.

    Why is lines of code (LoC) a poor measurement of programmer productivity?

    This is a question that just won't go away. Every programmer should be ready with the following answers:

    - A skilled programmer is likely to improve code by removing lines rather than adding them. Clear code is partly a function of how many lines of code must be read, and so removing lines of code while retaining clarity and functionality is worthwhile.
    - The corollary of the first point is that an unskilled programmer is more likely to add unnecessary lines of code (see also question 10).
    - LoC is a measurement that is easy to artificially inflate. After a programmer is aware that "productivity" is measured by lines of code then he or she tends to optimize for that measurement.
    - The number of lines in a body of code does not often correlate to the difficulty or producing those lines. An application's "secret

sauce" (the thing that gives it a competitive advantage or a unique ability) is unlikely to be the largest section of code. More often it is the code generated automatically by the form designer of an IDE that contains the most lines.

LoC is a measurement of *quantity not quality*, and it is therefore inappropriate to use as a measurement of programmer productivity. Deriving any meaningful conclusion from counting lines of code is difficult if not impossible.

31. Is the goto statement really that harmful?

Most programmers have been instilled with a strong sense of certainty that the goto statement is a source of untold misery and that it must be avoided at all costs.

Explain why the goto statement is considered harmful.

This bit of programming lore is handed down to every new generation of programmers, usually accompanied by a warning that using goto leads to *spaghetti* code and *unstructured* code and all manner of foul outcomes.

The origin of this lore is not hard to find. The idea that the goto statement is harmful was popularized by Edsger Dijkstra in in a letter published by the Association for Computing Machinery (ACM) in 1968. In this letter Dijkstra writes:

The goto statement as it stands is just too primitive; it is too much an invitation to make a mess of one's program.

To understand this criticism you need to understand what Dijkstra means by "too primitive."

You know that all programming languages have constructs for controlling the flow of the program. You know about the for loop, the while loop, and if you are lucky you know about the try-finally construct.

What would happen if all of these constructs were taken away and in their place were left just a goto and an if statement?

Well, obviously there would be a lot of angry programmers, but after the dust had settled then these programmers would get back to work and the first thing they would do would be to reinvent all of these control constructs using if and goto!

The point is that the goto statement is a foundational building block and, therefore, banning it is just as foolish as using it when better control structures are available.

Without `goto` you would not be able to construct the more advanced flow-control structures. Let's respect it for what it is and not ban something so useful because programmers sometimes write poor code.

32. Should software managers have technical backgrounds?

Should software development managers have technical backgrounds? To ask this another way, can a software development manager without a technical background be effective? (Notice that no stipulation exists that this technical background is necessarily programming experience.)

I can only answer this from my own experience, because I don't have an industry-wide study on the effectiveness of non-technical development managers. I also note that this question tends to divide the programming community, with both sides telling stories of the best manager they ever had who was, of course, "technical" or "non-technical."

From my own experience my answer is, "All other things being equal then, yes, an effective manager should have a technical background" and here are some reasons why:

- An effective manager needs to understand technical issues without being spoon-fed.
- The manager is an ambassador for the team and will speak on the team's behalf. A non-technical manager will struggle to do that effectively and consistently.
- An effective manager must trust the team but be capable of double-checking facts when the need arises.

You might suppose that for all of these points the non-technical manager can delegate responsibility to a technical person, and you would, of course, be correct. The question then becomes which manager is more effective: the one who can *choose* to delegate or the one who *must* delegate?

I look forward to hearing your views on this one.

33. Should application architects know how to write code?

Similar to the question about technical and non-technical managers, another question I often hear is whether application architects should be capable of writing code. What is your opinion?

Perhaps to a greater extent than the development manager, the application architect should be capable of writing code. That is not to say that the architect should spend all (or even a significant portion) of her time coding, but rather that the architect should be capable of writing a prototype to demonstrate her ideas. The architect must also be capable of understanding alternatives and must be able to hold meaningful and in-depth discussions with the developers who will implement the designs and plans laid down by the architect. There's nothing worse (for the programmer) than an architect who has lost touch with reality. As an application architect, keeping your feet on the ground and your head in the clouds is part of the job.

34. What is your desert-island "best practice"?

If you could choose one so-called "best practice" that everyone in your team (or, if you prefer, the world) would instantly start following, what would it be?

I suspect that by asking this question I have entered a depth of subjectivity from which I might not emerge unscathed. Every programmer with experience will have a first-hand account of how a particular approach has revolutionized the way they do software development. I won't persuade these programmers (nor should I try to persuade them) that my view is better than theirs. What I will say is that over the decades many approaches have been hailed as revolutionary, and I don't think the story of programming has yet been concluded.

At the time of writing this book some of the most popular approaches include:

- Unit testing and test-driven development
- Agile
- Functional programming

Looking back further in time you see:

- CASE tools and so-called 4GLs
- Object-oriented programming
- Client-server and *n*-tier architecture
- RAD and JAD

Looking back even further you see:

- The approach that is now known as "waterfall"
- Procedural and modular programming

So, considering all of this history and the fanfare that accompanied each of these approaches, which "best practice" would I magically ensure that every programmer follows?

That's easy: If you are a programmer then with the power of my magic wand I decree that from now on you must *think for yourself.*

Preparing Your Cheat Sheets

Despite the name of this section, nothing is underhanded about preparing for an interview. Take advantage of the time you have available before the interview to think about questions you might be asked, how you would answer them, and what questions you will ask if given the opportunity. You should consider what you say when asked tough questions about (for example) gaps in your work history, why you've changed jobs twice in the past year, and so on.

Use the questions in this section to prepare your cheat sheets. Go through this list and think about how you would answer each question if you were asked it at a phone or in-person interview.

Some of these questions will not apply to you or your circumstance, so you can freely ignore those. Use the programming concepts section to quickly see whether areas exist in which you need to brush up.

Look in particular for questions that you might find difficult to answer during the phone interview. Make brief notes that you can quickly refer to during a phone interview. Remember not to write too much or you will tend to read your answer rather than speak it as you would naturally. You also want to avoid making notes that are cryptic or too brief. Personally, I find some of the questions listed in this appendix a bit clichéd and I (as the interviewer) would be unlikely to ask them at an interview. Many other interviewers have no such qualms and are likely to ask you (to pick a classic example) about your "main strength and your main weakness." You should give these at least a moment's thought before an interview so that you don't burst out laughing when they are asked.

It is important that every claim of skill and expertise is supported by evidence. Interviewers love to ask the follow-up question "Can you give me an example?" Also note that *verifiable outcomes* are the best kind of evidence. Saying that you worked with C# since version 1.0 is all well and good, but saying that you wrote the core libraries for the successful AcmeWidgets product is even better.

As you work through these questions you might find reviewing the early chapters in this book for ideas and insight into the interviewer's motivation helpful.

NOTE Before you begin answering some of the questions in this Appendix, you might consider reading or reviewing Chapters 2 and 3, which both have information on what to do in interview situations, both on the phone and in person.

General and Behavioral

This section contains question that you might encounter concerning your past programming experience, your personal goals, your attitude towards groups, and working with others as well as how you would handle certain work situations.

What do you know about this company?

Briefly talk me through your work history.

Describe your most recent role in more detail.

Tell me about the last team you worked with.

What motivates you?

Tell me about the most difficult project you've worked on.

What is your proudest achievement at work?

Describe a work situation where you had to resolve a conflict with a peer.

What kind of role do you typically play in a team?

Tell me about a time when you argued in favor of an unpopular decision.

Describe how you handled a situation where you disagreed with a decision for technical reasons, but were overruled for business reasons.

What would your previous boss say about you if I were to call her?

What aspects of your experience make you a good fit for this job?

What things have you learned from you last job?

Tell me about your most recent project experience.

What are you least skilled at (non-technical)?

Describe the best/worst team you've been part of.

Programming, General

The questions in this section are what you might call "soft ball" questions. The answers to these questions tend to be based more on your opinions and personal experience rather than on textbook facts or specific technical knowledge.

What is your favorite programming book?

Do you participate in any programming communities, either online or in person?

What makes you stand out from all the programmers we could interview?

How would you describe your approach to software development?

How do you rate yourself in each of the major technologies mentioned in the job description or advertisement?

Can you name someone, not necessarily someone well-known, who has influenced the way you approach software development?

Describe a bug or a problem that you couldn't resolve.

What is your worst technical skill?

What experience do you have that is relevant to building large-scale web applications?

What experience do you have of designing multi-threaded applications?

Describe some of the pros and cons of using a relational database rather than, say, an XML-based data store.

What do you like best about the ___ programming language?

Do you prefer to work on the front-end or back-end of applications?

Give me an example of a good coding standard for the ___ programming language.

What is your most-used command-line tool or utility?

Programming Concepts

This is a list of "pop-quiz" type questions that an interview might use for an initial phone interview. You should review this list to be sure you can confidently and succinctly answer each one.

What is the difference between *overriding* and *overloading*?

What is a *critical section*?

With is the difference between a *value* type and a *reference* type?

In terms of memory management, what is the *stack*, and what is the *heap*?

In SQL, what is the difference between an *inner join* and a *left join*?

What is a *strongly typed* programming language?

Describe the difference between *valid* and *well-formed* XML.

What is the relationship between *threads* and *processes*?

What does *immutable* mean?

What is *revision/version control*?

What does the *V* in *MVC* stand for, and what does it signify?

What is the difference between a *class* and an *object*?

Why would you ever want to create a *mock object*?

What is *unit testing*?

Name and briefly describe three different kinds of testing that might be performed on an application before it is released to live.

What is the *Liskov substitution principle*?

What is *test-driven development*?

What is the difference between *iteration* and *recursion*?

What is *loose-coupling*?

Can you give a practical example of a recursive algorithm?

What is *time complexity*?

What is an *associative array*?

What is a *stateless* system?

What is the difference between an *interface* and an *abstract class*?

What is *SQL injection*?

What is the result of *1 XOR 1*?

What is a *regular expression*?

What is an *undirected graph*?

What are some important differences between a *linked list* and an *array*?

Why is *code clarity* important?

Work History

This section lists some questions about your work history that you might find difficult to answer unless you give them some thought before the interview. Answering these questions well—in a positive and honest way—will increase your chances of getting hired. Not all of these questions will apply to everyone.

Why are you looking to leave your current employer?

Why did you leave your last job?

Which is more important: getting things done or doing things properly?

You haven't been with your current employer for very long—why are you looking to move so soon?

You were in your last job for a long time, what prompted you to leave?

Can you explain this gap between jobs in your work history?

You were in your last job for a long time, why weren't you promoted in that time?

Can you explain why you have had a lot of jobs in a short space of time?

Why are you changing jobs so soon?

You have been looking for a job for some time, why haven't you found one yet?

Looking through your work history your career seems to have gone up and then down—what is the story behind that?

Don't you think this job is a step down from what you were doing previously?

Questions to Ask, If Given the Opportunity

Now it's your turn. You've answered all the questions your prospective employer will ask you for the time being and you have an opportunity to ask questions of your own. Remember that *what* you ask can say a lot about you. At the same time, you want to ensure that this job is the right one for you. The following questions might help you accomplish that:

How long has this job vacancy been open?

Why did the last person leave?

What is the best/worst thing about working for this company?

How long have you been with this company?

What does a typical day/week in this job involve?

What is the most/least enjoyable aspect of this job?

Would it be possible to see the working area?

Could you tell me a bit more about the team?

Could I meet someone (else) on the team?

What are the immediate challenges of this job?

What do you expect the challenges of this job will be over the next few months?

What are the most important day-to-day responsibilities of this job?

Index

NUMBERS

1NF. See first normal form
2NF. See second normal form
3.5NF. See Boyce-Codd normal form
3NF. See third normal form
4GLs, 393

SYMBOLS

& operator, 172
&&= operator, 205, 237
>> operator, 336

A

abstract classes, 31, 79, 125, 398
abstract dependencies, 246
abstraction, 384
accessors, 80
accomplishments
  CV highlighting, 11
  vague or nonspecific, 13
ACID, 81–82
ACM. See Association for Computing
  Machinery
active listening, 47
ADO.NET, 143
agile, 177, 393
Ajax, 82
algorithms, 64

Algorithms (Sedgewick and Wayne), 64
Amazon, 40
anchors, 85–86
AND gate, 312, 345, 346, 347
AND operator, 308
angles, 324–326
anonymizing data, 270–271, 286–287
anonymous inner class, 225–226
anonymous types, 135–136
Any CPU, 267, 278–280
application architects, 357, 392–393
Arctic, 321
arguments
  C functions, 173
  checking, 204–205, 234–235
  null, 234
  by value, 173
arithmetic shifts, 336
arrays
  associative array differences, 93, 95
  C, 174–175
  fundamentals, 68–69
  linked list differences, 93, 95, 398
  lookup, 129–130, 141–142
  time complexity, 129–130, 141–142
  transform to dictionary, 315–316,
    348–349
  traversal, 130, 142

as keyword, 199, 222
ASCII, 67–68
ASP.NET, 9, 369
assertions, 390
Association for Computing Machinery (ACM), 391
associative array, 69, 93, 95, 398
assumptions, 317
automated builds, 385
automated tests, 246
automatic semicolon insertion, 216
averaging measurements, 118
awk, 265, 270, 285–286, 288

B
backreferences, 90
bad habits, 179–184, 377
balance, 306, 326–328
barewords, 234
base case, 75
BCNF. *See* Boyce-Codd normal form
BDD. *See* behavior-driven development
bears, 304, 321
behavioral questions, 43
behavior-driven development (BDD), 247
best practices, 357, 393–394
BFS. *See* breadth-first search
bigint, 194
big-*O* notation, 113–117
  defining, 113
  using, 116–117
binary, 64–68
  converting hexadecimal to, 66–67
  set bits, 309, 338
binary fractions, 194–195, 208–211
binary point, 194, 209
binary search tree (BST), 70–71, 93
  self-balancing, 96
binary tree, 70–71
  breadth-first search, 93–94, 97
  depth-first search, 94, 98
Bing, 387
birthday problem, 306–307, 331–332
bitboards, 378

bits
  set, 309, 338
  tricks with, 308–309
bitwise operations, 308–309
block scope, 196–197, 213–215
blocking, 164
blocks
  catch, 179, 180, 185, 191, 366
  instance initializer, 225–226
  JavaScript scope, 196–197, 213–215
  labeled, 200–201, 226–227
blogs
  company information from, 40
  job searching and, 25–26
bonuses, 54
Boolean expressions, 131, 144–145, 147
Boolean values, 134
Boyce-Codd normal form (BCNF), 169–170, 188, 190
brain-teasers, 304–306
branching, 274
  integer comparison without, 309, 334–337
  in Subversion, 295–297
breadth first, 72
breadth-first search (BFS), 41
  for binary tree, 93–94, 97
  defining, 93, 96–97
break statement, 200–201, 226
brevity, 140
Brooks, Fred, 360
BST. *See* binary search tree
B-tree, 70–71
bubble sort, 73, 74
bug reports, 248
bug-tracking software, 370
build failure, 385
Build Solution, 266, 275–276
Build targets, 267
Bureau of Labor Statistics, U.S., 54

C
C
  arrays, 174–175
  function arguments, 173

passing values and references, 175–177
pointers, 171–177
whitespace, 172
C#, 198–199
  as, 199, 222
  >> operator, 336
  BigInteger, 194
  Boolean values, 134
  data types, 70
  DebuggerDisplay, 199, 220–221
  debugging, 220–221
  eight queens solution, 340–342
  enumeration, 128, 134
  Fizz Buzz, 347–348
  inheritance, 135
  inheritance control, 124
  iterators, 137
  locks, 184, 186
  magic number avoidance, 198–199, 218–220
  Monty Hall problem simulator, 329–330
  paths, 199, 220
  race conditions, 160
  remainders, 349–350
  reserved words, 134
  sorting in, 73
  String.Formats, 271
  strings, 198, 218
  Tower of Hanoi solution, 344–345
  transforming array to dictionary, 348–349
  verbatim string literals, 199, 222–223
C++
  function arguments, 173
  pointers, 171
  unit testing, 249
California Labor Code, 59–60
candidate composite key, 169, 189
captures
  backreferences, 90
  regular expressions, 89–90
CareerBuilder, 15
cargo cult, 181, 370

cargo-cult programming, 353, 370–371
Carnegie, Dale, 46
CASE tools, 393
casting, 222
catch blocks
  empty, 180, 366
  exception catching, 179, 185, 191
  ignoring exceptions, 179
  placeholders, 180
chaining, 70
character classes, 86–88
chars, 172
cheat sheets
  building networks, 19
  general and behavioral, 396
  managers using for interviews, 8
  phone interview preparation, 32
  phone interview templates, 35–38
  programming, general, 397
  programming concepts, 397–398
  questions to ask, 399–400
  work history, 398–399
CHECKSUM, 242
child nodes, 70–71
CI. See continuous integration
circular wait, 166, 186
clarifying questions, 43, 316–317, 320
classes, 76–78, 398
  abstract, 31, 79, 125, 398
  anonymous, 225–226
  character, 86–88
  constructors, 184
  coupling and cohesion, 380
  inner, 225–226
  Interface Segregation Principle, 124–125
  Liskov Substitution Principle, 123–124
  mock, 126
  objects and, 31, 398
  Open/Closed Principle, 123
  partial, 31
  Single Responsibility Principle, 121–123
  SOLID principles, 122–126
Clean Solution, 276

clear code, 110–111, 140
clever code, 354, 377
client-server architecture, 393
clock hands, 305, 324–326
cloned functions, 183
CLR exceptions, 276–277
cmdlets, 287
CMS. *See* content management systems
code clarity, 353, 365–366, 398
code comments, 138–139, 149
  in code reviews, 366
  downsides, 353, 371–373
  as duplication, 41, 373
  received wisdom about, 359
  superstitions, 181
  useless, 371
Code Complete (2nd edition) (McConnell),
  179, 371
code coverage, 255, 263
code duplication, 126–128, 131–132,
  145–147, 366
  comments as, 41, 373
code metrics, 385
code pages, 68
code quality, 109, 360
  acceptability of low, 353–354, 373–374
  avoiding duplication, 126–128
  clarity, 110–111, 365–366
  efficiency and performance, 112–119
  expressiveness, 112
  large projects, 375
  modular design, 119–120
  SOLID principles, 121–126
  standards, 356, 389
code reuse, 126, 152
code review, 293
  comments in, 366
  red flags in, 353, 366–367
coding questions, 315–316
coding standards, 356
  continuous integration, 385
  important, 356, 389–390
  programming wisdom in, 359

quality influence, 356, 389
coding superstition, 181–182
Coffman conditions, 166, 186
cohesion, 354, 380
coins, 305, 323–324
collation order, 207, 240–241
command-line tools, 268–271
comments. *See* code comments
common sense, 178–179
communication
  demonstrating, 304
  effective, 49–51
  product owner, 387
  programming as, 388
companies
  culture, 40–41
  information sources, 40
  websites, 21
compiler warnings, 367, 376
composition, 78
  Liskov Substitution Principle, 124
computer science
  big-O notation, 113
  formal education in, 63, 113
  hard problems, 92–93
ComputerJobs, 15
concrete dependencies, 246
concurrency, 158–166
  deadlocks, 165–166, 186, 332
  dining philosophers problem, 332–
    333
  interview questions, 307–308
  libraries, 160
  livelocks, 166
  locks, 160–165
  race conditions, 158, 160, 249
Concurrent Versioning System (CVS),
  273
Cone of Uncertainty, 363
constant time, 113–114
construction metaphor, 360–361
content management systems (CMS),
  82

context
  functions sensitive to, 204, 231
  of performance, 118
contingency basis, 16
continuous integration (CI)
  benefits, 385
  defining, 355, 384–385
  drawbacks, 293
  gated check-in and, 273, 293
  unit tests in, 385, 386
contracts
  evaluating, 59–60
  negotiating, 59–60
  standard, 60–61
conventions, 182
copying and pasting, 182–183
corflags.exe, 279–280
correlated subqueries, 207, 238–239
could haves, 57
coupling, 245, 354, 380
CppUnit, 249
CPU targeting, 267, 278–280
critical section, 397
critical thinking, 179
cross-cutting concerns, 122
CRUD (create, read, update, delete), 167, 306
cryptography, 93
CSS, 82
Cunningham, Ward, 381–382
curriculum vitae (CV)
  accomplishment highlighting, 11
  common blunders, 13–14
  experience, 9–10, 12
  goal of, 11
  graduate, 11–12
  keywords, 9
  layout, 11, 13–14
  length, 10
  matching job advertisement, 10
  personal interests, 11
  phone interviews and, 30
  preparing, 8–14

  unexplained gaps, 10–11
  unprofessional e-mail addresses, 14
  when returning to work, 12–13
  writing, 9
customer satisfaction, 33
CV. See curriculum vitae
CVS. See Concurrent Versioning System
CWJobs, 15

D
data persistence, 370
data structures
  arrays, 68–69
  hash tables, 69–70
  understanding, 68–72
data types
  new, 368
  numbers, 194–195
data warehouse, 170, 190
database constraints, 170
databases
  denormalization, 170, 185, 190
  design, 167, 168
  mock objects, 251
  normalization, 168–170, 185, 188–190
  populating normalized, 170–171
  relational, 167–171
dates, 133
  ISO 8601 standard for, 240
  overlapping, 152–155
  ranges, 152–155
  T-SQL, 207, 239–240
DateTime, 154
deadlocks, 165–166, 186, 332
DebuggerDisplay, 199
debugging
  C#, 220–221
  for getting familiar with projects, 369
decimal data types, 194–195
decimal fractions, 194, 208–209
decimal point, 194
declarative languages, 206

declarative referential integrity (DRI), 167

Deep Blue, 76

default.htm, 369

defensive code, 281

Delphi, 250, 378

DeMarco, Tom, 58

denormalization, 170, 185, 190

dependency
  abstract, 246
  concrete, 246
  external, 246
  partial, 169, 189
  transitive, 169, 190

dependency injection, 125–126, 253

Dependency Inversion Principle (DIP), 125–126

depth first, 72

depth-first search (DFS), 41
  for arbitrarily large tree, 94, 100–101
  for binary tree, 94, 98
  defining, 93, 96–97

design issues
  common sense, 178–179
  performance, 178
  YAGNI, 177–178

design patterns, 201, 227, 359

design problems, 43

deteriorated code bases, 375–376

development opportunities, 4

/dev/null, 284

DFS. *See* depth-first search

Dice.com, 15

dictionaries, 148
  transforming array into, 315–316, 348–349

Dictionary, 70

Dijkstra, Edsger, 332, 391

dining philosophers problem, 307–308, 332–333

DISTINCT keyword, 371

distributed version control system (DVCS), 274

divide and conquer, 75
  in optimization, 118–119

divide-by-zero errors, 349

documentation, 370
  generated, 385
  specifications, 387

document.writeln(), 197–198, 216–217

domain-specific enumerations, 151

double brace initialization, 200, 225–226

down-sizing, 12

dressing appropriately, 42

DRI. *See* declarative referential integrity

dumbing it down, 7

DUnit, 250

DVCS. *See* distributed version control system

E

eager loading, 183–184

Eclipse, 265

ECMAScript, 9, 215–216

edge cases, 167, 262

edges, 72

efficiency, 112–119

eight queens problem, 309–310, 338–342

elements, 68

e-mail
  contacting potential employers, 21
  CV layout, 11
  follow-up, 21
  job notifications, 14
  job searching, 18
  regex validating address, 84, 91
  unprofessional addresses, 14

empty catch blocks, 180, 366

encapsulation, 80

encodings, 67–68

enumeration
  C#, 128, 134
  domain-specific, 151
  SOLID principles, 132–133, 150–151
  Swiss Army, 150–151

equality, 196, 212–213

escalation, 61

estimates
  improving, 352, 363–365
  interview questions, 303–304
  risk management, 364
  uncertainty, 363
eventual consistency, 167
exceptions
  base, 185, 191
  call stack reset by, 179–180
  catching, 179, 185, 191
  CLR, 276–277
  coding standards, 390
  hidden, 266–267, 276–277
  ignoring, 179
  mishandling, 179–180
  null reference, 180
  re-throwing, 179–180
experience
  brain-teasers, 328
  CVs, 9–10, 12
  justifying claims of, 9–10
  phone interview questions on, 31
  of recruitment agents, 16
  relating in phone interviews, 32–33
  summarizing, 11
exploratory code, 261
expressive code, 112, 129, 138–141
external dependencies, 245
Extreme Programming, 111

F

F#, Fizz Buzz, 348
Facebook, 20
  job searching with, 23–24
false dilemma, 33
Feathers, Michael, 121, 376
Federal Trade Commission (FTC), 24
Fibonacci sequence, 75–76
fields, 80
FIFO. See first in, first out
file descriptors, 284
file handles, 272, 290
file permissions, 64
final keyword, 124
Find Your Ninja, 27

firing, explaining, 12
first in, first out (FIFO), 70
first normal form (1NF), 168–169, 189
Fizz Buzz, 315, 347–348
Flash, 82
floating point numbers, 194–195, 211
flow-control structures, 391–392
for loop, 391
foreign keys, 169, 189–190, 370
formal education, 63
frameworks, 182
Friedl, Jeffrey, 92
FTC. See Federal Trade Commission
full-stack web development, 82–83
functional programming, 81, 360, 393
functions, 81, 120, 151–152
  argument by value, 173
  C, 173
  C++, 173
  cloned, 183
  context-sensitive, 204, 231
  hash, 69–70
  inner, 215
  Java, 175
  long, 366
  main, 369
  pointers to, 173
  scope, 214
  undo, 357

G

gaps between jobs, 10–11
gated check-ins, 273, 293
gawk, 286
general intelligence test, 44
generic code, 126
Get-Date, 287
getters, 80
git, 274–275
  basics, 298–299
  finding bad commit, 299–302
git bisect, 275, 299–302
git checkout, 275
global variables, 355, 359, 380–381
global.asax, 369

golf balls, 303–304, 316–319
Google, 14, 40, 303, 387
goto statement, 356, 359, 391–392
graduate CVs, 11–12
grammar, 13
graphs, 72, 93
  representations, 96
  traversal, 72
  undirected, 398
greedy matching, 91
grep, 265, 269, 282–283, 288
groups
  introverts and, 19
  of processes, 122
  regular expressions, 89–90
Guiness, Ed, 362

H

half-adder, 314, 347
Hall, Monty, 306, 328–330
hand gestures, 49–50
handoff, 293
hard problems
  in phone interviews, 33–34
  recognizing, 92–93
hash, 69
hash collision, 70
hash functions, 69–70
hash map, 69
hash tables, 69–70, 148
heap, 397
heap sort, 74
hexadecimal, 64–68
  converting to binary, 66–67
hidden exceptions, 266–267, 276–277
hiding, 80
Hoare, Tony, 332
Hofstadter, Douglas, 364
Hofstadter's Law, 364
hoisting, 214
hold and wait, 166
How to Win Friends and Influence People
  (Carnegie), 46

HR. *See* human resource departments
HTML, 82
  regular expressions matching, 92
HTTP. *See* Hypertext Transfer Protocol
human resource departments (HR), 8,
  17–18
  contracts and, 60
Hungarian notation, 371
Hunt, Andrew, 371, 383
Hypertext Transfer Protocol (HTTP), 83

I

IDateRange, 152
idealism, 58
idioms, 193, 390
if statement, 391
immutability, 398
  strings, 186–187, 199, 224
incentive schemes, 54–55
inconsistencies, 367
incremental build, 275
index, 68
index keys, 158
index.htm, 369
inheritance, 78, 128–129, 135
InMail, 24–25
inner class, 225–226
inner functions, 215
inner join, 398
inorder, 72
inorder traversal, 98–100
in-person interviews
  communicating effectively, 49–51
  design problems, 43
  dressing appropriately, 42
  general intelligence test, 44
  knowing what to expect, 40–41
  practicing for, 41
  preparing for, 39–45
  question categories, 42–45
  rapport in, 45–48
  researching for, 40–41
  showing competency in, 48–49

social and behavioral questions, 43
stress test, 44–45
structure of, 41
technical pop-quiz questions, 43–44
insertion sort, 74
instance initializer block, 225–226
integers, 194
  comparing without branching, 309,
    334–337
  pointers to, 172
  powers of 2, 309, 337–338
integration testing, 255, 259–260
intellectual property (IP), 59–60
intelligence tests, 44
interface, 31, 398
Interface Segregation Principle (ISP),
  124–125, 374, 386
interpersonal skills, 7
interview approaches
  planned expansion, 3–5
  replacing someone, 6–7
  specific projects, 5–6
interviewers, motivation and approach
  planned expansion, 3
  replacing someone, 6
  specific projects, 5
int.MinValue, 336
introverts
  networking by, 18–20
  talking to groups, 19
intuition, 328
IoC containers, 4–5
IP. See intellectual property
IP addresses, 8
  regular expression matching, 94, 108
IP networks, subnet masks, 64
IQ questions, 44
irrational numbers, 194
ISO 8601 standard, 240
isolated components, 246
isolating problem sources, 368
ISP. See Interface Segregation Principle
iteration, 398
iterators, 137

J
JAD, 393
Java, 82, 200–201
  BigInteger, 194
  data types, 70
  design patterns, 201, 227
  double brace initialization, 200,
    225–226
  function arguments, 175
  inheritance control, 124
  iterators, 137
  labelled blocks, 200–201, 226–227
  Perl differences from, 204–205, 234–
    235
  regular expressions, 92
  strings, 186, 200, 224–225
  unit testing, 250
java.math.BigInteger, 194
JavaScript, 9, 195–198
  block scope, 196–197, 213–215
  equality testing, 196, 212–213
  floating point numbers, 211
  global object, 217–218
  NaN testing, 197, 216
  regular expressions, 84
  return values, 215–216
  strings, 195–196, 211–212
  this, 197–198, 216–218
  type coercion, 212
job advertisements
  emphasizing skills matching, 10
  online, 14–15
job fairs, 20
job offers
  analyzing numbers, 54–57
  considering whole package, 55–56
  MoSCoW technique for analyzing,
    56–57
  negotiating, 53
  recruiting agents in negotiating, 57
  understanding market and, 54
job requirements
  lack of fit to, 3–4
  for planned expansion hires, 3–5

understanding, 4–5
job searching, 17–22
  approaching potential employers,
    20–21
  emerging alternatives for, 22–27
  Facebook for, 23–24
  Find Your Ninja, 27
  finding potential employers, 20
  LinkedIn for, 24–25
  networking, 18–20
  persistence in, 21–22
  Stack Overflow for, 26–27
  timing in, 22
  Twitter for, 22–23
job sites
  comparison of major, 15
  using, 14–15
job specifications, for specific project
    hires, 5–6
job titles, 10
Jobserve, 15
jQuery, 82, 296
JSON, 82
JUnit, 250

K
Kaplan, Abraham, 265
Kasparov, Garry, 76
keys
  in arrays, 68
  in BST, 71
  candidate composite, 169, 189
  database normalization, 169
  in dictionaries, 348–349
  foreign, 169, 189–190, 370
  in hash tables, 69, 148
  index, 158
  learning data models with, 370
  natural, 169
  partial dependencies, 169, 189
  primary, 169
  registry, 272, 291–292
  surrogate, 169
key-value pairs, 167

keywords
  CV length, 10
  in CVs, 9, 10
  inheritance prevention, 124
  Stack Overflow careers, 26
knitting, 379–380

L
labelled blocks, 200–201, 226–227
lambda expressions, 198
last in, first out (LIFO), 70, 225
The Law of Leaky Abstractions (Spolsky),
    355, 384
law of the instrument, 265
layout
  logical, 11
  unclear or cluttered, 13–14
lazy loading, 183–184
leaky abstraction, 355, 384
leap years, 254–255
learning
  code bases, 370
  from firings, 12
  as part of job, 3–4
left join, 398
LIFO. *See* last in, first out
linear time, 113, 114–115
line-endings, 265
lines of code (LoC), 356, 390–391
linked lists, 93, 95, 398
LinkedIn, 20
  job searching with, 24–25
LINQ, 73, 136, 193
Liskov Substitution Principle (LSP),
    123–124, 398
listening, 47
Lister, Timothy, 58
lists
  linked, 93, 95, 398
  sorting, 73, 228–231
List<T>, 69
livelocks, 166
LoC. *See* lines of code
locations, 289

locks, 160–165
  deadlocks, 165–166, 186, 332
  livelocks, 166
  ordering, 184, 186
  shared data, 160–165
  on strings, 184, 186–187
  on "this," 184, 186
  threads, 161, 164
logarithmic time, 114, 115
logging, 368
logic gates, 311–314
long values, 336
loops, 129, 136–138, 391
  indexes, 137
  Perl, 232–233
loose-coupling, 398
LSP. *See* Liskov Substitution Principle

M

magic numbers
  avoiding, 198–199, 218–220
  as red flag, 367
main function, 369
main points, repeating, 50
malloc(), pointers, 172
managers
  interview cheat sheets, 8
  researching, 41
  talking to, 7–8
  technical backgrounds, 356, 392
market, understanding, 54
Martin, Robert, "Uncle Bob," 121
Mastering Regular Expressions (Friedl),
  92
Math.Min(), 309
McConnell, Steve, 136, 363, 365, 371
meaningless names, 366
Memcached, 167
merge sort, 73, 74
merging, 358
metaphors, 8, 360–361
methodology
  common sense and, 178–179
  effectiveness, 355

software development, 355, 386–387
methods
  long, 366
  object references, 175
  overloads, 43–44
Microsoft, 40, 81, 303
Microsoft Unity, 4–5
Microsoft Visual Studio Unit Testing
  Framework, 250
minimax algorithm, 76, 378
mirroring, 5, 47
mirrors, 305, 322–323
mishandling exceptions, 179–180
mock classes, 126
mock objects
  on programming concept cheat sheet,
    398
  reasons to use, 255, 260
  testing with, 246, 251–253
mocking frameworks (Moq), 253
modeling, 76–80
modular design, 119–120
  code reuse, 126
modular programming, 393
MongoDB, 167
Mono, 199
Monster.com, 15
Monty Hall problem, 306, 328–330
Monty Python, 1–2
Moq. *See* mocking frameworks
MoSCoW. *See* Must Should Could
  Won't
Mount Fuji, 304, 319–321
MS Access, 30
MSBuild, 278
MSDN, 242
MSTest.exe, 250
multitasking operating systems, 160
must haves, 56
Must Should Could Won't (MoSCoW),
  56–57, 58
mutual exclusion, 166
MVC, 398
The Mythical Man Month (Brooks), 360

N

NaN, testing for, 197, 216
NAND gate, 312, 313, 346–347
natural keys, 169
navigating code bases, 370
NBehave, 247
negotiation, 53
  analyzing numbers, 54–57
  contracts, 59–60
  escalation and ultimatums in, 61
  MoSCoW technique, 56–57
  problems in, 60–61
  recruiting agents and, 57
  silent treatment in, 61
  starting, 57–58
  tips for, 61–62
  understanding market for, 54
.NET, 3, 43, 82
  arrays in, 69
  call stack resetting, 179–180
  DateTime, 154
  function arguments, 175
  platform targets, 267, 278–280
  PowerShell integration, 271, 287–288
  regular expressions, 84, 92
  sorting in, 73
  String.Formats, 271
  strings, 186, 224
  Task Parallel Library, 160
  testing, 257
  time constants, 154
  unit testing, 249
networking, 18–20
  building, 19
new programmers
  advice for, 356, 388–389
  usual suspects question, 158
nibble, 66
Nimzowitsch, Aron, 63
no preemption, 166
nodes, 70–71, 72
noncompete clauses, 60
non-profit organizations, 11
nonsolicitation clauses, 60

non-zero values, 129, 135–136
NOR gate, 312, 313, 346
normalization, 167, 185, 188–190
  BCNF, 169–170, 188, 190
  database design, 167, 168
  denormalization, 170, 185, 190
  first form, 168–169, 189
  populating database, 170–171
  rules of, 168–170
  second form, 169, 189
  third form, 169, 190
North Pole, 321
NoSQL, 82, 167, 360
NOT gate, 312
NP-Complete, 93
NP-Hard, 93
n-tier architecture, 393
NUL device, 284
null, 234
nullable objects, 180–181
NullReferenceException, 154, 180
number systems, 66–68, 194
NUnit, 249, 250

O

object pipeline, 288
object-oriented programming, 360, 393
  Liskov Substitution Principle, 124
  modeling with, 76–80
  Open/Closed Principle, 123
object-relational mapping (ORM), 167, 370
objects, 76–78
  classes and, 31, 398
  global, 217–218
  locking references, 186
  mock, 246, 251–253, 255, 260, 398
  modifying, 187
  nullable, 180–181
  pass by value, 175, 185, 187
  PowerShell, 288–290
  references, 175
OCP. See Open/Closed Principle
octal, 64–68

Office of National Statistics, UK, 54
OLAP. *See* online analytical processing
1NF. *See* first normal form
online analytical processing (OLAP),
    170
online job advertisements, 14–15
Open/Closed Principle (OCP), 123
optimization, 117, 130, 142–143
    benchmarking, 309
    divide and conquer approach, 118–119
    goals, 118
OR gate, 312, 313–314, 345, 347
OR operator, 308
Oracle, 81, 167
ORM. *See* object-relational mapping
ORM frameworks, 82
out modifier, 185, 187–188
overcommitting, 58
overloading, 397
overloads, 43–44
overriding, 79, 397

P

packing efficiency, 318
parallel assignment, 236
parallelism, 160
paranoia
    in regular expressions, 108
    useful, 180–181
parsing, 131, 143–144
partial classes, 31
partial dependency, 169, 189
pass by reference, 31, 173, 175–177
pass by value, 173, 175–177, 185, 187
patches, 274
paths, 199, 220
Peopleware (DeMarco and Lister), 58
performance
    averaging, 118
    code quality, 112–119
    context, 118
    design, 178
    measuring, 117–118
performance/timing benchmark, 309

Perl, 201–202
    argument checking, 204–205, 234–235
    backreferences, 90
    barewords, 234
    bigint, 194
    command-line tools, 268–269
    context-sensitive functions, 204, 231
    Fizz Buzz, 348
    Java differences from, 204–205, 234–
        235
    looping, 232–233
    null, 234
    pragma directives, 234–235
    regular expressions, 84, 90, 92
    Schwartzian Transform, 193, 203–204,
        230–231
    sorting, 73, 203–204, 228–231
    strings, 202, 227–228
    testing, 250
    transforming array to dictionary, 349
    unit testing, 250
persistence, 21–22
pessimization, 117
phone interviews
    answering hard questions in, 33–34
    asking good questions, 34–35
    cheat sheet preparation for, 32
    cheat sheet templates, 35–38
    checklist for, 35
    CVs and, 30
    recent experience questions in, 31
    relating experience in, 32–33
    technical questions in, 31
    what to expect, 30–32
PHP
    regular expressions, 92
    testing, 250
PHPUnit, 250
pirates, 305, 323–324
plain old unit testing (POUT), 245
plain text, 67
Planck Time, 194
planned expansion, 3–5
PL/SQL, 145–147

pointers, 193
  assignment with, 172
  C arrays, 174–175
  C function arguments, 173
  declaration, 172
  defining, 171
  reassigning, 95
  untyped, 173
  value and reference passing, 175–177
polar bears, 321
politeness, 45
polymorphism, 78–80
polynomial time, 93
poor design, 177, 367
poor risk management, 361–362
poor writing, 9
pop-quiz questions, 43–44
postorder, 72
postorder traversal, 98–100
potential employers
  approaching, 20–21
  finding, 20
  information from recruitment
    agencies on, 40
POUT. *See* plain old unit testing
PowerShell, 271, 287–290
practice
  improving ability, 377–378
  for in-person interviews, 41
  spontaneity and, 51
pragma directives, 234
The Pragmatic Programmer (Hunt and
  Thomas), 179, 371, 383
preorder, 72
preorder traversal, 98–100
primary key, 169
prime numbers, 94, 104–108
privacy, 24
private builds, 293
private scope, 214
probability problems, 306–307
procedural programming, 393
Process Explorer, 272, 290

Process Monitor, 272, 291–292
processes, 398
  deadlocks, 166
  groups of, 122
product owners, 356, 387–388
productivity, 390–391
profilers, 119
programmer productivity, 356, 390–391
programming
  cargo-cult, 353, 370–371
  as communication, 388
  explaining non-technically, 354,
    379–380
  functional, 81, 360, 393
  modular, 393
  object-oriented, 76–80, 123–124, 360,
    393
  superstitious, 180–181
programming ability, improving, 354,
  377–378
Programming by Coincidence, 371
programming wisdom
  coding standards, 359
  disagreeing with, 352, 358–360
project configuration, 268, 280–282
project management, 361–362
puzzles, 304–306
Python, 250
PyUnit. *See* Unittest

Q

quadratic time, 116
quantifiers, 88–89
query optimizer, 239
question types, 42
  design problems, 43
  general intelligence test, 44
  social and behavioral, 43
  stress test, 44–45
  technical pop-quiz, 43–44
queues, 70, 72, 97
quicksort, 73, 74
quirks, 193

R

race conditions, 158, 160, 249
RAD, 393
radix point, 194
rambling code, 147–149
random rows, 207–208, 241–243
rapport, 45
  establishing, 46–47
  working on, 47–48
RDBMS. *See* relational database
  management system
readability, 389
realism, 58
Rebuild Solution, 266, 275–276
received wisdom, 352, 358–360
recognizing hard problems, 92–93
recruitment
  for planned expansion, 3–5
  reasons for, 2–7
  to replace, 6–7
  for specific projects, 5–6
recruitment agencies, 8, 15–17
  agent experience, 16
  contingency basis, 16
  employer information from, 40
  job offer negotiation role of, 57
  working with, 17
recursion, 75–76, 81, 398
  algorithms, 309–311
  eight queens solution, 339
  Tower of Hanoi solution, 343–344
red, green, refactor, 247
Redis, 167
redundancies, 12
Reed, 15
`ref` modifier, 185, 187–188
refactoring, 355, 382–383
reference type, 397
reflection, 319
registry keys, 272, 291–292
regression tests, 249
regular expressions, 83–92, 398
  anchors, 85–86
  character classes, 86–88
  gotchas, 90–92
  greedy matching, 91
  groups and captures, 89–90
  for IP addresses, 94, 108
  quantifiers, 88–89
  word boundaries, 85–86
rehashing, 70
relational database management
  system (RDBMS), 81–82, 167, 360
  synchronized data access, 160
relational databases, 167–171
remainders, 316, 349–350
replacement, recruitment for, 6–7
reproducing problems, 367–368
requirements, 356, 387–388
resumé. *See* curriculum vitae
return values, 215–216
returning to work, CVs for, 12–13
reverting committed changes, 274,
  297–298
revision control, 357–358, 398
risk management
  estimation, 364
  poor, 361–362
root nodes, 70–71
Ruby, 82, 205, 250
  &&= operator, 237
  parallel assignment, 236
  sorting, 73
  strings, 205, 235
  swapping variables, 235–237

S

school bus, 303–304, 316–319
Schwartzian Transform, 193, 203–204,
  230–231
SDLC. *See* software development life
  cycle
`sealed` keyword, 124
search box, 387
second normal form (2NF), 169, 189
`sed`, 265, 270–271, 286–287

Sedgewick, Robert, 64
SELECT statements, 371
self-balancing binary search tree, 96
set bits, 309, 338
set-based thinking, 82
setters, 80
SHA1 hashes, 274
share options, 55
shared data
  access management, 160–161
  locks, 160–165
shelveset, 292
shelving, 273, 292–293
should haves, 56
showing competency, 48–49
side effects, 81
sieve of Eratosthenes, 107
silent treatment, 61
Silverlight, 82
Single Responsibility Principle (SRP),
    121–123, 150–151, 366, 386
skills
  gaps in, 3
  interpersonal, 7
  matching advertisements, 10
sleeping barber problem, 308, 333–334
slicing text files, 270, 285–286
smalldatetime, 239
smiling, 45
social and behavioral questions, 43
The Social Network (film), 23
software development life cycle
    (SDLC), 37
software development methodologies,
    355, 386–387
software development tools, 265
*Software Estimation: Demystifying the
    Black Art* (McConnell), 363, 365
software projects
  adding programmers to, 352, 362
  construction metaphor, 360–361
  controlling large, 354, 375
  deteriorated code bases, 375–376
  estimating, 352, 361, 363–365

getting familiar with, 353, 369–370
late and over budget, 352, 360–362
pride in, 354, 378–379
requirements, 356, 387–388
risk management, 361–362
software quality, 33
software testing, 37
SOLID principles, 109
  compromising, 374
  defining, 121
  Dependency Inversion Principle,
    125–126
  enumerations following, 132–133,
    150–151
  Interface Segregation Principle,
    124–125
  Liskov Substitution Principle, 123–124
  Open/Closed Principle, 123
  Single Responsibility Principle,
    121–123
  testable code with, 386
sort, 269–270, 283–284, 285
sorting
  .NET, 73
  Perl, 73, 203–204, 228–231
  Ruby, 73
  types of, 73–74
source code
  adding features, 354, 375–376
  getting familiar with, 353, 369–370
  managing, 272–275, 292–302
  revision control, 357–358
  unfamiliar, 354
source control, 352, 357–358
South Pole, 321
space complexity, 113
spaghetti code, 391
speaking slowly, 50
specific projects, recruitment for, 5–6
specification documents, 387
spellcheckers, 9
spelling, 13
Spolsky, Joel, 355, 384
spontaneity, practicing, 51

SQL, 81–82, 145–147, 206, 397. *See also*
  Transact-SQL
  procedural, 206
  set-based, 206
SQL injection, 398
SQL Server, 167, 207, 240, 241
SRP. *See* Single Responsibility Principle
stack, 397
Stack Overflow, 362
  careers at, 26–27
stacks, 70, 72, 97, 225
standard contracts, 60–61
standard streams, 269
stderr, 269, 270, 283, 284–285
stdin, 269, 283, 284
STDIN, 84
stdout, 269, 283, 284, 285
stress test, 44–45
String.Formats, 271, 287–288
strings
  .NET, 186, 224
  C#, 198, 218
  immutable, 186–187, 199, 224
  interned, 187
  Java, 186, 200, 224–225
  JavaScript, 195–196, 211–212
  locks on, 184, 186–187
  Perl, 202, 227–228
  permutations, 94, 101–104
  Ruby, 205, 235
  T-SQL, 206–207, 237–238
  verbatim literals, 199, 222–223
strongly typed programming
  languages, 398
structs, 172
subnet masks, 64
subquery, correlated, 207, 238–239
subtrees, 71
Subversion, 273–274, 294–298
  basics, 294–295
  branching and tagging, 295–297
  reverting committed changes, 297–
    298
superstition, 181–182

surrogate keys, 169
swapping variables, 205, 235–237
Swiss Army enumeration, 150–151
Sysinternals utilities, 265, 272, 290
System.Numerics.BigInteger, 194

T

TABLESAMPLE, 241–242
tagging, 274, 295–297
tail, 269
Task Parallel Library (TPL), 160
TDD. *See* test-driven development
Team Build, 273
Team Foundation Server (TFS), 273,
  292–293
teams
  conventions, 182
  phone interview questions, 31
  working against, 182
tech talk, 7–8
technical debt, 355, 374, 381–382
technical pop-quiz questions, 43–44
technical questions, in phone
  interviews, 31
test harness, 119
test values, 255, 262–263
Test::Class, 250
test-driven development (TDD), 245
  BDD, 247
  benefits, 246–247
  as best practice, 393
  on interview cheat sheet, 398
  red, green, refactor, 247
  writing tests, 254–255, 257–259
testing, 245
  code coverage, 255, 263
  edge cases, 262
  mock objects, 246, 251–253
  slow things, 249
  what to test, 254, 256–257
Test::Unit, 250
text files
  plain, 67
  slicing, 270, 285–286

TFS. *See* Team Foundation Server
things in common, 7
third normal form (3NF), 169, 190
this
  JavaScript, 197–198, 216–218
  locking on, 184, 186
Thomas, Dave, 371, 383
threads, 158–159, 398
  deadlocks, 165–166
  locks, 161, 164
  order of execution, 162–164
time complexity
  array lookup, 129–130, 141–142
  array traversal, 130, 142
  big-*O* notation, 113–117
  constant, 113–114
  linear, 113, 114–115
  logarithmic, 114, 115
  polynomial, 93
  programming concepts cheat sheet,
    398
  quadratic, 116
timing, 22
Titus Livius, 110
Tower of Hanoi, 310–311, 343–345
TPL. *See* Task Parallel Library
Transact-SQL (T-SQL), 194, 206–207,
    237–243
  collation order, 207, 240–241
  correlated subqueries, 207, 238–239
  dates, 207, 239–240
  selecting random row, 207–208,
    241–243
  strings, 206–207, 237–238
transitive dependency, 169, 190
trees, 70–71
  arbitrarily large, 94, 100–101
  DFS on large, 100–101
  sub, 71
  traversing, 98–100
troubleshooting, 353, 367–369
trunk, 296
truth tables, 311–314
try-finally construct, 391

T-SQL. *See* Transact-SQL
Tuple.Create, 43–44
Twain, Mark, 39
Twitter, 19, 20
  job searching with, 22–23
  tips for using, 23
type coercion, 212

U
ultimatums, 61
unclear code, 110–111
undirected graph, 398
undo function, 357
Unicode, 67–68
uniq, 270, 284, 285
unique characters, 149–150
unit constants, 141
unit testing, 245, 259–260, 393, 398
  benefits, 255, 260
  frameworks, 249–251
  limits, 255, 260–262
unit tests, 246, 254
  continuous integration, 385, 386
  failing helpfully, 248
  learning code bases with, 370
  mock classes, 126
  self-contained, 248–249
  self-evident, 248
  simplicity, 248
  speed, 247, 249
  testing, 263–264
  writing, 247–249
Unittest, 250
universal gates, 346
UNIX, 265, 268
unstructured code, 391
untestable code, 367
user interface, 158
utilities, 265
UX, 82

V
value type, 397
variables

global, 355, 359, 380–381
  hoisting declarations, 214
  swapping, 205, 235–237
verbatim string literals, 199, 222–223
version control, 398
Vim, 68
Visual Studio, 265
  Build and Rebuild, 266, 275–276
  Build targets, 267
  Clean Solution, 276
  CPU targeting, 267, 278–280
  Debug mode, 268, 280–282
  debugging, 220–221
  exploring, 266–268
  hidden exceptions, 266–267
  project configuration, 268, 280–282
  registry keys, 272, 291–292
  Release configuration, 268, 280–282
  unit testing framework, 250

W
wait and retry, 166
warm-up questions, 63
waterfall approach, 393
Wayne, Kevin, 64

web developers, 10
  full-stack, 82–83
web-scale, 167
weighing, 306, 326–328
while loop, 391
window, 217–218
won't haves, 57
word boundaries, 85–86
work history, 398–399
working directory, 289–290
Working Effectively with Legacy Code
  (Feathers), 376
writing, on CV, 9

X
XML, 82, 360, 398
XOR gate, 312, 313, 314, 346–347
XOR operator, 236, 308
XOR swap, 236
xUnit, 249–250

Y
YAGNI, 111, 177–178
Yahoo!, 14, 387
You Ain't Gonna Need It. *See* YAGNI